Hunting & Stalking Deer throughout the World

Hunting & Stalking Deer throughout the World

G Kenneth Whitehead

St. Martin's Press
New York

Copyright © *G. Kenneth Whitehead* 1982
For information, write: St. Martin's Press,
175 Fifth Avenue, New York, N.Y. 10010

Printed in Great Britain

Library of Congress Cataloging in Publication Data

Whitehead, G. Kenneth (George Kenneth), 1913–
  Hunting and stalking deer throughout the
world.

  1. Deer hunting.   I. Title.
SK301.W45 799.2´77357   81-21471
ISBN 0-312-40156-6   AACR2

First U.S. Edition

Contents

Acknowledgment

No single person, no matter how widely he may have travelled the world, can claim to be an authority on the subject of deer hunting in any country other than perhaps his own. In the preparation of this book, therefore, I have received considerable assistance from innumerable friends and sportsmen whom I have been fortunate enough to meet during various hunting trips in different parts of the world, and in particular, I wish to thank the following for their invaluable help so readily given.

C Allison (Australia); T Aman (Switzerland); Luděk Bartoš (Czechoslovakia); Arthur Bentley (Australia); A J Hettier de Boislambert (France); Karl Draskovich (Austria); Howard Egan (New Guinea); Dr J J Eshuis (the Netherlands); L H Harris (New Zealand); Lennart Hedberg (Sweden); Hans-Heinrich M Hatlapa (West Germany); Ing. Josef Hromos, Csc (Czechoslovakia); Finn Kristoffersen (Denmark); Dr Ing. Jerzy Krupka (Poland); Prof. Teppo Lampio (Finland); Dr A Starker Leopold (Mexico); Raul Mandojana (Argentina); A Morrisey (Eire); Hisashi Nagata (Japan); W H Nesbitt (Administrative Director of the Boone and Crockett Club); L Petyt (Belgium); M Piodi (Italy); Jorge de Andrada Roque de Pinho (Portugal); Ricardo Medem Sanjuán (Spain); Mr Schanen (Luxembourg); Robert Scott (Northern Ireland); Jack Shepherd (New Caledonia); Alexander F Skutch (Central America); Prof. Dr H Stubbe (East Germany); Dr L Studinka (Hungary); J O Thate (the Netherlands); Dr Werner Trense (West Germany); G A Treschow (Norway); V Varicak (Yugoslavia); Rule Graf von Bismarck (Chile); Prof. P L Wright (United States of America – Chairman, Boone and Crockett Club).

I am equally indebted to the C.I.C. (Conseil International de la Chasse) and Paul Parey Verlagsbuchhandlung, the Boone and Crockett Club of North America and to Norman Douglas for their kind permission to include some of their formulae for measuring deer trophies, thus permitting the reader an opportunity to study the three methods and decide for himself which, in his opinion, is probably the most accurate and fair to both hunter and trophy. The Boone and Crockett Club has also kindly permitted me to use a number of their photographs to illustrate some of the best trophies taken in North America, for which I am most grateful.

ACKNOWLEDGMENT

I would like to acknowledge the loan of photographs from: Joël Bouëssée, R E Chaplin, Göran Ekström, Roy A Harris and K R Duff, Leonard Lee Rue III, Dr Studinka, Grösta Tysk and the Boone & Crockett Club.

Finally, I acknowledge the kind permission of the Hayward Art Group to reproduce the maps which they originally prepared for my book *The Deer of the World*.

Introduction

Of the forty living species of deer in the world which represent just under 200 subspecies, no fewer than twenty-five of the former and over eighty of the latter are indigenous to Asia. Sadly, many of these deer are now included in the *Red Data Book* of the I.U.C.N. (International Union for Conservation of Nature and Natural Resources) as being either endangered, vulnerable or rare, and even if their native habitat was open for hunting, until their numbers had recovered to permit some limited harvesting, none should be considered as game by the trophy hunter.

Already during the past fifty years, the unique deer of Thailand – the beautiful Schomburgk's deer *Cervus schomburgki* – has become extinct, and the world population of at least one species – the Persian Fallow deer *Dama dama mesopotamica* – reduced to under a hundred, with several other species below the thousand mark. When population levels reach these figures, the point of no-return is not far off, and the hunter *must* respect this fact.

Many of the deer of northern India, Tibet and China are much reduced in numbers to what they were at the beginning of the century, and in almost every case the reason has been the same – over-hunting and loss of habitat, the former undoubtedly made more effective by the accuracy of the modern firearm. It has not been sport hunting, however, that has been a major factor, but the slaughter of stags – particularly of the genus *Cervus* – whilst their antlers are in velvet, for the latter, ground up and dried, are used in the preparation of an aphrodisiac – one of which is called Pantocrin. In recent years, however, it has been found possible to farm deer for the sole purpose of producing antlers which can be harvested without the stag having to be killed – an operation which cannot, of course, be done with the wild deer, but one which, unfortunately, must involve considerable pain, for the growing antler is then at its most sensitive state. So great is the demand for antler velvet that deer farms are being set up in many parts of the world outside Asia, and deer farming is already big business in New Zealand and is starting to develop in Europe.

Whilst one cannot condone a practice that involves any cruelty to a living animal, so long as the demand for antler velvet persists, deer farming may, fortunately, take the pressure off hunting – and killing – the wild herds and thus allow stocks to build up. The question is, therefore, should farmed deer be allowed to suffer to ensure survival of the species, for if banned, decimation of the wild herds would undoubtedly result. Removal of the growing antler must be done under a local anaesthetic.

Despite the reduced population of so many species, deer in general have a much wider distribution in the world today than they had at the beginning of the last century, for until about 1813 the whole of Australasia, which included Australia, New Zealand, New Guinea and New Caledonia, were without any members of the *Cervidae*. Now at least ten species of deer introduced not only from the Nearctic and Palearctic regions, but also Indo-Malaya, have established themselves in a feral state, and indeed it is to Australasia where one must now go to hunt some species of the Indo-Malayan deer.

In Britain, when anyone goes deer hunting, it is assumed that it entails the use of horse and hounds, whilst tracking deer on foot is generally referred to as stalking. In North America the pursuit of all game, be it with gun, rifle or hound, is always referred to as 'hunting' – a term which has more international usage than 'stalking' and one which I have adopted for this book.

Seventy years ago, any hunter with time and money could hunt, more or less, in any part of the world that he chose. Today, due to political unrest, the hunter's world has shrunk and although the jet age has reduced the duration of an overseas safari from months to days, many parts of the eastern world have now closed their doors to the visiting sportsman, who must now content himself with hunting some of these eastern deer as exotics in the western world and elsewhere. Even a short trip to Europe today after a stag or buck is probably beyond the pocket of the majority of hunters, for the cost of a good medal class trophy could well run into two or three thousand pounds, for trophy hunting is now very big business.

Compared to Europe, the cost of hunting deer in North America is still very reasonable with a fixed licence fee of about $25 to $50 (£12 to £25) for a Whitetail or $225 (£112) for a Wapiti and Whitetail (or Mule Deer), as well as a bear, in Montana, irrespective of the size of trophy taken. Hunting, however, in the United States can be very 'crowded' and any visiting sportsman would be well advised to spend as much money as he can afford in arranging a hunt with a good outfitter in an area as remote as possible from the more accessible hunting grounds where competition with other hunters is considerable, and with such pressure it is not surprising that the deer soon move to quieter pastures.

Costs, due to inflation, can change daily so it must be appreciated that licence and trophy fees mentioned in the text usually refer to 1979–80. Whilst it can be assumed that they will not get less in the foreseeable future, they will at least act as a guide to show how the trophy fees are calculated in each country. Generally, since the 1979–80 season, fees have increased by approximately 5 to 10 percent.

I have avoided giving any reference or advice on suitable rifles for this is not only a matter of personal taste but also depends on the type of deer being hunted. Personally, for almost fifty years, I have found the 7 mm Rigby firing the 140 grains bullet a very reliable all-round deer rifle, but more recently I have been using a .30-06, finding a 150 grain bullet quite adequate for all species of deer except Elk, Moose, Wapiti and Caribou for which the 220 grain bullet is preferred. In the end it is, of course, the man behind the rifle who really counts, for that great elephant hunter 'Karamojo Bell' (WDM Bell) frequently used his .275 Rigby, firing a 200 grain bullet, on this large pachyderm, and was of the opinion that 'if wrongly placed, the 800 grs from the .400 had no more effect than the 200 grs from the .275' (*The Wanderings of an Elephant Hunter*). On occasions he even used his .256, and concludes by saying 'Each hunter should use the weapon he has *most confidence* in'.

Although at one time meat was the primary reason for killing deer and other game animals, today it is the trophy, and the larger the antlers the better satisfied the hunter will be. To suit the whims of the trophy hunter, a system of assessing trophy value had to be developed, and during the past fifty years a number of different systems have evolved, and these are described in Chapter 11. Hunting is an international sport, and it would have been preferable if only one system could have operated throughout the world, but this, unfortunately, has not been possible and seems hardly likely in the foreseeable future. At present three different systems operate: in Europe (C.I.C.), in North America (Boone and Crockett), and in Australasia (Douglas), not to mention one or two others, less well known, for measuring exotics on the Texan game ranches.

The mere fact that a trophy scores more points does not necessarily make it any more attractive, but it gets a high place in the Record Book which is what the average hunter desires and pays for.

Anyone planning a hunting trip in a foreign land must have a contact to start his enquiries. In the Appendix, therefore, I have included a number of addresses that may help the deer hunter to start planning his trip. Reference to the appropriate ambassador can also be very helpful, and travel agencies usually have some useful information.

In his quest to add a rare trophy, however, a hunter must never endanger a species. Live animals can perpetuate a species – a stuffed head on a wall cannot.

Part I
Europe

EUROPE

There are five indigenous and five exotic species of deer distributed in the countries of Europe (except the U.S.S.R. which appears in Part II) as follows:

INDIGENOUS

Red deer
Cervus elaphus
Austria
Belgium
Bulgaria
Czechoslovakia
Denmark
England
France
Germany (East)
Germany (West)
Hungary
Ireland
Italy
Luxembourg
Netherlands
Norway
Poland
Portugal
Romania
Scotland
Spain
Sweden
Switzerland
Yugoslavia

Roe deer
Capreolus capreolus
Austria
Belgium
Bulgaria
Czechoslovakia
Denmark
England
France
Germany (East)
Germany (West)
Hungary
Italy
Luxembourg
Netherlands
Norway
Poland
Portugal
Romania
Scotland
Spain
Sweden
Switzerland
Yugoslavia

Fallow deer †
Dama dama
Austria
Bulgaria
Czechoslovakia
Denmark
England
France
Germany (East)
Germany (West)
Hungary
Ireland
Italy
Netherlands
Poland
Portugal
Romania
Scotland
Spain
Sweden
Wales
Yugoslavia

Elk
Alces alces
Czechoslovakia
Finland
Norway
Poland
Sweden

Reindeer
Rangifer tarandus
Finland*
Iceland
Norway
Sweden (domestic herds only)

EXOTIC DEER

Sika deer
Cervus nippon
Austria
Czechoslovakia
Denmark
England
France
Germany (West)
Ireland
Poland
Scotland
Switzerland

Axis deer or Chital
Axis axis
Yugoslavia*

Muntjac
Muntiacus
England

Chinese Water-deer
Hydropotes inermis
England

White-tailed deer
Odocoileus virginianus
Czechoslovakia
Finland

* No hunting permitted
† A large number of Fallow deer are in enclosed parks or reserves

1 Great Britain and Ireland

GREAT BRITAIN

In the United States of America and in many other countries, shooting – whether it be deer or birds – is generally referred to as 'hunting'. In Great Britain, however, the word 'hunting' is reserved for any sport that entails the use of hounds. Thus deer hunting would indicate hunting deer with hounds as is currently practised by the staghounds and buckhounds of southern England. 'Stalking', therefore, is the term usually applied to shooting deer with a rifle irrespective of whether it is on foot or from a high seat. This is the term, therefore, that will be used when referring to the shooting of deer in Britain.

And there are other words closely associated with the sport of stalking. In Scotland, deer terrain is always referred to as 'forest', even though the area may be a forest in name only, completely devoid of any trees. The professional keeper on a 'deer forest' is called the 'stalker'; his assistant is called the 'ghillie', or he may be the 'ponyman' should ponies or 'garrons' still be used to bring in the deer. The sportsman is generally referred to as the 'rifle', though in former days he often went by the name of 'the gentleman'. Other terms in common usage are the 'glass' when referring to the telescope, and 'piece' for the luncheon packet, whilst in the presence of deer the 'stalker' may point out to the 'rifle' which 'beast to take', i.e. shoot. After the shot the deer will be 'gralloched', i.e. will have the stomach and intestines removed.

Six species of deer – Red, Roe, Fallow, Sika, Muntjac and Chinese Water-deer are available for stalking in the wild in Britain – the first four in Scotland and all six in England.

All species of deer except the last two mentioned now have close seasons during which it is illegal to shoot any deer except to prevent marauding. Unfortunately legislation in England is different from that in Scotland, and this has resulted in a variation of open-season dates between the two countries (*see the appropriate species*).

Firearm requirements also vary between the two countries. In England the *Deer Act* 1963 makes it illegal to shoot deer with any rifle having a calibre of less than .240 in. (6.1 mm) or a muzzle energy of less than 1700 ft/lb (238 metre/kg) and whilst it is permissible to use a shotgun, it must be 12-bore gauge or larger and the cartridge must not be less than A.A.A. (i.e. loaded with pellets of 5.16 mm or .203 in. diameter) or rifled slug (*Wildlife and Countryside Act* 1981).

In Scotland the *Deer (Scotland) Act* 1959 makes no such restriction and provided the weapon is one 'as defined in the *Firearms Act* 1937, other than a prohibited weapon', a rifle or gun of any calibre or bore may be used.

Both the crossbow and bow-and-arrow are prohibited weapons for deer in England.

No one in Britain is permitted to use a rifle unless in possession of a firearm certificate obtainable from the police at a cost of £25 and valid for three years. A game licence costing £6 per annum, and obtainable from a post office, is also required to shoot wild deer.

Except in the case of marauding on crops or forestry on *enclosed* land, deer may be shot *only* during the period commencing one hour before sunrise and ending one hour after sunset.

It is legal to shoot deer on a Sunday and although much practised in England, it is seldom done in Scotland.

Deer stalking by day or weekly permits for Red, Roe, Fallow and Sika deer are available from the Forestry Commission on many forests in both England and Scotland, and whilst shooting fees vary according to species, conditions, terms and charges are more or less standard throughout.

In making a reservation, a non-returnable booking fee of about £10 is required, in some conservancies, to be paid in advance, and anyone in possession of a permit should give at least seven days' notice of his intended visit.

No one will be allowed to stalk on Forestry Commission ground unless accompanied by a Commission Ranger. Stalking is normally undertaken during the hours of early morning and evening, and for each period of three hours a stalking fee of £21.90 is charged (1981), with an addition of £7.30 for every hour in excess of three. An outing is defined as the time spent with the ranger. Stalking on Sunday and on certain public holidays is not normally permitted on a Forestry Commission permit.

Where, by special arrangement, the permit is shared between two stalkers, the stalking fee will be 150 percent of the normal rate.

In addition to the stalking fee, there will be a shooting fee which will be assessed according to the quality of the head, the latter being the property of the permit holder. The scales of shooting fees vary from species to species, and appear on page 19 (Red deer), page 26 (Fallow deer), page 24 (Roe deer) and page 27 (Sika deer).

Should a permit holder miss a deer, he will incur a minimum penalty charge of £10 but if the deer is hit and runs off only slightly wounded, the charge will be £15. Should, however, the deer be badly wounded and not recover, in addition to the £15 penalty fee the client will be charged the value of the lost venison.

Should a deer be shot in such a way that the amount of usable venison is substantially reduced – i.e. a haunch-shot beast – or the carcase cannot be recovered within twelve hours, the Forestry Commission reserve the right to charge the permit holder the market price for the carcase, which will then become his property.

All prices quoted include V.A.T. at 15 percent.

In the forests in England any rifle that meets the minimum requirements of the *Deer Act* 1963 is acceptable to the Forestry Commission, but in Scotland where there is no such restriction, the Forestry Commission has imposed its own restrictions and whilst the North Conservancy have adopted the minimum requirements for a deer rifle in England, other Conservancies have stipulated that the rifle must have a calibre of not less than .222 in. (5.7 mm) and soft or hollow nosed bullets with a published muzzle energy of not less than 1100 ft/lb or 155 metre/kg. Nowhere in Britain, however, may a permit holder use a shotgun whilst stalking on Forestry Commission ground, and no private estate would permit any stalking guest to use any weapon other than a rifle of suitable calibre.

In addition to a valid firearm certificate, all permit holders must have a third party insurance cover to the value of at least £100,000.

Red deer *Cervus elaphus* Sp.

In Great Britain, the main concentrations of Red deer *C.e.scoticus* are in Scotland, and in particular on the mountains north of about latitude 56° where the deer are well distributed not only on the recognized deer 'forests' but also on adjacent grouse moors and marginal sheep ground. They are also present in the hills and woodlands of Galloway in south-west Scotland as well as on a number of the west coast islands, which include Arran, Rhum, Islay, Mull, Skye, Harris and Lewis. In England, however, except in parts of northern Cumbria and in the south-west, the majority of deer are true woodland creatures.

Throughout Scotland, the total Red deer population is estimated to number about 250,000 animals, of which around 40,000 will be shot each year by stalking.

In England, apart from Martindale Forest in Cumbria, which is the last remaining true deer forest south of the Scottish border, the majority of Red deer are to be found in plantations and woodlands belonging to the Forestry Commission, such as Grizedale in Cumbria and Thetford in Norfolk, and in these areas, apart from still hunting or stalking in the more open localities, most of the shooting will be done from a high seat.

There is also a large stock of Red deer on the moors and in the wooded combes around Exmoor in south-west England, but this is the centre of stag hunting in England, the deer being regularly hunted by the three surviving packs of staghounds – the Devon and Somerset, the Tiverton and the Quantock.

In Scotland the stalking party will generally set out at about 8.30 or 9.00 a.m. and in this respect stalking the Scottish Red deer differs considerably

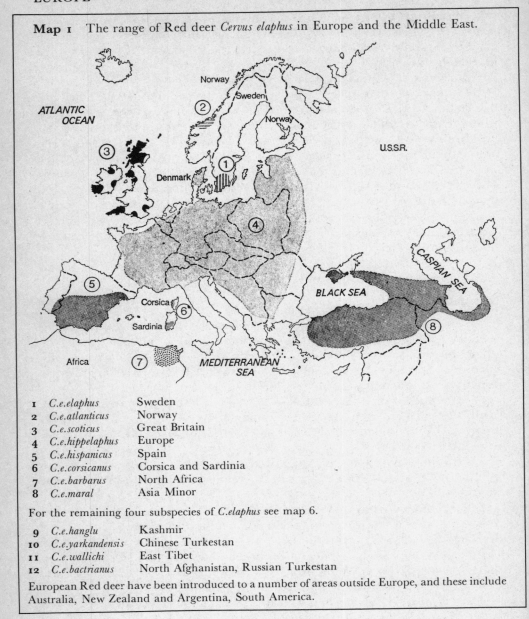

Map 1 The range of Red deer *Cervus elaphus* in Europe and the Middle East.

1	*C.e.elaphus*	Sweden
2	*C.e.atlanticus*	Norway
3	*C.e.scoticus*	Great Britain
4	*C.e.hippelaphus*	Europe
5	*C.e.hispanicus*	Spain
6	*C.e.corsicanus*	Corsica and Sardinia
7	*C.e.barbarus*	North Africa
8	*C.e.maral*	Asia Minor

For the remaining four subspecies of *C.elaphus* see map 6.

9	*C.e.hanglu*	Kashmir
10	*C.e.yarkandensis*	Chinese Turkestan
11	*C.e.wallichi*	East Tibet
12	*C.e.bactrianus*	North Afghanistan, Russian Turkestan

European Red deer have been introduced to a number of areas outside Europe, and these include Australia, New Zealand and Argentina, South America.

from its pursuit in England or on the continent, where a much earlier start is essential, the reason being that in Scotland, due to the fact that the deer are on the open mountain and easily located, the stalk and shot can be taken during the middle part of the day, even though most of the deer will probably be resting. In dense woodland habitat, however, the shot normally has to be taken when the deer are at feed or on the move, and this is only possible at dawn and dusk – otherwise during the middle hours of the day they will be lying up in the thickest part of the forest and quite impossible to locate.

In Scotland the stalking party may be accompanied by one or more ponies dependent on how many deer it is intended to kill. Before the Second World War the pony – or 'garron' – was the only means of bringing back the deer carcases from the hill, but today, in many forests that are not too rocky or precipitous, the pony is gradually being replaced by track-driven vehicles some of the larger ones being capable of recovering four or five carcases at a time, and this picturesque means of transport is fast disappearing from the Scottish scene.

In spying for deer on the open hillside, most professional stalkers use a telescope, for with its greater power of magnification over binoculars, it enables the quality of antlers of individual deer at extreme ranges to be more easily assessed. The use of a telescope requires practice, and people unfamiliar with its use will find binoculars much easier to handle. Binoculars, however, are essential for woodland stalking or shooting from a high seat. One great disadvantage of the telescope over binoculars is that during wet weather – and unfortunately there are many such days in Scotland – it easily becomes fogged up and is then quite useless.

The same also applies to the telescopic sight on the rifle, and for open hill stalking in Scotland, provided one's eyesight is good, the open sight is probably best, for even on fine days it is often difficult to keep the telescope dry during a crawl through long heather and grass that has previously been saturated by rain or mist. However, for woodland stalking, a telescopic sight is essential for it enables shots to be taken at dawn and dusk when accurate aiming through the open sight is an impossibility.

During the early part of the season, and until about the third week in September, the stags will mainly be in large parties and a stalk after an individual stag in a herd that may number anything from perhaps a dozen to over a hundred beasts is a real test of fieldcraft. By the end of September, however, and into October the rut will be under way and once the stags have broken out and joined the hinds, stalking becomes much easier. During a rain storm or misty weather, the sound of roaring during October will also help to keep the stalking party in touch with the deer.

Just as much of the approach work during a stalk will have to be taken at the 'crawl', so will the majority of shots have to be taken in the prone position, generally at ranges from about 100 to 150 yards (90 to 135 metres) but considerably longer by those who dislike a long crawl!

In Scotland the stalking of stags finishes on 20 October, but during the winter months good sport can be had with the hinds, the open season for which lasts until 15 February. Hind stalking in winter, however, can be very cold work – and on occasions more to be endured than enjoyed! In England hinds may be shot until the end of February and stags until the end of April.

Reference has already been made to two inescapable features of stalking in Scotland – rain and the crawl – and these alone dictate that whatever clothing is worn must be warm and loose fitting. On the continent a Loden jacket or cape is a popular garment for all shooting but it is not suitable for Scotland, the best material being tweed of suitable colour to blend into the hillside. Plus-four trousers are unquestionably better than close-fitting knee breeches, for no matter how wet they may become, once the rain stops, the loose-fitting part around the knees will soon dry out in the wind. Waterproof leggings should never be worn, for not only are they uncomfortably hot at times, but are extremely noisy, especially when crawling. If a raincoat is worn, it must be short so as to leave the knees free when crawling.

Stalking Red deer in the forests of England is very much the same as elsewhere in Europe, and as already mentioned, most woodland stags will be shot at dawn or dusk, either by 'still hunting' or from a high seat. During the rut it is possible to call the stag either by imitating its roar with a horn, or by pinching one's nose in an attempt to imitate the nasal bleat of a hind. Neither method, however, is as much practised in England as on the continent.

Although it is rare for Scottish Red deer heads to exceed sixteen tines, the ideal trophy is the 'royal' (12-pointer) but to fulfill this description it must have six tines on each side, with the top three in the form of a crown. A really good trophy should have an antler length of about 36 in. (92 cm); a beam circumference of 5 in. (13 cm) and an inside span of at least 30 in. (76 cm).

In the woodlands of England and in particular from Thetford Forest in Norfolk, larger stags have been killed and three from this area at Budapest were awarded Gold medals – the best obtaining 201.03 C.I.C. points. Even larger trophies have come from south-west England, and in 1950 a magnificent 20-pointer came from Endsleigh, Devon, with a C.I.C. score of 224.50 points. No stalker, however, had the satisfaction of shooting this British record trophy, for it unfortunately met with an accident and was killed.

In Scotland the open season for shooting stags is of considerably shorter duration than in England, lasting about sixteen weeks as compared to thirty-nine weeks in the latter country. This is due to the different habitat, for whereas the bulk of deer in Scotland live on the mountains with little or no access to woodland in winter for shelter, the majority of Red deer in England are true forest dwellers, and if the open season terminated in October, as in Scotland, it would be impossible to kill sufficient numbers to keep the population under control. Furthermore, it is only during the early spring that the staghounds in south-west England hunt the young stags. The open seasons for killing Red deer in both England and Scotland are, therefore, as follows:

	England	Scotland
Stags	1 August–30 April	1 July–20 October
Hinds	1 November–28/29 February	21 October–15 February

Anyone wishing to stalk deer in Scotland should approach one of the agencies who cater for sportsmen and advertise regularly in the sporting press. Some of the hotels also provide stalking by the day for their guests, whilst permit stalking by the day is also available from the Forestry Commission.

As to the cost, much will depend on the length of the lease, quality of the forest and whether lodge accommodation is included. As a rough guide, stalking from a hotel or lodge with everything provided, including accommodation, the cost will work out at about £150 to £220 per beast. For instance, a week's stalking from a lodge in Sutherland during which six stags can be shot, will cost about £1250 or £208 per beast.

As already mentioned, permit stalking on Forestry Commission ground costs (1981) £21.90 per outing of three hours' duration, with an extra £7.30 per hour thereafter. The shooting fee will be assessed according to the quality of the trophy and will vary from about £52 for a beast with antlers of fewer than five tines (points) to almost £400 for a head of fourteen tines. Any trophy with twelve or more tines will be assessed under the C.I.C. formula and should it be in the medal class, additional fees will be charged as follows:

Medal class	England	Scotland	Extra charge £ per C.I.C. point
Bronze	165.0–179.9 points	160.0–167.9 points	£1.12
Silver	180.0–194.9 points	168.0–179.9 points	£1.85
Gold	195.0 points and over	180.0 points and over	£2.42

Any freak head or hummel will be subject to local negotiations and agreement. Stags under two years old, hinds and calves will be charged £29.

Under the above named charges, the best Scottish trophy exhibited at Budapest in 1971 (180.73 C.I.C. points) would have cost about £833. It is, however, impossible to say what the 20-pointer from Thetford (201.03 C.I.C. points) would have cost, for having more than fourteen tines, the final charge would have been 'by negotiation'. It would certainly not have been less than £900.

In some areas of Scotland, hind stalking for a period of five days, or until eight deer have been shot (whichever shall come the sooner) is available from the Forestry commission for a charge of £160, the fee being inclusive of any stalking time lost through the weather.

Roe deer *Capreolus capreolus capreolus*

Two hundred years ago the Roe appears to have been extinct throughout much of southern Scotland, and also in most of England as well. Today, however, as a result of a number of introductions at the beginning of the last century, there is not a county in Scotland which does not now hold a stock of Roe. The position is similar in the south of England, and most southern counties as far north as Wiltshire and Berkshire now have a thriving Roe population and during the next few years the spread will doubtless continue to spread northwards.

Roe are also present in East Anglia, the present population being descended, it is thought, from animals brought from Württenberg in Germany and introduced to Thetford in about 1884. Although the Roe has never been entirely absent from the extreme north of England, in recent years it has been slowly but surely spreading southwards and has now reached mid-Lancashire and the Yorkshire Wolds. It has, however, not yet penetrated into central England or into Wales, where it became extinct during the seventeenth century.

Apart from the above mentioned deer from Germany to Thetford, all the other introductions to southern England appear to have come from either Scotland or Cumbria, the first liberation being some Perthshire Roe to Milton Abbas in Dorset about 1800.

Medal wise, the strongest antlers come from the Roe of southern England, and in particular from Surrey and Sussex, and although the trophies from this area, with their massive, well-pearled beams and bulbous-shaped coronets score heavily in weight and volume, they seldom score many points for span, being on the whole rather narrow and upright. Far more appealing to the eye are the lyre-shaped antlers of the Wiltshire bucks – a county that has produced a number of Gold medal trophies in recent years. The highest number of C.I.C. points, however, belongs to a buck that was shot in Hampshire in 1974, and although this trophy has not yet been officially measured by an international jury, provisionally it has been assessed at 238.55 C.I.C. points – almost ten points more than the existing world record from Hungary (228.68 C.I.C. points).

At first glance the antlers of this Hampshire buck have a somewhat peruke appearance, for they grow from two pedicles of considerable circumference and development, and as a result, weigh on frontal bone no less than 1032 g, the volume being 404 ccm. With such exceptional figures it is not surprising that the head has such a high score. The antlers are quite hard, and appear to be of normal texture, if a trifle brittle towards their extremities. There is little doubt that on score alone, the Hampshire trophy is a world record – but whether it will ever be officially accepted as such, on the grounds that 'an abnormal development of the trophy does not permit an official valuation according to the Formulae of the International Hunting Council for the Preservation of Game' is extremely doubtful, for I don't think anyone would claim that the head was anything but abnormal.

At the International Exhibition held in Budapest in 1971, all but one of the twenty-two British Roe trophies on view were in the Gold medal class, and all but two came from the south of England, the best being a Sussex buck with a C.I.C. score of 173.15 points. Better trophies, however, have since come out of Sussex, the best – shot in 1971 – had an official score of 210.25 C.I.C. points at the World Exhibition of Hunting in Plovdiv, Bulgaria, in 1981, where forty of the British Roe heads were awarded Gold medals, with a further twenty receiving Silver and the remaining five, Bronze medals.

Whereas the bucks in south-east England produce such extremely strong antlers, those from Thetford are poor in comparison, and are the lowest standard in the south of England.

It is rare, however, for any trophy from the north of England to achieve Gold medal standard, and any score in excess of 140 C.I.C. points would be exceptional.

Some extremely good trophies, however, have come from Scotland, particularly from Perthshire, which has produced a number of trophies with a score around the 140 point mark, the best – shot in 1976 – having a provisional assessment of 203.60. Aberdeenshire and Moray have long been famous for good quality bucks but it is only during the last ten years that some exceptional trophies have been taken in southern Scotland, the best that has been measured to date coming from Berwickshire (1973) with a score of 181.73 C.I.C. points.

It is, however, only since the late forties that any Roe heads have been measured under the international formula – or indeed by any method at all, for prior to that date the manner in which the British sportsman treated the Roe is something better forgotten! Pre-war, Roe stalking with a rifle was practised by only a dedicated few, the majority being shot during the course of a drive in winter, by which time most of the bucks had shed their antlers. Small wonder, therefore, that there were very few antlers to measure! The shotgun was, unfortunately, the usual armament, and needless to say, with game pellet shot many deer escaped peppered but not for the pot.

Fortunately, on many estates – which include those belonging to the Forestry Commission – these shotgun drives are now a thing of the past, and although in both England and Scotland the shotgun is still a legal weapon for all species of deer, in the former country the weapon and shot size must not be smaller than 12-bore and S.S.G. respectively.

High seats first started to appear in Britain about 1956 in some of the Forestry Commission plantations, and are now a regular feature of their woodlands wherever deer occur, particularly in England. Now the fashion is catching on in private woodlands, especially those that cater for the overseas permit shooter. They come in a variety of sizes and designs, from a mere ladder leading to a seat of wood supported between two branches to almost a tree house, complete with roof, and whilst the latter structure is unnecessarily elaborate, I believe it essential for the seat to be made as comfortable as possible. Otherwise there will be many aches and pains during a two to three hour vigil and too much fidgeting may well disturb an approaching deer. Furthermore, there should be some support not only for the feet to rest on but also to provide a rest for the rifle so as to ensure steady, accurate shooting. Some trees – particularly yew – if conveniently placed, often provide a suitable 'structure' in which to incorporate a seat, whilst the portable high seat is particularly useful when the movement pattern of deer is uncertain, or a temporary seat has to be 'rushed' into position to deal with marauding deer.

Constructed basically of aluminium so as to be both light and noncorroding, the portable seat, with a total weight of under 36 lb (16 kg) should be capable of being dismantled so as to be easily portable through thick cover.

The main advantage of shooting from a high seat is that being elevated ten or more feet (3 metres) from the ground, human scent is generally carried over the head of any approaching deer, and being undisturbed, the animal will probably be in view for several minutes, thus enabling the stalker to be selective in what he shoots. A shot from a high seat is, also, much safer than one taken at ground level.

Sitting in a high seat is a good opportunity to use a 'call' during the rut, the object of the exercise being to imitate the peeping noise made by a doe when searching for a buck. The expert caller will probably just pluck a beech leaf from a nearby tree, and after trimming it down with a knife to the required size, place it to his lips and start to produce the required bleep and then hopefully await the arrival of a buck.

There are other factors which may nullify even the best produced sounds, for should the local buck already be with his doe when the peeping starts, it is unlikely he will be attracted by another call. Furthermore, the success or otherwise of calling depends very much on weather conditions; a still, warm day being more fruitful than one that is cold, wet or windy. Whilst the continental Roe stalker is undoubtedly more successful in calling Roe than the average British stalker, the lack of success of the latter *may*, in the majority of cases, be due to the fact that he seldom has the opportunity to call under such ideal conditions as generally prevail on the continent. Nevertheless, I have seen Cumbrian bucks, which generally ignore my own calling efforts, readily respond to the 'squeaks' made by a German friend of mine using his carefully tailored beech leaf, even though weather conditions have, at times, been far from ideal.

For those unable to prepare their own calls, a wide variety of artificial aids are available – some manufactured from wood or plastic such as the German Hubertus or British made Acme, to the Orlovsky Universal Roe luring whistle from Czechoslovakia, which consists, principally, of a 6-in. (15-cm) rubber tube. All the above-mentioned types need lung power to produce the required sound, the first two by blowing and the last mentioned by sucking, the variation in sound being produced by digital pressure on the rubber tube. Another favourite call is the Buttolo – which operates rather like an old-fashioned motor horn, the sound being made by squeezing a rubber bulb instead of lung power.

Whatever type of call is used, however, one cannot hope to succeed unless by pure fluke, without practice – and this means frequent opportunities to hear the real thing. Unfortunately, it is only on comparatively rare occasions when weather conditions are ideal, that one has the opportunity to hear a doe 'peep-peeping' for her buck, a sound that seems only audible on the stillest of days. So, lack of success may well be due to the fact that the caller, never having heard the real thing, is unaware of what sort of sound he should be making with his call.

Frequently a doe will respond to the call – and if during the rut, one happens to disturb a buck, his retreat can often be arrested with a few 'peeps' on the call, and if uncertain as to the cause of the disturbance, may even be encouraged to retrace his steps for a closer inspection.

In areas where a large number of does have to be killed due to the short daylight hours of mid-winter, it will be impossible to achieve the cull by stalking or shooting from high seats alone, so the majority of these will have to be shot during the course of drives – or more correctly, as a result of moving deer operations. Moving deer is quite distinct from driving, for the object of the exercise is to persuade deer to vacate a block of woodland in as leisurely fashion as possible. This is achieved by three or four beaters entering the wood downwind of the deer, so that as they advance their scent will reach the deer long before their arrival, and thus persuade them to move to a new area, quietly along their accustomed paths of exit which will be covered by two or three concealed rifles. On no account must the beaters talk or shout, and apart from an occasional light tapping with a stick, which is necessary, particularly in thick cover to maintain contact with each other, the 'drive' must be kept as quiet as possible, for it is scent rather than sound which is to move the deer. Dogs should never be allowed to run free during a 'drive', but one should always be in attendance in case a wounded deer has to be trailed. Shots at fast running deer should not be encouraged, for not only is the chance of wounding or damage to venison increased, but a barrage of missed shots around a fleeing deer is unlikely to be forgotten quickly, and the next time the wood is driven the deer will waste no time in clearing out.

Roe in Britain are seldom seen in the fields to the same extent as in many countries of Europe, but in some areas in the north of England and Scotland they frequent quite mountainous terrain, well away from forestry, and here they can be stalked in much the same fashion as Red deer. They can often be seen sunning themselves on some sheltered heathery knoll, or feeding among the straggling silver birches scattered along the glens and burns so typical of highland scenery. In addition to binoculars, a telescope is of considerable help in this form of stalking, for the Roe is a small animal, and many miles of walking can often be saved if the small blob of red picked up some distance away by the binoculars can be positively identified as a deer, and more important, as a buck, with the telescope.

In woodland stalking, however, the telescope is useless, for ranges are short and a wide field of vision, as given by binoculars, essential. In this form of stalking, one cannot go slowly enough, and in most woodland terrain one mile an hour (1.6 km) is quite fast enough. At such a slow speed of progress, physical effort is, of course, minimal, but the 100 percent concentration required throughout can mentally be very exhausting.

Although Roe occur along both sides of the border between England and

Scotland, due to a difference in dates for open and close seasons between the two countries, the position could arise during the last ten days of October when a deer standing in England could be legal game one moment and out of season the next, having travelled the few yards across the border into Scotland.

The open seasons for shooting Roe in Britain are as follows:

	England	Scotland
Bucks	1 April–31 October	1 May–20 October
Does	1 November–28/29 February	21 October–28/29 February

Although the majority of private estates are only interested in letting Roe stalking for a period of, say, three to five years, permit stalking by the day or week is available from the Forestry Commission, who, in addition to a fixed stalking fee (*see page 14*) use the following basic scale to calculate the charge applicable (1981) to the quality of deer shot:

Antler length cm	6 or 5 points (tines) £	4 points (tines) £	3 points (tines) or fewer £
32 and over	66		
30.0–31.9	65		
28.0–29.9	64 Plus medal	52	44
26.0–27.9	61 fee (*see*		
	below)		
24.0–25.9	56	44	
22.0–23.9	50	29	29
20.0–21.9	44		
18.0–19.9	37		
16.0–17.9	29	18	18
under 16 cm	18		

Heads with more than six points will be charged an extra £5.57 per point in excess of six.

Antlers of five points or more and minimum length of 22 cm will be assessed by the C.I.C. formula and if found to score 105.0 points or greater, will have the following medal fees added to the above basic scale:

Medal class	C.I.C. points	
Bronze	105.0	£132 plus £2.90 per C.I.C. point or part point up to 114.9
Silver	115.0	£174 plus £4.40 per C.I.C. point or part point up to 129.9
Gold	130.0	£305 plus £10.20 per C.I.C. point or part point thereafter.

Large freak heads will also be assessed under the C.I.C. formula, but the charge for smaller heads will be subject to negotiation. A doe may be shot for £7.30

All prices are inclusive of V.A.T. at 15 percent.

Based on the above mentioned charges, the Sussex buck which scored 210.25 C.I.C. points at the 1981 Plovdiv Exhibition would have cost about £1187, whilst the fee for the large Hampshire trophy, killed in 1974 (238.55 C.I.C. points), would have been in the region of £1462.

Fallow deer *Dama dama dama*

There has always been considerable doubt as to whether the Fallow deer is indigenous to England, or was originally introduced by the Romans or by the Phoenicians. Whatever may have been its origin, it has long been present both as a wild animal in the forest and in the deer park. Today, in England, among the forests where wild deer occur are Epping Forest (Essex), Dean Forest (Gloucestershire), Rockingham Forest (Northamptonshire), the New Forest (Hampshire) and Cannock Chase (Staffordshire).

In Scotland feral herds are to be found in at least nine counties, the most important wild population being at Dunkeld (Perthshire). Small numbers also exist on the islands of Islay, Mull and Scarba. There are also a few in various parts of Wales, having formerly escaped from deer parks.

Fallow deer are mainly a woodland species, and like other woodland deer, the best opportunity for shooting a buck is at dawn or dusk, either from a 'high seat' or by stalking, particularly during the rut which takes place mainly in October. In some localities, such as Cannock Chase and Dunkeld, which have large areas of heathland intermixed with forest, the deer can also be stalked throughout the day.

There are many different colour varieties, ranging from black, brown, spotted to white, all of which differ to a greater or lesser degree from one season to another.

Not many Fallow buck antlers have been measured under the C.I.C. formula, but it is doubtful if many will better Bronze or Silver, the best trophies coming from the south of England.

In the New Forest, Fallow are hunted by the New Forest Buckhounds, but only the bucks are taken. This is the only area in Britain where Fallow are hunted with hounds.

In pre-war days, when there was a larger Fallow deer population, the Buckhounds would account for about thirty-five bucks per season, but latterly it has only been about eight or nine.

In both England and Scotland bucks may be shot from 1 August until 30 April, but for does in Scotland the open season is slightly earlier than in England, running from 21 October to 15 February, as compared to 1 November to 28/29 February in England.

A limited number of bucks are available on Dunkeld Forest in Perthshire, at a fee of about £50. The majority of wild Fallow deer, however, frequent

Map 2 The range of Fallow deer *Dama dama* in Europe.

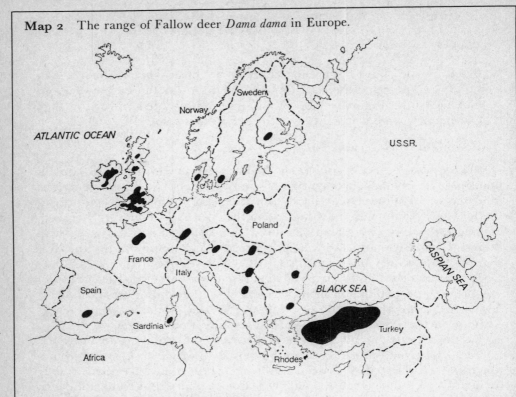

Dama dama dama Europe and Near East*
See also map 17 for range of *D.d.mesopotamica*

*The original home of *D.dama dama* was the Mediterranean region of southern Europe, including Anatolia and Island of Rhodes. It has been introduced to many countries of Western Europe, although in some (marked with an asterisk) their existence has only been maintained in fenced-off reserves or parks; Austria, Belgium*, Bulgaria, Czechoslovakia, Denmark, England, Finland, France, Germany, Hungary, Ireland, Italy*, the Netherlands*, Norway*, Poland, Portugal*, Romania, Sardinia, Scotland, Spain, Sweden, Switzerland*, and Yugoslavia. It has also been introduced to Australia, Tasmania, New Zealand, North America, Africa and South America.

Forestry Commission property, and their charge (1981) in addition to outing fee, are based on antler measurements, and range from about £28 for a two-year-old pricket with spike antlers under 10 cm in length to £216 for a Forestry Commission Gold medal category buck – i.e. a buck with antlers averaging at least 60 cm in length, and a palm width of 12 cm and over.

A doe may be shot for £14.

Sika deer *Cervus nippon* Sp.

Sika deer were first introduced to Britain during the latter part of the last century, and wild herds are now well established in many counties of both

England and Scotland. Animals vary tremendously in size from one locality to another, and it is apparent that more than one subspecies has been introduced, but unfortunately no record has been kept of their source. In England feral herds occur in a number of counties which include Dorset, Hampshire, Lancashire and Yorkshire, whilst in Scotland this deer is plentiful in parts of Argyllshire, Caithness, Inverness-shire, Peebles-shire, Ross-shire and Sutherland. In south Cumbria Sika deer have been crossing with Red deer, and similar hybridization is suspected in parts of Argyllshire.

The rut will start towards the end of September and continue throughout October.

Weights vary considerably from one area to another, and adult stags can weigh anything from about 100 lb (45 kg) in Scotland to about 150 lb (68 kg) in the south of England.

Length of antlers also varies considerably from one area to another, and whilst anything over 40 cm (16 in.) would be good for western Scotland, 55 to 60 cm (22–23 in.) would be nothing unusual for England.

In Scotland, where the deer live principally in small patches of scrub and woodland – mainly birch and bracken – stalking is the usual method of shooting, particularly at dawn and dusk when the deer emerge from cover to feed. Another method which I used to employ during my younger days whilst stalking Sika in the Mull of Kintyre, was to walk through endless patches of bracken in the hope of disturbing a beast during its mid-day siesta. With luck, a deer flushed in this fashion would often stop after having run, perhaps a hundred yards (91 metres) to see what had caused the disturbance, thus giving the chance of a quick shot if the bracken was not too high.

In woodland habitat such as the New Forest, most shooting will be done from a high seat.

The open season for shooting Sika deer in Britain is as follows:

	Stags	Hinds
England	1 August–30 April	1 November–28/29 February
Scotland	1 August–30 April	21 October–15 February

Occasionally Sika stalking on private estates, particularly in Scotland, is available through an agency and a typical charge, inclusive of lodge accommodation for four stags during a week's stalking would be about £800 to £850, which works out at about £200 per beast. On a daily basis, without accommodation, the charge would be approximately £120 + V.A.T. per day, with the expectation of shooting one stag. Probably the best chance is on permit through the Forestry Commission who, in addition to its standard outing fee (*see page 14*) calculate the shooting fee in accordance with the number of tines (points) and length of antler. Thus a typical 8-pointer, with an antler length of 50 cm or over would cost £169 which would be increased to £249 should the head have had eleven tines. A 4-pointer, on the other hand, with an antler length of 35 cm, would cost £37, but if under four points, the fee would be £29.

EUROPE

Medals will be awarded by the Forestry Commission for heads of eight tines or more as follows:

Gold Length over 50 cm
Silver Length 40 to 49.9 cm and beam of 9 cm or greater
Bronze Length of 40 to 49.9 cm and beam of 8 to 8.9 cm

Any freak head will be subject to local negotiation and agreement. A Sika deer hind may be shot for £14. The best Sika trophy from England at Plovdiv 1981 had a C.I.C. score of 295.10 points.

Muntjac *Muntiacus*

Muntjac from both India *M.muntjak* and China *M.reevesi* have been liberated in England and whilst the majority of deer now belong to the latter, a few cross-bred animals probably exist as well. The original deer were introduced to Woburn, Bedfordshire, about 1900 by the eleventh Duke of Bedford, and have now spread their range into a number of counties of central England.

The Muntjac has no fixed rutting time, and bucks in hard antler can be seen at all times of the year, but principally in winter, which is the best time to hunt this small deer, either by stalking or from a high seat, for the foliage is then at its minimum.

A feature of this deer, which stands only about 20 in. (51 cm) high at the shoulder and weighs about 25 lb (11.2 kg) clean is the short antlers supported on long, skin-covered pedicles which continue down the forehead as convergent ridges, thus giving the deer the name of Rib-faced. It is also known as the Barking deer, due to the characteristic barking sound it makes.

A good pair of Reeves antlers will measure about 7 to 8 cm (about 3 in.). The bucks also have small canine tusks about 22 mm ($\frac{7}{8}$ in.) in length. Measured under the C.I.C. formula (*see page 307*) any Reeves antlers with a score of 56.00 points are above average.

Chinese Water-deer *Hydropotes inermis*

Due to escapes from both Woburn Park and nearby Whipsnade Zoo – both in Bedfordshire – this small deer has now established itself in a feral state in the surrounding countryside, but not to the same extent as the Muntjac.

A feature of this deer, which stands about 20 in. (51 cm) high at the shoulder and weighs about 28 lb (12.6 kg) clean, is that neither sex has antlers, the bucks being furnished with long canine tusks about $2\frac{3}{4}$ in. (70 mm) in length, those on the doe being considerably shorter. For C.I.C. formula in measuring tusks, see page 00. The rut takes place about December.

This deer prefers open grassland to cover, and although many are shot during a drive, stalking which may involve some crawling obviously provides the best sport.

IRELAND

Although politically Ireland is divided into two – Northern Ireland and the

Republic (Eire) – most of the data presented here refers to the country as a whole.

In the Republic, the Department of Lands and Forests is the major landowner with more than a million acres (404,000 hectares) under its control. A considerable acreage of both mountain and bogland is also in private ownership, and this applies particularly to deer country in the counties of Wicklow, Cork and Kerry, and in the high country of Tipperary and Wexford. Game rights in State forests, as well as on some of the privately owned mountain land, are rented to individuals or gun clubs, at fairly low charges. In Northern Ireland, State forests come under the control of the Ministry of Agriculture, Forestry Branch.

Until *The Wildlife Act* 1976 came into operation, deer in Eire had not been regarded as game under the *Game Preservation Act* 1930 and were therefore shot freely throughout the year. More recently, as a result of the *Wildlife* (*Wild Mammals*) (*Open Seasons*) *Order* 1979 all species may now only be hunted during the following open seasons:

	Males	**Females**
Red deer*		
Fallow deer	1 September–28 February	1 November–28 February
Sika deer		

* No open season for Red deer in Co. Kerry.

Under the above mentioned Order, deer may only be shot with rifle but for security reasons no licence will be granted for a rifle of heavier calibre than .22, the 22/250 and the 5.6 × 57 coming within this category. A minimum bullet weight of 55 grains should be used. Automatic or gas-operated rifles are banned, and it is illegal to use a smooth bore shotgun for deer.

Firearm certificates, costing £5.00, are obtained from the Department of Justice but will only be issued to an applicant who has already obtained a hunting licence, the latter being issued free of charge by the Department of Fisheries and Forestry in Dublin.

In applying for a hunting licence the applicant must state the make and calibre of the rifle he intends to use, and if a visitor, must also state the areas in which he has permission to hunt, and supply written proof of this. All firearm certificates and hunting licences are valid until 31 July and must be renewed annually. Visiting sportsmen to the Republic must obtain both firearm certificate and hunting licence before arrival, as both documents will have to be presented to Customs at the point of entry.

In Northern Ireland, although deer at present may legally be shot throughout the twelve months of the year, it is the practice of the two large estates of Baronscourt and Colebrook, who supply deer-stalking facilities for visiting sportsmen, to observe the following unofficial close seasons:

| Stag (Japanese Sika) | 1 April–31 July |
| Hind (Japanese Sika) | 1 March–31 August |

At present there are no restrictions as to the type and calibre of firearm that may be used on deer, but eventually it is hoped that all deer shooting in Northern Ireland will be restricted to rifles of calibre not less than .236 in. (6 mm) with the use of any smooth bore shotgun being illegal.

Three species of deer are found in Ireland – the Red deer which, in a wild state, is restricted to the Republic; the Japanese Sika deer and the Fallow deer.

Red deer *Cervus elaphus* Sp.

The Red deer is restricted to the Killarney district of Co. Kerry, the mountains of Co. Wicklow and the Glenveagh Forest Co. Donegal. Straying beasts can also be expected elsewhere in the form of park escapees.

The deer in Co. Kerry are the only Red deer in Ireland that are descended from indigenous stock – even so, early in the century a park stag from Windsor Great Park and some stags from Scotland were introduced, the latter going to Muckross Forest and the former to Derrycunnihy Forest.

Trophy wise, the antlers of the Killarney deer are nothing exceptional, but the weights are far superior to those of stags killed in Scotland and three beasts shot during 1964–5 had an average weight of 27 stone 11 lb (176 kg) clean, without heart and liver. A good pair of antlers will have a length of about 37 in. (94 cm) and carry twelve to fourteen points (tines).

Until the early twenties there were no wild Red deer on the Wicklow Hills but during the 1922 Rebellion some of the deer from Powerscourt Park escaped and since then a small feral population has remained in the area. The majority of heads in this area, although strong in the beam, are inclined to be narrow and the tops rather wild. Average weights are also good, with many adult stags scaling over 20 stone (127 kg). Unfortunately, Red deer have been crossing with the more numerous Japanese Sika deer which frequent the same area.

At one time dogs were frequently used in Wicklow for driving deer to hunters armed with rifles but the use of dogs for this purpose is now illegal, and deer can only be hunted by dogs under licence granted by the Minister – a licence which will, in effect, only be granted to a recognized pack of staghounds (Sect. 25–2 *Wildlife Act* 1976).

Stalking in the traditional manner, however, is practised on Glenveagh which was first afforested in 1891 when a deer fence was erected and deer obtained from Scotland introduced. Subsequently a number of other introductions were made from parks both in England and Ireland and these continued until about 1950 when the deer stock at Glenveagh was estimated to be about 1100 head. The total acreage originally fenced off was about 23,000 acres (9300 hectares) but during the troubled times of the early twenties the deer fence was broken in several places and a number of deer escaped to populate the surrounding countryside. Stags weigh considerably lighter than those of Killarney and although a number in excess of 20 stone

(127 kg) have been killed, the average is around the 15 stone (95 kg) mark and comparable to weights from some of the better Scottish forests.

Hunting the carted deer (Red deer) is still practised in Ireland where two packs – the Ward Union in Co. Wicklow and the Co. Down in Northern Ireland – regularly meet during the winter months.

In hunting the fox, hare or *wild* deer, the aim is to kill the animal; in hunting the carted deer the main consideration is to avoid killing or even harming the quarry. One of the advantages of hunting the carted deer is that the blank day can generally be eliminated, though it does sometimes happen that the two deer normally taken to a meet both prove to be non-runners.

Japanese Sika deer *Cervus nippon nippon*

The most abundant deer in Ireland today, both in Northern Ireland and in the Republic, is the Japanese Sika which, for over a hundred years has been leading a feral existence in some areas.

In the Republic the largest population of Sika deer is to be found in Co. Kerry, particularly around Muckross, whilst the species is also plentiful in the woods bordering the Wicklow mountains, having originated as escapees out of Powerscourt Park. Unfortunately, the Sika deer have been crossing with the Red deer which frequent the same area.

In Northern Ireland feral Sika are present in considerable numbers both at Baronscourt Newtonstewart, Co. Omagh and at Colebrooke, Co. Fermanagh, and both estates offer stalking facilities for visiting sportsmen. At Baronscourt, where the deer can be stalked over approximately 5500 acres (2200 hectares) of woodland and surrounding forestland, the charges for a week's stalking during the 1981–2 season, which includes the right to kill three stags is £275 plus V.A.T., which works out at £91.67 per stag. Any stags shot in excess of three are charged at £110 plus V.A.T., there being no additional charge for trophy merit. Hinds may be shot without charge.

Few Sika heads have been measured, but antlers with a length of about $22\frac{1}{2}$ in. (57 cm) would be good for Co. Kerry. In 1980 a trophy from Wicklow had a C.I.C. score of 243.50 points (antler length 52 cm (L) and 50.5 cm (R)).

Fallow deer *Dama dama dama*

Fallow deer are present in a number of counties both in Northern Ireland and in the Republic, but nowhere can they be said to be numerous. Their presence everywhere is due to escapism from the many deer parks scattered throughout the country.

From the few heads that have been measured, trophies would appear to be only average.

2 Western Europe

AUSTRIA

Red and Roe deer are the two principal species of deer that are available for hunting by the visiting sportsman, and although several tourist resorts and a few hotels have their own hunting grounds for use by their guests, the majority of hunting leases are to be obtained from the private landowner, contact with whom can often be established by advertising in one of the Austrian sporting journals such as *Österreichs Waidwerk*, *Der Anblick* or *St Hubertus*.

Fallow and Sika deer also occur in Austria but the majority are in enclosed parks and only about 350 of the former and 500 of the latter are living in the wild.

Before one can hunt in Austria, it is necessary to obtain both a shooting licence (*Behördliche Jagdkarte*) and a shooting permit (*Jagderlaubnis*), the former being issued by the local district authorities (*Bezirkshauptmannschaft*) and the latter from the owner of the land over which it is intended to hunt. Before the shooting permit will be granted, the applicant must produce, to the authorities, proof of identity (valid passport), and Austrian third party hunter's insurance certificate (*Jagdhaftpflichtversicherung*), a passport photograph and proof of his hunting ability. Should the applicant not be in possession of an earlier Austrian *Jagdkarte* or a valid certificate of a hunting organization of his home country, then he would have to obtain a membership card of an Austrian provincial hunting organization or pass the hunting examination.

Hunters from abroad can usually obtain the necessary documents (*Jagdkarte* and third party hunter's insurance certificate) from the owner of the ground (*Revierinhaber*) in question, the fees varying from province to province, and may vary from as little as £5 to about £50 for a complete year, with resident hunters having to pay about a third of this price. In several provinces it is possible to obtain a temporary visitor's card (*Jagdgastkarte*) at a reduced rate. For the services of the *Jäger* (forester), the fee varies from about AS100 to AS500 (about £3 to £17) per day.

Foreigners can import, duty-free, into Austria two unloaded rifles with up to 100 cartridges per firearm. For deer, the minimum calibre required is 5.6 mm.

A shooting agreement for, perhaps, a day or single kill is considered to have been made when the visiting huntsman has reached an amicable agreement with the lessor about the date of the hunt, and when 50 per cent of the cost of the shoot has been paid in advance as a deposit.

Acceptance of this deposit obliges the owner of the shoot (or his representative) to provide a professional *Jäger* whose main task is to see that the sportsman is brought to within shooting distance of the game being hunted. In mountainous terrain about 200 metres (218 yards) is considered to be a reasonable range.

For a deer which has been wounded but not recovered, it is customary for the full price to be paid unless some other arrangement has previously been made. In the case of a missed shot, the hunt will continue but should there be further misses, it is custom, on many estates, for part of the shooting cost to be paid.

Roe deer *Capreolus capreolus capreolus*
Local names: Roe, *Reh*; Buck, *Rehbock*; Doe, *Rehgeiss*.

The Roe has a wide distribution throughout Austria, being most numerous in the lowlands and hilly districts, and becoming progressively sparser as the altitude increases.

In 1979 the Roe population in Austria was estimated to be about 470,000. During the 1978–9 hunting season 233,481 Roe were shot.

As is the practice in West Germany, Roe bucks are divided into 'quality categories' and although the hunting season for the bucks starts, in some areas, on 16 May and in others on 1 June, generally speaking it is only the Class III quality bucks which may be killed during the first few weeks of the season. Termination of the buck shooting season also varies from area to area, ending in Ober Österreich (Upper Austria) as early as the end of September but in others *may* continue until the end of the year.

In the Tirol and Vorarlberg does may be shot as early as 1 June, a month earlier than in Salzburg – but elsewhere the opening day will be between 1 August and 1 September, the season for shooting of kids being the same as for does. It is only in recent years that the practice of shooting does in summer has been permitted, the intention being that yearling does should be shot before they become pregnant. In the hands of responsible hunters it has proved beneficial, for it has enabled the full number of female deer to be taken before the season is over.

The normal method of hunting Roe in Austria is by stalking, calling during the rut or shooting from a high seat.

Prices for shooting Roe bucks differ from one estate to another, and could vary from about £50 for a small buck with average antlers to over £500 for a very good trophy. In 1978 a buck, shot at Kaunteral, had antlers of 165.50 C.I.C. points.

Red deer *Cervus elaphus hippelaphus*
Local names: Red deer, *Rotwild*; Stag, *Hirsch*; Hind, *Hirschtier*, *Tier*; Calf, *Kalb*.

EUROPE

Red deer are to be found throughout Austria, being particularly plentiful in the provinces of Nieder (Lower) and Ober Österreich, Steiermark and the Tirol. The species is also reasonably abundant in Salzburg, Voralberg and Karnten. In 1979 the Red deer population was estimated to number about 115,000. During the 1978–9 season 42,466 deer of both sexes were shot.

Environment plays a significant part of the deer of Austria, and those deer which enjoy the luxuriant pastures of the Danubian Plain will often weigh as much as 570 lb (258.5 kg), whereas a stag from the Alpine region would do well to scale 350 lb (158.7 kg), both weights clean (without stomach).

In most provinces stags may be shot from 1 August until the end of the year, but may be extended to mid-January – the normal date for the termination of hind shooting. In some areas prickets may be shot during June or July.

As is the practice in West Germany, the stags are placed in categories, and both the duration of the season and the number allowed to be shot of the better quality animals strictly controlled.

The charges for shooting Red deer vary from one estate to another, ranging from about £100 for a cull type stag (*geringerer Hirsch*) to about £3400 for a really good trophy (*kapitaler Hirsch*). A stag was shot at Blühnback (1979) with a trophy of 232.09 C.I.C. points.

BELGIUM

Both Red and Roe deer are present in Belgium but the opportunities for a non-resident, unless invited by friends, to stalk or partake in a deer drive are really insignificant and hardly worth pursuing. Shooting is principally organized on a syndicate basis, and occasionally one or two days' shooting can be leased by a visitor to join a syndicate hunt. Anyone wishing to do so would be advised to advertise the fact in the St Hubert journal called *Chasse et Nature*. Should, however, a foreigner wish to lease an area – and this would probably be for a minimum period of nine years – he would have to tender for the shoot by putting in a price together with a signed agreement by two Belgian citizens prepared to guarantee payment should he default.

Normally, a day's driving consists of four or five separate drives, with rifles spaced out at perhaps 100 to 300 yards (90 to 270 metres) intervals, depending on the terrain, so as to surround completely the section of wood being driven. In the majority of cases, the game will be driven across a ride or clearing, and the rifles are invariably located on the edge of the wood being driven, so that shots can be taken as the deer run across the drive, having left the wood. Normally, shots are not allowed to be taken before the game has left the section being driven, but in broken country, where shots can safely be taken at game within the drive, areas where such shooting is permissible is clearly shown by a line of paint on trees – the safety arc being indicated by yellow or white paint and the no-shooting areas clearly marked in red.

Quite often it is the rifles posted along the side from where the driving starts who will get most of the sport, for the game will frequently break back through the drivers, who are assisted by a medley of dogs. The sound of running dogs, as they bring game towards your butt or blind, is quite the most exciting part of this form of sport which, however, can never be compared to stalking, for success is largely a matter of luck, keeping awake *and* dead quiet.

For both Red and Roe deer the minimum rifle calibre is 6.5 mm. Shotguns are also permitted, provided only ball or rifled slug are used.

There are three types of licences: (a) a full licence for daily use costing (1981) BFr.6600 (about £85); (b) a licence to hunt on a Sunday, costing BFr.4620 (about £60); and (c) a foreign visitor's licence costing BFr.1650 (about £22), valid for five consecutive days. The first two must present their examination certificate on application, but for a foreign visitor the certificate of his country of residence is acceptable.

Red deer *Cervus elaphus hippelaphus*
Local names: Stag, *Cerf*; Hind, *Biche*; Calf, *Faon*.

Red deer are plentiful in parts of the Plateau de l'Ardenne, and in particular in the provinces of Liège and Luxemburg. A few also occur in the province of Namur. The deer keep exclusively to the forest, and in the main, are prevented from wandering on to agricultural land by deerproof fencing. In the lease of many hunting grounds, the provision of artificial feeding during winter by the shooting tenant or syndicate is mandatory.

Throughout the whole of Belgium it is estimated that the Red deer population numbers about 5850 animals, of which some 1800 will be killed each year, the majority being shot during the autumn and early winter drives – a form of sport very popular with the Belgian hunter. A few stags will be shot from the high seat, but stalking, or still hunting, is seldom practised after the first two or three weeks of the season.

On the few estates – which include both private and State owned – where stalking is practised, inspired by German methods, *Abschuss* or shooting plans are being observed, and the shooting in these areas is becoming more selective.

By Belgian law it is permissible to kill stags from 25 September until end November, whilst hinds and calves may be shot between 15 October and 30 December. Not all class of stag, however, is legal game throughout the season, for during the first week when stalking, or shooting from a high seat is the usual method of hunting, only stags with antlers showing twelve points or more may be killed. Then, between 1 and 11 October, all stags except spikers (*daguets*) may be shot, but thereafter, for the remaining seven weeks of the season (12 October to 30 November) when the majority of deer will be killed, it is illegal to shoot *any* stags carrying *fewer* than ten tines. Penalties for breaking this law are severe, and may result in the forfeiture of hunting licences. Hunting at this time of year is almost entirely by driving the deer with beaters and dogs to sportsmen posted around the forests.

From a management point of view this is not a reasonable law, for as a result, switch-type heads and ugly 6-pointers – the very class of animal which should be taken out – enjoy a close season lasting almost fifty weeks, thus

35

ensuring that the majority of them will become the future stud animals.

Quick assessment of a deer's head – particularly of a running animal during a drive in woodland – is not easy, and at times it is almost impossible to judge whether or not the animal bears the necessary ten tines to make it a legal target. When mistakes occur, and perhaps an 8-pointer has been killed, it is sometimes impossible to discover which of the shooting party – which may number sixteen or more rifles – was responsible, for no one is prepared to admit to an action which could result in the loss of his hunting licence! A stag was shot at Wellin (1965) with a trophy of 211.75 C.I.C. points.

Roe deer *Capreolus capreolus capreolus*
Local names: Buck, *Brocard*; Doe, *Chevrette*; Kid, *Chevrillard*.

The Roe has a wide distribution throughout Belgium, and can be described as being plentiful in the provinces of Luxemburg, Liège and Namur, much of which is covered by the Plateau de L'Ardenne. A few occur in suitable localities in the province of Hainaut, but elsewhere its occurrence is rare. Throughout the whole of the country, the Roe population is estimated to be about 18,000 animals, of which about a third will be shot each year.

The hunting season for bucks is divided into two parts, the first, lasting from 1 May to 15 May and the second from 15 July to 15 August, which covers the period of the rut. A third season from 1 October until 30 November allows for the driving season's shooting, when deer of either sex may be taken.

During the July–August season, when the rut is on, the bucks are usually stalked, or shot from a high seat, when calling is practised. At this time, it is illegal to shoot bucks of fewer than six points. During the May season, however, only bucks with fewer than three points on one antler may be shot.

The quality of trophies is not high and few reach Gold medal standard, one of the best being shot at Cednogne in 1963 (159.10 C.I.C. points).

Roe are also hunted by two packs of hounds. One, the Rallye Campine Hunt, which was founded in 1919, hunts some 19,760 acres (8000 hectares) of forest – half private and half State-owned north-west of Maastricht in the province of Limbourg. The other, which has been in existence since 1844, is known as the Rallye Vielsalm, and their territory is some 29,640 acres (12,000 hectares) near Vielsalm, which is situated some 27 miles (45 km) south-east of Liège in the Ardennes. Both packs are Gascons-Saintongeois hounds, the former numbering forty-five and the latter sixty.

DENMARK
Four species of deer are found in Denmark; Red, Roe, Fallow and Sika, the last mentioned having been imported in 1900 and now occur in a number of localities both within a fenced reserve and in the wild. Occasionally an Elk has swum across from south Sweden and settled down in the Helsingör district of Frederiksborg, but have seldom remained on Danish soil for long.

In Denmark the shooting rights belong to the landowner who can let the shooting right to individual tenants or to a syndicate. Generally speaking, these shooting rights are only available on some of the larger estates who will sell the right to shoot a proportion of the males to be shot during the season. Normally this will be done through one of the travel agencies who arrange hunts for overseas sportsmen. Costs will vary, of course, from one agency to another, but one company who has the Roe stalking on a number of Danish estates, was quoting (August 1979) a figure of between £115 to £180 per buck regardless of size with, perhaps, an additional charge for trophies that attain medal class.

The same agency was offering Fallow buck stalking on four different Danish estates, the price varying from estate to estate, and depending on size of trophy. The price varied between £180 to £455 according to size of trophy, so for an average well-palmated trophy the charge would probably be about £350.

All sportsmen must be in possession of a Danish game licence costing DKr 104,00 (about £7) and foreigners may obtain this by showing or sending a valid game licence from their native country to Vildtforvaltningen, Strandvejen 4, DK 8410 Rønde, Denmark.

For all species of deer except Roe, a minimum calibre of 6.5 mm is mandatory. A shotgun, however, may be used for shooting Roe deer, and although there is no restriction as to pellet size, no.3 shot is the one normally selected, the maximum effective range being considered about 22 yards (20 metres). Brenneke ball is not used in Denmark.

Red deer *Cervus elaphus hippelaphus*
Local name: *Krondyr.*

Apart from about 200 animals in the royal deer park at Klampenborg near Copenhagen, all the wild and other enclosed Red deer populations are found in Jutland, with the biggest concentrations in the Toft Skov – Lille Vildmose area (about 400 deer) and Lindenborg Roldskovdistrikter (about 320 deer) of east Jutland. In west Jutland, the largest herds are at Klitplantagerne (about 285) and Statsskovdistrikt (about 175), whilst in mid-Jutland there are four areas where the population exceeds a hundred deer, the largest number being at Harreskov M.fl.Plantager (about 130). Throughout the whole of Jutland, the latest count (1975) suggested that the Red deer population was slightly in excess of 3000 animals.

Jutland is comparatively flat, with no ground rising above 565 ft (170 metres) above sea level. Much of it is, of course, under agriculture but there are also considerable areas of woodland (mainly spruce, pine, oak, beech and birch) as well as heath. The deer live principally in the woods and since they have access to agricultural land as well as, in most areas, to the seashore, they are able to keep in good heart throughout the year with none of the privation that deer in Scotland have to put up with in winter. Notwithstanding the facilities that are available to the deer, a few estate owners also feed them during spells of severe weather, if only to keep them from straying off their own ground.

One would expect that deer living under such favourable conditions would grow exceptionally fine heads but probably due to the sandy nature of the soil, they are nothing remarkable, and it is rare for a stag living in the wild to produce antlers with more than twelve points, the record being a 15-pointer from Påböl Plantage, Ribe County, killed in 1968 with 204.30 C.I.C. points. In the deer parks heads of up to twenty tines have been shot. The best trophy yet recorded for Denmark came from Jagersborg Deer Park. It was shot in 1972 and has been assessed at 232.80 C.I.C. points.

As mentioned previously, the deer, in many localities, keep mostly to the woods and during the autumn, should the weather be fine, a quiet approach on foot over the carpet of crisp leaves and twigs is almost an impossibility. A method much practised in former days on some estates, particularly during the rut when the majority of trophy stags will be shot, was to use a horse and trap in which to approach the deer. In this vehicle the sportsman, accompanied by the driver and keeper, drove about through the woods until the deer were seen. Should there be a shootable beast in the herd, the carriage would be driven in a large but gradually narrowing circle until within about 100 yards (90 metres) of the deer. Then, choosing a suitable opportunity, the sportsman would slip off the carriage *whilst it was still in motion* and take up a position behind a tree, from where a shot could be taken. Generally, the deer are not unduly disturbed by the sight or sound of a horse-drawn vehicle in the wood, for woodmen are constantly passing to and fro with their timber wagons. But under no circumstances must the trap stop, otherwise the deer become suspicious and move off. If this should happen they seldom travel far, and a fresh approach is generally possible. Single stags are often easier to drive up to than a stag with hinds, for the latter seem far more apprehensive of the carriage. It does not matter very much, however, how much noise is made, and provided the sportsmen chooses a suitable moment to slip off there should be little difficulty in getting a shot.

This was the manner in which I shot my first Danish stag at Mejlgaard in 1951, but in recent years this method has largely been replaced by a quiet approach before dawn to a favoured rutting area of the stags, or perhaps a wait at dusk in some 'hide' on the edge of a clearing in order to catch the deer emerging from the woods for their nightly foray to the fields.

During the winter months battues are held on the larger estates when the deer will be driven to sportsmen posted in the forest, offering, in the majority of cases, a moving target.

A wild stag, before gralloching, will weigh approximately 352 lb (160 kg) or about 264 lb (120 kg) clean.

The hunting season for Red deer in Denmark is as follows:

Stags 1 September–28/29 February   Hinds 1 October–31 December
Calves (both sexes) 1 September–28/29 February

Roe deer *Capreolus capreolus capreolus*
Local name: *Rådyr.*

Roe are by far the most common deer to be found in Denmark and are present almost everywhere, including many of the larger and smaller islands in Danish waters. Some of the best heads are to be found in the eastern part of Denmark, especially in the Bornholm County.

The majority of landowners feed their Roe in winter time with either kale, sugar beet or clover hay. In order to prevent the deer doing damage to young trees, all plantations are adequately fenced off until they have grown to a sufficient height to be past damage.

Roe bucks are generally shot in the spring by stalking at dawn or in the late evening, when some very fine sport can be had in trying to approach an animal, say, feeding out in the centre of a field extending to some 50 acres (20 hectares) or more, especially when surrounded by perhaps half a dozen other deer.

Throughout the whole of Denmark during the 1976–7 season, about 38,000 Roe were killed, which was an increase of some 2000 on the previous year. An adult Danish Roe buck weighs about 38 to 44 lbs (about 17 to 20 kg) clean.

There are two open seasons for hunting bucks in Denmark – a summer season from 16 May until 15 July, and an autumn season from 1 October to 31 December when does and kids (both sexes) may also be shot. It will be appreciated, therefore, that the buck may not be shot during the period of the rut, and since most of the older bucks will start to shed their antlers from October onwards, the autumn season is unsuitable for the trophy hunter. Shooting of Roe bucks from a high seat is not much practised in Denmark.

The best Roe head to come out of Denmark to date was shot at Fredenslund, Northjylland County in 1955 with a C.I.C. score of 158.50 points, thus beating by 0.4 points the previous record shot at Dybdal, Jutland, in 1944.

Fallow deer *Dama dama dama*
Local name: *Dådyr.*

Fallow deer are present in both the wild state and in the deer park, and some of the finest specimens are those to be seen in the royal park at Klampenborg. In the wild, the best populations are to be found on the bigger estates in the eastern parts of Denmark, which include the islands of Fyn (on the Wedellsborg estate), Samsö and Langeland, as well as in several of the woods in south Zealand. They also occur on the islands of Lolland in the area of Saksköbing and Holeby, whilst north of Copenhagen there are about 425 at Grib Skov. No up-to-date figures are available for the total population of

Fallow deer in Denmark, but in 1970 it was estimated to be about 3850. About 1500 deer will be shot each season.

The finest trophies have come off the Wedellsborg estate, the best being a buck killed in 1968 which scored 213.26 C.I.C. points.

In some areas in Jutland, for example, at Rold Skov, and on the Sostrup estate, there are also a few.

Apart from deer killed during winter battues, stalking is the normal method of hunting trophy bucks.

The hunting season for Fallow deer is the same as for Red deer.

Sika deer *Cervus nippon nippon*

The first Japanese Sika deer to reach Denmark were released in a fenced area on the estate of Svenstrup, near Copenhagen, about 1900 and it is believed they came from Ireland. A second introduction took place in 1909 when some Sika deer from Hagenbeck in Hamburg were released in a deer park on the Knuthenborg estate. These two introductions have probably been the source of all subsequent releases, although there is some doubt about the origin of the deer on the Frijsenborg estate in Jutland which was the first free-ranging population in Denmark, and numbering about 200, is now the largest feral herd. Other free-ranging herds in Jutland include Kathom in Arhus county, where the herds number about 100 animals, at Hals, near the coast east of Aalborg, at Ormstrup-Tange and Sophiendal-Hemstok in central Jutland, but on none of the last three areas do the numbers exceed about thirty, and they may well be on the way out.

On Zealand there exist two feral populations of Sika deer, one numbering about forty animals at Gribskov in the north – a State-owned forest of about 12,350 acres (5000 hectares), and the other in western Sjælland (Zealand) which started in 1936 when three deer escaped from a deer park on the estate of Gunderslevholm, and now number about seventy.

Altogether it is estimated that the total population of Sika deer in Denmark numbers about 700 animals, of which just over half will be free-ranging. About 200 deer are shot each year, at least 50 percent of which will be taken from the feral herds.

Stalking is the usual method employed for hunting Sika deer, the deer at Kathom producing the best trophies.

The hunting season for Sika deer is the same as for Red deer.

FINLAND

Of the four species of deer that are at present leading a wild existence in Finland, only two – the Elk and the introduced White-tailed deer from North America – are available for hunting on the mainland, and although a certain amount of Roe hunting is permitted on Åland, their numbers elsewhere are insignificant and the species is at present totally protected throughout the year. In 1902 there was an unsuccessful attempt to introduce Roe – locally referred to as *Metsäkauris* – to southern Finland.

The same applies to the wild Reindeer which occurs along the eastern border with Russian Karelia, but the herds there are steadily increasing and at some future date it seems probable that some hunting will probably be permitted.

Fallow deer occur on a few private estates, such as at Kytäjä near Hyvinkää in central Finland, where they are confined within a fence, and on the Hättö reserve which consists of about thirty small islands in the archipelago to the west of Helsinki. During the rutting season bucks frequently swim from one island to another in search of does. The first Fallow, a buck and two does, came to Hättö from Slottsparken in Gottenburg, Sweden, in 1938, since when further animals from other Danish parks have been added. A few animals are shot each year.

Red deer in 1938 and Roe in 1955 were also introduced to Hättö but within two years the former had to be killed off owing to damage they were causing to trees.

During the sixteenth century there were also some Red deer on Åland, but the species has long been extinct.

The Elk, therefore, is the principal deer species to be hunted in Finland, and any hunting party that consists of more than one person must have an appointed leader and deputy who will be responsible for the conduct of the hunt. Their names must be notified to the local police chief, as well as those of all members taking part in the hunt, and details of the weapons that will be used.

Elk may only be shot with rifles and soft-nosed bullets which weigh at least 10 g (154 grains) and whose hitting energy is at least 3000 Newtons (2210 ft/lb) at a distance of 25 metres (about 27 yards) from the mouth of the barrel. The cartridges must be factory made. For Whitetail, the hitting energy required is reduced to 2500 Newtons (1843 ft/lb) at 25 metres.

On a privately owned shoot every hunter must wear a red or orange cap, but if the area is State-owned, such as in northern Finland, where more than one hunting party may be operating in the same area, it is mandatory for both hunters and beaters to wear in addition to the cap a clearly distinguishable waistcoat or jacket.

Importation of weapons into Finland is easy. For those arriving at Helsinki by air, all that is required is for the visitor to fill in an application form at the airport, and a temporary licence will be issued immediately. For those arriving at other airports, by boat or by road, the firearm has to be left at the Customs office until a temporary licence has been obtained from the local police station, which will enable the weapon to be released by the Customs office.

Before hunting Elk, a hunter must pass a test which consists of three shots at a standing silhouette, and three shots at a moving target – range 75 metres. Any person who has passed a hunter's test in one of the following countries need not take an Elk shooting test in Finland: the Federal Republic of Germany, the German Democratic Republic, Austria, Switzerland, Spain,

Poland, Romania, Czechoslovakia and the Soviet Union. An Elk-shooting test passed in Sweden or Norway is also acceptable in Finland.

Elk *Alces alces alces*
Local name: *Hirvi*.

The Elk has a wide distribution, stretching from Lapland in the north to Helsinki in the south, with the heaviest population being found in the south-eastern, south and south-western coastal regions where the density is around four or five Elk per 1000 hectares. At present (1981) it is estimated that the winter population throughout Finland exceeds 100,000 animals and although 34,626 animals – which included 13,138 bulls – were legally taken by Finland's 65,000 Elk hunters during the 1978 season, it was insufficient to check the increasing population, and today the cull exceeds 55,000. Each year about 30 to 50 percent of the year's calves will be shot. Fifty years ago the Elk population was estimated to number only about 10,000 animals, and the annual cull was then about 2000. In 1980 the figure was 53,762.

Elk are also to be found on the former royal hunting reserve of Aland.

The hunting season, lasting two months, opens in Lapland on 1 October but elsewhere on the mainland a fortnight later (15 October), finishing on the 30 November and 15 December respectively.

The antlers are of two distinct types, those in the south and central part of Finland being mostly of cervine type with little or no palmation, whilst those in the north and east are principally of palmate type.

Hunting with Elk hound, following the tracks in snow, or driving, are the usual methods for hunting Elk in Finland.

A licence has to be obtained for each Elk it is intended to kill, the cost of which varies not only from area to area, but also according to the age of the animal, which varies from about £18 for a calf to about £60 for an Elk of more than one year of age.

Licences have to be applied for before the end of April, but will be refunded if the hunter has been unsuccessful. A licence, however, will be granted to an applicant only if he has a hunting area of at least 1000 hectares (2470 acres). In practice, therefore, a visiting sportsman will not be in a position to apply personally for a licence, so this will have to be done by his Finnish host.

Unless, therefore, the visitor is a guest, most foreign hunters will be charged not only for participating in a shoot but will probably have to pay a trophy fee as well. There is no fixed figure for these charges, but the Hunters' Central Organization has recommended to hunting clubs who organize most hunting for visiting sportsmen, to make the following charges:

1 For participation in a hunt organized by the Club, Fmk 1000 (about £116)
2 For killing an Elk of either sex, Fmk 1000
3 If the Elk killed is a bull, then in addition to the Fmk 1000, Fmk 150 will be charged for each prong (about £18 per prong).

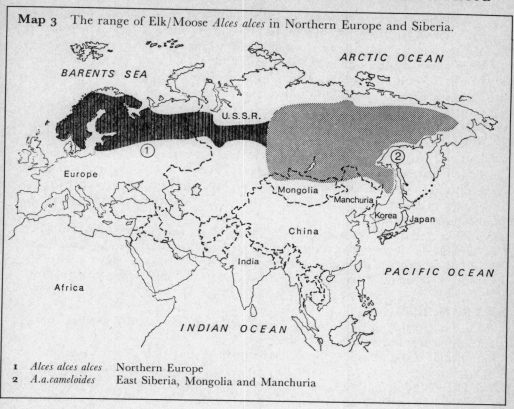

Map 3 The range of Elk/Moose *Alces alces* in Northern Europe and Siberia.

1 *Alces alces alces*   Northern Europe
2 *A.a.cameloides*   East Siberia, Mongolia and Manchuria

4 Should the trophy be of medal standard, then instead of charge (3) the
   following prices will apply:
   Bronze standard Fmk 3000 (about £350)
   Silver standard Fmk 4000 (about £466)
   Gold standard   Fmk 6000 (about £700)

If an animal has been clearly wounded but has not been recovered within one
day, it is recommended that there should be a fine of Fmk 1000. Every effort,
however, will be made subsequently to recover the wounded beast.

Accommodation, food and transport will, of course, be extra. The visitor is
entitled to take away the head with antlers, hide and hooves of any animal
killed, if he so wishes.

White-tailed deer *Odocoileus virginianus borealis*

In 1934 five White-tailed deer arrived in Helsinki from Minnesota and were
placed in a large fenced-in enclosure at Vesilahti near Tampere where they
remained until 1938 when the only male in the enclosure escaped and then it
was decided to release all the females. The deer acclimatized themselves well,
and by 1947 the population was estimated to be about ninety. The following

year six more deer, consisting of three male and three female calves, were again obtained from Minnesota and after a short stay in the enclosure at Vesilahti, were also liberated to join up with the feral herd, which by 1955 were estimated to number between 200 and 300 animals. Apart from local transfers from one area to another, no other introductions have been made.

At the present time White-tailed deer are distributed over a large area in south-central Finland, ranging from Kouvola in the east to Turku in the west, and from Pihtipudas in the north to almost Helsinki in the south.

The hunting season for Whitetail opens on 15 October and runs until the end of the year, and during the 1978 season some 9437 deer of both sexes, of which 3859 were bucks, were killed legally. Today the cull has been increased to around 15,000. The licence for each animal costs Fmk 105 (about £12) but will be granted to applicants only if they have a hunting area of at least 500 hectares (1235 acres).

One of the best trophies taken in recent years was shot in 1966 and when measured in centimetres under the Boone and Crockett formula, had a score of 419.2 – or 165 when converted into inches. In Minnesota – the source of the Finnish Whitetail – the best trophy has a score of $206\frac{5}{8}$ (measured in inches).

FRANCE

Hunting, either with rifle or on horseback following hounds, is available to the visiting sportsman to France.

So far as sport with rifle is concerned, foreigners may hunt on private estates – generally by invitation only – and on State grounds which are managed by the Office National des Forêts (O.N.F.) which is the equivalent to the Forestry Commission in Great Britain, who will issue individual licences. From a forestry point of view the O.N.F. manages about 3,705,000 acres (1,500,000 hectares) of State forests, but only a small portion of this area is available for licensed stalking, the remainder being leased or loaned to shooting syndicates: At the present time there are twenty-two O.N.F. hunting areas open to licensed stalking, on eleven of which Red deer can be stalked, Roe on nine and Sika deer on one. In the near future this number could well be increased, for the O.N.F. policy is to extend as much as it can its licensed areas for stalking, particularly for hinds which at present, in some areas, are too numerous and will have to be drastically reduced. Shooting on State grounds is normally by stalking or shooting from high seats, but whichever method is used, the sportsman must at all times be accompanied by an official guide. No special formalities are required for a foreign sportsman stalking on O.N.F. ground, but he may be requested to shoot at a target before the hunt to prove his ability and accuracy of his rifle.

Throughout most of France, deer can be hunted only within the limits of the annual *plan de chasse*, or 'bag limit' which has been set by local authorities for each hunting area. In many *departements* the *plan de chasse*, in addition to the number of deer to be killed, also states the age and quality of male Red deer allowed to be shot, and within 48 hours of having been shot, the complete head has to be available for examination to see that the *plan de chasse* has been observed. It seems probable that, in the very near future, the same regulations will be applied to Roe bucks shot during the rut. It is only since January 1979 that the *plan de chasse* became operative in all regions.

Hunting deer with horse and hound – *chasse à courre* – is still a very popular sport in France and more than eighty packs are actively hunting either stag or Roe buck – or both – throughout the country as follows:

	Hunting stag only	Hunting Roe buck only	Hunting both stag and buck
North (Paris region)	15	5	1
North-west	13	18	5
Central France	1	3	–
South-west France	1	17	–
South-east France	1	3	–
North-east France	1	–	–
Total = 84	32	46	6

(Extracted from J Bouéssée's *Vénerie d'Aujourdhui*, 1975.)

It will be noted that most of the hunting takes place in the north and north-west of the country, being almost absent from the eastern regions, where, in fact, the most important populations of wild deer – both Red and Roe – are to be found.

Any foreign visitor wishing to follow a day's hunting with hounds should contact Société de Vénerie in Paris and apart from the rent of a horse, there should be no other cost. However, if, after the kill, the visitor should receive the 'foot honour' – presentation of a slot from the stag – this would entail an expensive tip of about FFr. 300 to 500 (about £30 to £50) to the *equipage* (pack) for the honour. By tradition, this tip to the hunting pack was the equivalent of a gold 'Louis' – about the same value as the sovereign.

Fallow deer *D.d.dama* – locally referred to as *le daim* – were formerly hunted by hounds in the Forêt de Compiègne, near Paris, as well as in one or two other areas. At the present time, apart from about 400 wild animals in Alsace, in the Selestat region (Bas-Rhin), the remaining Fallow deer are in private parks. Trophies are generally poor in the wild population, but some good park heads are occasionally shot.

Sika deer *C.n.nippon* from Japan were introduced into the Rambouillet park at the end of the last century, being the gift of the Mikado to the French president, and they soon established themselves. In 1948 an area between Nantes and Rennes was stocked with deer from Rambouillet and they, also, established themselves well. In eastern France, in the Parc de Salzlecke – an enclosure of about 300 hectares (720 acres) in the Forêt de la Harth near Basel – licences costing FFr. 1000 to 3000 (about £100 to £300) according to quality, are available from the O.N.F. for stalking Sika deer.

Since 1976 the Comité National de Mensuration des Trophées is recording trophies of all big game species shot in France, and provided the score of a Red deer or Roe deer trophy is at least 165 C.I.C. points or 105 C.I.C. points respectively – the minimum scores for Bronze medal standard in Western Europe – it will be accepted for inclusion in the Record Book. The scores of trophies of any species shot in parks or enclosures are listed separately.

Although trophies shot under licence in the national forests are charged for according to trophy merit, the method of calculating this charge is not based on the C.I.C. score, as is the practice in many European countries, but under a system known as the O.N.F. score (*fiche de notation*).

This system, which is calculated only on physical measurements so as to avoid any discussion that might arise between client and keeper over weight or beauty points, is purely a commercial one in order to establish the correct price to charge a client for his trophy. The following example, based on the measurement of the record trophy stag shot in 1977, shows how the system works:

Details of measurement	Left cm		Right cm	Total	Divide by factor	O.N.F. points score
Length of antlers	111.2	+	111.3	222.5	40	5.56
Length of brow tines	27.2	+	28.5	55.7	80	0.69
Length of tray tines	32.6	+	32.6	65.2	80	0.81
Circumference of coronets	25.6	+	26.0	51.6	20	2.58
Circumference, lower beam	17.5	+	18.2	35.7	10	3.57
Circumference, upper beam	18.2	+	18.0	36.2	10	3.62
Number of points (tines)	8	+	9	17	10	1.70
Inside span*		66.0				0
				Total score		18.53

* This figure is multiplied by 2 and divided by the total length of both antlers. If the resultant figure is under 0.7 or greater than 1.2, 0 points are awarded; but 0.1 to 0.3 points are awarded for any figure between 0.7 (0.1 point) and 1.2 (0.3 point).

Charges for shooting Red deer vary from about £40 for a stag with an O.N.F. score of nil to about £790 for one with antlers of Bronze medal standard, and over £3000 for a Gold medal trophy. The latter, however, would be exceptional for France.

With only three measurements to take, the O.N.F. score panel for Roe buck antlers is much simpler to calculate, as shown by the example of a Bronze medal trophy which under the C.I.C. formula scored 105.02 points.

Measurements	Left cm		Right cm	Total	Divide by factor	O.N.F. points score
Length of antlers	25.0	+	28.3	53.3	12	4.44
Volume of antlers (in cm/3)				138	20	6.90
				Total O.N.F. score		11.34

The charge for shooting a Red deer hind (*biche*, *bichette*) or calf (*faon*) is

FFr.400 and FFr.300 respectively – double the prices required for shooting a yearling Roe buck (*chevrillard*) and doe (*chevrette*).

In addition to the trophy fee there is an outing fee, morning or evening, of FFr.100 which will be increased at the rate of FFr.30 per hour should the period exceed five hours.

Game wounded but not found will be charged according to the species, sex and quality, varying from about FFr.150 for a Roe doe to FFr.3000 for a trophy stag (*cerf à chandelier*). A trophy Roe buck will be about FFr.700.

If the client happens to shoot stag or buck other than the one designated by the keeper, he will be fined 120 percent of the price that would normally be charged for that particular trophy, or FFr.1000, whichever is the greater. For Red deer hinds or calves the fine is also FFr.1000, but reduced to half for the Roe does and kids (*chevrette, chevrillard*).

To summarize, therefore, the above charges, if a sportsman was fortunate during the course of two outings in a State forest of France to shoot a stag or Roe buck with antlers of Bronze medal standard, the charge would be approximately FFr.7800 or just over £700 to FFr.3700 (say about £340) respectively.

With regard to firearms in France, it is only with a very special authorization that one is allowed to use a rifle of military calibre, so in order to avoid any difficulties with the Customs or police, visiting sportsmen would be well advised not to bring in any rifle chambered for a cartridge in use in any army of the world. This would include .308; .30–06; .223; 7 × 57 and 8 × 57. Automatic rifles must be limited to 3-shot capacity (one in barrel and two in magazine).

Although in all O.N.F. licensed areas only the rifle is allowed, elsewhere for Red deer, provided the rifle is of no less calibre than 5.6 mm or ball shot is used, shotguns are permissible. For Roe, however, pellet shot under 3 mm (no.4 shot) is permissible in some *departements*, as Roe are often shot during small game drives. Shot, however, is forbidden in the three eastern *departements* of Bas-Rhin, Haut-Rhin and Moselle.

Red deer *Cervus elaphus hippelaphus*
Local names: Stag, *Cerf*; Hind, *Biche*; Calf, *Faon*.

Red deer are to be found in many scattered populations in northern and eastern France, being most plentiful in the large forests to the north and east of Paris right up to the Ardennes and the frontier with West Germany. These include the forests of Villers Cotteret (near Soisson), Marchenoir (on the Loire) and Sedan (Ardennes). They are absent, however, from the Pas-de-Calais area east of Boulogne.

In northern France, near the Normandy coast, Red deer can be stalked in the State forests of Roumare (Seine-Maritime) near Rouen, and Cerisy (Calvados) near Bayeux, whilst south of Lille the forest of Mormal has recently been opened up for licensed shooting. In Lorraine, near the German frontier, stalking can be had in the forest of Dabo (Moselle) and Haslach (Bas-

Rhin), and also in Haut-Rhin near Basel. Further south, near Geneva, stalking is now available in the Jura forests – an area which in 1977 produced one of the best trophies yet recorded for France (216.19 C.I.C. points). In the south-east, in the Dauphine area, stalking in State forests is available at Durbon (Hautes-Alpes), Vaucluse (near Avignon), Drôme and Isère (near Grenoble). In addition to deer it is possible to hunt mouflon in Drôme, and both mouflon and chamois in Isère, so a combination hunt after these typical European game animals should be an attraction to foreign sportsmen. In the north-west, the species has a moderate distribution in Normandy, particularly in parts of Calvados, but in forests along the coast it is subject to considerable disturbance from holiday makers in the area. The same also applies in other areas within easy reach of city dwellers, particularly in Alsace where deer are most plentiful. In the Forest of Rambouillet, south of Paris, which is hunted by hounds, there is a fair stock of Red deer and one or two fine trophies have been shot in adjacent woods.

In the south of the country, Red deer are not plentiful but numbers are increasing in the Herault district to the west of Montpellier. The Corsican Red deer *C.e.corsicanus* is now believed to be extinct in Corsica.

Since 1950 possibly a thousand deer or more have been caught up in Chambord, and introduced into areas devoid of any Red deer. Chambord, extending to about 12,350 acres (5000 hectares), is an enclosed forest in Loir et Cher, near Orleans, belonging to the State, its main 'sporting function' being to provide large 'official drives' at wild boar. In addition to the boar, the park also contains a very large quantity of Red deer, but owing to the sandy nature of the soil, are of poor quality. However, once released into new terrain both weight and trophy qualities have improved tremendously, and this is particularly noticeable in the deer introduced to Jura forest which are 100 percent 'Chambord' blood, for prior to 1951 Red deer were extinct in the area. Now, in a forest area of about 37,050 acres (15,000 hectares) there is a stock of about 700 deer, which include many stags having a potential trophy value of 195 C.I.C. points or more. In fact, it was in the Forêt de Chaux, Jura, that the best trophy yet recorded for France was killed during a *battue* in 1977 (216.19 C.I.C. points).

In Syndicate shoots, driving – *battue* – is the normal method of hunting, but in the State forests generally only boar are shot at the *battue*, stalking – *approche* – or waiting in high seats being practised on deer.

The season for hunting deer with rifle is decided by the central authority, Direction de la Protection de la Nature, in Paris, whilst the *plan de chasse* is decided by a Commission seated in each *departement*, so conditions will vary from one *departement* to another. Furthermore, the three *departements* of the east, Bas-Rhin, Haut-Rhin and Moselle, have their own game laws which are completely different to those operating elsewhere in France, but almost similar to German methods, and this has resulted in a higher deer population in these *departements*. Generally, the open season for both sexes runs from about the end of September until the end of the first or second week of January, although in some areas the shooting of hinds may be restricted to only a day or two. Latterly, however, the owners of a *plan de chasse* have been granted, in many *departements*, special authorization to stalk stags from 1 September even though the general season may not open until 25 September or even later.

The season for hunting the stag with hounds is considerably longer, opening during the last week of September and extending to the end of April – a total of seven months.

Altogether, as a result of the shooting and hunting with hounds, just over 7000 deer of both sexes, including calves, are being killed annually.

Roe deer *Capreolus capreolus capreolus*
Local names: Roe, *Chevreuil*; Buck, *Brocard*; Doe, *Chèvre, Chevrette*; Kid, *Faon, Chevrillard*.

The Roe deer has a wide distribution in France, being particularly plentiful in Alsace, Ardennes and the Seine valley of Normandy. In Brittany it occurs in most woods, as well as on moorland where there is broom and bracken to provide shelter. In the Charente-Maritime *departement* north of Bordeaux its main haunts are the Forêt de Benon and Forêt de La Coubre. It is, however, absent from the area around Perpignan, in the extreme south, and also in Provence, north of Marseilles.

Until the early fifties the only methods for hunting Roe in France were driving – *battue* – and hunting with hounds – *chasse à courre* – and since both these activities took place during the winter months, very few trophy bucks in hard antler were ever killed. In fact in 1954 it was illegal in many parts of France to hunt Roe before November.

However, in recent years there has been a growing interest in stalking Roe buck, for this deer is now considered as the game animal of the future, and every effort is being made to increase the Roe populations at the expense of the Red deer, owing to the greater damage caused to forestry by the latter. Already medal class trophies are being taken and since about 1950 over twenty trophies of Gold medal standard have been taken in various parts of the country, the best being a buck shot in the Aisne *departement*, some 42 miles (70 km) north-east of Paris in 1978, which has been assessed at 190.87 C.I.C. points. This is the second Gold medal buck to have come from this area, the previous one having been shot in 1959 (158.62 points).

Unless one is stalking as a guest on private land, the best chance for a foreigner to hunt Roe in France is to apply to the Office National des Forêts, for stalking is available on at least nine of their State forests, which include Mormal (Nord); Dabo (Moselle); Haslach (Bas-Rhin); La Harth and Kastenwald (Haut-Rhin); and Auberive (Haute-Marne); all of which, except Mormal, are in the eastern part of the country.

During the 1976-7 season about 63,200 Roe (both sexes) were killed in France, both by shooting and by hunting.

In all forests managed by Office National des Forêts for licensed stalking, the hunting season normally extends throughout the *general* hunting period,

49

i.e. end of September to mid-January. Stalking Roe bucks during the rut, however, is now becoming popular and since 1979 has been allowed on special terms from 1 July to 30 August.

GERMANY, WEST (FEDERAL REPUBLIC OF GERMANY)

In no country in Europe is hunting more steeped in tradition than in Germany, many of the customs dating back to the seventh century when the sovereigns of Europe practised the right to hunt as the sole prerogative of the Court. In those days game was divided into two groups: *Hochwild* and *Niederwild* – literally 'high' and 'low game', but now known as 'big' and 'small game'. *Hochwild*, which included the Red deer, was reserved for the sovereign and his guests. *Niederwild*, which included the Roe, was hunted by people of lesser rank, but then only with the sovereign's permission.

By 1500 more ceremony was being introduced and in order to entertain in lavish fashion, the large hunting parties assembled for the sport, great hunting castles – *Schloss* – were erected. Large scale drives – *Treiben* – were the order of the day, and large numbers of deer and boar were driven into confined areas to be shot at by the assembled hunters.

This form of sport was very popular with the nobility, and continued in fashion until the beginning of the nineteenth century, when the royal hunting prerogative virtually disappeared, and the title of much of the land, previously controlled by feudal lords, passed to the common people.

In 1848 hunting rights became connected to real estate titles, and landowners were entitled to hunt the game on their own property. With their new-found freedom to hunt, the result was inevitable, and it was not long before uncontrolled hunting had seriously reduced the deer population, and in the case of the Red deer, almost to a point of extinction. Fortunately the situation was noticed in time, and during the early part of the present century, due to sound legislation, Germany's stock of game was restored.

Probably the most important piece of hunting legislation in Germany's history was the law of 1934 which was enforced by the federal hunting master, *Reichsjägermeister*, and as a result the *Reichsregierung* was able to exercise almost complete control over the country's hunting activities.

This law was subsequently replaced by the 1952 Federal Hunting Law – which remains in effect today – and although it follows the pattern of the 1934 law it also recognizes the hunting sovereignty of the separate States, *Länder*. The position today is, therefore, that whilst the Federal Hunting Law defines hunting rights, open seasons, minimum size of hunting areas and licensing requirements etc., the *Länder* are able to impose their own regulations within this framework and to suit their own particular requirements.

Hunting land in Germany is divided into areas averaging 1000 to 2000 acres (400 to 800 hectares) called *Reviere*. The right to hunt deer in these areas can be owned or leased by anyone of the following: the F.R.G., a State, individual or syndicate, or a community. Whoever owns or leases hunting property, therefore, is automatically the holder of the hunting rights. The

Federal Hunting Law establishes *minimum* sizes for various categories of *Reviere*. The principal *Revier* classifications are:

1 *State and federal hunting.* These areas usually consist of woodland belonging to a State or the F.R.G. In most state forest *Reviere*, the Forestry Department exercises control of the hunting rights through the forestry official in charge of the *Revier*. These hunting rights may, however, be leased to private citizens.

2 *Hunting co-operatives.* These consist of a number of parcels of land which, when combined, have a minimum area of 625 acres (250 hectares) and are owned by a community or a group of citizens. Hunting rights in the combined area – known as a *Gemeinschaftlicher Jagdbezirk* – are usually leased to the highest bidder.

3 *Private areas.* The hunting rights in these areas – known as *Personengemeinschaft* – belong to the property owner, and may be exercised by him, or leased to others.

Areas in any of the above mentioned groups may be leased to individuals or groups for varying periods, twelve years being the usual lease for Red deer and nine for Roe.

Whoever holds the hunting rights, *all* are bound by law to manage and conserve the game so that an equitable balance is maintained between the available feed and cover, and the adverse effects of crop damage. This is called the *Abschussplan* – the shooting plan. In order to make this plan, the holder of hunting rights must take an annual census of all cloven-hoofed game (*Schalenwild*) except boar on his shooting ground, and from this a shooting plan will be prepared and then submitted to a county hunting authority for approval. In addition to the number of deer on the ground, the shooting plan will indicate the sex ratio, approximate age groups, and the number of deer, including the class of trophy, it is planned to kill. The hunting authority will then evaluate the plans and in the light of crop damage, and any other factors that might have occurred during the previous year, approve or amend accordingly. Once approved, the shooting (harvest) plan becomes mandatory and will be enforced, should it be necessary, by forestry officials.

In Germany holders of hunting rights are also required by law to own, or have available, a dog capable of searching for wounded game. Many breeds of hunting dogs are used for this purpose, but for deer, probably the most popular are those of Bloodhound type – *Schweisshund*.

In order to decide which animals are to be shot, and which are to be preserved for breeding, all cloven-footed game are classified in two divisions (1) virility and; (2) quality.

In Red and Fallow deer male specimens belong to one of three virility classes: (I) strong; (II) medium; and (III) inferior. For male Roe deer, however, only (I) strong and (II) inferior are considered.

With regard to quality standards, animals placed in Class A are good, both in body and antler, and are the ones to be preserved for breeding. Class B animals, on the other hand, display some weakness in either physical or antler development, which may be hereditary and should, therefore, be culled. Aged animals, barren females, late or weak calves etc., all come into this category also.

In an attempt to improve game quality, weak animals and those of poor trophy potential are culled if possible during the weeks prior to the rut. On the other hand, prime trophy stags and bucks that have reached full maturity will normally be killed during and after the rut, and in the majority of cases will be shot from a *Hochsitz*, high seat, which gives the best opportunity to make a careful appraisal of the deer before the shot is taken, so essential if the shooting has to be selective.

One of the first customs a visitor to Germany, and also to Austria, will notice is the plume of hairs worn by hunters in their hats. These hairs – known as a *Bart* – may be either chamois, Red deer or wild boar. In chamois (*Gams*) the hairs used for making into a *Gamsbart* are plucked from an animal in full winter pelage, and come from the hairs which run along the backbone of animals of both sexes, and in particular those of advanced years. For a *Saubart* the guard or crest hairs that grow along the back of a mature boar (*Sau*) are also taken. In Red deer (*Hirsch*) the hairs for a *Hirschbart* are taken from the mane of a rutting stag, the best coming from those of middle age. Of all the *Bart* trophies, the *Gamsbart* is the most coveted, and in the Bavarian and Austrian alpine regions is considered a status symbol. In Germany, a good *Gamsbart* will sell for about DM400 to DM500, with outstanding examples costing double that amount – say about £90 to £110.

Another custom a visiting hunter is soon to become acquainted with is the use of the greeting *Waidmannsheil* and *Waidmannsdank* – literally 'hunter's greeting' and 'hunter's thanks'. Not only is it a general term of greeting between one sportsman and another, but during the hunt, following a successful shot, the *Jäger* (keeper) or person guiding the hunter, will take a small branch – *Schützenbruch* – (hunter's branch) and after dipping it in the blood of the deer, will place it on his hat or on the blade of his hunting knife, and present it to the successful hunter with the word *Waidmannsheil* (hunter's greeting) – who will accept it and after placing it on the right side of his or her hat, will respond with the words *Waidmannsdank* (hunter's thanks). Even when hunting alone, it is customary for a hunter, after making a kill, to place a small branch in his hat, thus informing anyone met on the way home that the hunt has been successful.

When an animal has been wounded, and finally tracked down by a dog, the dog handler will present the branch to the hunter, who will then break a piece off and hand it back to the dog handler, part of which will then be attached to the dog's collar thus denoting that success has been achieved only by the combined efforts of hunter, dog-handler and dog.

Branches are also used in many other ways during the course of a hunt, such as to indicate the point where a wounded deer was first hit, and to indicate the direction in which it went off. The branches are always broken from the living tree, and only those trees native to Germany are used. These include oak, alder, pine, fir and spruce.

Normally, according to German practice – *Waidgerechtigkeit* – if a deer is shot in one *Revier*, but escapes to die on a neighbouring *Revier*, the hunter is not entitled to leave his ground to take possession, but must mark the point where the deer crossed the boundary, and inform as soon as possible the holder of the hunting rights of the area in question. A number of estates, however, have an agreement that if a wounded deer is visible on a neighbour's ground, the animal may be given a finishing shot, and although it must then be gralloched (stomach removed) under no circumstances may the carcase be removed.

The use of the hunting horn is another aspect of the hunt that has persisted through the centuries. At one time the carrying of the hunting horn was the exclusive privilege of the large game hunter. Now, in modern Germany, a social hunt is not complete unless buglers are present with their hunting horns, not only to pass information and instructions to those partaking in a hunt – this is particularly important during a drive – but also to play a *Totsignal* (last post) during the closing ceremony. Altogether there are over forty distinct hunting calls in use in Germany today – some instructive, such as informing beaters and hunters that game has broken back, and the drive will be retaken – others ceremonial, particularly to mark the end of a hunt when all the game will be laid out in proper order, each beast lying on its right side, with Red deer occupying the first row, stags at one end and calves at the other. If any Fallow deer have been killed they will occupy the second row, and in the mouth of every male deer will be placed a small branch as a token of respect, indicating the 'last bite' – *letzter Bissen*. It is also customary to place a branch, referred to as 'ownership branch' – *Inbesitznahmebruch* – over the bullet hole in the body. For male animals, the broken end of the branch points towards the head – for females the branch is reversed with the tip pointing in the direction of the head.

The buglers take up their position behind and to the right of the rows of game, whilst behind them stand the dog handlers with their dogs. The third row will be taken up by the beaters. To the front of the game, with the host standing in the centre, are the hunters, and after the former has announced the total number and species of game taken, he will hand out a shooter's branch, *Schützenbruch*, to every hunter who has shot a cloven-footed game (*see also below*). The host may also name the king of the hunt – *Jagdkönig* – the hunter who has killed most game. The buglers then present the appropriate *Totsignal* for each species killed, and close the ceremony with the two calls – *Halali* and *Jagdvorbei* – the hunt is over. Throughout the ceremony it is customary for the party to stand at ease, with head gear removed, and on no account should anyone step over a carcase, but always walk round.

Following a day's driving there is generally a festive meal or gathering held at a hunting lodge or guest house – *Schüsseltreiben* or *Knödelbogen* – literally the 'last drive', and all hunters who have participated in the day's sport are expected to attend.

The Saint Hubertus holiday is observed by all hunters in Germany on 3 November, and the Hubertus hunt is generally considered the outstanding social function of the hunting calendar. During the hunt practically all the hunting customs are employed, ranging from the various bugle calls to the most commonly used branch signs and display of game.

Deer in Germany are hunted by one or a combination of the following methods. (1) Stalking (*die Pirsch*), a technique which is the same the world over. (2) Sitting or waiting (*Ansitz*). Most Germans prefer to wait for deer at dawn or dusk coming to a favourite feeding place or rutting ground. Normally the hunter will sit on an elevated platform which may vary from a seat supported on a ladder (*Leiter*) to a more solid and permanent construction generally referred to as a high seat (*Hochsitz*). Should the latter have a roof and door, making it a small one-room unit equipped, perhaps, to sleep two hunters, it will be called a *Kanzel* (pulpit). The advantages of a high seat are that the hunter is out of range of the deer's keen sense of smell, and the shooting is not only safer, but can be more selective. (3) Driving or stand hunting (*Drückjagd*). This is the most effective way of killing a large number of deer and is only practised towards the end of the season when a number of hinds and inferior stags have to be killed to complete the cull for the shooting plan. It only requires a small number of beaters who should move slowly and with as little noise as possible through the woods so as not to panic the deer into hasty flight, thus giving the rifles posted around the wood etc. the chance of a quiet shot at a slow-moving animal. Only Red and Fallow deer are normally hunted in this fashion in Germany, for it is seldom for Roe to be driven.

Under the Federal Hunting Law it is illegal to use any rifle of calibre under 6.5 mm (.256 in.), and whilst it is in order to use for Roe deer a cartridge whose knockdown energy or shooting power at 100 metres (E-100) is less than 100 kilopondmeter (981 joule or 726 ft/lb), for Red and Fallow deer the cartridge must either produce a minimum velocity of 850 metres per second (2789 feet per sec.) at 100 metres (V-100) or the bullet must weigh at least 10 g (154.32 grains). This provision, however, is not universal throughout Germany, for local variations exist in some States. For instance in Baden-Württemberg, should a rifle of calibre greater than 6.5 mm be used, then for Red and Fallow deer, no bullet weighing less than 8 g (123.6 grains) and producing less than 200 kpm (1446 ft/lb) at 100 metres (E-100) may be used. Bavaria and the Saar have a similar restriction but include the Roe as well.

Shotgun slugs (Brenneke) are legal for short-range shooting and are often used during drives for Red deer and wild boar. The use of shot of any size is forbidden for all cloven-hoofed game.

In Germany all hunters must pass an examination before obtaining a hunting licence. This compulsory examination – which is in two parts, written and practical – is normally preceded by a series of lectures covering all aspects of hunting, i.e. use of weapons, gun safety, hunting laws, game animals and birds, customs etc. As a result of these examinations, just over a quarter of a million people are in possession of hunting licences. The cost of a hunting licence (*Jagdschein*) in Germany is DM80 (about £18) plus another DM60 for insurance.

A foreigner may hunt anywhere in Germany if he is invited by the proprietor of a private shoot, or if he purchases the right to shoot a deer in one of the Government forests. A trophy fee will be added.

At the end of the season, each hunting association holds an annual trophy presentation at which Gold, Silver and Bronze medals are awarded to any trophy that scores sufficient C.I.C. points. In some cases, a local hunting association may award a bronze medal to the oldest or most unusual trophy.

Red deer *Cervus elaphus hippelaphus*
Local names: Red deer, *Rotwild*; Stag, *Hirsch*; Hind, *Alttier* or *Tier*; Calf, *Kalb*.

Although Red deer are present in many parts of West Germany, their presence is not popular in many areas due to damage they cause to forestry and agriculture. In north Germany the main herds are to be found in the Schleswig-Holstein district and in Niedersachsen. A few occur in the forests around Kleve near the Dutch border, but the quality here is not good.

In the Eifel forest district Red deer are numerous between the Mosel river and the Belgian border. They are also plentiful in the Soon-Wald forest which lies south of the Mosel, their range spreading right up to the Luxembourg frontier.

South-east of Hannover there are a fair number in the Harz mountains where, in the past, deer from Rominten in former East Prussia – renowned for their excellent quality – have been introduced. They are tolerably plentiful also in the alpine district of southern Bavaria. In few parts of Germany, however, owing to numerous introductions in the past of fresh blood, can the deer be said to be of pure indigenous stock.

In 1980 it was estimated that the total stock of Red deer in West Germany was about 90,000 head, the cull for the 1979–80 season being approximately 32,000 of which one-third came from Bayern.

As already mentioned, Red deer are divided into three virility classes I, II and III and within these three classes are further subdivisions based on antler weight, configuration and probable future development. The following classifications, with some regional variations, apply throughout Germany.

Class I A. To qualify for this class, stags must be at least ten years old, display a trophy that meets the conservation standard established for that particular region, and the trophy must weigh a minimum of 3.5 kg (about $7\frac{3}{4}$ lb). The antlers must be symmetrical, consisting of well-pearled, heavy beams that are long-pointed and well crowned on both sides. The spread of antlers must measure at least 60 percent of the average beam length.

Class I B. To qualify for this class, stags must be at least ten years old and carry a trophy that weighs at least 3.5 kg, but with antlers that do not meet established conservation standards. Stags in this category are generally those with asymmetrically formed antlers, with narrow spread beams and short tines, and display a crown on one side only.

Class II A. Stags of this category are animals between four and nine years of age, whose physical and trophy characteristics suggest that they will eventually qualify for Class I.

Class II B. Stags of this category are those animals whose weight of antlers range from 1.5 kg to 3.5 kg (about $3\frac{1}{4}$ to $7\frac{3}{4}$ lb), and whose general substandard physical condition or defective antler formation would indicate that they will never advance to Class I.

Class III A. Stags of this category are those animals between the years of one and three, whose physical and trophy characteristics are proportionally well-developed and likely to reach conservation standards. Two year old stags displaying massive or forked antlers over 20 cm (about $7\frac{3}{4}$ in.) in length, three year olds exhibiting 6-pointed antlers, and four year olds carrying 8-pointed antlers with well developed tines, all belong to this category.

In some States the above animals may be designated II A.

Class III B. Stags in this category display antlers that weigh less than 1.5 kg and are substandard or defective in form.

In West Germany an average stag will weigh about 275 lb (124.7 kg) with those in alpine areas being some 30 to 40 lb (13 to 18 kg) lighter.

The seasons for hunting Red deer in Germany are as follows:

Stags (*Hirsch*) and mature hinds (*Alttiere*)	1 August–31 January
Spikers (*Schmalspiesser*)	1 June–28 February
Young hinds (*Schmaltiere*)	1 June–31 January
Calves – male (*Hirschkalb*), female (*Tierkalb*)	1 August–28 February

Roe deer *Capreolus capreolus capreolus*
Local names: Roe deer, *Rehwild*; Buck, *Rehbock*; Doe, *Rehgeiss*, *Ricke*; Kid, *Kitz*.

Roe deer are plentiful throughout West Germany, from the plains right up to the timber line of the Alps. It is also abundant on some of the islands along the North Sea coast. In some areas, especially in a district west of Hannover, melanistic Roe occur in fair numbers. In 1980 the stock of Roe in West Germany was estimated to number about 1,700,000 of which about 669,000 would be shot during the hunting season.

The usual method for hunting Roe is either by stalking during the early morning or evening hours, or waiting up a high seat that has been sited at the edge of a wood overlooking a meadow that is frequented by deer. During the rut (*Blattzeit*), particularly during warm, still weather, the use of the call can often lead to success. There are a number of calls, but an imitation of the doe – either by means of a leaf or using one of the artificial calls – is probably the most productive.

The seasons for hunting Roe in Germany are as follows:

Bucks (*Böcke*)	16 May–15 October
Does (*Ricken*)	1 September–31 January
Yearling does (*Schmalreh*)	16 May–31 January
Kids (*Kitze*)	1 September–28 February

Roe bucks are divided into two categories – strong and inferior – and these are again subdivided into three classes according to virility and quality of antler development as follows:

Strong bucks: Category I
Class I. Bucks of this category are those with massive antlers which weigh, including the nasal bone, at least 200 g. The animal should be at least six years of age and be in good physical condition. The antlers of Class A bucks should have three well-formed tines on each side – *kapitaler sechser Bock* (exceptionally good 6-pointer buck).

Inferior bucks: Category II
Class II A. Bucks in this class are young animals whose trophies weigh less than 200 g, but whose promising physical and trophy characteristics suggest that they will eventually become Class I.
Class II B. Bucks of this class are those animals whose physical and trophy development does not meet the required standard, and with little chance of the trophy reaching 200 g minimum weight necessary for a Class I trophy buck.

It is estimated that road casualties amongst Roe in West Germany number about 70,000 per annum.

Fallow deer *Dama dama dama*
Local names: Fallow deer, *Damwild*; Buck, *Damhirsch*; Doe, *Damtier*; Fawn *Damwildkalb*.

The bulk of the small population of Fallow deer in West Germany is found in northern areas, and in particular in the Schleswig-Holstein district north of Hamburg, and in Niedersachsen, with an estimated population (1978) of about 4100 in each *Länder*. Overall, the total Fallow population in West Germany is estimated to number about 30,000 (1980).

Fallow deer may be hunted during the following seasons:

Bucks (*Damschaufler*) and adult does (*Damtier*)	1 September–31 January
Spike bucks (*Damspiesser*)	1 July–28 February
Young does (*Damschmaltier*)	1 July–31 January
Fawns – male (*Damhirschkalb*), female (*Damlierkalb*)	1 September–28 February

Similar to Red deer, Fallow deer are divided into three virility Classes I, II and III, and within these categories are further subdivisions based on antler weight, configuration and future development. The following classifications apply:

57

Strong bucks: Category I

Class I. To qualify for this class bucks must be at least ten years old, and their trophy must weigh at least 5½ lb (2.5 kg). This figure of 2.5 kg, however, may be raised or lowered by an intermediate hunting authority to suit local conditions should it be thought necessary. The conservation standard required for a Class I buck (*Schaufler*), is that the antlers must have fully developed palms or shovels without any major irregularities, and the antlers must have a good span.

Medium bucks: Category II

Class II A. Bucks of this class are five to ten year old animals whose physical and trophy potential suggest that they will develop into Class I bucks.

Class II B. Bucks of this class are animals of five years of age or older but whose antlers weigh less than 2.5 kg and whose physical condition or undesirable antler formation would rule out any chance of advancement into Class I.

Inferior Bucks – Category III

Class III A. Bucks of this class are those animals between two and three years old whose physical and trophy potential are such that advancement to a higher class can be expected. No trophy weight limitation is imposed.

Class III B. Bucks under five years old whose formation of antler is below the minimum standard required.

Sika deer *Cervus nippon*

Sika deer have been introduced to a number of areas in north Germany, which include Nord Westfallen and Rundhof in Schleswig-Holstein. Some of the best trophies at the International Hunting Exhibition in Plovdiv, Bulgaria, in 1981 came from the former area.

In 1981 the stock of feral Sika was estimated to number about 1000 head.

ICELAND

Reindeer *Rangifer tarandus tarandus*

First brought to Iceland from Norway during the years 1780–91, they have remained there for almost 200 years.

The first shipment seems to have died off soon after arrival, but the second consignment was released on a small peninsula on the south coast where they soon established themselves in considerable numbers. Unfortunately, due to over-hunting, the herds in this locality were eventually exterminated, the last cow being shot in 1913.

The third shipment landed in east Iceland and they, too, increased rapidly. However, due to a combination of hard weather conditions and over-hunting, they, too, had almost reached the point of extinction when just before the Second World War, all hunting was forbidden, and this remained in force until 1960 when a limited amount of hunting was again permitted every second year. This resulted in a slow but steady increase in the Reindeer population, and by 1977 it was estimated that there were about 4500 to 4800 animals in Iceland, of which about a quarter are allowed to be shot each year.

At the present time, however, only landowners and farmers, and the occasional V.I.P. are permitted to hunt.

ITALY

Red, Roe and Fallow deer all occur in Italy but stocks are insufficient to provide any hunting for the visiting sportsman. Furthermore, any foreigner wishing to hunt in Italy must obtain a gun licence which will be granted only after an examination has been taken before the relevant authorities.

The hunting season for all species runs from the third Sunday in September until 31 December and the majority of trophies have come from fenced-in reserves.

Red deer *Cervus elaphus hippelaphus*
Local name: *Cervo.*

Red deer are not plentiful in Italy, and apart from those in some of the large deer parks, few are living in the wild. In the north about 100 deer are established in the Aosta Valley on the borders of Switzerland, whilst further east deer from the Swiss National Park near St Moritz frequently cross into Italy where their chief haunts are the Valle di Sotto, Valle di Dentro and the Stelvio National Park in Lombardy where the resident population is estimated to be about 200. A few deer also occur in the Bolzano district. Other deer have entered northern Italy from Austria and taken up residence in the Veneto region and around Pieve di Cadore east of the Dolomites, whilst others are to be found near the Yugoslavian border.

About 300 to 400 deer are maintained in the Mandria Park just north of Torino (Turin) whilst some 30 miles (50 km) to the west about 400 to 500 deer frequent the Valle di Susa and in particular in the Gran Bosco Park, which is a mountainous area with the deer mainly living at an altitude of between about 3936 to 6560 ft (1200 and 2000 metres). Some of the stags in this area grow extremely strong antlers and recently a pair of cast antlers were recovered which it was estimated must have weighed, on the skull, about 24 lb (11 kg). It was an uneven head of nine points with a massive crown on the left side.

Small groups of deer are to be found in central Italy on private estates such as Montalto di Castro near Civatavecchia and on the presidential estate of Castel Ponziano in Rome. Red deer from Switzerland have been released into the Casentino State Forest near Arezzo where the original stock was completely destroyed during the war. There are also a few deer on a private estate at Mesola east of Ferrara, near the mouth of the river Po.

In Sardinia *C.e. corsicanus* is now reduced to possibly under 200.

EUROPE

Roe deer *Capreolus capreolus capreolus*
Local name: *Capriolo.*

The Roe occurs in a number of locations in Italy but nowhere can it be said to be common.

Fallow deer *Dama dama dama*
Local name: *Daino.*

Fallow deer occur only in parks and reserves such as the presidential estates of San Rossore (Pisa), Castel Proziano (Rome) and on private estates of Montalto di Castro and Migliarino (Pisa), where the hunting is retained by the owners.

LUXEMBOURG
Red deer, in small numbers, are resident mainly in the northern parts of Luxembourg, in the Ardennes Forest and each autumn their numbers are increased by an influx of stags coming in from Belgium and Germany for the rut. It is doubtful if the total wild population of Red deer much exceeds 200 animals.

There are also some Red deer enclosed within a 1200 acre (500 hectare) reserve near the town of Luxembourg which belongs to the Grand Duke. A considerable number of Red deer are living free on the hunting ground of the two grand-ducal castles of Colmar and Fischbach, from where they spread after the rut, as far as the Moselle river which separates Luxembourg from Germany, in the south-eastern part of the country.

Roe are plentiful throughout the country. It is forbidden to shoot bucks during the rut, and no animal under the age of one year may be killed at any time.

Hunting seasons are:

Red deer
Stags	10 October–30 November
Hinds and calves	15 October–31 December

Roe deer
Bucks	1–15 July
	15 September–20 October
Does	10 October–15 November

Unless one is hunting as a private guest, the opportunities for foreign visitors to stalk deer in Luxembourg are not worth considering.

THE NETHERLANDS
Only two species of deer, Red and Roe, occur outside the deer parks in the Netherlands, and wild populations of the former can only be described as scarce, with an overall population under 1000. Roe, however, occur in most suitable localities, whilst in the Royal Crownland Het Loo park, as well as in

Het Deelerwoud and several other private parks, Fallow deer are maintained.

Despite the widespread distribution of Roe, the number of deer permitted to be shot on each estate is strictly controlled by allocation granted by the Directeur Faunabeheer of the Ministry of Agriculture and Fisheries. In consequence, the majority of landowners retain the shooting for themselves and their friends, and permits are never available for foreigners who have not rented the shooting rights. The possibility of shooting, therefore, in the Netherlands is by way of a personal invitation only. Opportunities to hunt either Red or Fallow deer on one of the Government properties may, however, be available, and enquiries should be made to the Koninklijke Nederlandsee Jagersvereniging in Amersfoort.

Large herds of Fallow deer are also maintained at Elspeeter Bosch and Dekkerswald – two private parks situated at Elspeet, near Apeldoorn and at Groesbeck, near Nijmegen, respectively.

Anyone invited to shoot in the Netherlands will have to purchase a Dutch game licence, and before this can be issued, the following documents will have to be presented:

1 Copy contract of insurance, which must include a special *shooting risk* policy. Furthermore, the insurance company must have a representative in the Netherlands.
2 A copy of both game licence and firearm certificate.

A non-resident game licence costs 30 Dutch florins (about £6) and is valid for six consecutive days mentioned on the licence. A resident game licence, valid from the 1 April to 1 April following, costs Dfl. 70 (about £14) and will only be granted to applicants who can prove that they have passed a hunting examination or can prove that for three consecutive years between 1972 and 1977 they have been granted a game licence.

Sunday hunting is not permitted. It is also forbidden to shoot on New Year's Day, Easter Monday, Whit-Monday, Christmas Day and Ascension Day.

Driving game is not permitted in the Netherlands nor may deer be hunted in time of snow by following their tracks.

There are also special instructions regarding the calibre of rifle that may be used. For Red deer the calibre must not be less than 6.5 mm and the hitting power at 100 metres must be at least 2206 joules (1632 ft/lb). The use of a bullet with a hitting power of 980 joules (725 ft/lb), however, is acceptable for Roe deer. The importation of a firearm for hunting should offer no difficulty and will be applied for and issued along with the game licence.

Any hunting ground must have an adjoining area of at least 99 acres (40 hectares) without any interruptions, where the licensee has the sole right of shooting. The width of the adjoining area must be at least 327 yards (300 metres). The shooting tenant is responsible for damage to crops etc. done by game, and is therefore responsible for payment of compensation. All shooting, however, is forbidden on any plot situated between two hunting grounds which has a length of under 218 yards (200 metres).

The minimum period for which a hunting ground may be leased is six years, but in some cases permission may be granted by the Minister of Agriculture and Fisheries to extend the lease to twelve years.

Roe deer *Capreolus capreolus capreolus*
Local names: Roe, *Ree*; Doe, *Reegeit*; Yearling doe, *Smalree*; Buck, *Reebok*; Kid, *Reekalf*.

The Roe deer has a wide distribution being particularly plentiful in the Utrecht and eastern provinces of Gelderland, Overijssel, Limburg, Dresthe and Noord-Brabant. They are less plentiful in the provinces of Noord Holland, Zuid Holland, Zeeland, Friesland and Groningen, but are entirely absent on the isles in the Waddenzee (Texel, Terschelling, etc.). There are a number of melanistic Roe in south-east Netherlands and although their numbers may have decreased in recent years, black Roe are still not rare.

Concerning the number of melanistic Roe in many places in the Netherlands, twenty-five years ago, on an estate at Vorden in Gelderland, it was estimated that about 15 percent of the Roe were black, and on several occasions I saw a normal coloured doe with black twins, or a black buck chasing a red doe during the rut. Today it is estimated that the percentage has dropped to about 4 or 5, and I understand that similar reductions have been noted elsewhere.

It is estimated that the total Roe deer population in the Netherlands numbers about 25,000, of which about 6800 (2950 bucks, 2100 females and 1750 kids) will be killed by shooting. In addition, apart from those taken by natural predators such as fox, a considerable number are killed by traffic accidents, poaching and dogs running uncontrolled in the woods.

Although the open season for shooting bucks lasts for twenty weeks from 15 May until 1 October, it is intended that only yearlings should be shot during the opening month. Does and kids are shot during the first two and a half months of the year (1 January to 15 March). Stalking, waiting up high seats and calling during the rut are the customary methods for hunting the buck.

Red deer *Cervus elaphus hippelaphus*
Local names: *Hert, Edelhert, Hoogwild* and *Roodwild*.

Although indigenous, Red deer leading a completely wild existence are not very plentiful in the Netherlands, and an estimate taken during the spring of 1978 suggested that the population outside the deer parks stood at about 820 animals, consisting of 330 stags, 340 hinds and the remainder calves of the previous summer. Most of the wild population are located in the province of Gelderland, and in particular in the sparsely populated district known as the Veluwe, which is considered capable of supporting no more than about 700 to 800 deer in the spring before the crop of calves arrives. Red deer are also present in the De Onsalige Bossen and nearby Imbosch, both of which are unfenced.

A considerable number of Red deer are also maintained in parks or fenced-in reserves, which include the Royal Crownland Het Loo (26,182 acres or 10,600 hectares) near Apeldoorn, the National Park De Hooge Veluwe (14,820 acres or 6000 hectares) near Arnhem, and in Het Deelerwoud, which lies between Apeldoorn and Arnhem, and belongs to the National Nature Conservation Trust.

As a result of the annual spring count, a decision is made on the number of deer to be culled that year, and for each animal to be shot, a licence is issued. During the 1978–9 season a total of 367 deer were shot, of which 115 were stags, 95 were hinds, 30 yearlings and the remainder, calves of the year.

An owner or tenant of a shooting ground wishing to shoot a Red deer can apply to the Department of Agriculture for a licence, and a licence for each deer to be killed on his ground will be issued free of charge, provided the applicant is in possession of a general shooting license. With the licence will be issued a tag which will be attached to the right hind leg of every animal killed, and without the tag attached, the transport of any deer carcase is forbidden. Furthermore, whenever a stag has been shot, the appropriate Government department has to be informed so that the animal can be inspected.

Each year there is an exhibition of trophies, and although it is not mandatory, most hunters do submit their trophies for assessment. At the exhibition the heads are placed into one of five categories – A1 and A2 are animals of not less than ten years of age; B1 are younger animals which show good potential and should not have been killed until they were at least ten years old; B2 are also middle-aged animals but not likely to develop into anything very good, and C are poor animals that hold no future and should be killed at an early age. If a hunter is found to have killed, say, a B1 animal in its sixth or seventh year, a red point will be glued to the skull for all to see at the exhibition.

During the last war the fences of the National Park De Hooge Veluwe were destroyed in places, and as a result a number of deer escaped into the surrounding countryside and subsequently mated with the native deer. The deer in the park, however, were no longer 100 percent native stock, for at the beginning of the century Prince Henry of the Netherlands, in an effort to improve the quality of deer at Veluwe, had imported deer from Germany, Rominten, Spain and Czechoslovakia, and more recently deer from Scotland. This infusion of park blood, and in particular the deer from Rominten, has undoubtedly improved the standard of trophy, for whereas fifty years ago it was difficult to find a stag with a 12-point head, today there are many in this category. One of the best trophies to come off Veluwe since the war was a 12-pointer, shot in 1952, which had an antler length of $42\frac{1}{2}$ in. (108 cm).

Adult stags outside the parks weigh approximately 265 lb (120 kg) complete, with hinds weighing about a third lighter. In Het Loo, which extends to some 26,500 acres (10,725 hectares) the best stags at rutting time weigh about 265 to 287 lb (120 to 130 kg) complete with head, skin and legs but without stomach. The deer in the park are artificially fed both during the winter and spring, the feeding at the present time being mostly dried sugar beet pulp. At one time a small amount of sesame was added to the feed in the springtime to help with antler growth.

Apart from a special licence being issued by the Minister for Agriculture and Food for a few deer to be shot, there is no open hunting season for Red deer in the Netherlands. As a result of these special licences, about fifty deer are shot each year in the Veluwe either by stalking or from a high seat.

It is legal to shoot Red deer of either sex as from 1 September, and whilst the hunting season for stags terminates on 20 February, hinds and calves may be killed until 15 and 31 March respectively.

NORWAY

Four species of deer – Elk, Reindeer, Red deer and Roe deer – are available for sportsmen visiting Norway where the hunting and shooting rights are the property of either the Government or the landowner, from whom permission to hunt must always be obtained.

Visiting hunters can lease the right to hunt Elk on some of the larger properties, whilst a number of hotels hold the right to hunt wild Reindeer in the district, which are available for hunting by resident guests on payment of the required fee.

Norwegian citizens who wish to hunt have to pay a Game Fund tax, amounting to Nkr. 10 (about £1) for each municipality in which it is intended to hunt, or Nkr. 50 (about £5) with no area limits, the season extending from 1 April to 31 March. No one under sixteen years of age is permitted to use a firearm.

Before a hunting licence is granted, the applicant must show that the area in which he intends to hunt meets the minimum area stipulated by the Directorate of Game and Freshwater Fish. For Elk, Red deer and Roe deer the area must be mainly woodland and bogs, whilst for Reindeer, only mountainous region. The size of the minimum area varies from one municipality to another, and may also vary within the individual municipality.

Foreigners wishing to hunt in Norway must obtain a licence costing Nkr. 50 (about £5). This fee, which is the same as the Game Fund tax for Norwegian residents, can be obtained from any post office and is valid for the whole of the hunting year – 1 April to 31 March.

The fee in itself, however, does not confer the right to hunt anywhere, and this, as mentioned above, can only be obtained from the landowner. There is no trophy fee charged on any game.

Provided the firearm fulfilled certain regulations and the visitor, on entry, can produce a licence of ownership issued by his own country, there is no problem in bringing a weapon into Norway, but there is a duration limit of three months for any foreigner retaining a firearm in the country. Ammunition must be of the expanding type (soft nose, hollow point or similar) with an energy of not less than 200 kg at a distance of 300 metres (327 yards). Special dispensation may, however, be granted for other calibres provided

Spying for deer on a Scottish deer forest — for long-distance viewing the telescope is preferable to binoculars.

In former days the pony was the usual form of transport to bring in the stag from the h

Today the pony is being replaced by mechanical transport.

A good Scottish Red deer stag during the October rut.

In Scotland a number of stags never produce any antlers and are known as hummels.

Above In parts of southern England the diminutive Chinese Water-deer, introduced early in the century, can be stalked.

Right Muntjac buck – a small Asian deer that can now be stalked in many parts of southern England. (*Roy A Harris & K R Duff.*)

In Belgium the majority of deer are shot during a drive – a typical stand for a deer drive in the Ardennes.

Staghunting in France – the stag is brought to bay. (*Joël Bouëssée.*)

In Europe, deer in woodland are
generally shot from a high seat –
hochsitz which may take the form
of a portable metal construction
(*above left*) or be something more
permanent (*above right*)
(*Dr Studinka.*)

Red deer at dawn near
a high seat (*right*).

In both Austria and Germany, hunters adorn their hats with a plume or *bart* – in this case a bunch of hairs taken from the mane of a stag – called a *Hirschbart*.

The canine teeth of stags – often referred to as tushes or *grandeln* – are much prized by continental hunters, many of whom keep them in special display cabinets.

Fallow deer can be stalked not only in many countries of Europe, but also in North America, Argentina, New Zealand and Australia.

Roe buck in late summer – British Roe antlers are fully up to the standard of continental Roe. (*R E Chaplin.*)

the ammumition is considered suitable for Reindeer, and application should be addressed to the Direktoratet for Viltog Ferskvannsfisk, Elgeseter gt. 10, 7000 Trondheim. When hunting Reindeer it is not permitted to use a magazine or automatic rifle unless the magazine or repeater mechanism has first been immobilized and sealed by the police, the object being to ensure that only one shot can be fired each time the action is cocked. On completion of the hunt, the rifle must be presented to the police for removal of the seal. Many foreigners object to this regulation, because in many rifles one or two small holes may have to be drilled in order to attach the tag securely.

Every hunter intending to hunt deer must pass an annual test in marksmanship, consisting of six shots fired at a standard 60 cm circular (23.6 in.) target at a range of 100 metres. The firing position is optional, but the use of a rest is not allowed. The test must be carried out with the same rifle and with the same expanding bullets it is intended to use in the field, and to qualify, a minimum of thirty-six points out of sixty must be scored.

Visiting sportsmen, however, may hunt without having to undergo a shooting test in Norway, provided a written certificate from his own country is produced testifying to his marksmanship.

Elk *Alces alces alces*
Local name: *Elg*.

Elk are well distributed in all suitable localities throughout Norway, being most plentiful in the valleys of Gudbrandsdal and Østerdal in central Norway, and in the two Trøndelag provinces, Nord (north) and Sor (south) of Trondheim right up to the 65th parallel, with scattered individuals occurring as far north as Finmark.

Until 1952, apart from a few exceptions under special licence, the Elk hunting season lasted only five days, during which period hunters could shoot an unlimited number of animals. Since then, however, it has been extended to a fortnight, commencing in September and terminating in October, the actual dates varying according to district, the more northerly forests having an earlier season than those in the south. Thus, north of Trondheim the season takes place during the latter part of September whilst in the south the opening date will not be until early October. During the 1980 season about 19,000 Elk of both sexes were shot throughout Norway, which is almost five times more than was possible some thirty years ago. This gives some indication of the increase in the Elk population during recent years.

Since the extension of the open season to a fortnight, a licence system has been introduced, and dependent on the size of the estate, each landowner is given permission by the local game board – *Viltnemnda* – to shoot a certain number of animals – divided into bulls, cows and calves – the minimum area required for each varying from one locality to another depending on local stocks and damage done in that particular district. As a rule, the minimum requirement per animal varies from about 100 to 1000 hectares (247 to 2470 acres).

Hire of the best hunting terrain is normally around Nkr.3000 (about £260) per Elk, but such terrain is difficult to hire as the demand is greater than the supply. Moreover the price will vary considerably according to the class of trophy taken.

Apart from stalking or still-hunting there are three other methods for hunting Elk which involve the use of hounds – namely driving, tracking with a hound-on-leash (*band-hund*) and hunting with a loose-hound (*lös-hund*) – but although driving, particularly in Sweden, accounts for the majority of Elk killed, it is poor sport when compared to the other methods.

Hunting the Elk with an Elk-hound, either on leash or loose, offers not only excitement but a real test of physical endurance. Moreover, working with such a highly intelligent animal as the Elk-hound adds greatly to the enjoyment of this particular sport.

Whether the hound being used is running 'loose' or 'on leash', it is essential that it has a good nose, for the hunter relies solely on this to bring him in contact with his quarry. It is essential, also, that a hound running loose must give tongue only when it has brought the Elk to bay. Then it should keep up an incessant barking until such time as either the hunter has arrived on the scene or the Elk has moved off, when the whole procedure of running the animal, and bringing it to bay again, will have to be repeated. I have been told that a good *lös-hund* will, in order to maintain contact with his hunter, occasionally run back or even draw the Elk towards him, but none of the hounds I worked with had developed such sagacious tactics. A hound-on-leash, however, should always remain silent, even though an Elk may be standing in full view only a short distance away. Under such circumstances one has only to look at the hound to realize what tremendous self-control these animals possess, for it is against their nature to be silent when close to, and in sight of, stationary Elk.

Of the two hound methods, loose-hound hunting is unquestionably the more exacting on both hound and hunter. It can, however, be successfully carried out only in fairly thick forest; otherwise the Elk may run completely off your ground before being bayed. In the preliminary stages the hunter, accompanied by the pilot (man in charge of hound), takes a cast or two through the forest to see if the hound can pick up a fresh trail. When this has been accomplished, if the slot marks indicate that the animal is a good-sized bull, the hound will be unleashed and, unless advantage can be taken of any high ground in the vicinity from which there will be a better chance of hearing the hound when it starts to bay, the hunter will now have to wait and hope that the hound will be able to stop and bay the animal before it has run out of earshot.

As soon as baying is heard, the hunter must run to the spot with all speed. Should the bay be downwind, a detour will have to be made so as to avoid the chance of any human scent being carried to the Elk. Should this happen the Elk may be lost for the day for, although more annoyed than frightened by the baying hound, it cannot stand human scent.

66

Probably, before the hunter has run half the distance, the baying will cease, which indicates that the Elk is on the move again, so this will necessitate a further wait, until the sound of baying can be heard again. This sort of thing may be repeated for several hours, during which time the hunter may have run many miles over the worst possible country before eventually coming up to the Elk. It is essential, therefore, that the hunter must be fit before tackling this form of sport. Even then there is no certainty of a shot, for the Elk may be standing at bay in a thick clump of trees and, at the last minute, may succeed in slipping away unseen, or perhaps offer only a stern shot, which should not, of course, be taken. Whatever animal your hound is baying, however, will generally have to be shot, even though it may be only a cow or small bull; otherwise the hound may be so discouraged that it will not give of its best on future occasions. If the shot has been successful, the hound will race in and start to pluck mouthfuls of hair out of the Elk as though to satisfy itself that the animal has been successfully disposed of. Some hounds will then place themselves on top of the carcase and defy anyone, including their owners, to touch it. The majority of hounds, however, are quite docile, and, as often as not, are so exhausted after the chase that even while the Elk is being gralloched and cut up, are more interested in sleep than in aggression.

Undoubtedly the best way to obtain a big head is to work with a leash-hound, for it is unnecessary to shoot every beast that the hound has been following and one can, therefore, be more selective. As in loose-hound work, one starts the day by taking a few casts in the forest, but as soon as an Elk is winded, instead of letting the hound run loose, the hunter allows it on-leash, to lead him up to the quarry.

The hound generally follows the trail by airborne rather than ground scent, and several times I have been led up to an Elk without having seen any slot marks. On such occasions, however, the trail will seldom be a long one, and is generally the most profitable, for the hunter knows the Elk must be to the windward. It is extraordinary how clever the hounds are at avoiding obstacles that will entangle the leash. When close in to Elk it is prudent to stop and listen every 50 yards (45 metres) or so for, if the animals are feeding their presence will be betrayed either by sound of movement in the forest or, perhaps, by the mooing or grunting of one animal to another. When getting near the Elk, particularly if it is in the middle of the day, it is a wise precaution to work the hound somewhat downwind of the trail, for the animal may be resting and, before doing so, a sagacious bull will often make a sweep back, so as to take his siesta downwind of his tracks. My impression was that the Elk's eyesight is not particularly good, but liberties can not be taken with the wind, for he has a keen nose.

Once the animals have been located the hunter should proceed forward alone. Despite its size, the Elk blends wonderfully well with its surroundings, and every bush must be carefully scanned before further approach is made. As often as not, only the light-coloured legs, or perhaps a massive antler, are all that will be visible, but once the beast has been found, patience should bring its reward. If only a cow or a calf is first visible, the hunter should not be too discouraged, for Elk are frequently found in family parties and the bull may temporarily be hidden from view. It will be appreciated, therefore, that for selective shooting, leash-hound hunting is the only certain way of trying to get the big heads, for generally speaking, the hound, having been tethered a short distance away, may never see the quarry until it is shot, and if the hunter has decided that the trophy is not good enough, and no shot is taken, then no harm is done to the dog.

An average full grown Elk in Norway will weigh over 660 lb (300 kg) with exceptional bulls – locally referred to as *Okse* or *Bringe* – reaching 1100 lb (500 kg), whilst cows (*Ku* or *Kolle*) will weigh around the 484 lb (220 kg) mark. The average carcase weight of an adult bull is 487 lb (221 kg).

The rut takes place from about mid-September to mid-October, and by the beginning of January the older bulls will have started to cast their antlers. Probably the best trophies are to be found in Nord Tröndelag, the area around Lake Siesjöen north of Snaasa being particularly good. During a five-day visit there in 1952 I saw several good bulls and shot two, one of nineteen points and the other of twelve. Much of this area belongs to the Government who let the hunting annually on a sealed envelope highest bid basis.

The Elk has few natural predators in Norway but many are killed on the roads and railways.

Reindeer *Rangifer tarandus tarandus*
Local names: *Rein* or *Villrein*.

There are many vast expanses of mountain moorland which provide excellent ground for Reindeer. Their distribution can be roughly divided into four main groups, each separated from the other by natural or artificial barriers.

In the central-southern part of the country wild Reindeer are to be found on the high mountain-plateau that rises from the valleys of Setesdal, Sirdal and Suldal, much of which is known as the Njardarheim preserve. In central Norway Reindeer are widely distributed over the desolate Hardangervidda plateau, but the Telemark to Haukeli highway would appear to restrict any movement of deer between these two areas. North of Hardangervidda, across the main Oslo to Bergen railway, a number of deer frequent the Hallingdal and Jotunheimen range, but the valley of Gudbrandsdalen prevents them joining up with the large herds which roam the beautiful Dovrefjell and Snehetta range. Further to the east, across the valley of Østerdalen a herd of tame Reindeer has been introduced and now leads a feral existence, whilst other tame herds are preserved in parts of southern Norway. There are also large herds of tame Reindeer belonging to the Lapplanders on both sides of the Norwegian border with Finland and Sweden, in Finnmark, Tromsø, Nordland and Nord-Trøndelag.

There is little doubt that on occasions, animals from some of these tame herds have been allowed to mingle with the wild Reindeer, particularly in the Njardarheim preserve and on Hardangervidda, and as a result, the deer in

Map 4 The range of Reindeer *Rangifer tarandus* in Northern Europe and Siberia.

1	*Rangifer tarandus tarandus*	Norway to Russia
2	*R.t.fennicus*	European Russia, from Karelia to Sakhalin Island
3	*R.t.platyrhynchus*	Spitsbergen

these two areas have deteriorated, both as regards body-weight and antler development. The Snehetta and Dovrefjell herds, however, have not been contaminated to the same extent and generally speaking, the bulls are not only larger, but carry better antlers. The presence of a number of white animals in a herd is generally an indication of tame stock.

In recent years attempts have been made with the aid of aeroplanes, to take a census of Norway's wild Reindeer population, but the results are not considered entirely satisfactory, due to the fact that the herds, sometimes to the number of a thousand or more, are constantly on the move. A conservative estimate, however, suggests that the stock of wild Reindeer in Norway is about 50,000 to 55,000 animals, the largest population being on Hardangervidda. About 10,000 animals were killed in 1980, the season for hunting extending for three weeks during the latter part of August and into September.

Most of the Reindeer grounds are State owned, and in consequence, during the shooting season, the animals are continually being disturbed by several hunters all operating in the same district.

Permission to hunt wild Reindeer is granted by the Directorate of Game and Freshwater Fish in Trondheim, and generally speaking, the system for issuing Reindeer licences is as follows. Prior to the season a decision will be made as to the number of deer that can be killed in each district and licences will be allotted accordingly. Districts are comparatively small and may only extend to one or two valleys. There is nothing, however, so long as licences are available, to prevent a hunter taking out one or more licences in different districts – and many of the peasants do this – but under no circumstances can the number killed in any particular area exceed that shown on the licence. The same applies to privately owned ground, though the owner himself may decide to reduce the permitted number of Reindeer that have been allocated to be shot by the authorities. He will, moreover, only pay the fee for the actual number killed.

It will be appreciated, therefore, that during the opening week of the season, when the majority of hunters will be out, some of the shooting grounds become considerably overcrowded, and under such conditions not only are the Reindeer continually on the move, but the chance of a stalk being effected undisturbed is pretty small.

Very little stalking or selective shooting is done by the majority of peasant hunters, whose main concern is venison for the winter. Many hunters, therefore, as soon as it is light, make for some favourite pass in the mountains, and there they will wait until sooner or later a herd will pass their way. When this occurs, it is often met by a fusilade of bullets which will continue until an animal or two have fallen or the herd has disappeared around the next mountain. Some Norwegian Reindeer hunters, however, are extremely skilful, and the manner and speed with which they are able to approach a moving herd of deer is literally, quite breathtaking!

The Norwegian Government, in an attempt to minimize the wounding that inevitably occurs from 'browning' into the herd, introduced the law that anyone hunting Reindeer must have the magazine of the rifle sealed off so that only one round could be fired without re-loading the rifle (*see page 65*). Until recently it was also illegal to use any rifle of calibre of less than 8.0 mm, but this has now been relaxed, and the only restriction is that the bullet must have an energy of not less than 1446 ft/lb (200 kgm) at a distance of 327 yards (300 metres). ·

Whilst the prohibition of the magazine has undoubtedly reduced the number of wounded animals which is bound to result from irresponsible firing into a herd, it has also, in some instances, caused the loss of a wounded animal due to the delay in getting in a quick second shot. In some respects, therefore, it might have been advisable to have retained the minimum calibre restriction of 8.0 mm for the crippling effect of a large bullet, even though badly placed, greatly reduces the chance of a wounded animal escaping.

If the Reindeer have been plentiful in any particular district, then, after about the first week or ten days, most of the hunters will have shot their quota and returned to the valleys. The latter part of the season, therefore, is the best time in which to seek big heads, for not only is there less chance of a stalk being spoilt by other hunters but with the rut at hand, the big bulls are more in evidence.

Reindeer hunting, however, is a chancey affair, and a change in wind may shift all the animals out of your district, never to return until the season is over. This is exactly what happened to me at Hardangervidda in 1952, and although up to the day prior to my arrival the ground had been simply crawling with Reindeer, during the full seven days I was there not a shootable beast was seen! On the last but one day the wind changed to the north and late in the afternoon a seemingly endless column of Reindeer, several thousand strong, could just be seen through the telescope many miles away travelling upwind, and apparently making a bee-line for my ground. The change of wind, however, brought snow and when I awoke the following morning a raging blizzard prevented any idea of taking to the hill until the afternoon. Whether the herd had passed through my ground during the night it is impossible to say, for the snow had obliterated all tracks. There was certainly no sign of them that afternoon. Even early in September a raging snow blizzard may keep you in your hut for a day or more on end. Thus, if you only allow yourself the last week of the season, you undoubtedly run the risk, for one reason or another, of failure, therefore as much time as possible should be allowed when hunting Reindeer.

Stalking a big bull in the middle of a herd, which may be a thousand strong, can be highly exciting, and if the animals are on the move, it is also extremely arduous. My first bull in 1953 was a case in point.

He was first spotted standing among, perhaps, 300 other animals on a flat plateau with no cover for approach within a mile. Fortunately, the wind was favourable, and with the aid of frequent snow showers which kept giving temporary concealment, I eventually reached a point about a quarter of a mile (400 metres) from the herd. By this time, however, the animals, although unaware of my presence, were on the move and so for the next hour it was a case of crawling or running as the occasion demanded – and it was generally the latter – if contact was to be maintained. However, eventually I reached the cover of some rocks and as the herd passed by some 150 yards (136 metres) away, the bull, pausing to take a bite of moss, stood momentarily separated from his companions, and thus gave me the chance I had been wanting. At times, however, when dealing with large herds, the manner in which smaller beasts continually cover the bull selected can be extremely tantalizing and many chances have been lost in this fashion.

By this time, the night was fast approaching, and the trek home, over 10 miles (16 km) of rough mountain country in the dark, was long and tiresome, for even on flat ground a large Reindeer head is an awkward and weighty thing to carry. However, my companion knew the ground, and with the aid of our compasses when the snow showers were on, we eventually reached the hut.

Compared to Elk hunting, the cost of Reindeer hunting in Norway is not particularly expensive, but due to the fact that the demand for licences generally exceeds the number available, it is difficult for foreigners to get one. The main difficulty is the law which permits only Norwegian citizens to hunt on State owned property. On Hardangervidda, for instance, which covers some 1,729,000 acres (700,000 hectares) more than half of this mountainous terrain is owned by the State, and therefore virtually closed to foreigners, whose only chance would be to hunt on a resident's licence, which would cost NKr.700 (about £60 to £70) per animal. A few licences may also be available to hunt on private land, and these would generally include hut accommodation which would not be included in the licence to stalk on Government land. Adequate accommodation, however, can generally be obtained at one of the numerous tourist hostels which the State have erected on many of the Reindeer grounds, some of which are tucked away in the mountains 20 to 30 miles (32 to 48 km) from any road or track. If the weather is favourable, a small float plane can be chartered and a landing made on a lake near one of the huts, otherwise all travelling on the ground would have to be done on foot. It is essential, therefore, to travel light.

In former days it was comparatively easy to find guides and horses to accompany the hunting party into the hills, but today both are virtually impossible to find, the latter being replaced on the small farms by mechanized transport. On the other hand, float planes are more easily available, and these are being used not only to take the hunters in and out of the mountains, but also to carry out the meat. Many of the local hunters, on killing a beast, just cut off sufficient for their immediate requirements, and *cache* the rest for collecting when their hunting is finished. Cool days and frosty nights will keep it fresh.

Although sharing the ground with a number of other hunters can, at times, be exceedingly irksome for one never really knows when a shot from an unknown quarter may prematurely end your stalk, there are many compensations, and stalking the bull Reindeer in the mountains of Norway compares very favourably with deer stalking in Scotland, except that the life is harder and considerably more primitive.

At one time it was the practice to use a leash-hound, as it is used today for hunting Elk, for finding and trailing Reindeer, but this method is no longer used.

The rut starts about the third week of September and lasts about a month. Early in the century, the best trophies generally came out of the southern reserves of Lyseheien and Auredalen which, at that time belonged to Dr Thv. Heilberg but subsequently became part of the Government controlled Njardarheim reserve. One of the best trophies from this area was a 25-pointer (11 + 14) shot by Robert L Scott in 1910, which had an antler length of $59\frac{1}{2}$ in. (151 cm), beam circumference of $5\frac{5}{8}$ in. (14.2 cm) and an inside span of $41\frac{3}{4}$ in. (106 cm). Such a trophy, however, would be extremely rare today, and anything over 45 in. (114 cm) can be considered good.

An adult bull will have a carcase weight of about 110 lb (50 kg) whilst adult cows will weigh some 33 lb (15 kg) less.

Red deer *Cervus elaphus atlanticus*
Local names: Stag, *Hjort*; Hind, *Hind* or *Kolle*.

Red deer are to be found in a number of districts along the west coast, ranging from Boknfjorden in the south to the island of Otterøen, near Namsos in the north. Included in this range are areas around Hardangerfjord, Sognefjord, Inner Sogn, Nordfjord, Nordmøre, as well as the large islands of Hitteren and Tusteren, and some of the smaller islands. The large estate of Sognli in South Trøndelag, which now belongs to the Government, also has a large stock. In recent years, they have been gradually increasing their range, and wandering animals are frequently met away from their main centre of distribution.

The Norwegian Red deer is a typical coast dweller, which prefers the mild coast climate where it can find forested country. During the spring and summer months they frequent the steep, wooded mountain sides, but on the onset of winter, when the snow comes, they move toward the coast and often swim to the islands which are dotted along the coast line, where they remain until the spring.

The hunting season runs for thirty days, commencing in September and terminating during October, the first part of which normally coincides with the beginning of the rut. As with the Elk, the local game board *Viltnemnda* decide how many deer are to be shot, the normal minimum requirement of land per animal being about 247 acres (100 hectares), but this figure may be adjusted if conditions warrant.

About 7800 deer were shot in 1980, it being legal to kill deer of either sex, but not yearlings. Farmers, however, have the right to shoot deer marauding their crops at any time of the year, but any deer killed must be reported to the police and the venison surrendered. The average weight of an adult Norwegian stag varies from about 242 to 331 lb (110 to 150 kg) and hinds will weigh about 40 percent less.

Roe deer *Capreolus capreolus capreolus*
Local name: *Rådyer*.

Roe deer are well distributed throughout the eastern part of southern Norway, being particularly plentiful in the provinces around Oslofjord and their numbers are steadily increasing and spreading out. Most of central Norway is unsuitable for this deer, but scattered populations occur as far north as Nord-Trøndelag and the 65th parallel.

Up to date little attention has been paid to hunting this deer in Norway, and since the three months open season does not open until 1 October, it only allows a week or two before the older bucks will start to shed their antlers. The season ends on 23 December, by which time approximately 6000 deer will have been shot, the greatest number being taken in the provinces of Østfold, Akershus, Hedmark, Opland and Vestfold. A great number are also killed by hounds running loose in the forest.

Until recently, the Roe was completely protected in the south-western

EUROPE

provinces of Telemark, Vest Agder, Øst-Agder and Rogaland but stocks have
increased and hunting is now permitted. The species, however, is still partly
protected in the provinces of Hordaland, Sogn and Fjordane, and Møre and
Romsdal.

The rut, as elsewhere in Europe, commences about the middle of July and
runs to the latter part of August.

Up to date some of the best trophies have come out of Hedmark, including
one killed in 1973 which not only had the best antlers yet recorded for Norway
(184.95 C.I.C. points) but was also exceptionally heavy, having a live weight
of 84.8 lb (38.5 kg). At least two other bucks with carcase weights of about
55 lb (25 kg) have also been taken. Such weights are well above the average
for Western Europe.

PORTUGAL

Twenty or more years ago the Roe deer *Capreolus capreolus capreolus* was
extremely scarce in Portugal, and at one time it was thought to be extinct.
Now it is described as quite plentiful in the north-east and in particular in
the region of Bragança (Trás-os-Montes). At present (1981), however, the
species is entirely protected but the question of allowing a short open season
for hunting this deer is currently being pursued, and may be authorized in the
near future. Only rifle will be permitted.

Red deer *Cervus elaphus hispanicus* are increasing in the Preserve of Herdade
da Contenda Moura which is situated in eastern Alentejo near the Spanish
border. At present the species is entirely protected.

Fallow deer *Dama dama dama* were once plentiful in a number of private
parks in Portugal but were almost exterminated after the Revolution of 25
April 1974. The species, however, is abundant in the State park of Mafra
which lies some 30 miles (40 km) north-west of Lisbon. No hunting, however,
is permitted in the park.

Whilst it seems probable that some deer hunting, particularly for Roe deer,
will shortly be possible in Portugal, it is most unlikely that any, in the
immediate future, will be available for the visiting sportsman.

SPAIN

For variety of fauna and sport, few countries in Europe can surpass Spain, for
not only is shooting of Red, Roe and Fallow deer available for the visiting
sportsman, but also excellent stalking, after the unique Spanish ibex and
diminutive Cantabrian chamois, not to mention boar and wolf etc.

The traditional manner of hunting the Red deer in Spain is the *monteria*,
and during the year about 35,000 stags, as well as boar and a few wolf, will be
killed by this method.

Only on one day in the year does a *monteria* take place in any one area –
indeed in some areas or *fincas* as they are called, two years may elapse
between such events. Only stags are shot, and the inevitable result is, of
course, that most areas are now vastly over-populated with hinds, which is

74

having a serious effect on the quality of the deer. Not only are they small in size but very few stags have the chance to reach maturity. In consequence, trophy heads are few and far between.

The size of the operations for a *monteria*, which take place between 10 October and 20 February, differ from one locality to another but on the larger ones as many as a hundred rifles spread over about 2000 acres (800 hectares) with, perhaps, two to three hundred hounds to move the game, may take part.

The majority of the hounds – a mixture of *podencos* and *mastines* – are in small packs – *rehalas* – of perhaps twenty to thirty animals which belong to individual huntsmen called *perrero*. Each *perrero* carries a horn which is blown at frequent intervals to keep in touch with his own particular hounds, some of which have bells attached to their collars.

Some of the senior *perrero* also carry a musket – *trabuco* – which is fired (blank shot) from time to time to encourage the hounds or whenever game is roused. There are also a few beaters (*ojeadores*) – but not many – as the hounds are better able to penetrate the almost continuous thickets consisting, in many areas, of the gum-cistus, which is a sticky-leaved shrub growing to shoulder height even on the stoniest ground. The principal trees are ilex, cork-oak and alder. Thorns are everywhere, and spikes of burnt cistus are a constant hazard to both man and beast walking through the undergrowth. To protect the legs, many sportsmen and beaters wear leather skirts called *zajones*.

The rifles generally assemble about 8.30 in the morning and as each one's name is called by the 'shoot president', a card is drawn out of a hat indicating where his stand or blind (*puesto*) will be for the day. By 9 o'clock the draw should be complete and the rifles, in parties of about ten, start to move off, being guided to their *puesto* by a *postor*, some of which may be as much as 10 miles (16 km) distant from the assembly point. In some *fincas* these stands can only be reached on foot, or by mule or horse – *caballerias* – in others, a rough forest track may enable the rifles to be conveyed by mechanized transport to within a short walking distance of the stands.

Rifles – dependent on the terrain – are spaced about 400 yards (360 metres) apart, encircling the whole area – referred to as *mancha* – to be driven, with probably, two lines of rifles called *traviesas*, posted diagonally through the centre. However, this is not as dangerous as it may seem, for since the ground in most areas is broken and rugged, shooting is generally permissible in any direction except when the beaters are in close proximity. Generally speaking, although there was a fair amount of shooting by neighbouring rifles, I never felt that at any time was my life in jeopardy although on at least two occasions I heard the whine of a bullet as it passed overhead.

Many of the *perrero* with their *rehalas*, as well as some of the beaters, will have had to start out long before the meet in order to reach their allotted starting-off point by about 11.30 or 12 noon, by which time most *monterias* are scheduled to begin. All the rifles should be in position by this time, and once your *puesto* is reached, under no circumstances should it be vacated until the drive is complete, which will generally not be before 4 or 5 p.m. There is only one drive in the day, and it is a long one, as the *rehalas*, working from all four sides, attempt to move the game towards the centre, but of course a number of deer and boar always succeed in breaking back through the line.

Over the years I never seem to have the best of luck at deer drives, and during the three days of *monteria*, apart from a single spiker stag which, like hinds, should not be shot, I saw only female deer. Had I drawn a post on a *traviesa*, I might have been more fortunate, for it would appear that those posted in the centre generally have the most shooting.

Game was certainly not scarce, and on the first day I counted no fewer than about 470 shots, which resulted in a bag of 80 stags and a boar or two. When one realizes that this number of stags came off an area of about 2000 acres (800 hectares) – and that hinds probably outnumbered stags by four to one – the deer density per acre works out at not less than one deer per 5 acres (2 hectares) and probably even higher. This is vastly overstocking for vegetation is scarce, with large areas of sterile rock or scree.

On the second day about 45 stags were shot and although on the third it was suggested that the bag might even exceed 100, stags were extremely scarce and only about 64 and a few boar were accounted for, one of the latter falling to my rifle. But even these bags are somewhat dwarfed by the 360 trophies killed in a day's *monteria* at Los Alarcones in 1973 which beat the previous record of 238 trophies shot in a day in 1969 at San Calixto, quite near La Baja, where I was hunting on the third day.

It is always difficult to know exactly what the bag has been, for at the end of the *monteria* one never sees all the game collected and brought to one spot, as is normal custom in deer drives elsewhere in Europe. At the end of the drive each successful sportsman generally cuts off the head of any deer or boar shot, and this is carried back with him on his mule or other transport. The headless carcases will later be collected by *caballerias*, their location being indicated by a piece of white paper attached to a nearby bush to facilitate discovery. There seems to be no serious effort to follow up any game suspected of having been wounded – nor indeed, is any systematic search made over the area with dogs on the following day for such animals, so it is inevitable, unfortunately, that a number of wounded animals are never recovered. I understand, however, that a few days after the *monteria* has occurred, circling crows and hawks will generally record where a wounded deer or boar has died – but then, of course, it is too late for any venison to be in an edible condition although at least the trophy – if the beast carried one – can be recovered. One seldom, therefore, has a chance of seeing what has been shot, for in many cases, as soon as the rifle reaches his car, he is away. Of the twenty or more beasts I did see being loaded in to cars, only about three were really mature stags, the best being a strong 12-pointer comparable to a really good Scottish head. The rest were all young animals, the majority being little or more than two or three years old. Clearly, a *monteria* is not – nor can be – selective, and a sportsman will be extremely lucky to shoot a really good trophy.

What a contrast is the end of a Spanish *monteria* to a deer, boar or even a pheasant shoot in Germany, where at the end of the day, all the game is neatly laid out, the sportsmen gather together and whilst the *jägers* sound a 'last post' on their hunting horns, the party will often doff their hats in respect of the fallen – a ceremony which I always find rather stirring. In Spain such a ceremony is just not possible, for the *monterias* cover such huge areas of country and consequently to bring all the carcases to one place would take many hours and could not be achieved before nightfall. Furthermore, a stream of *caballerias* bearing headless carcases would be neither informative nor a pretty sight to end a day's sport!

To the Spanish sportsman a *monteria* is a highly popular sport, and all *fincas* are fully subscribed. The fee for Spanish sportsmen to attend a *monteria* varies from about 60,000 to 150,000 pesetas (about £340 to £900) per day, depending on the area. This money is paid to either the owner of the land, or to the sporting tenant. Arrangements for a visiting sportsman to participate in a *monteria* can be made through a sporting agency, the cost of which would be around £320 to £350 with no extra charge for any game shot. Except under very exceptional circumstances, the venison is retained by the owner of the land, the rifle only taking the trophy. Whether you are fortunate enough to get a shot or not, there is an unquestionable thrill as the sound of running hounds approaches your post – or maybe the adrenalin starts working overtime as rustling in the nearby undergrowth suggests that game is close and may break cover at any moment. Absolute quietness and a hundred percent attention is, therefore, essential during the course of the drive, for should concentration lapse for even a 40 second snooze, as often as not this will be the one moment when a deer or boar breaks cover to give you the one chance of the day.

Luck in the draw undoubtedly plays a most important part in a day's *monteria* for if one has drawn a bad stand there is nothing one can do except listen to the shots of other sportsmen more favourably placed and just hope that something may eventually come your way. Conversely, if you are favourably placed, and an expert marksman at hitting running game with a rifle, you might have the opportunity to kill twelve or more stags and boar in a day.

A *monteria* is a most sociable occasion and to those sportsmen of advanced years or strictly limited time for sport, it has its undoubted attractions; for anyone still capable of physical effort, however, it can never compare or replace hunting a game animal by fair stalking – or at the *pirsch* as it is generally referred to in Europe.

Licences to hunt in the Government Game Reserves – principally for ibex and chamois – are available through the Spanish State Tourist Department in Madrid. The number of permits available, however, is strictly limited. Hunting can also be obtained through a sporting agency called Caza y Naturaleza, S/A (Cazatur) and although more expensive, this is possibly the most convenient way for a visiting sportsman wishing to trophy hunt in

77

Spain, for this organization takes care of everything from the moment of arrival in Madrid to departure, including all transport, licences and accommodation, etc.

Whatever the species of deer being hunted, there is a fixed daily Safari Basic Fee which, according to the composition of the hunting party, will vary from US $345 per day (about £180) for one guide per client, to US $195 (about £100) if the guide is shared by three sportsmen. The normal duration of the hunt is of three to five days for each animal to be hunted. Many of the species are available in El Castano, a private hunting reserve of about 15,000 acres (6000 hectares) controlled by Caza y Naturaleza.

There is also a Basic Trophy fee payable only when the trophy has been taken, which varies from US $1950 for a Red deer stag, to US $1200 and US $1300 respectively for a Roe or Fallow buck. Should, however, the client miss three reasonable chances of getting his trophy, and subsequently fail to take a trophy during the hunt, he may be charged 25 percent of the trophy fee for the animal being hunted. For any animal wounded but not recovered, the charge will be 50 percent of the trophy fee.

Until recently, Spain had its own formulae for measuring big game trophies, but in 1977 it was decided to change over to the C.I.C. formulae which was the accepted method elsewhere in Europe for European trophies. Why this decision had not been taken twenty-five years earlier is hard to understand, for it was in Madrid in 1952 that the present C.I.C. formulae were adopted for general use in Europe. Nevertheless the old formula is still being used by the Game Department (Institute for the Conservation of Nature – referred to as I.C.O.N.A.) and Cazatur when deciding whether there should be a trophy surcharge for heads of exceptional merit.

For instance, a surcharge for a Red deer trophy is only levied when the points score (I.C.O.N.A.) exceeds 155, whilst for Roe and Fallow deer the surcharge only applies after 108 and 180 points respectively.

The following, based on 1980 charges, is how the system works.

	Basic trophy fee *	trophy surcharge
Red deer (Good representative trophy, 146 pts)	US $1950	Up to 155 pts no surcharge 156–165 pts $80 per point 166–175 pts $100 per point 176–185 pts $150 per point Above 185 pts $220 per point
Roe deer (Good representative trophy 95 pts)	US $1200	Up to 108 pts no surcharge 109–113 pts $80 per point 114–118 pts $100 per point Above 118 points $150 per point

Fallow deer	Basic trophy fee*	trophy surcharge
(Good representative trophy 170 pts)	US $1300	Up to 180 pts no surcharge
		181–190 pts $80 per point
		191–200 pts $100 per point
		Above 200 pts $220 per point

* For trophies with fewer than 12 points (tines) the basic trophy fee is reduced to $825.

These charges apply to game stalked and not shot during a *monteria*.

Females of all species, when available may be shot for $250. If, however, a female deer is shot in mistake for a male, the charge will be half the basic fee for the species.

Under the above mentioned charges, a good representative Red deer trophy of over twelve points would cost about US $2500 (about £1300).

Medals awarded for trophies assessed under I.C.O.N.A. system are:

	Bronze	Silver	Gold
Red deer	152.01–162 pts	162.01–173 pts	over 173 pts
Roe deer	106.01–112 pts	112.01–116 pts	over 116 pts
Fallow deer	175.01–188 pts	188.01–198 pts	over 198 pts

Red deer *Cervus elaphus hispanicus*
Local name: *Ciervo* and *Venado*.

Apart from a population of about 500 deer in the ancient royal hunting ground of El Pardo, just north of Madrid, the majority of Spain's Red deer are to be found in the mountain ranges of the provinces of Toledo and Cuidad Real, in the provinces of Caceres and Badajoz in the west, and in the Sierra Morena de Andujar and Sierra Morena de Cordoba in the south, where they are the most plentiful. Other herds frequent Las Marismas of the Coto Doñana and adjacent areas along the Guadalquiver river and marismas of Huelva province.

Throughout the whole of Spain it is estimated that the total Red deer population may be about 350,000 animals of which, perhaps, 2000 are centred around Coto Doñana.

For a number of years, mainly due to differences in size and weight, it was considered that Red deer in Spain – often referred to as the Western Red deer – were represented by two subspecies – *C.e.bolivari* over much of its northern range, and *C.e.hispanicus* in the Coto Doñana and adjacent areas, the deer in the latter area being considerably smaller. This difference, however, seems due to habitat, for the deer of the Coto Doñana live in scrubland terrain which is both flat and sandy, and is in marked contrast to the sierras of central Spain, where pasture is both rich and varied, with forests of oak and cork to give the deer shelter in winter.

Although more trophy stags are now being shot by stalking than formerly, the majority of Red deer in Spain are killed during the *monteria*. Occasionally, however, in the Coto Doñana area, the deer are hunted on horseback with a rifle.

The shooting season for Red deer extends from early September until about 20 February, although the best time to hunt for a trophy stag is during the rut, which commences about 10 September and continues for about a month.

The best trophies have come from the Montes de Toledo and Sierra Morena where a good representative trophy will have antlers about 34 in. (86 cm) in length, with twelve points (tines) or more.

Fallow deer *Dama dama dama*
Local name: *Gamo*.

The principal population of Fallow deer in a purely wild state is in the Coto Doñana, south of Sevilla where they roam the scrubland in their hundreds. Other populations occur at El Pardo, an ancient hunting ground of the kings of Spain, and at Viñuelas, north of Madrid, whilst the El Castaño reserve in the mountains of Toledo holds a fair number.

The open season for shooting Fallow deer runs from the beginning of September until the end of February, but during the rut in October is the best time to hunt for a trophy buck.

Roe deer *Capreolus capreolus capreolus*
Local name: *Corzo*.

The main distribution of Roe in Spain is along the foothills of Cordillera Cantabrica in the north with scattered populations occurring in all suitable localities from the provinces of Navarra and Soria in the north-east to Asturias and Gallicia in the west. In central Spain a few occur in the Sierra Guadarrama and Montes de Toledo, north and south of Madrid respectively, with others in the Sierra Morena near Cordoba, and at La Almoraima near Algerciras, in the extreme south of the country.

Until recently, when the open season for hunting Roe of both sexes was from 1 October to 15 February, the majority were killed during a drive. Latterly, however, the open season for bucks has been changed to run from April to October inclusive, and a greater interest in stalking is being developed. Like their chamois, Spanish Roe trophies are not particularly large, the best so far recorded being a buck killed in 1966 with 138.85 C.I.C. points.

SWEDEN
Elk, Red deer, Roe deer and Fallow deer are the species of deer which can be hunted by sportsmen in Sweden today. A fifth, the Reindeer, occurs only in domestic herds in the north where it is estimated about a quarter million animals are being herded by the Lapps, the last truly wild deer having been killed about 1865.

The Elk is Sweden's most important big game animal for the overseas visitor and during 1979 over 2000 licences were issued to foreign hunters wishing to participate in Elk hunting. Indeed, I understand that the increasing number of foreign hunters visiting Sweden is causing concern to Swedish hunters who fear that this overseas interest in their sport can only lead to their sporting rents being increased. In consequence, many Swedish hunters prefer to offer Elk hunting to foreigners on an exchange basis for, perhaps, the opportunity to hunt boar, Red deer or mouflon, and thus avoid any monetary transaction taking place.

Anyone wishing to hunt in Sweden must first apply to the police at the point of entry for a firearm licence on which will be entered details about yourself, homeland hunting licence, rifle and ammunition, and movements in Sweden. This will cost Sw.Kr.40 (about £4).

Danish, Finnish and Norwegian citizens may, however, bring in such weapons and ammunition without licences, provided they arrive *direct* from Denmark, Finland or Norway. The weapons, however, may not remain in Sweden for a period longer than three months.

For hunting in Sweden both a firearm licence and a Swedish hunting licence must be carried, the latter, costing Sw.Kr.75 (about £8) (1979) being valid for one year (1 July to 30 June). This licence can be applied for in advance, and will normally be done by the hunting host. It is also necessary for every sportsman to have adequate insurance cover for both third party liability and accident insurance cover in case of disablement and death, and unless these insurances are covered by his own personal insurance at home, these insurances can also be arranged by the hunting host, who will also arrange for the visitor to become a member of the Swedish Hunting Association. A membership, including both these insurances, costs Sw.Kr.33 (about £3.50) (1979).

The minimum calibre permissible for Elk hunting is 6.5 mm and although shooting slugs from shotguns is forbidden, it is allowed to use a combined shotgun/rifle firearm, provided the latter is of sufficient calibre. The bullet (soft-nosed) must weigh at least 139 grains (9 g) and have a power of 1998 ft/lb (2700 joules) at a distance of 109 yards (100 metres) from the rifle. If the bullet weighs 154 grains (10 g) or more, the power must be at least 1480 ft/lb (2000 joules). As two or more shots may have to be taken at an animal not downed with the first shot, a rifle that can hold four or five cartridges in the magazine or a repeating rifle is the most suitable. Fully jacketed bullets are not allowed. For Elk hunts appropriate rifles may be hired for a period not exceeding fourteen days to anyone in possession of a gun licence entitling him to carry a weapon suitable for Elk hunting and who has already passed the shooting test.

Test shooting at a distance of 87 yards (80 metres) at an Elk-silhouette of natural size is regularly undertaken by both visiting and Swedish hunters before a shoot. The test comprises a series of four shots at a stationary target, and two series each of four shots at a target travelling at about 16 ft (5 metres) per second. The travelling target is visible during 25 yards (23 metres) of running. For a pass, all four shots at the fixed target and at least three for each series of the moving target are required. A hit is reckoned to be a shot which strikes within the marked area (lung, heart) of the target figure. Lennart Hedberg, an experienced Elk hunter, recommends that the most lethal shot on Elk is to hit the lungs and he illustrates this by what he calls the 'Elk clock' which depicts the different shooting angles that may be presented to the hunter wishing to achieve a 'lung shot'. (*Shooting Times and Country Magazine*, 17–23 May 1979.)

The use of shotgun for Roe during the winter months is permitted. Since 1971 Brenneke slug have been banned for use in Sweden, and only pellet shot of maximum circumference of 4 mm (no. B.B. shot) are permitted for use with shotguns.

In Sweden shooting generally is forbidden after sunset, but district officials are empowered to vary this regulation in order to extend the time for shooting Roe until one hour after sunset.

Elk *Alces alces alces*
Local names: $\bar{A}lg$; Bull, *Tjur*; Cow, *Ko*; Calf, *Kalv*.

From almost being on the point of extinction in the late eighteenth century, the Elk has made a remarkable recovery and in some areas – notably in middle Sweden – a maximum tolerable density has already been reached, if not exceeded, to the detriment of forestry and agriculture. Up to 1789 the hunting of Elk was reserved for the monarchy but in that year King Gustav III declared that hunting should be *free to all* landowners, and this was considered one of the main causes of its decline. Predation by wolves also played a part, but only up to the middle of the last century, for by 1865 they were practically extinct in Sweden. Nowadays, however, Sweden once again has a small population of wolves.

Shortly after 1924, following a five year suspension of all Elk hunting, the Elk population started to increase, and despite increased culling, has done so ever since. It is believed that most of the very rapid increase in Elk population during the last decade has been due to insufficient pressure being put on to the cull of calves, and it is recommended that about 30 to 40 percent of the annual cull should be in this age group.

In 1941 the total cull of Elk for the whole country was about 10,000. Since that date Elk have now spread over the whole of Sweden, except on the island of Gotland, and in 1978 it was estimated that the total population was around 300,000 animals of which a fifth were in Värmland. During the 1978 hunting season the total cull in Sweden was 94,217 Elk and in the following year this was increased to 115,800 of which Värmland's contribution was 15,338 – about 5000 short of the number of Elk licences issued for that *län*. It is not surprising, therefore, that the Elk population in Värmland continues to increase, particularly in the south where it is estimated, according to an aerial survey, that there were probably 74 per cent more Elk there than in the previous year. As a result it was decided that during 1980, in areas where up to 200 Elk are licensed to be shot, hunters would be allowed sixty days of hunting, whilst in areas where a cull of more than 200 was planned, the open season would run from 13 October until 31 January – a total of 111 days.

In addition to those animals killed by hunters, in the whole of Sweden a further 3000 to 4000 Elk annually become road or rail casualties, which may result in severe human injury and on occasions, loss of life, quite apart from damage to vehicles. There are two periods in the year when traffic accidents are most likely to occur – one in the late spring and early summer when the cow is attempting to drive away the previous year's calves prior to calving herself, and the other in the autumn when the Elk have their rutting season.

Most Elk in Sweden are killed during the course of a drive, when as many as twenty or more rifles may be involved. In every hunting party one leader is responsible for the day's hunting, for Elk driving, particularly on some of the larger estates, requires a considerable amount of organization. For instance, before each drive can take place, each rifle will have to be allotted a stand where he will have a reasonable field of fire without endangering the lives of other members of the party be they fellow sportsmen or beaters.

In 1951 I had two days' Elk driving in central Sweden and I was much impressed with the excellent organization that marked the whole proceeding. There were three drives each day and before each took place the estate manager called all the sixteen rifles together, handed each a large-scale map to show how the other rifles were placed, and also, by means of arrows, which routes the dog patrols would be taking and which were the safe directions for firing. As often as not the stand was on a road, with dense forests bordering it on either side, and the field of fire was, in consequence, rather limited.

Nowadays, in order to avoid any misunderstanding due to language problems, it is normal practice for the host to provide an interpreter for each foreign guest, and he will accompany him throughout the day.

Despite the size of the Elk – a full-grown bull stands some 70–79 in. (178–200 cm) at the shoulder and may weigh about half a ton (508 kg) or more – it is remarkable how such a large animal can move so quietly in the forest, and, unless the waiting rifle keeps a sharp look-out, a beast may easily slip across the road unseen. The animals are driven forward by both men and Elk-hounds, and, although moving shots have frequently to be taken, it is seldom that the animal is more than ambling along. During these drives it is customary to shoot both bulls and cows, as well as calves. During the two days I had driving, eleven Elk were killed, of which only two were young bulls, the remainder being cows.

Elk driving is not only a sport, but also a business, for it is the only method by which a sufficient number of animals can be killed in the time available. For the hunter, particularly one who has had little experience of this form of hunting, it has its moments of thrilling expectancy, such as when a running hound, hidden to view, starts to bay an Elk close by, or perhaps the cracking of a twig or two nearby advertises the approach of an Elk. One has, however, to be extremely lucky to shoot, during a drive, a real trophy bull, for I have the impression that few bulls in areas that are frequently driven, have the chance to reach full maturity and those that do owe their survival to the fact that they realized at an early age that to break back through the line of beaters was the best route of escape.

A far more exciting and exacting method of hunting Elk is for a single hunter, accompanied only by a dog-man, to use a hound to bring him in contact with an Elk. The hound can either be allowed to run free – *lōshund* – or kept on a leash – *ledhund* – methods which have been described in Elk hunting in Norway, so need not be repeated here (*page 66*).

In the north of Sweden, the hunting season opens during mid-September but in the south it will be a month later, and according to district and hunting area, may vary in length from only two to five days, and up to three or four months on the largest estates.

Sverek, who arrange hunting in Sweden for foreign sportsmen, offer a number of three-day hunts after Elk in various forests, which include both driving and stalking. In the Risebo-Smaland area, which extends to about 7410 acres (3000 hectares) some 14 miles (24 km) south of Åtvidaberg, hunting by *battue* is available for parties of eight but individual applicants will be placed in groups to make up the required number for the shoot. The Elk population in this area is said to have increased in recent years, and during 1978 twenty animals were released to augment the stock.

In addition to a 'permit documentation' fee of about Sw.Kr.350 (about £35) the daily charge for each hunter taking part in a *battue* is about Sw.Kr.1607 (about £164) – a figure which includes the hire of beaters, dogs etc. but not accommodation. A trophy fee, ranging from about £120 for antlers bearing six to eleven tines (points) to about £600 for heads of twenty-one tines or more will be charged only if the hunter takes the antlers away with him. A three-day hunt, therefore, at Risebo, during which a 16-pointer bull may have been shot, will cost about £1000.

For the trophy hunter, a two or three day hunt in the Misterhult State Forest, which is situated some $15\frac{1}{2}$ miles (25 km) north of Oskarshamn, might be more productive, for this forest contains some good trophy bulls, and in recent years bulls with antlers bearing fourteen tines or more have been shot.

Normally, hunting of Elk in State forests is reserved for State officials, but prior to the opening hunt towards the end of October, a permit is available, costing about £470 for a three-day hunt, for two hunters to shoot two bull Elk, one of which can be a trophy animal. These will be shot by one hunter accompanying a guide with hound on leash – *ledhund* – whilst his companion will be posted in a hide.

Trophy charges on a State forest are about double those charged elsewhere, varying from about £175 for a small Elk to over £900 for a bull of sixteen tines or more. Should a hunter fail to take advantage of a chance to shoot during the first two days a bull bearing more than five tines, half the shooting fee will be charged, whilst during the last day of the hunt, this condition will apply to animals of all categories. Half the approximate fee will also be charged for any Elk missed or wounded during the hunt.

Assuming the party, therefore, was successful in bagging two bulls, one a 16-pointer and the other a small 4-pointer, the total cost of the three-day hunt, exclusive of accommodation – would be around £1400.

Roe deer *Capreolus capreolus capreolus*
Local names: *Rådjur*; Male, *Råbock*; Female, *Råget*; Kid, *Kid* or *Killing*.

The Roe deer are plentiful throughout most of southern and mid-Sweden, but north of about latitude 61° they become progressively fewer until by latitude 65° they can be described as rare. However, a few occur right up to the Arctic circle, principally in coastal regions, and have now spread their range around the Gulf of Bothnia into Finland. A few Roe were imported to the island of Gotland in the Baltic Sea shortly before the war, and the species is still extant there. During the 1977–8 season some 66,900 Roe were killed in Sweden.

Roe bucks may not be shot in Sweden until 16 August by which time the rut in some areas will be practically over. From then on, until the end of the month, bucks may be shot with rifle only, the use of hounds during this period being prohibited. From 1 October until the end of the season, which varies according to district, some terminating on 31 October, some on 30 November with the majority continuing until the end of the year, both sexes may be killed. Hounds may also be used after 1 October as the majority of deer will be shot during drives at which both rifle and shotgun are permitted, the smallest gauge of the latter allowed being 20 bore. In regions where there is a high population of Roe, special licences may be granted to stalk buck with rifle only, during September. On the Isle of Gotland, however, it is forbidden to hunt Roe at any season.

The best trophies come from the south of Sweden, and at the 1971 World Exhibition of Trophies at Budapest all forty-three Swedish exhibits were in the Gold medal class, the best, killed at Börringe in 1928, attaining 176.40 C.I.C. points. Since then, however, a number of better trophies have been taken, the best being a buck at Widtskofle in 1975 (208.50 C.I.C. points).

Not many opportunities are available for an overseas visitor to hunt Roe buck in Sweden, for most landowners keep the stalking to themselves and for their friends. When available, compared to prices in Eastern Europe, Roe stalking in Sweden is not too expensive, and a three-day hunt – including accommodation – during which a 6-point buck may be shot, should not cost more than about £150 to £175.

Sverek annually offer a three-day 'package hunt' for three hunters during which the party – not each hunter – will be allowed to shoot one Red deer, one Roe deer and five wild boar, for a total cost of under £500, including accommodation.

For any deer wounded but not found the full shooting fee for the game in

85

question will have to be paid – approximately £12 to £70 depending on whether the buck's antlers have under six tines (points) or is a 6-pointer or more.

Red deer *Cervus elaphus elaphus*
Local names: *Kronvilt*; Male, *Kronhjort*; Female, *Hind*: Calf, *Kid* or *Calf*.

There is a small population of Red deer in the county of Skåne in the south, the majority of animals being centred on the Häckeberga estate, near Genarp, but all hunting is private. In Skåne, where the total population of Red deer is under 200 animals, about thirty will be killed during the open hunting season, which in 1979–80, opened for both sexes on 16 October, terminating on 15 November for stags, and at the end of November for hinds and calves. In three other southern districts, the open season is slightly longer, opening on 10 October and running until the end of November. Every year a few Red deer wander from the Norwegian Atlantic coast into central Sweden.

About 1955, seven Red deer (a 14-pointer and six hinds) were caught-up at Häckeberga and transferred to an enclosure at Halleberg in central Sweden for subsequent release in the district. This was done in an attempt to move the native Red deer into an area where it was hoped they would do less damage than was occurring in the more agricultural south.

Opportunities to hunt Red deer seldom occur, but occasionally the odd deer may be included in the game to be hunted in the Agusa game preserve in Skåne.

Fallow deer *Dama dama dama*
Local names: *Dovvilt*; Male, *Dovhjort*; Female, *Hind*; Fawn, *Kid*, *Calf*.

Fallow deer exist in small scattered colonies in southern Sweden up to about Stockholm, which includes Adelsnäs near Linköping, and on the island of Öland. Stalking the bucks, and driving are accepted methods of control, and over 2000 deer will be shot.

In southern Sweden, bucks only may be shot throughout September, but for does and fawns there are two open seasons, one lasting three weeks, 1–20 October inclusive, and the other of about six weeks, starting on 16 November and running until the end of the year. In two districts of mid-Sweden, however, and on the isle or Gotland, the hunting of Fallow deer is forbidden.

Each season it is estimated that just over 2000 Fallow deer will be shot. In 1978 the official figure for *both* Red and Fallow deer was 2470 killed.

SWITZERLAND

Switzerland is divided into twenty-five cantons – the equivalent of a county in Britain – and each has its own individual law as to hunting etc.

Briefly, there are two hunting systems – one similar to the German system which operates in the nine *Revierkantone* and the other in the sixteen *Patentkantone* with a *Patentjagd* or hunting examination which each hunter has to pass before being issued with a licence which will specify both the kind and amount of game he is allowed to shoot.

The average size of a *Patentkanton*, which means 'people's hunting', is about 523,800 acres (212,000 hectares), and is about double the size of a *Revierkanton*. In a *Revierkanton* every village or city leases a territory of land for a period of eight years, in which a group of hunters may shoot and hunt. Roughly speaking the northern cantons are *Revierkantone*, whilst the middle and south-western cantons are *Patentkantone*. Scattered about among the *Patentkantone* are a number of federal reserves where no hunting is permitted, with heavy penalties for infringement. These reserves serve as a reservoir to prevent the game being decimated in the *Patentkantone* where the hunting, as mentioned above, is public for the people. Reserves also exist in the *Revierkantone*, and although they make a useful contribution to general game conservation, their role is not so vital as hunting pressure is less dominant.

So far as deer are concerned, three species are available for hunting, Red, Roe and Sika deer, but there are very few of the latter.

Any foreigner can hunt in Switzerland for a restricted period, the length of which varies according to the canton, provided he can produce a hunting licence of his country of origin.

The cost of hunting licences also varies from one canton to another. In Canton Zurich, for instance, it will cost the *lease holder* as well as the gamekeeper, SFr.20 (about £5) but guest licences vary according to duration or whether the guest is a Swiss citizen or foreigner. For instance, the annual licence for a Swiss citizen living within Canton Zurich will cost SFr.100 (about £25) but if resident outside the Canton the cost will be double – the same price as a foreigner living within the canton would have to pay. Foreigners living outside the canton, however, have to pay SFr.400 (about £100). Licences for shorter periods of a week or even two days are also available, the latter, for a non-resident, costing SFr.24 (about £6). Persons who have not passed the hunter's examination may only apply three times for two-day licences, or once for a one-week licence during a calendar year.

In Pantentkanton Graubünden, however, the cost of licences, particularly for foreigners, is considerably higher. For local citizens of the canton the annual cost for a licence is SFr.240 (about £60), whilst for other Swiss citizens the price varies from SFr.700 (about £175) for those who have lived in the canton for at least ten years to SFr.1200 (about £300) for other Swiss citizens. The annual licence for a foreigner, however, costs SFr.4800 (about £1200) – an inflated price obviously designed to discourage 'outsiders'.

Nowhere in Switzerland has any trophy fee to be paid.

Firearms can be imported freely but there are strict rules as to calibre which again, vary from canton to canton. Canton Zurich, for instance, requires a minimum energy for stag and wild boar of 1446 ft/lb (200 mkg) but 150 mkg is acceptable for chamois and 723 ft/lb (100 mkg) for Roe deer. Full patch bullets are not permitted. In the Pantentkanton Graubünden (Grisons) and in several other *Pantentkantone* the 10.3 calibre is allowed but telescopic sights may not be used by those under forty-five years of age. This rule applies to everyone, whether glasses are worn or not. Whilst this regulation is obviously made to prevent long range shooting at chamois and stag, and to encourage the hunter to stalk as close as possible to his quarry, it is, in my opinion, a mistake, for the challenge of hunting is in the approach work and not the shot, and all modern facilities available to make the latter as precise and humane as possible, irrespective of the age of the hunter, should be used.

In Canton Zurich and one or two other cantons, the shotgun can be used for deer, but *only* during a drive.

Except in the three *Patentkantone* of Graubünden, Glarus and Tessin, hunting and shooting on Sundays is forbidden.

Red deer *Cervus elaphus hippelaphus*
Local name: Stag, *Hirsch*; Hind, *Tier*.

Although practically extinct in Switzerland at the beginning of the last century, Red deer are now established in sixteen cantons, the majority being found in Canton Graubünden/Grisons. Throughout the whole of Switzerland, the spring population of Red deer is estimated to be about 20,000 animals, divided between *Patentkantone* and *Revierkantone* as follows:

	Census (April 1978) Stags and hinds	Numbers killed (1978)			
		Stags	Hinds	Calves	Total
Patentkantone	19,040	1344	1240	288	2872
Revierkantone	1119	162	183	62	407
Total	20,159	1506	1423	350	3279

Trophy stags from Switzerland are only moderate, and of the eighteen heads displayed at the Budapest Exhibition of 1971 only two reached Silver medal standard – the best, shot in 1953, coming from Ebnat-Kappel with a score of 175.28 C.I.C. points. The national record trophy (217.17 C.I.C. points) was shot in the Canton Valais in 1976 and exhibited at the Marseilles Exhibition of 1977.

The season for hunting Red deer stags in Canton Valais runs from 1 September to mid-December.

Roe deer *Capreolus capreolus capreolus*
Local name: *Reh*; Buck, *Reh männlich*; Doe, *Reh weiblich*.

The Roe has increased in numbers considerably in recent years, and now occurs in every canton, being most plentiful on the plains lying between Jura and the Alps.

According to federal statistics, the estimated population and cull of Roe in 1978 was as follows:

	Census (April) Bucks and Does	Number killed			
		Bucks	Does	Kids	Total
Patentkantone	53,500	8303	7013	3327	18,643
Revierkantone	52,800	10,520	9441	4697	24,658
Total	106,300	18,823	16,454	8024	43,301

In some cantons the Roe population is considered too high and efforts are being made to reduce the number. In Canton Zurich, for instance, during the 1977–8 season over 50 percent of the estimated population based on the spring census was killed but even this was not considered sufficient and during the following season the cull was increased to 63 percent. The full figures for these two seasons were as follows:

	Census Bucks and Does	Number of Roe deer killed Bucks (including yearlings)	Does	Total
1978	6517	3777	4276	8053
1979	5870	3906	4632	8538

Over the whole canton the sex ratio is thought to be about 1 to 1.3 with an average density in forest areas of about 28.9 deer per 247 acres (100 hectares) – i.e. about one deer per 8.5 acres (3.4 hectares) – which is fairly heavy stocking.

Although in the *Revierkantone* the open season for shooting bucks starts on 1 June, the closing date, as well as the open season for hunting does varies according to *Revierkanton*, in some terminating at the end of November but in the majority, continuing until the end of the year.

The class of animal which may be shot during the open season also varies. In Canton Zurich, for instance, only yearlings and cull-type bucks may be shot before August. Kids are to be shot during September from does with twins, the weaker being taken. For the remainder of the season after 1 October, additional kids which are weak or orphaned should be shot.

Swiss Roe trophies are, in my opinion, some of the most attractive from the whole of Europe, being not only well pearled but with sufficient span to give an attractive appearance. The best heads have come from Cantons Zurich, Schaffhausen and Aargau, with the highest scoring trophy at Budapest (183.22 C.I.C. points) being shot in the Revierkanton Zurich.

Sika deer *Cervus nippon nippon*
Local name: *Sikawild*.

Prior to 1939 Japanese Sika deer were kept in a park near the Rhine on the Swiss frontier facing Kaiserstuhl. During the war the park was opened up and the majority of deer killed. However, a few managed to escape and now lead a feral existence in some of the woods on both sides of the frontier. They are not plentiful and according to a census taken in 1978 numbered about thirteen in Canton Zurich and 130 in Canton Schaffhausen.

Normally, about thirty Sika deer will be shot each year, but during the 1978 season, at the request of the Forestry Department, the number was increased to fifty (23 stags, 20 hinds and 7 calves).

3 Eastern Europe (excluding U.S.S.R)

BULGARIA

In recent years Bulgaria has been designating certain areas for the development of international hunting and fishing, and Balkan Tourist now has available for the visiting sportsman about fifty hunting areas for both big and small game. Included among the former are Red, Roe and to a lesser extent, Fallow deer.

Special hunting lodges are available in most of the hunting areas but sportsmen wishing to use them must make a reservation when booking the hunting trip.

Hunting of all species of deer is by stalking, or shooting from a high seat, but never driving. Group hunting with the use of hunting dogs is, however, the normal method of hunting bear and wild boar.

For stalking deer, no more than three hunters are allowed in any one hunting area at the same time – hunting being permitted throughout the week, Sundays included.

The tourist prices for all species of deer are calculated on a trophy weight basis, heads (antlers on skull with full upper jaw) being weighed twenty-four hours after cleaning.

A fine of $22.50 (about £10) will be incurred if a Red deer stag or Fallow buck is missed, whilst for a Roe the penalty is reduced to half. For a wounded deer that is not recovered the fine will vary from $167 (about £80) for a Roe buck to as much as $1112 (about £550) for a Red deer stag – which is double the amount for a lost Fallow buck. Fines for lost hinds, does, calves and fawns are correspondingly less.

Guides are charged for at about £5 to £6 per day, and should a cart or motor vehicle be required, this will be charged accordingly.

Red deer *Cervus elaphus hippelaphus*

Thirty years ago Red deer were so scarce in Bulgaria that all hunting of this deer was forbidden, and as a result the species is now well established in all suitable localities, being particularly plentiful in the deciduous forests along the foothills of the Stara Planina in the north, where the best hunting areas include Vidin, Belogradchik, Berkovitza, 'Vitinia', Koprivshititsa, Lovech, Gabrovo and Veliko Turnovo.

South of Sofia, Red deer are to be found in the Rila, Pirin and Rhodopi Planina mountains where the principal hunting areas for stag are around Samokov, Borovetz, Kustendil, Razlog, Sandoniski, Gotre Delehev, Velingrad and Devin (Pamporovo).

In eastern Bulgaria, where the country is less mountainous, Red deer are to be found around Kolarovgrad in the north-east, hunting being permitted in the areas around Varna, Shumen, Targovishte, Razgrod, Silistra and Tolbuhin.

Further south they occur throughout east Stara Planina and Strandja Mountains, the principal hunting areas being centred around Nessebur, Aetos, Sliven, Kazanluk and Topolovgrad.

There is a five-month open season for hunting stag, opening on 1 September and continuing until the end of January. The rut normally commences during the first week of September and lasts about a month.

The minimum charge (1979) for shooting a stag, based on skull and antler weight, is US $236 (about £107), and this will steadily increase to about £2750 for a trophy weighing 12 kg with an additional £14 for each 0.1 kg increase.

Based on these charges the average cost of shooting a Gold medal stag in Bulgaria would range from about £740 to over £2700.

In 1975 a magnificent 18-pointer, with a skull and antler weight of 33 lb (14.99 kg) was shot by Todor Zivkov in 'Irry Hissar', a flat forest area in the district of Silistra of north-east Bulgaria, with a C.I.C. score of 253.62 points, which became the new world record. Three years later the same hunter shot an even larger trophy (256.78 C.I.C. points) but weighing almost one pound lighter (32 lb or about 14.56 kg). This stag was shot in the same area as the previous one, which was believed to have been its father. To a visiting sportsman the charge to shoot either stag would have been in excess of £3000.

Roe deer *Capreolus capreolus capreolus*

Roe deer are plentiful in all suitable localities and hunting is available in all localities mentioned under Red deer.

The best trophies have mainly come from the Stalin district of north-east Bulgaria, the record for the country being a buck shot at Kavarna, near the Black Sea coast in 1976 (176.40 C.I.C. points).

The open season for bucks extends from 1 June to 31 January, but does may be killed only during November.

Charges (1979) for shooting Roe buck, based on skull and antler weight, vary from about £17 for small heads under 200 g weight to around £830 for a trophy head weighing 550 g with an additional £12 for each g above.

At the International Hunting Exhibition in Plovdiv, 1981, two trophies had weights in excess of 600 g, the heaviest – shot in 1976 – having a weight of

637 g and a score of 175.78 C.I.C. points. Based on the above mentioned charges, this trophy would have been priced at around £1400.

Fallow deer *Dama dama dama*

Fallow deer has a limited distribution in Bulgaria, the best trophies having come from Voden which is situated in the district of Razgrad in the north-east, and from Studen Kladenetz, which is adjacent to the dam 'Studen Kladenetz' in the district of Kurdjaly in south-east Bulgaria.

The open season for hunting bucks extends from 1 October to 31 January.

Charges (1979) for shooting Fallow buck are based on upper skull and antler weight, and range from about £132 for a small head weighing under 2.5 kg to approximately £1930 for a trophy weighing 5.0 kg with an extra £19 for each 0.1 kg increase.

CZECHOSLOVAKIA

Before describing the deer of Czechoslovakia, it should be mentioned that this Republic is based on two distinct nations: Czech and Slovak, each with a different, but similar, language. Since 1968 the Republic has had the official designation of 'Federation'.

Hunting for Red, Roe and Fallow deer is available for the sportsman visiting Czechoslovakia, and some excellent trophies can be taken. During the last century Sika deer *Cervus nippon* and White-tailed deer *Odocoileus virginianus* were introduced, and are now established in several localities both free-living and enclosed, but at present only the former may be hunted by foreigners, hunting of the latter being restricted as numbers at present are considered insufficient for hunting. The Sika deer were introduced in 1897, with the initial stock coming from Hagenbeck, and a recent estimate suggests that the total stock living in the wild may number around 1500 animals, the majority being centered around Manětín and Konstantinovy Lázně (west Bohemia). There is also a small population around Šumperk in Moravia.

In some areas the habitat is shared with Red deer and as is currently occurring elsewhere in the world, it is believed that some hybridization may be taking place. In 1953 a few Sika deer were introduced into a park of about 200 acres (80 hectares) at Zahrádky, which lies some 43 miles (70 km) north of Praha (Prague) but they did not remain there long. There are, however, two game preserves where Japanese Sika deer *C.n.nippon* are maintained – one at Janovice near Heřmanův Městec in eastern Bohemia and the other at the town of Velké Meziříčí in Moravia. There are also some Dybowski Sika *C.n.hortulorum* at Opočno in eastern Bohemia, whilst both Japanese and Dybowski are in a park at Lány just west of Praha.

White-tailed deer first came to Czechoslovakia in 1840 and now frequent the Dobříš area some 18 to 25 miles (30 to 40 km) south of Praha. They are free-living, and at the end of 1980 were estimated to number about 250 head. The original deer were supplied by the animal dealer Hagenbeck, the deer having come from Canada, so they were probably of the northern woodland type *O.v.borealis*. The open season for hunting White-tailed deer is from 1 September until the end of the year, during which period about thirty will be shot.

Unfortunately, the Whitetail are subject to parasite infection which, it is thought, is being transferred to domestic stock, so at present a large enclosure of approximately 4940 acres (2000 hectares) is being constructed at Dobříš, to which it is intended to transfer the bulk of these animals.

Between 1965 and 1970, as a result of helminthological investigation of thirty-three deer from the region Brdy-Hřebeny, twenty-six species of parasitic worms were found, and according to Ing. Alois Kotrlý and Dr Božena Kotrlá (1972) 'the most frequent parasites of White-tailed deer are *Spiculopteragia böhmi* (66 percent); *Fascioloides magna* (57 percent), *Ostertagia asymetrica* (40 percent) and *Elaphostrongylus cervi* (33 percent).'

Many years ago the Elk *Alces alces* became extinct on the territory of present-day Czechoslovakia, but during the past twenty years a few have started to reappear, having wandered in from Poland. Their number, however, is probably under ten and hunting is not permitted.

Apart from a minimum charge for shooting a male of Red, Roe or Fallow deer, the prices are fixed according to the points value of the trophy when assessed under the relevant C.I.C. formula, and based on 1981 prices, the charges work out approximately as follows:

Red deer stag

Minimum – (up to 130 C.I.C. points) $151.60 (about £77)
Bronze medal – up to $1165.40 (about £595)
Silver medal – up to $2961.70 (about £1511)
Gold medal – minimum $3087 (about £1575), and thereafter increased by $214.40 (about £109) per point up to 220 C.I.C. points, and beyond that score, by $357.30 (about £182) per point.

Fallow deer buck

Minimum – (up to 100 C.I.C. points) $81.40 (about £42)
Bronze medal – up to $645 (about £329)
Silver medal – up to $793 (about £379)
Gold medal – minimum $768, thereafter increased by $39.40 (about £20) per point.

Roe deer buck

Minimum – (up to 40 C.I.C. points) $30 (about £15)
Bronze medal – up to $341 (about £174)
Silver medal – up to $576 (about £294)
Gold medal – minimum $594 (about £303), plus $30 (about £15) per point thereafter.

For Red and Fallow deer trophies taken in an enclosure, prices are increased by about 10 percent.

Based on these charges, the best Czechoslovakian trophies at Budapest would have been priced approximately as follows:

Red deer (240.65 C.I.C. points) $12,377 (about £6314)

Fallow deer (191.56 C.I.C. points)	$1223 (about £624)
Roe deer (176.72 C.I.C. points)	$1995 (about £1018)

Fines for animals that escape wounded vary from about £105 for a stag, £55 for a Fallow buck to £25 for a Roe buck, while for a complete miss, the approximate fines incurred are £36 (Red), £30 (Fallow) and £14 (Roe). Should the hunter take a shot at an animal other than the one designated by the keeper, irrespective of whether the beast is killed, wounded or missed, he will be charged a figure equivalent to the full estimated price of the trophy.

In addition to the keeper, each visiting hunter will be accompanied by a Cedok interpreter for which there will be no payment. There is, however, an 'organization' charge of approximately £9 for each day actually spent hunting.

A licence to hunt in Czechoslovakia costs about £14 for one full month, or about £30 for the calendar year and this covers insurance.

Rifles can be hired if necessary at about £4 per day each, with cartridges extra at about 50 pence each, but if the hunter has his own weapon, twenty rounds of ammunition can be imported duty free.

Red deer *Cervus elaphus hippelaphus*

Local names:	Czech	Slovak
Stag	*jeleň*	*jeleň*
Hind	*laň*	*jelenica*
Calf	*kolouch*	*jelienča*

Red deer are well distributed throughout Czechoslovakia, particularly in the western half of the federation, their main haunts following the woods which cover the mountains along the frontier with Austria and Germany. Away from the mountains it only occurs in the larger woodland areas situated principally between Brno and Šternberk and between Plzeň (Pilsen) and Praha (Prague). In the east it occurs along the Carpathian foothills and the Polish border.

The red deer of the west are smaller than those in eastern Czechoslovakia, which gradually assume the magnificent proportions of the Carpathian stag. This difference in size has led some authorities to suggest that two subspecies are represented – *C.e.hippelaphus* in the west and *C.e.montanus* in the east, but modern opinion considers them all one subspecies.

For about 200 years there has been a small herd of white Red deer in a park at Žleby near Čáslav, some 40 miles (64 km) east of Praha. The true origin of these white deer is unknown, but it would appear they came to Czechoslovakia about 1780. The herd at present numbers about sixty head.

The Red deer population was not much affected by the war, and today it is more numerous than it was during the thirties. In 1978 the stock of Red deer was estimated to number 45,605 head, consisting of 17,647 stags, 18,229 hinds and 9729 calves. About a quarter of the Red deer population is kept in preserves, the remainder being free-ranging. At the present time about 24,631

Red deer are being killed annually, of which about 7511 will be trophy stags, the best coming from the east towards the Carpathians. One of the best trophies so far taken in Czechoslovakia (240.65 C.I.C. points) was shot at Kriváň, Low Tatras, in 1961.

The open season for shooting stags opens on 1 August and extends until 31 December. Hinds are shot during the same period.

Roe Deer *Capreolus capreolus capreolus*

Local names:
	Czech	Slovak
Buck	*srnec*	*srnec*
Doe	*srna*	*srna*
Kid	*srnče*	*srnča*

The Roe has a wide distribution throughout Czechoslovakia, being particularly plentiful in the plains of Bohemia and Moravia. A census taken in 1978 estimated that the total stock of Roe throughout the federation amounted to 311,915 of which 116,559 were bucks, 122,545 does and the remainder kids.

On average, Roe in the east weigh approximately 14 percent heavier than those in the west, weights of 44 to 55 lb (20 to 25 kg) without stomach often being attained. Similarly, the heaviest antlers also come from eastern bucks, the best trophy (201.70 C.I.C. points) being shot at Opatovice near Zidlochovice, just south of Brno, in 1938.

Towards the end of the last century several attempts were made to introduce the larger Siberian Roe *C.c.pygargus* but the results seem to have been a failure. One of the areas where Siberian Roe were liberated was at Valč, some 17 miles (28 km) south-east of Karlovy Vary (Carlsbad) in western Bohemia.

The open season for hunting Roe bucks in Czechoslovakia is from 16 May until 30 September whilst does may be shot during the period September to December. Stalking on foot, shooting from a high seat or driving around in a carriage are the methods normally employed for hunting this deer. The annual cull is around 110,000 animals, of which about 40,000 will be bucks.

At one time the principal predator of the Roe in the east was the wolf, but there are not many now. Throughout the whole of the country a certain mortality among kids is caused by fox and wild boar.

Fallow deer *Dama dama dama*

Local names:
	Czech	Slovak
Buck	*daněk*	*daniel*
Doe	*daněla*	*danielica*
Fawn	*dančе*	*danielča*

The term *lopatař* is used for a strong buck.

Scattered populations of Fallow deer occur throughout much of the country away from the mountains, and although the majority are enclosed in parks – varying in size from 740 to 1235 acres (300 to 500 hectares) – there are also a fair number leading a wild existence. In 1978 the total stock of Fallow – about half of which were in preserves – was estimated at about 8897 of which 3257 were bucks, 3609 does and the remainder fawns of the year. On occasions fresh blood has been obtained from Gyulaj in Hungary.

Some excellent Fallow trophies have come from Obora Soutok near Břeclav in south Moravia, the best (203.73 C.I.C. points) being shot in 1975.

The open season for hunting bucks opens on 1 September and continues until the end of the year. Does may be shot during the same period. In former times many deer were killed during the course of large drives, sewelling or *lappen* (pieces of cloth or feathers attached to a long length of cord) being used to divert deer towards the rifles. Driving is now completely forbidden throughout Czechoslovakia and the deer are shot by stalking or from a high seat.

Each year about 3000 deer – which include some 800 bucks – are taken from the herds and whilst the majority will be shot, a number are caught up for transfer to other areas.

EAST GERMANY (GERMAN DEMOCRATIC REPUBLIC)

At the present time there would appear to be no possibility of any hunting being available in the German Democratic Republic for foreign visitors coming from a capitalistic country. There are, however, some State-owned hunting areas where sportsmen from a non-capitalistic country may hunt on invitation. The management of these areas comes under the Ministerium für Land-, Forst- und Nahrungs-güterwirtschaft. As the only hunting by visiting sportsmen is by invitation, no trophy fees are charged as is general practice in other countries of Eastern Europe.

Although there are certain calibre restrictions for hunting deer, Brenneke slug is permitted for all species, but seldom used for Red deer. The most popular rifle calibres used are 8×57, 7×57, 7×65 and 7×64.

The best trophies shot in the Democratic Republic are measured and displayed each year at the *Landwirtschaftsausstellung* (agricultural show) in Leipzig – Markkleeberg. In 1971 a 21-pointer stag was shot at Hagenow with a C.I.C. score of 231.87 points. Eight years later a 15-pointer from Genthin had a C.I.C. score of 232.60.

At the International Hunting Exhibition in Budapest, 1971, ten of the thirty Red deer trophies gained Gold medal awards, the best having a score of 225.85 C.I.C. points.

The standard of Roe trophy is also good, and forty-nine Gold medals were awarded to trophies shot since 1958, the best having a score of 182.73 C.I.C. points.

The hunting seasons for deer in the German Democratic Republic are as follows:

	Stags/Bucks	Hinds/Does
Red deer	16 August–31 January	16 September–31 January
Fallow deer	1 September–31 January	16 September–31 January
Roe deer	1 May–15 October	16 September–31 January

Hunting Reindeer in the mountains of Norway – after a successful stalk a good bull is gralloched.

A trophy bull Elk in Sweden. (*Göran Ekström.*)

A bull Elk being bayed by a hound in Sweden (*Grösta Tysk.*)

Elk hunting in Norway.

In Hungary, the shooting of Roe bucks in the fields is generally done from horse-drawn carriages. (*Dr Studinka.*)

Hunting facilities in Hungary – a shooting cabin on the left, a horse-drawn vehicle in the centre and a large 'high seat' on the right from which deer crossing any of six rides may be observed. (*Dr Studinka.*)

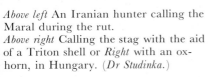

Above left An Iranian hunter calling the Maral during the rut.
Above right Calling the stag with the aid of a Triton shell or *Right* with an ox-horn, in Hungary. (*Dr Studinka.*)

Japanese Sika deer have been introduced to the U.S.A., New Zealand and many countries of Europe, and provide good stalking.

Axis deer or Chital – a native of India and Sri Lanka – can now be hunted in North America, Argentina and Australia.

The Rusa deer – a native of Indonesia – can now be hunted in New Guinea and elsewhere in Australasia.

The Sambar – a native of most Asian countries – can now be hunted in New Zealand and Australia.

Typical deer country of South Island, New Zealand.

Bull Moose during the rut. (*Leonard Lee Rue III.*)

14-pointer Bull Wapiti. (*Leonard Lee Rue III.*)

Barren-ground Caribou bull. (*Leonard Lee Rue III.*)

White-tailed buck of nine points. (*Leonard Lee Rue III.*)

GREECE

Hunting is permitted, upon payment of a fee, on most State-owned property in Greece, but the only large game available for hunting is the wild boar (15 October to 10 February).

HUNGARY

Visitors to International Hunting Exhibitions in Europe, and in particular to the one in Budapest in 1971 or the one in Bucharest, Romania in 1978, cannot fail to have been impressed by the wonderful quality of antlers produced by the Red, Roe and Fallow deer of Hungary. How has this excellent standard been attained?

In the first place, there are no private hunting grounds owned or leased by an individual, but areas can be rented by a hunting association or syndicate. At the present time about 22,000,000 acres (8,800,000 hectares) are regarded as hunting territory and this is divided into State forests, State agricultural farms and association blocks leased to hunting societies.

Pre-war the average area of a hunting territory – the majority of which were privately owned – was about 296 acres (120 hectares) in one block. Now the territories for deer management vary between 12,000 and 48,000 acres (4800 and 19,200 hectares) and consist of a mixture of deciduous woods with dense undergrowth, and arable, providing ideal conditions for the deer. Any Hungarian wishing to hunt must be a member of one of these associations, but before being accepted as a member, he must pass a test of knowledge and marksmanship. Fees for membership vary according to district, but they are not expensive – about 250 forints (about £3.50). An association member is permitted to introduce a Hungarian guest, but should he be a foreigner, approval will first have to be obtained from the Ministry of Agriculture.

Each association block belonging to a hunting society – which on average has about thirty-two members – is divided into smaller blocks, and whenever a local hunter goes out he must give due notice of his intentions and of the locality in which he wishes to hunt. If any other hunter is already using that block on that particular day, he will probably be diverted to another area – or have to change his hunting dates.

Each hunting association is responsible for making an annual census each spring, of the game present in its hunting area, and in the case of male deer, these will be divided into two categories – trophies and cull types – and from this information a shooting plan will be decided upon. Since most of the best hunting is usually sold to foreigners, it is seldom that a member has the opportunity to kill a really good trophy.

Each association is responsible for feeding the deer in winter when necessary. In practice, deer are fed only in time of deep snow and the feed consists mainly of lucerne, augmented by maize and roots when the weather is really hard. In an average winter there are only about fifteen to twenty days, the most occurring in the north of the country where the highest altitude is only about 2460 ft (700 to 800 metres), the highest peak being Mátra at 3312 ft (1010 metres) above sea level. On the other hand, the annual rainfall is only

97

about 24 to 25 in. (about 62 cm). Chestnuts are also collected and given to the deer in spring prior to the new grass emerging.

Deer stocks are kept at a level in accordance with their environment and in the most favourable areas the average deer density is about 1 deer per 70 acres (28 hectares), which is reduced to under half of this population in the least favourable areas. The deer density is based on woodland only, i.e. if only half of an area covering, say, 200 acres (80 hectares) is wood, then only 100 acres (40 hectares) is considered. The sex ratio is tried to be kept at 1:1.

Another interesting feature is that game density is based on 'deer units' per hectare, and for this purpose a 'game unit' consists of either one Red deer, two Fallow deer, three mouflon, three Roe deer or five boar. .

If anyone kills a stag that is considered too young for culling, he is given a 'minus point' by the Trophy Commission, and although at one time there was some punishment given to anyone who had accumulated two or three 'minus points', latterly no disciplinary action has been taken but nobody is proud of being given a 'minus point'!

Trophy fees paid by foreign sportsmen, which, as will be explained later, may run into several thousand pounds per beast, are paid in hard currency to Mavad who in turn will pass on the fee in Hungarian currency to the association or to the State-run territory in whose area the beast has been shot.

Whilst membership of a local hunting association is usually very cheap for a Hungarian hunter who could not, anyway, afford to pay very much for his sport, trophy fees for a foreigner for all species of large game are as high as anywhere in the world.

For instance, measured in accordance with the C.I.C. formula, and based on the weight of the skull and antlers, the *average* trophy fee for a Gold medal Red deer stag will be about £1750 to £2000 with exceptional heads costing up to £5000 or more. Even a Roe buck trophy of exceptional merit, if shot by a foreign sportsman, might require a fee approaching £1500. Similar charges are made for Fallow buck, and an average Gold medal trophy will not leave much change out of £1200, with outstanding trophies considerably higher.

An interesting feature of trophy prices in Hungary is that for stags killed after the rut, i.e. 30 September and Roe bucks killed after 14 August, even though the antlers may weigh the same as in the earlier part of the season, there is a slight reduction in cost. Misses are also slightly cheaper. Fallow bucks shot at Gyulaj, which produce some of the best antlers in the world, although priced slightly cheaper than elsewhere are, in fact, slightly more expensive, as a 20 percent supplement for quality is charged here. A similar supplement is also added to the charges for all big game shot in the forests of Gemenc and Gödöllö, in the territories of Keselyüs and Valkó respectively.

Misses can also be expensive, ranging from about £75 for a stag to £12 for a Roe buck. However, should the foreign hunter subsequently succeed in shooting a beast of the same species during his stay, the fine is waived. A wounded deer, however, if not recovered can be very expensive, for the fine is based on half the *estimated* weight of the antlers and this could well involve a fine approaching £1000 or even more for a lost Gold medal stag. One might imagine that the fee for wounding might involve a certain amount of argument but I understand this seldom occurs, for the weight of the trophy has generally been *estimated* by both stalker and guest *before* the shot is fired.

Every trophy taken in Hungary has to be sent to Budapest for official measurement by the Game Department and on these official measurements will the trophy fee be assessed. During the height of the stag season in September about forty-five trophies a day are being measured, whilst during July, Roe buck heads number about a hundred a day.

Roe deer *Capreolus capreolus capreolus*
Local name: *Öz*.

Roe deer, estimated to number about 200,000 animals, are found throughout most of Hungary and as a result of large-scale agricultural schemes, larger areas have become attractive to them and are being populated. It would appear that some of the best antlers are now coming from bucks shot in recently populated areas – a similar situation to that which has been occurring in the south of England where Roe are likewise extending their range.

Roe terrain in Hungary can be divided into three categories: (1) areas of large-scale agriculture on the plains, from which most of the best trophies have come; (2) mixed plain and hill districts with a number of small woods; and (3) hilly areas with large woods. Roe stocks are highest in the first mentioned areas, where density is kept at about 1 Roe per 30 acres (12 hectares).

Early in the century a number of Roe from Denmark were introduced to some estates which were then in private hands.

In the fields, the bucks are mostly shot from horse-drawn carriages, the hunter often alighting to take the shot whilst the carriage continues on its way. Stalking on foot, or shooting from a high seat is also much practised.

The season for shooting bucks opens on 1 May, and continues until 15 October. During the 1978 season, however, an experiment was made to permit during the first fifteen weeks until mid-August only 'cull type' bucks to be shot, for it was realized that since bucks were easier to locate in May than in August, this had resulted in the over-shooting of the best bucks in the majority of areas before they had had the chance to go to the rut.

During the 1978 season, prior to 15 August, 4032 bucks were shot by foreign sportsmen, with a further 517 in the period afterwards. The experiment, however, was not repeated in 1979.

Prices, which are calculated on the weight of antlers on frontal bone, range from about £27 for a small head of under 200 g to about £1300 for a trophy weighing 550 g with an additional £17 for each gram above. Antlers are weighed twenty-four hours after boiling.

For trophies shot after 14 August there is a slight reduction of about 1 percent. For trophies that attain medal standard there is a 10 percent supplement for Bronze; 15 percent for Silver and 20 percent for Gold.

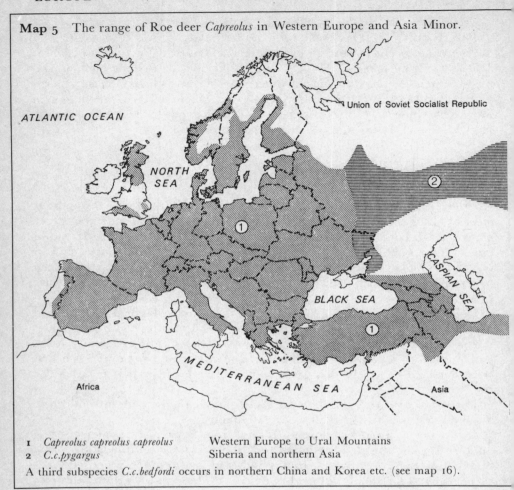

Map 5 The range of Roe deer *Capreolus* in Western Europe and Asia Minor.

1 *Capreolus capreolus capreolus*   Western Europe to Ural Mountains
2 *C.c.pygargus*   Siberia and northern Asia

A third subspecies *C.c.bedfordi* occurs in northern China and Korea etc. (see map 16).

Based on these charges, the record buck for Hungary, weighing 766.50 g and scoring 228.68 C.I.C. points, would have cost about £5000.

The fine for missing a buck is about £12 – subject to 1 percent reduction after 14 August, but if a buck is wounded and lost, the fine, as already stated will be 50 percent of the estimated trophy fee.

Red deer *Cervus elaphus hippelaphus*
Local names: Red deer, *Gimszarvas*; Stag, *Gimszarvas bikia*; Hind, *Gimszarvas teheni*; Calf, *Borju*.

Red deer are well distributed throughout most of the hills and wooded areas, avoiding only the more open plainland of the eastern part of the country which lies along both banks of the Tisza river. The best deer are all to be found west of the River Duna (Danube) in the comitat districts of Tolna, Zala, Baranya and Somogy. Throughout Hungary, the estimated population is about 25,000 of which about a quarter will be killed each year. During the 1977–8 season a total of 2078 stags were killed by foreign sportsmen, of which 1450 were trophy animals shot during the rut.

Environmental circumstances basically define the quality of deer and antler. The southern Trans-Danubian plain and forest clad hills which are interspersed with arable land provide better living conditions than the almost continuous belt of forests which cover the medium-sized hills of northern Hungary, and it is, obviously, the former areas that one can expect to provide the best trophies. From such localities, the average clean weight of a stag is about $27\frac{1}{2}$ stone (about 175 kg) whilst in the less favourable areas it will be some 5 stone (about 32 kg) lighter. From the former area an average good pair of antlers will weigh about $18\frac{3}{4}$ lb ($8\frac{1}{2}$ kg) but in the poorer areas not much over 13 lb (5.9 kg).

In 1970, 9800 deer were killed, of which 987 trophies were in the medal class. Ten years previously, 221 medal class deer were obtained out of a total 5700 killed, whilst before the war in 1937 approximately sixty of the 6400 stags killed would have carried medal class antlers. Such impressive figures prove the splendid improvement that has been achieved in recent years in the development of Red deer antlers.

The rut only lasts about three weeks, starting at the beginning of September and being practically over by the 25th of the month. In the southern parts, especially near the Duna, it commences slightly earlier than in the more mountainous areas of the north and north-east.

Dependent on the weather, a considerable movement during the early winter months and again in early spring has been observed, particularly south of Lake Balaton between the Duna and the Drava, from Mohács northward to Szekszárd and Tolna. It would appear, however, that these seasonal activities follow no set migrational routes.

The usual methods for hunting are from high seats, or by stalking on foot or in a horse-drawn carriage. Calling with the aid of a Triton shell or ox-horn, is also practised during the rut but it is illegal to shoot deer of any species or sex during a drive in Hungary.

Red deer trophies are priced according to weight of antler on upper skull and range from about £190 for a small head of under 3 kg to about £4200 for a trophy weighing 12 kg with an extra £20 for every 10 g over this weight. Weights are taken twenty-four hours after boiling. For trophies taken after 1 October there is a slight reduction of about 1 percent.

Based on these charges the best Red deer trophy for Hungary exhibited at the Budapest 1971 Exhibition, weighing 12.45 kg and scoring 251.83 C.I.C. points, would cost over DM.25,000 – say about £6000.

If any stag is wounded and lost, 50 percent of the price, based on the estimated weight of the antlers, has to be paid.

The cost for shooting a hind or calf is about £36 and £16 respectively, half of which will be paid should an animal be wounded and not recovered. The fine for a complete miss, however, will be about £7 for a hind but only half this sum for a calf.

Fallow deer *Dama dama dama*
Local names: Fallow deer, *Damvád*; Buck, *Lapátos*; Doe, *Tehen*; Fawn, *Corju*.

Fallow deer occur in seven to eight scattered populations throughout Hungary, with the majority of Gold medal trophies, including the world record (220.31 C.I.C. points) coming from the Gyulaj Forest, which is situated west of the Duna near Tamási. Extending to about 40,000 acres (16,000 hectares) this forest holds about 950 Fallow deer as well as about 330 Red deer, eighty Roe and some wild boar. Throughout Hungary the estimated population of Fallow is about 5500, all of which are living under free-range conditions.

Depending on the weather, the rut, lasting about three weeks, takes place during October or early part of November. Hunting methods are the same as for Red deer. A good buck will weigh about 154 lb (70 kg) with stomach removed. The hunting season for Fallow deer extends from 1 October until 31 December. During the 1977–8 season 210 bucks were shot.

Trophy prices outside Gyulaj Forest, based on skull and antler weight, range from about £220 for a small head weighing under 2.50 kg to about £2850 for a trophy weighing 5.0 kg with an additional £25 for each 10 g in excess of this figure. At Gyulaj, although the above charges are reduced by about 1 percent, owing to the exceptional quality of the bucks in this forest, there is a 20 percent quality supplement added to the charge.

Furthermore, any trophy shot anywhere in Hungary that reaches medal standard will have the charge increased by 10 percent for Bronze, 15 percent for Silver and 20 percent for Gold.

Antlers with skull and full upper jaw are weighed twenty-four hours after boiling.

Based on these charges, the price of a former record trophy (217.25 C.I.C. points) taken in 1970 with a weight of 5.15 kg would be just over £4000 whereas the existing record (220.31 C.I.C. points) shot in 1972 and weighing a full kilogramme lighter would, in consequence, have cost about a third of this price!

Bucks wounded and not recovered are charged for on half the estimated trophy fee, whilst the fine for a complete miss at a buck would be about £50, but correspondingly less for does (£6) and fawns (£2). To shoot a doe the charge is about £27, with fawns costing half this figure.

POLAND
Hunting in Poland is organized by the Polish Hunting Association, which is a social organization with a membership of over 60,000 hunters spread among over 2400 clubs.

The State is divided into hunting districts, which vary in size from about

7410 to 24,700 acres (3000 to 10,000 hectares), and these are leased to the hunting clubs for a period of ten years, during which time each club is responsible for the hunting economy of the district on lease, both as regards hunting and breeding. These clubs also organize, through the Polish Travel Bureau Orbis, and other agencies in Europe, hunting for both small and large game in Poland by foreign hunters.

Included among the game animals available for hunting by visiting sportsmen are Red, Roe, Fallow and Elk, and all four species have shown a remarkable increase in numbers during the past seven years, as the following figures show:

| | Estimated population | | Percent increase |
	1972	1978	
Red deer	40,300	64,700	61%
Roe deer	235,000	363,800	55%
Fallow deer	2700	3800	41%
Elk	1700	5100	200%

There are also a few Sika deer *Cervus nippon nippon* which, in 1980, were stated to number 150 animals in the Kadyny district near Elblag in the north of the country, and a further 100 around Pszczyna near Katowice. In both areas they are free living.

For all species of deer, trophy fees are charged according to the weight of the skull weighed twenty-four hours after cleaning (*see under each species*). In addition, for driving only, but not individual hunting, there is a small daily charge for organizing the hunt, which varies from about £15 to £20, depending on the species being hunted. All formalities concerning both hunting and gun importations are made by the travel agency concerned.

Provided the Polish Consulate is advised of the make, calibre and serial number of the firearm, there is no restriction on the temporary importation of firearms into Poland. The minimum calibre required for Red deer is 6.5 mm but for Elk it must be at least 7 mm.

Red deer *Cervus elaphus hippelaphus*
Local names: Red deer, *Jelén*; Stag, *Byk*; Hind, *Lania*; Calf, *Ciele*.

With an overall population of about 64,700, Red deer are well distributed throughout the great forests of Poland and about 12,900 (stags and hinds) will be shot each year. The best trophies come from the eastern part of Carpathies and in particular from the forests of Krepna and mountains around Bieszczady. The Pilska forest area of the north and both Bialowieska and Knyszyńska forests in the north-east, also produce fine trophies.

In the north-east corner of Poland lies the former East Prussian forest of Rominten Heide, which during the thirties was producing some of the best trophies in central Europe. Only a small part of Rominten is now in Poland, the remainder, including the part around Kaliningrad (Konigsberg) being in Russian hands.

The record trophy for Poland was shot at Krynki, in the Chief Forest District Waliwy near Bialystok in 1978 (252.00 C.I.C. points).

Prior to the war, in order to improve the deer in the Bialowieska forest, some Carpathian deer were introduced, the animals coming from Pszczyna, south of Stalinogród (Katowice).

The heaviest stags occur in the east Carpathian mountains, and beasts weighing up to 550 lb (250 kg) have been killed.

The shooting season for both stag and calf runs from 21 August until the end of January, whilst hinds may be shot from 1 September to the end of January. Stags are normally stalked, particularly during the rut – about 15 September to 5 October – but on occasions a drive for stags may be authorized by the forestry inspector. The majority of hinds, however, will be shot during the course of a drive.

Red deer trophies are priced according to weight of the complete skull, twenty-four hours after cleaning, starting (1981–2 season) at about £325 for a trophy weighing under 5 kg, to about £2500 for one in the 10 kg class. To shoot a hind the charge is £23, whilst for a calf the price is £20.

In the areas Bieszczady, Augustów and Bialystok, however, there may be a 20 percent surcharge on the above prices.

A wounded stag costs £250, a hind £23.

Fallow deer *Dama dama dama*
Local names: *Daniel*; Buck, *Byk*; Doe, *Lania*.

Fallow deer, first introduced during the sixteenth century by King Jan Kazimierez, are, apart from the few Sika deer, the least numerous of the four species of deer present in Poland, and the total population of the whole country is about 3800 animals, of which about 374 beasts will be shot each year. Most of the deer occur in the north of the country, particularly in the area between Grudziadz and the Gulf of Gdańsk. There are also some Fallow deer around Poznań (Posen). Two heads from Radom were exhibited at Budapest in 1971, but neither was particularly good, and only one reached Bronze medal standard.

Trophies are charged according to weight, starting (1981–2 season) from about £200 up to about £1500. An animal wounded and lost is charged the former price. A doe or fawn costs £30 – the same price being charged if wounded and lost.

The hunting season for both buck and doe runs from 1 October until the end of January.

Elk *Alces alces alces*
Local names: Moose, *Loś*; Bull, *Byk*; Cow, *Klempa*; Calf, *Loszak*.

Prior to the First World War the Elk population in Poland was in excess of 3000 head, but by 1938 this number had been reduced to about half. During the Second World War, however, the herds were heavily shot almost to the point of extinction, with the result that by 1950 about forty animals remained, the majority of which were in the great forest of Augustów and in the boggy areas near Rajgród situated in the extreme north-east of the country. However, a complete ban on the hunting of Elk for a period of sixteen years, together with the introduction of a few animals to Bialowieska, and one or two other areas in the north, enabled stocks to recover sufficiently for hunting to be restarted in 1966, when the Elk population was estimated to be about 500. Six years later, the population had increased to about 1700 and in 1972 the cull was 286 – a figure which was obviously well below the annual increment of calves – so stocks continued to rise and by 1978 had reached about 5100. In that year 780 Elk were shot.

The best areas for hunting Elk in Poland today are the forest of Augustów and in areas north and east from Warsaw. The four month hunting season for bulls commences on 1 September and runs to 31 December, whilst cows and calves may be shot between 1 October and end of December.

Elk trophies, in common with other species of deer, are charged according to weight starting (1981–2 season) from about £350 to £1800. An animal wounded and lost also costs £350. A cow or calf may be shot for £80, the same price being charged should the animal escape wounded.

The best head so far recorded was killed in 1938 at Wiado, which is now in Soviet Union territory. At the 1971 Budapest Exhibition this head was awarded a Gold medal (333.20 C.I.C. points). In recent years, however, it would appear that nothing better than Silver medal class trophies have been shot.

Roe deer *Capreolus capreolus capreolus*
Local names: Buck, *Koziol*, *Rogacz*; Doe, *Koza*; Kid, *Sysak*, *Koźle*.

The Roe has a wide distribution in Poland, but it is only in the forests of the west and south-western parts of the country that it can be said to be really plentiful. The strongest animals are to be found in central Poland, in the Lódź region and near Warsaw and Lublin. In 1972 the total Roe population in Poland was estimated to be about 235,000. Six years later it had increased to 363,800 – an increase of 128,800. In 1978 67,200 deer were shot.

The season for shooting Roe buck opens on 11 May in those areas west of the Vistula river, but not until 21 May in other parts, terminating everywhere at the end of September. Does and kids may be shot from the beginning of October until the end of January.

The bucks of eastern Poland often weigh as much as 66 lb (about 30 kg).

The best trophies come from near Radom and Kielce, which are situated south of Warsaw.

For many years the world record trophy (196.00 C.I.C. points) came from Poland. It was shot in 1896 at Nienadowa in Count Mycielski's forest by the Count's chef! Nienadowa lies close to the Russian frontier on the River San. The best head in recent years was shot at Skuly, near Warsaw in 1967 (192.28 C.I.C. points).

Roe trophies are charged according to weight, starting (1981–2 season) at about £50 for a head weighing under 300 g to £600 or more for those in the 500 g category. For a doe or kid the price is £20.

A number of trophies weighing more than 500 g have been shot in recent years, the heaviest being one of 623 g killed in 1968. Although this head did not have a particularly high score (147.37 C.I.C. points) the charge, calculated on a weight basis, would have cost the hunter about £1800.

The charge for wounding a buck is £125, whilst for a doe or kid it is £20.

ROMANIA

Some of the finest Red deer *Cervus elaphus hippelaphus* in Europe come from Romania, their principal habitat being in the north, which includes the southern part of the Carpathian mountains. In the last ten years at least three trophies with a C.I.C. score in excess of 240 points have been taken, the best being shot in 1980 scoring 261.25 points – a new world record.

Roe and Fallow deer are of equally high quality, particularly the former which has a wide distribution in Romania, with the best trophies coming from the old province of Walachia in the vicinity of the rivers Prahova and Olt. It was from the former area where the record Roe trophy for Romania with a score of 211.67 C.I.C. points was shot in 1976.

Fallow deer occur, principally, in fenced-in reserves, the best trophies coming from Socodor Arad near the border with Hungary. No Fallow trophy has yet quite achieved a C.I.C. points score of 200, the best, shot in 1969, missing it by just over half a point (199.48).

Stalking is the most usual method of hunting all species in Romania.

Unfortunately the stalking of deer in Romania is at present completely closed to foreign hunters.

YUGOSLAVIA

Of the three species of deer available to be hunted by the overseas sportsman in Yugoslavia, the Red deer achieve the highest standard of trophy, and several heads have exceeded 240 C.I.C. points. Some extremely fine Roe trophies have also been taken but the small Fallow population offers few chances to an overseas sportsman for a really good trophy.

At the beginning of the century some Axis deer or Chital *Axis axis axis* from India – locally known as *Aksis jelen* – were introduced to the island of Brioni off Istra in the Republic of Croatia by a Mr Kuppelwieser where they established themselves well and now number over 1000 animals. They have also been introduced to the island of Cres as well as to some of the other Adriatic islands and more recently, since 1953, to one or two localities on the Istra peninsula. They have no fixed breeding season, calves being born at all seasons of the year. There are no predators on Brioni but it is possible that on some of the other areas of release, where jackals occur, calves may be taken.

Brioni is a national park, and apart from selective shooting for control work, no hunting is permitted. Its main function is to act as a breeding area for catching-up animals for re-stocking elsewhere. In the areas of more recent release, stocks at present are insufficient to permit any hunting.

Prices for shooting trophy deer in Yugoslavia are calculated in acordance with the score obtained when measured under the C.I.C. formula. Thus, in 1979 the approximate prices for shooting the various species of deer were as follows:

	Red deer stag £	Fallow buck £	Roe buck £
Minimum price	85	51	21
Bronze medal standard	300–560	380–680	170–255
Silver medal standard	560–1320	680–850	255–760
Gold medal standard	1320 minimum	850 minimum	760 minimum

Whilst hunting Red and Fallow deer there is a daily charge of about £10 and for Roe about £8.

For Red and Fallow deer it is not permissible to use a rifle of calibre less than 6.9 mm but for Roe 5.6 mm is allowed.

Hunting deer with dogs of any kind is forbidden.

Red deer *Cervus elaphus hippelaphus*
Local names: Stag, *Jelen*; Hind, *Košuta*.

Red deer are principally in the three federal states of Croatia, Slovenia and Serbia, being most abundant in Croatia in the large forests along the rivers Drava, Sava and Danube in province Slavonia (not to be confused with Slovenia). There are also a few in the Republic of Macedonia. The deer in the plains of Slavonia are considerably larger and stronger than those living in the high mountains of Slovenia and it is in the former area where all the best trophies have been shot. Many trophies from Slavonia frequently exceed 230 C.I.C. points, whilst anything over 210.00 points is very good for Slovenia.

Throughout the length of the long frontier of Croatia with Hungary, where equally high quality Red deer are to be found, animals, particularly stags, are frequently crossing the rivers Drava and Danube from one side to the other. In Slovenia, following the revolutionary year of 1848 when many deer were exterminated, fresh stock was imported, before the close of the century, both from Bavaria and the Carpathians.

Throughout Yugoslavia the estimated Red deer population is about 13,500, of which almost half will be in Croatia. About 3000 deer are killed each year.

The rut generally commences about 10 September and continues until about the end of the first week in October. The hunting season for stags opens on 1 August and continues until the end of the year, whilst hinds and calves may be shot during a four month season, starting on 1 September.

Whilst the average weight of a stag (without stomach) will be around 330 lb (150 kg) exceptional beasts have been double this figure. Hind weights vary from 154–309 lb (70 to 140 kg).

Trophy stags are generally shot during the rut either by stalking or from high seats. They are priced in accordance with the points scored when assessed under the C.I.C. formula ranging from about £85 for a small head of under 130 C.I.C. points to about £300 for Bronze medal, £680 for Silver and £1320 for Gold medal increased by £170 for each C.I.C. point over 210.00.

For a wounded stag not recovered with the aid of a *Schweisshund* (tracker dog) a fine of approximately £128 is charged. A charge of about £13 is made for shooting a hind or male calf, but should either be wounded and lost, fines of approximately £53 and £32 respectively are incurred.

The best trophy so far recorded for Yugoslavia, which was exhibited at the 1971 Budapest Exhibition, was assessed at 248.55 C.I.C. points. Based on the above mentioned charges, the price of this trophy would be over £7700.

Roe buck *Capreolus capreolus capreolus*
Local names: *Snrjak*; Buck, *Rehbock*; Doe, *Ricke*; Kid, *Rehkitz*.

Except on the littoral of the Adriatic, Roe are plentiful throughout most of Yugoslavia, where the total population is estimated to be in excess of 200,000 animals, of which about 30,000 will be shot annually. In some areas, a considerable number of Roe are taken by wolves, whilst in the mountains, during periods of heavy snow, mortality is high.

The usual method of hunting is by stalking or shooting from a high seat.

The hunting season for bucks opens on 16 May and continues until 31 October, whilst does and kids can be shot between 1 September and 15 January. Rutting takes place for about three weeks from 25 July until 15 August.

Probably one of the heaviest bucks to come out of Europe this century was shot in 1921 by Dr M Zoričič near Dugoselo in Croatia. It weighed about 90¾ lb (41.20 kg) *with stomach removed* – a weight one might expect from a Siberian Roe.

The prices for shooting Roe bucks commence at about £21 for a button buck (yearling) to £740 or more for a buck of Gold medal standard (130 C.I.C. points or greater).

All trophies are weighed with full upper skull.

Whilst about £10 is the price required to shoot a doe or kid, should the animal escape wounded and not be recovered, fines of approximately £16 and £8 respectively are incurred.

Based on the above mentioned charges, the price of the record buck from Yugoslavia (183.15 C.I.C. points) shot in 1955 would be approximately £5250.

Fallow deer *Dama dama dama*
Local names: *Damjek*; Buck, *Schaufler*; Doe, *Tier*; Fawn, *Kalb*.

Only about 2000 Fallow deer are kept in Yugoslavia, the best trophies coming from Kunjevci near Vinkouci, Lipovica near Beograd (Belgrad) and Vorovo near Ilok. There are also a few on the island of Brioni.

Charges for shooting Fallow deer in Yugoslavia start at about £50 for a small head under 110 C.I.C. points to about £680 for a Bronze medal; £900 for a Silver and at least £1060 for a Gold, with an additional £170 for each C.I.C. point over 180.

For a doe or fawn the price is about £8 but if any deer is wounded and not recovered, the following approximate fines are incurred – buck £170; doe £64 and fawn £34.

The best trophy yet recorded for Yugoslavia was shot in 1955 by President Tito at Kunjevci near Vinkouci. It had a C.I.C. points score of 192.10. Priced under the above mentioned trophy rating, this trophy would have cost over £3000.

Part II
U.S.S.R., Asia
and Australasia

4 Africa, Asia, the Middle East and U.S.S.R.

Of the forty living species of deer in the world, which represent just under 200 subspecies, no fewer than twenty-five of the former and almost a third of the latter, are indigenous to Asia. Sadly, many of these unique deer are now included in the *Red Data Book* of the I.U.C.N. (International Union for Conservation of Nature and Natural Resources) as being either endangered, vulnerable or rare, and even if their habitat was open for hunting – which, in the majority of cases, it is not – present numbers of some species are insufficient to stand much hunting pressure.

Many of the deer of northern India, Tibet and China are much reduced in numbers to what they were at the beginning of the century, and in almost every case, the reason has been the same – over-hunting and loss of habitat, the former undoubtedly made more effective by the accuracy of the modern firearm. It has not been sport-hunting, however, that has been a major factor, but the slaughter of stags – particularly of the genus *Cervus* – whilst their antlers are in velvet, for ground up and dried they are used in the preparation of an aphrodisiac much cherished in the far east.

Amongst the most endangered are the Yarkand deer *Cervus elaphus yarkandensis* of Chinese Turkestan and the Shou *Cervus elaphus wallichi* of south-east Tibet and adjacent valleys of Bhutan, and indeed the *Red Data Book* suggests that both might now be extinct. No recent information is available, either, concerning those other two deer of Tibet and western China, namely M'Neill's deer *Cervus canadensis macneilli* and Thorold's or White-lipped deer *Cervus albirostris* – but at the beginning of the war the population of the former was thought to be around 5000 whilst in 1964 Thorold's deer was already described as 'very rare and in need of special protection'.

Rather more hopeful is the present status of both Kashmir deer or Hangul *Cervus elaphus hanglu* of Kashmir, and the Bactrian or Bukharian deer *Cervus elaphus bactrianus* of northern Afghanistan and adjacent parts of Russian Turkestan. Throughout the range of the Hangul in Kashmir and the Bactrian deer in Turkestan, hunting is totally prohibited, and although some poaching does occur, their numbers seem to be slowly building up. A fairly recent report suggests that the population of both species would appear to be around 900 each. In northern Afghanistan, too, despite lack of any legal protection, the

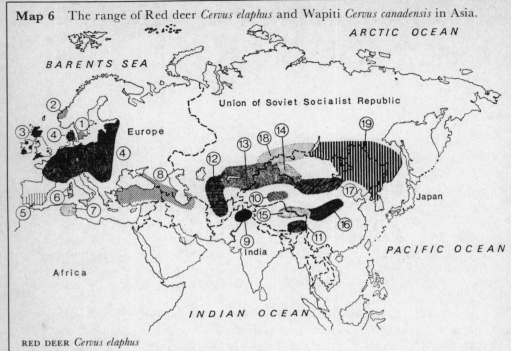

Map 6 The range of Red deer *Cervus elaphus* and Wapiti *Cervus canadensis* in Asia.

RED DEER *Cervus elaphus*

9	*C.e.hanglu*	Kashmir
10	*C.e.yarkandensis*	Chinese Turkestan
11	*C.e.wallichi*	East Tibet
12	*C.e.bactrianus*	North Afghanistan, Russian Turkestan

For the European and Middle East range of *C.elaphus* which include *C.e.elaphus* (1); *C.e.atlanticus* (2); *C.e.scoticus* (3); *C.e.hippelaphus* (4); *C.e.hispanicus* (5); *C.e.corsicanus* (6); *C.e.barbarus* (7); and *C.e.maral* (8) see map 1.

WAPITI *Cervus canadensis*

13	*C.c.songaricus*	Tien Shan Mountains, etc.
14	*C.c.wachei*	Western Mongolia
15	*C.c.macneilli*	Tibetan/Chinese border
16	*C.c.kansuensis*	Kansu, China, etc.
17	*C.c.alashanicus*	South-east Mongolia
18	*C.c.asiaticus*	Altai to Transbaikalia
19	*C.c.xanthopygus*	Manchuria and Mongolia

For the range of *C.c.roosevelti*; *C.c.nelsoni*; *C.c.manitobensis*; and *C.c.nannodes* in North America, see map 19.

deer is just about holding its own, and a 1974 estimate suggested that the population there might be around 150 to 200. The Hindustani name for this deer is Barasingha – a name by which the Swamp deer is often referred to.

In north Africa the status of the Barbary deer *C.e.barbarus* – the only indigenous deer of Africa – is slowly improving in Tunisia, but reports from Algeria are not so promising, poaching and loss of habitat being contributory factors. It remains, therefore, an endangered deer with an overall population of around 500 and totally protected by law throughout its range.

Other Asiatic members of the genus *Cervus* whose status is causing concern are the Swamp deer *Cervus duvauceli* of India, the Thamin or Brow-antlered deer *Cervus eldi* of Manipur and Thailand, and some of the Sika deer races *Cervus nippon* of China and Japan.

Of the two subspecies of Swamp deer, whilst the population of the northern race *C.d.duvauceli* – often referred to as *Gond* – which occurs principally in Uttar Pradesh, western Bengal and Assam, is now estimated at about 4500 animals, it is doubtful if more than about 100 animals remain of the southern

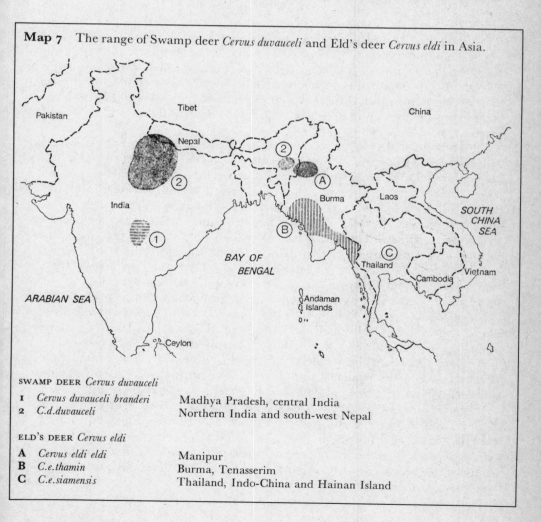

Map 7 The range of Swamp deer *Cervus duvauceli* and Eld's deer *Cervus eldi* in Asia.

SWAMP DEER *Cervus duvauceli*

1	*Cervus duvauceli branderi*	Madhya Pradesh, central India
2	*C.d.duvauceli*	Northern India and south-west Nepal

ELD'S DEER *Cervus eldi*

A	*Cervus eldi eldi*	Manipur
B	*C.e.thamin*	Burma, Tenasserim
C	*C.e.siamensis*	Thailand, Indo-China and Hainan Island

race *C.d.branderi* all located in the Kanha National Park, Madhya Pradesh. Unfortunately, the national park is also a reserve for the tiger – the principal predator of the Swamp deer – so any increase in the tiger population automatically increases predation on the Swamp deer.

Another deer of southern Asia which is becoming scarce is the Thamin or Eld's deer – sometimes called Brow-antlered deer – *Cervus eldi*, of which three subspecies are recognized – *Cervus e.eldi* from Manipur, where it is referred to as *Sangai*; *C.e.thamin* from Burma, Tenasserim and adjacent parts of Thailand, and *C.e.siamensis* from Thailand whose range also extends into Vietnam and Hainan Island.

Little is known about the present status of these races, but it seems that all are extremely rare. The principal habitat of this deer in the Manipur Valley is swampland, and their feet are modified to enable them to walk on such ground.

The plight of the Thai Brow-antlered deer *C.e.siamensis* is a little obscure, but in Thailand itself it is believed that only a few herds now remain at Nang Kong in the north-east and at Chieng Karn in the north. In Kampuchia (Cambodia), where it was at one time relatively common, the deer suffered heavy losses as the result of the war, since when however, several reserves have been set up and all hunting prohibited, but how successful these measures will be remains to be seen.

The Sika deer, *Cervus nippon* has a wide distribution in eastern Asia, and although some thirteen different races are recognized, many of these, and in particular those present in China, are now considered endangered species. These include *C.n.mandarinus* of north China, *C.n.grassianus* of the Shansi district of central China and *C.n.kopschi* of south-east China.

On the island of Formosa or Taiwan, there is an insular race of Sika deer – the Formosan Sika deer *C.n.taiouanus* – which, like some of the mainland forms, is now on the verge of extinction (if not already) – in a wild state.

So far as the six subspecies of Japanese Sika deer are concerned, apart from the Kerama or Ryukyu Sika deer *C.n.keramae* of the Ryukyu Islands, the status of the other five races causes no concern and hunting is permitted.

Of the five species of Muntjac *Muntiacus*, two are considered endangered – namely the Black or Hairy-fronted Muntjac *Muntiacus crinifrons* of eastern China and Fea's Muntjac *M.feae* of Tenasserim and Thailand.

Little is known of the status of any of the three species of Tufted deer *Elaphodus cephalophus* which occurs in northern Burma and in central and southern China, but it would seem to be rare in much of its range.

The diminutive Water-deer *Hydropotes inermis* – sometimes referred to as the Yangtze River deer – is still plentiful, however, in most of the central and eastern valleys of north-east China (*H.i.inermis*) and southern Korea (*H.i.argyropus*). Like the Musk deer, neither sex has antlers but the males are armed with long canine tusks about $2\frac{3}{4}$ in. (70 mm) in length, those on the does being insignificant.

Another Asiatic deer which although not endangered, is certainly 'rare' is

Map 8   The range of Tufted deer *Elaphodus* in Asia and the former range of Schomburgk's deer *Cervus schomburgki* in Thailand.

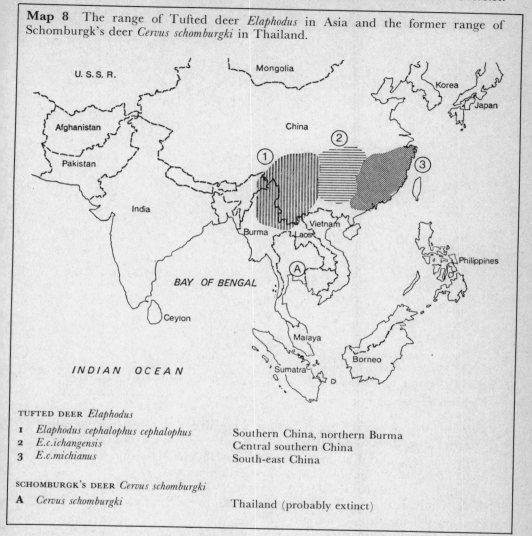

TUFTED DEER *Elaphodus*

1	*Elaphodus cephalophus cephalophus*	Southern China, northern Burma
2	*E.c.ichangensis*	Central southern China
3	*E.c.michianus*	South-east China

SCHOMBURGK'S DEER *Cervus schomburgki*

A	*Cervus schomburgki*	Thailand (probably extinct)

the Bawean or Kuhl's deer *Axis kuhlii* which is confined to the island of Bawean situated to the north of Java. The most recent estimate (1969) as to population suggests that there may be about 500 animals on the island, and although it is protected by law, this protection is not strictly enforced. Hunting by local fishermen, who are unable to put to sea during the early months of the year, is not considered as serious a threat as the clearing of forests to make way for increased cultivation, thus reducing the habitat areas. The real threat to their survival, however, would appear to come from American and Japanese oilmen prospecting for off-shore oil deposits and if oil was to be found, the situation could deteriorate rapidly.

Map 9   The range of Water-deer *Hydropotes* in Asia.

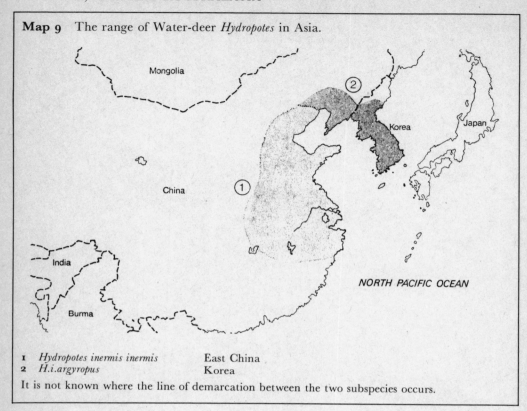

I *Hydropotes inermis inermis*	East China
2 *H.i.argyropus*	Korea

It is not known where the line of demarcation between the two subspecies occurs.

A very similar deer to *Axis kuhlii* is the Calamian deer *Axis calamianensis* which is restricted to the Calamian group of islands lying to the west of the main Philippine group, and in particular to the islands of Busuanga and Culion where the total population would appear to be about 900.

Until 1975 – the year the deer was first included in the *Red Data Book* of the I.U.C.N. – it was permitted to hunt the Calamian deer, the bag limit being two stags per hunting season per hunter.

The Calamian deer is the only deer on the Calamian Islands and the sole representative of the genus *Axis* found anywhere in the Philippines, all the other deer being Sambar *Cervus unicolor*.

Prior to 1972, the hunting of Sambar was permitted in the Philippines in areas outside national parks, game refuges and bird sanctuaries in any year divisible by five – i.e. 1960, 1965 etc. Since then, however, due to the ban on carrying guns by private citizens, all hunting has been suspended.

The most widespread species of deer in the Indonesian archipelago is the Rusa deer *Cervus timorensis* of which a number of insular races are represented, their principal distribution being as follows:

Islands

C.t.timorensis	Timor, Flores
C.t.floresiensis	Flores
C.t.russa	Borneo, Java
C.t.moluccensis	Moluccas
C.t.macassaricus	Celebes
C.t.djonga	Muna, Butang (Celebes group)
*C.t.renschi**	Bali
*C.t.laronesiotes**	Meeuwen

* These two may be insular forms of *C.t.russa*.

The largest of the Rusa deer, both in body and antler, come from Java with the best trophies coming from east Java. One of the best heads ever recorded from Java had an antler length of $43\frac{3}{4}$ in. (111.5 cm).

As regards the rut of Rusa deer in Indonesia, there appears to be no fixed pattern and calves have been recorded in almost every month of the year.

Rusa deer have been introduced to Australia, New Caledonia, New Guinea, and New Zealand, and in all areas hunting is available. Rusa deer have also been introduced to the island of Mauritius in the Indian Ocean.

Apart, therefore, from Mongolia, India, Japan and a few localities in the U.S.S.R. no hunting facilities are at present available for the visiting sportsman to hunt in Asia, although it seems probable that in the near future China may open up some areas for hunting.

INDIA, BURMA AND SRI LANKA

Although eight species – and more than a dozen subspecies – of deer are indigenous to India, only four – the Chital, Hog deer, Muntjac and Sambar – are sufficiently numerous to permit being hunted. The remainder, which include the Hangul or Kashmir stag, Eld's deer and Swamp deer, are now endangered and therefore totally protected, whilst the eighth – the antlerless Musk deer *Moschus* of the Himalayan region, is hunted only commercially for its musk which is used in the perfume industry. In the neighbouring Kachin State of Burma, this small deer is now thought to be extinct.

Compare this unhappy state of affairs to fifty years ago when not only were all the above mentioned species in abundance, but also many other fine game animals as well, such as the markhor, blue sheep and tiger, whose status today is causing concern. In those days some of the finest hunting in the world after both mountain and forest game could be had in India. Sadly, since the war, man both directly by over-hunting – legitimately or otherwise – and indirectly by over-grazing with domestic stock resulting in loss of habitat, has been the principal cause of the decline in the country's game – in some case almost to the point of extinction. It is to be hoped, therefore, that the existing game laws can be enforced so that these fine game animals can be restored to something like their former status, both within and outside the reserves which have been provided for their survival.

Map 10   The range of Musk deer *Moschus* in Asia.

1	*Moschus moschiferus moschiferus*	Northern India, Himalayas, etc.
2	*M.m.sifanicus*	West, central and southern China
3	*M. sibiricus sibiricus*	Siberia, north Mongolia and Korea
4	*M.s.sachalinensis*	Sakhalin Island
5	*Moschus berezovskii*	Szechwan, China

At the present time, therefore, the opportunity to hunt any big game in India is strictly limited and in some states completely prohibited. For instance, in the State of West Bengal, under the *Wild Life (Protection) Act* 1972, the hunting, shooting and capturing of all wild animals and birds – except certain species of vermin – is prohibited throughout the year, whilst in Haryana, Chandigarth in the Punjab the hunting of all species of deer has been banned throughout the year although there is a five month open hunting season for other big game animals extending from 1 October to 28 February.

In both Nepal and Uttar Pradesh, however, facilities to hunt deer and other species of big game are available, and one agency who is currently arranging shikars (hunting trips) to these States is Klineburger Worldwide Travel. In 1981 a seventeen day 'forest hunt' in Nepal, during which it should be possible to hunt Chital, Muntjac and Hog deer as well as Serow, will cost one client $6500 (about £190 per day). This price does not include the general hunting licence costing $175 (about £86) which enables the client to hunt all the above named species.

Parties assemble for the hunt at Biratnagar (Terai), the hunts taking place from December to the end of February.

The same agency also offers a seven to fourteen day forest hunt in Uttar Pradesh after Chital, Muntjac and Sambar as well as boar and the cost for a seven day hunt varies between $2447 (about £1040) and $2129 (about £906) depending on whether the party is for one or three clients. The cost of a fourteen day hunt is only about $600 to $800 more.

Forest hunting in Uttar Pradesh takes place from November to the end of April.

Whether the hunt is in Nepal or Uttar Pradesh, the period of the hunt will depend on the species being hunted, for not only are the chances of a good trophy best during the rut, it is pointless to shoot a stag with antlers still in velvet.

The rut of both Sambar and Hog deer generally takes place during December or early January and if only these two species were involved, then the New Year would be about the best time to hunt. If, however, a hunt after Chital was to be included, since this deer may not be rutting until about February or March, it is doubtful whether many stags will be in hard antler until about February. February, therefore, would appear to be the best month for hunting all three species and whilst March and April would also be suitable for Chital, most adult Sambar will have shed their antlers during the latter month. February would also be a good month for Muntjac.

Clients are advised to bring their own firearms and ammunition, for whilst the former can be supplied by the outfitter, no ammunition is available in India. Up to 200 rounds of ammunition, however, are allowed to be brought into the country duty free.

In Sri Lanka there are no facilities for hunting deer of any species, and the export of skins is prohibited by law.

A brief description of the range and habits of the four species of deer that can legally be hunted in India is as follows:

Chital or **Spotted deer** *Axis axis*
Local names: *Chitri* (Hindi); *Boro Khotiva* (Bengali); Male, *Chitra-jank* (Hindi); *Tic Muha* (Cingalese); *Pali-man* (Tamil).

The Chital or Axis deer *A.a.axis* although less numerous than formerly, is well distributed throughout the peninsula of India, occurring in all suitable localities south of about latitude 25°N. North of this line it occurs in parts of Uttar Pradesh and extends its range right up to the upper reaches of the River Indus and its tributaries in Pakistan. It also occurs sparingly in Bengal and parts of Assam.

Map 11   The range of Axis or Chital deer *Axis axis* in Asia.

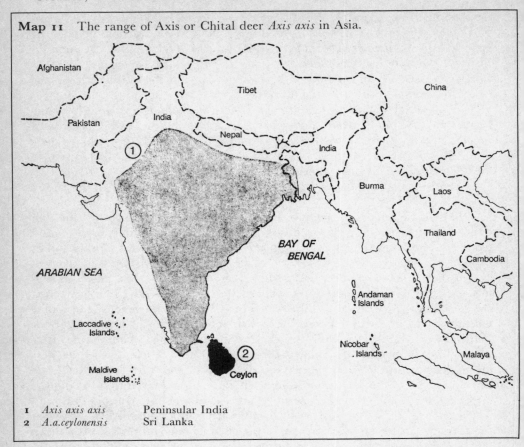

1	*Axis axis axis*	Peninsular India
2	*A.a.ceylonensis*	Sri Lanka

It does not, however, occur west of about latitude 74°E, being entirely absent from Sind and Baluchistan in west Pakistan.

Stalking in the early morning or evening, or waiting at drinking holes, is the usual manner in which this deer is hunted. In former days a popular sport with British officers stationed in India was to ride the deer down on horseback in much the same fashion as in pig-sticking, and dispatch it with a spear.

The majority of adult stags cast their antlers about August and September, and it will not be until about February or March that they will be in hard antler. Although new-born calves have been found at all seasons of the year, it would appear that most stags go to the rut during late April and May.

Hog deer *Axis porcinus porcinus*

Local names: *Párá* (Hindustani); *Nutrini haran* (Bengali); *Will-muha* (Cingalese); *Khar laguna* (Nepalese); *Darai* or *Dayai* (Burmese). In Sri Lanka the Hog deer is sometimes referred to as 'Swamp deer' – the true Swamp deer, however, is *C.duvauceli* of northern India.

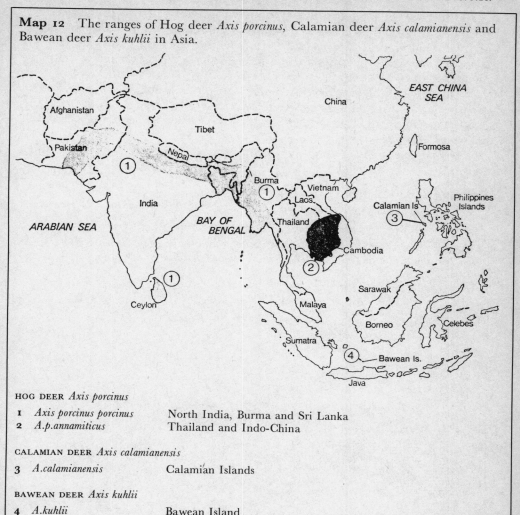

Map 12 The ranges of Hog deer *Axis porcinus*, Calamian deer *Axis calamianensis* and Bawean deer *Axis kuhlii* in Asia.

HOG DEER *Axis porcinus*

1   *Axis porcinus porcinus*   North India, Burma and Sri Lanka
2   *A.p.annamiticus*   Thailand and Indo-China

CALAMIAN DEER *Axis calamianensis*

3   *A.calamianensis*   Calamian Islands

BAWEAN DEER *Axis kuhlii*

4   *A.kuhlii*   Bawean Island

The hog deer is restricted to Sri Lanka and the low alluvial grass plains of the Indus and Ganges valleys, where it ranges from Sind in the west (about longitude 67°E) through the Punjab, Uttar Pradesh and Bengal to Assam in the east, and thence into Burma. Outside Sri Lanka, about latitude 24°N, and the Himalayan foothills, can be said to mark the extent of its range south and north respectively in India. In Burma the Hog deer occurs as far south as Tenasserim (about 14°N) whilst to the east, across the border into Siam (Thailand) a slightly larger race *A.p.annamiticus* occurs – locally known as *Con huū:*

At one time the Hog deer was extremely common, particularly in parts of Bengal, but not only has excessive hunting reduced the population in many areas, but cultivation of many of its former haunts has reduced its range. It is, however, reasonably abundant in areas where the grass lands remain uncultivated. It never ascends into the hills.

Unlike the Chital, Hog deer are not gregarious, and it is rare to see parties of three or four animals together. Generally, they are found singly or in pairs. It is fond of lying up in paddy fields, which has earned it the name of 'Paddy field deer'.

The rut takes place mainly during the months of November and December.

Sambar *Cervus unicolor*

Local names: *Samar* (Hindustani); Stag, *Jarao*; Hind, *Jarai* (Nepalese);

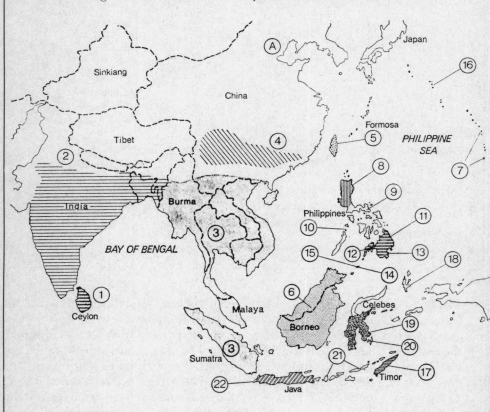

Map 13   The ranges of Sambar *Cervus unicolor* and Rusa deer *Cervus timorensis* in Asia. Also former range of Père David's deer *Elaphurus davidianus* in China.

Stag, *Gous*; Hind, *Bholongi* (East Bengal); *Khat-khowa-pohu* (Assam); *Connai*, *Tshat* (Burmese); *Gona*, *Rusa* (Cingalese).

Of all the species of deer in southern Asia, the Sambar has the most widespread distribution, for its range stretches from the Philippine islands in the east, through Indonesia, southern China, Burma to India in the west. Throughout its range, sixteen subspecies are recognized.

The typical race of Sambar – *C.u.unicolor* – is restricted to Sri Lanka (Ceylon) where it occurs in all suitable localities, right from the sea coast up to altitudes of 7000 to 8000 ft (about 2300 metres). Here it is sometimes referred to as 'Elk'.

In India the Sambar – *C.u.niger* – has a wide distribution, being found in all suitable localities right up to the foothills of the Himalayas where, on occasions, it has been found at altitudes as high as 9000 ft (2743 metres). It is

---

SAMBAR DEER *Cervus unicolor*

Cervus unicolor unicolor	Sri Lanka
C.u.niger	India
C.u.equinus	Burma, southern China, through to Sumatra
C.u.dejeani	South-west China
C.u.swinhoei	Formosa
C.u.brookei	Sarawak, Borneo
C.u.mariannus	Guam Island, Marianne Group (probably extinct)
C.u.philippinus	Luzon, Philippines
C.u.alfredi	Central Philippines
C.u.barandanus	Mindoro Island, Philippines
C.u.francianus	Mindanao Island, Philippines
C.u.nigellus	West Mindanao Island, Philippines
C.u.apoensis	South-east Mindanao Island, Philippines
C.u.basilanensis	Basilan Island, Philippines
C.u.nigricans	Basilan Island, Philippines
C.u.boninensis	Bonin Island (probably extinct)

Sambar have also been introduced to Australia and New Zealand.

RUSA DEER *Cervus timorensis*

Cervus timorensis timorensis	Timor and adjacent islands
C.t.moluccensis	Molucca islands
C.t.macassaricus	Celebes island
C.t.djonga	Muna and Buron islands (Celebes group)
C.t.floresiensis	Flores and Lombok islands, etc.
C.t.russa	Java

Rusa deer have also been introduced to south-east Borneo, New Guinea, Hermit and Ninigo Islands (Bismarck Archipelago), New Caledonia, Australia and New Zealand.

The former range of Père David's deer *Elaphurus davidianus* in China.

Elaphurus davidianus	Imperial Hunting Park, Peking*

Preserved at present in Woburn Park, England, and in many zoological gardens throughout the world.

---

absent from Baluchistan as well as from the barren plains of the Punjab, Sind and Rajasthan, and like the Chital, it can be said that about longitude 74°E marks the limit of its range in a westerly direction.

The Sambar – *C.u.equinus* – also has a fair distribution in Burma, where it is often referred to as *Connai*, being found at all elevations where there is sufficient cover, avoiding, however, areas of open scrub land.

In India most Sambar stags shed their antlers towards the end of March or early April, but as in some of the other species of Asiatic deer there is a certain amount of variation in date. In India the rut reaches its peak during December, which is almost two months later than in Sri Lanka. Dates, however, are inclined to be variable.

Most of the best trophies taken in India have come from Madhya Pradesh state, the best recorded coming from Bhopal with an antler length of $50\frac{1}{8}$ in. (127.3 cm). A good average length of antler for *C.u.niger* from India would be about 40 in. (102 cm). In Sri Lanka, however, anything over 30 in. (76 cm) would be good.

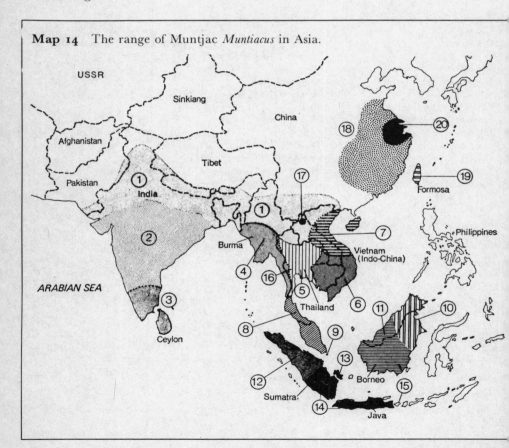

Map 14   The range of Muntjac *Muntiacus* in Asia.

Abnormal antlers are comparatively common and may range from a typical switch type of but two points (tines) to a multi-pointed head of, perhaps, twelve or more points.

Generally speaking, the habits of the Sambar are mainly nocturnal and unless disturbed, they are seldom seen about in the middle part of the day.

Muntjac, Barking deer or Rib-faced deer *Muntiacus*

Local names: *Maya* (Bengali); *Kolri* (Uttar Pradesh); *Kákar, Jangli-Bakri* (Hindustani); *Hugeri* (Assam); *Weli, Hulamuha* (Cingalese); *Kalai, Katu-ardu* (Tamil); *Ratwa* (Nepal).

The Muntjac, which includes five species and a number of subspecies, has a wide distribution throughout south-east Asia, ranging from India and Sri Lanka in the west, throughout Burma, Thailand, Vietnam to eastern China and the island of Formosa in the east. Its range also includes Indonesia but it is absent from the Philippines.

In India, where it is sometimes called the 'jungle sheep', three races of

MUNTJAC *Muntiacus muntjak*

1	*Muntiacus muntjak vaginalis*	Northern India to south-west China
2	*M.m.aureus*	Peninsular India
3	*M.m.malabaricus*	Southern India and Sri Lanka
4	*M.m.grandicornis*	Burma
5	*M.m.curvostylis*	Thailand
6	*M.m.annamensis*	Indo-China
7	*M.m.nigripes*	Vietnam and Hainan Island
8	*M.m.peninsulae*	Malaya
9	*M.m.robinsoni*	Rhio-Linga archipelago
10	*M.m.rubidus*	North Borneo
11	*M.m.pleiharicus*	South Borneo
12	*M.m.montanus*	Sumatra
13	*M.m.bancanus*	Billiton and Banka islands
14	*M.m.muntjak*	Java and South Sumatra
15	*M.m.nainggolani*	Bali and Lombok islands

FEA'S MUNTJAC *Muntiacus feae*

16	*Muntiacus feae*	Tenasserim and Thailand

ROOSEVELT'S MUNTJAC *Muntiacus rooseveltorum*

17	*M.rooseveltorum*	Indo-China

REEVE'S MUNTJAC *Muntiacus reevesi*

18	*Muntiacus reevesi reevesi*	South-east China
19	*M.r.micrurus*	Formosa

BLACK MUNTJAC *Muntiacus crinifrons*

20	*Muntiacus crinifrons*	East China

Muntiacus muntjak – generally referred to as the Indian Muntjac – have been recognized as follows:

1 *M.m.vaginalis* in the north, including Kashmir, Nepal, Uttar Pradesh, Bengal, Sikkim, Bhutan and Assam. This race extends its range eastwards into the northern parts of Burma, Thailand and Vietnam and into south-western China. In the Tenasserim area of Burma around Thaton, small populations of Fea's Muntjac *M.feae* occur.

2 *M.m.aureus* which has the widest distribution in India, being found throughout central and much of southern peninsular India.

3 *M.m.malabaricus*, which is restricted to southern India from about latitude 15°N southwards. This race, which is the largest of the above named three, also occurs in Sri Lanka, where it sometimes goes by the name of 'Red deer'.

The rut is variable but the winter months are as good a time as any to find a buck in hard antler. The largest trophies are produced by the typical race *M.m.muntjak* from Java, where antlers of 7 to 8 in. (17.5 to 20 cm) in length can be expected. Antlers of this length, however, would be exceptional for India.

IRAN

Until recently Iran was undoubtedly one of the foremost hunting countries – particularly for its mountain game – in the world, but with the overthrow of the Shah's regime, the country is now in such a turmoil that until the political scene has returned to something like normal, there would appear to be little or no opportunity for any hunting now being available for the visiting sportsman.

It was not until about 1967 that any organized safaris were operating in Iran, and one of the first organizations outfitting hunts there went by the name of Iran Safaris – which subsequently became known as Iran Shikar.

Of the three species of indigenous deer, the Maral is the most prized by the hunter, but the rare Persian or Mesopotamian Fallow deer *Dama dama mesopotamica* with a world population of probably under a hundred and in the wild now restricted to Iran, is, without question, its most important deer. In 1977 it was suggested that there were perhaps only about thirty or so deer in their natural habitat in Khuzistan, with perhaps a further fifty or so in captivity.

Owing to the scarcity of this deer it seems unlikely that it will ever, in the foreseeable future, be available for hunting except, possibly, as an 'exotic' on a game ranch.

Maral *Cervus elaphus maral*
Local name: *Gavazn.*

Maral are found in the forests that lie between the Caspian Sea and the northern slopes of the Elburz mountains, ranging from near Astara in the north-west, eastwards through the states of Gilan and Mazandaran until the forest zone terminates in the eastern side of the Mohammad Reza Shah National Park.

Maral are forest dwellers and keep almost entirely to the deciduous forests which cross the lower slopes of the mountains up to about 7500 ft (2280 metres) above sea level.

The rut starts during the first week of September and lasts for about three weeks, and this is the time when most trophies are taken. A favourite method of hunting is for the sportsman to try and simulate the roar of a rutting stag – the glass chimney of a hurricane lamp or an ibex horn being used for this purpose. Another method is to proceed very slowly through the forest in the hope of running into deer, and when a roar is heard, try and approach the roarer without being detected. This is exciting work, and so far as I was concerned, proved more successful than the simulated roar by my guide on his ibex horn.

A good Maral trophy head of twelve to sixteen tines will have an antler length of about 45 in. (114.3 cm) and score about 740 C.I.C. points.

Roe deer *Capreolus capreolus capreolus*
Local name: *Shuka*.

Roe deer are found in the northern forest belt of Iran from the Azarbaijan region in north-west Iran along the foothills of the Elburz mountains to the eastern limits of the Mohammad Reza Shah National Park, preferring areas of sparsely wooded valleys to the denser forests.

As in Western Europe, the rut takes place between late July and early August.

Roe antlers from Iran have not appeared at any of the European exhibitions of trophies, but it would seem that they are of only average quality.

JAPAN

Deer and other game in Japan belong to the nation and not to the landowner, so provided the sportsman has passed the required Governmental hunting examination, he is entitled to hunt deer whenever he wishes except on game reserves and a few other areas where no hunting is permitted.

For the resident hunter this offers no problems, but since hunting examinations, which *must* be passed by every hunter, are held only during the months of August and September – some three months before the start of the deer hunting season – this means that any visitor to Japan wishing to hunt deer must either spend at least three to four months in the country, or make a return visit there during the open season which, in Honshu, Kyushu and Shikoku, runs from 1 December to end of January, but in Hokkaido commences a fortnight earlier and finishes on 15 January – the same date as on Iwate. However, once having passed the examination, there is no difficulty in obtaining a licence. These cost about 20,000 Yen (approximately £40) and entitle the hunter to shoot, in one prefecture only, all species of legal game animals and birds, up to a maximum daily figure for each species, which for deer is one per hunter. Should he wish to hunt in other prefectures, a separate licence for each will have to be obtained.

Apart from the .22 rifle. which is entirely prohibited for *all* game shooting, deer may be shot with any rifle of larger calibre, and also the shotgun. Provided the visiting sportsman has obtained permission from the Japanese Public Peace Commission to have a firearm, the importation of firearms into Japan should not present any problem. He will still, however, have to pass the examination before being issued with a licence to hunt.

No professional guides or outfitters are available in Japan and any sportsman wishing to hunt will have to arrange it privately by contacting local hunters or farmers.

Due to the mountainous and afforested terrain of Japan, stalking or still hunting is seldom practised, and most of the hunting for deer is done with dogs, the principal breeds being Kishu, Akita and Beagle.

Japanese Sika deer *Cervus nippon*
Local pronunciation: *Shika*.

The only indigenous deer of Japan is the Sika – *Cervus nippon* – which has a wide distribution on many of the islands, and although zoologists have suggested that six subspecies may be represented, from a hunting point of view, only two need be considered – the Sika deer of Hokkaido *C.n.yesoensis* – locally referred to as the *Ezo-shika* – and the typical Japanese deer, *C.n.nippon* which occurs principally on Kyushu, Shikoku and Honshu, although Dr Kishida (1936) gave the deer of Honshu (Hondo) subspecies status of *C.n.centralis*.

Although similar in colour, the *Ezo-shika* – which gets its name from Yezo, the former name of Hokkaido – is the largest of the Japanese Sika deer with adult stags topping the 200 lb (91 kg) mark. The Honshu deer, however, are considerably lighter, averaging about 100 to 140 lb (45 to 63 kg) with exceptional beasts reaching the 180 lb (82 kg) mark.

The best areas for hunting Sika deer in Honshu are the prefectures of Iwate, Miye, Hyogo and Wakayama, whilst on Kyushu, the prefecture of Miyazaki is another very good hunting area. In each of the above mentioned prefectures over 2000 deer are shot annually.

Just over a century ago, in 1877, a canning factory was established in Chitose, near Sapporo and in the following year about 30,000 cans of venison were produced. The venture, however, did not survive long, for following a severe winter in 1879, there was considerable mortality among the deer and ten years later all hunting on the island was stopped.

In 1899 the Hokkaido prefectural Government re-opened the hunting and in the following year some 6000 Sika deer were shot – an insignificant number compared to the 76,000 deer which were being shot before the canning factory was established.

The deer, however, never recovered, and in 1920 the Japanese Government again closed all deer-hunting on Hokkaido. Yet, despite no legal hunting, by the late thirties the Sika on Hokkaido was near extinction, due mainly to predation by the wolf – locally known as the *Ezo-ookami*.

Map 15   The ranges of Sika deer *Cervus nippon* and Thorold's deer *Cervus albirostris* in Asia.

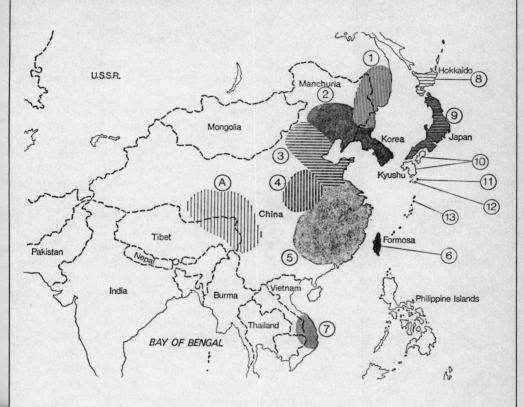

SIKA DEER *Cervus nippon*

1	*Cervus nippon hortulorum*	Ussuri district, Manchuria
2	*C.n.mantchuricus*	Manchuria, Korea
3	*C.n.mandarinus*	Northern China
4	*C.n.grassianus*	Shansi district, China
5	*C.n.kopschi*	South-east China
6	*C.n.taiouanus*	Formosa
7	*C.n.pseudaxis*	Vietnam
8	*C.n.yesoënsis*	Hokkaido Island, Japan
9	*C.n.centralis*	Hondo (Honshu) Island, Japan
10	*C.n.nippon*	Kyushu Island, Japan
11	*C.n.mageshimae*	Mageshima Island, Japan
12	*C.n.yakushimae*	Yakushima Island, Japan
13	*C.n.keramae*	Ryukyu Islands, Japan

THOROLD'S DEER *Cervus albirostris*

A	*C.albirostris*	Eastern Tibet, western China

Fortunately a few remained in the Hidaka district, and with the subsequent extinction of the wolf, deer stocks started to build up again. By 1951 the Japanese Government once more opened up hunting in the Minam i-Hidaka area, to be extended, six years later, to most of their other habitats in Hokkaido. The best hunting area at the moment is in the Hidaka district and in particular those areas facing the Pacific Ocean.

On both Kyushu, which is the third largest island of Japan, and Shikoku, the deer are reasonably well distributed, being most scarce in the extreme north of the former island.

South of Kyushu, on the small island of Yaku which belongs to the Kagoshima prefecture and is situated approximately 75 miles (120 km) south of Kagoshima City, Sika deer are comparatively numerous and hunting is permitted. The Sika of Yaku-jima (*jima* meaning island) have been given the subspecific name of *C.n.yakushimae*. This deer is similar in size to those on Kyushu with stags standing about 27 to 32 in. (70 to 80 cm) high at the shoulder, the hinds being about 4 in. (10 cm) smaller.

Mention should also be made of the Kerama Sika deer *C.n.keramae* which are to be found on the small uninhabited islands of Yagahi-jima, Kuba-jima and Agahi-jima near Okinawa. The Kerama Sika is an endangered deer, and the last estimate (1979) suggested that the total population on Yagahi, which extends to only 304 acres (123 hectares) was about forty, with a further ten on each of the other two islands – a slight increase on the number (30) estimated to be on the islands in 1969, but well below the figure of 160 for the late fifties. Needless to say, all hunting of this deer is completely forbidden.

Throughout Japan the deer live almost exclusively in the forests and only venture on to more open grounds in search of food. During the spring, summer and autumn months, herds will be found up to altitudes of 8200 ft (2500 metres).

The rut takes place from about mid-September until the end of October.

As one would expect, the largest antlers are produced by the deer (*C.n.yesoënsis*) on Hokkaido, where the average length for an adult stag is about $29\frac{1}{2}$ in. (75 cm) with occasional specimens running up to $31\frac{3}{4}$ in. (81 cm). A good pair of antlers from Hondo (*C.n.nippon*) will measure about $25\frac{1}{2}$ in. (65 cm) whilst $15\frac{3}{4}$ in. (40 cm) would seem to be about the average for stags from Shikoku and Kyushu. An antler length of $14\frac{1}{2}$ in. (37 cm), however, would be extremely good for Yaku-jima – the general average being about 11 in. (28 cm).

Incidentally, all Japanese hunters refer to an adult 8-point Sika stag as '*Mitsu-mata*' meaning, literally, 'three (*mitsu*) a side' – because in Japan the extremity of the main beam is not counted as a point.

MONGOLIA

Mongolia, at present, is the only country in north-east Asia where visiting sportsmen are welcome. These hunting trips are arranged by the National Tourist Office under the Ministry of Foreign Trade of the Mongolian People's Republic – referred to as Zhuulchin.

Whilst a hunt after the wild sheep – Argali – and Ibex in the Altai mountains is probably the greatest attraction to the visiting sportsman, forest hunts after Wapiti and Siberian Roe, and to a lesser extent Elk (Moose) can also provide some excellent trophies for the deer hunter.

Overseas sportsmen started to visit Mongolia in the mid-sixties. At that time the Mongolian Hunters' Association were anxious to invite foreign members to join their association and this one could do by paying an entrance fee of $50 and thereafter $100 annually. These fees have now been doubled. Once a member, a foreigner was allowed to 'hunt or fish in Mongolia once in two years'. Although on joining, a member may on his first hunting trip shoot an antelope and a number of birds free of charge, it will not be until his third year of membership that an elk and wapiti, along with argali, ibex and antelope, may be shot, the fee for each being reduced to 50 percent of the normal safari hunting prices. After six years' membership, hunting fees for the above species are further reduced to 40 percent.

Today, one does not have to belong to the Mongolian Hunting Association to hunt in Mongolia, and outfitters such as Klineburger Worldwide Travel, or Safari Outfitters Inc. are able to arrange, in collaboration with Zhuulchin, forest hunts after the above mentioned deer at the following charges (1980), which include all meals and accommodation (tents etc.) in the hunting area, transport to and from the hunting area, including the use of a horse for hunting when required; transport to and from the airport to Utar Bator where accommodation will be provided in transit; and also the provision of an interpreter.

Six days' hunt after Wapiti – locally referred to as *Maral* – in the Batkhan area, which is situated some 149 miles (240 km) west of Ulan Bator as follows:

One person	$2000 (about £1000),
two persons	$1700 (about £850), each,
party of three persons	$1500 (about £750) each.

These prices are based on the exchange rate of approximately $3\frac{1}{3}$ tugruks to the dollar.

These prices also include the trophy fee for one Wapiti, but if a second animal is taken, the additional charge will be $550 (about £275). The charge for a non-hunting companion is $600 (about £300). A Roe buck may be shot for $220 (about £110).

A fourteen-day forest hunt, for a party of three or more some 62 miles (100 km) from Bulgan near the Siberian border, will cost each client excluding any trophy taken, $4000 (about £2000) (non-hunting companions $1400 or about £700). These prices include the cost of the 248 mile (400 km) flight from and to Ulan Bator.

Trophy fees for animals taken, which will be paid for after the hunt, are as follows: Wapiti and Elk (when available) $550; Roe buck $220. If desired, the hunter may also have the chance to shoot a bear ($550) and boar ($220) on this trip.

131

Forest hunts take place between 1 August and 31 October, but only the Roe buck can be guaranteed to have the antlers clean of velvet during August.

Should a client collect a trophy larger than the national record, it automatically becomes the property of the Mongolian Government and may not leave the country. The client, however, will be permitted to have a further hunt without any additional charge. This principally applies to Argali.

Animals wounded and lost will cost the price charged for a second trophy, i.e. in case of Wapiti $550. It is forbidden to shoot any females or young animals and should any be taken then the cost will be based on 150 percent of the trophy price and the head confiscated.

Prior to making any firm arrangements Zhuulchin require a 25 percent deposit, the balance being paid on arrival at Ulan Bator.

Describing conditions of a Mongolian hunt, Roman Hupalowski from Chicago writes (1976), 'The Mongolian *Yurt* is more than adequate and could be considered the equivalent of a first class African Safari tent with the advantage of being insulated and having a stove for heat. The Mongolian ponies are extremely sturdy and carried the writer up and down mountains that had I been on a Canadian pack trip I would have had to walk up and down. Mongolian saddles are not very comfortable. . . .'

The deer species that may be hunted in Mongolia are as follows.

Wapiti *Cervus canadensis*

The Wapiti – generally referred to as the *Maral* in this part of Asia – has a fair distribution throughout most of the perimeter areas of Mongolia, but elsewhere, the vast Gobi desert area not only makes the more central part unsuitable, but also prevents general intergradation of the four subspecies found in the Altai – Trans Baikal – Amur area of central Asia.

Of the four subspecies found in Mongolia – the Manchurian Wapiti *C.c.xanthopygus* in the north-east; *C.c.asiaticus* (syn. *C.c.sibiricus*) in the north and north-west; together with *C.c.wachei* in the west, which may be a synonym of *C.c.asiaticus*; and the Ala-shan Wapiti *C.c.alashanicus* of the south, *C.c.asiaticus* is the most widespread, and this is the type which can be hunted by visiting sportsmen operating from Ulan Bator, the area most frequently hunted being the Khangai mountains. Apart from stalking, bulls are sometimes shot during the course of small impromptu drives.

Wapiti antlers will not be clean of velvet before the end of August or the beginning of September, and this has resulted in a number of trophy bulls having to be shot with antlers still partially in velvet by sportsmen trying to combine an August hunt after sheep with a forest hunt after Wapiti. September is also a good month for the other deer.

Elk *Alces alces cameloides*

The range of the Siberian Elk, which has a wide distribution throughout much of north-east Asia, from about the Yenisei river in the west to Manchuria and the Sea of Okhotsk in the east, just penetrates into northern

Mongolia and occasionally may be included among the game to be hunted during a fourteen-day general forest hunt.

In colour the eastern Elk is a much darker animal than the European form, particularly during the early autumn when some animals appear almost black. Later in the year, as the hairs lengthen and the natural gloss of the autumn pelage is lost, the general colour becomes lighter. The beard or 'bell' of this Elk is longer than in western types, and comparable to the 'bell' seen on the Moose of North America.

Roe deer *Capreolus capreolus*

Two types of Roe occur in Mongolia – the large Siberian Roe *C.c.pygargus* in the north and north-east corner, and the smaller Chinese or Manchurian Roe *C.c.bedfordi* – sometimes referred to as the Duke of Bedford's deer – in the south-east.

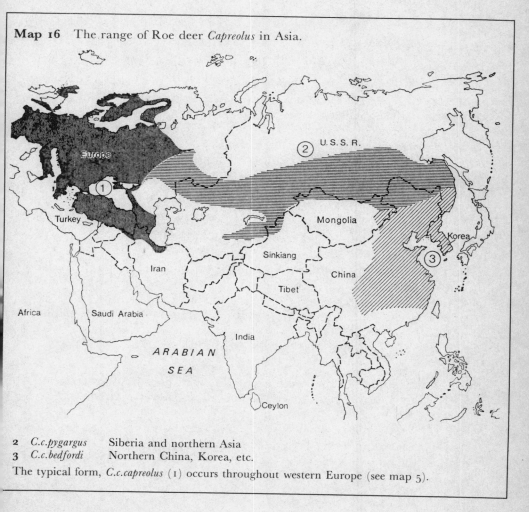

Map 16 The range of Roe deer *Capreolus* in Asia.

2 *C.c.pygargus*   Siberia and northern Asia
3 *C.c.bedfordi*   Northern China, Korea, etc.

The typical form, *C.c.capreolus* (1) occurs throughout western Europe (see map 5).

133

The main differences between the Siberian Roe *C.c.pygargus* and the European form *C.c.capreolus* is the size, a good buck standing about 33 to 35 in. (84 to 89 cm) high at the shoulder – a good 6 in. (15 cm) higher than the west European form – and weighing almost double. The antlers are also considerably larger, and are widely separated at the pedicles, the coronets never touching, as they frequently do in the latter. A good pair of antlers will measure 15 in. (38 cm) or more in length, will have deep pearling, and although basically 6-tined, the posterior point of the fork will often bifurcate to give it eight points.

The Chinese Roe *C.c.bedfordi* is similar but smaller than the Siberian type, and antlers appear to be more typically 6-pointed than 8-pointed.

Both Siberian and Chinese races rut during July and early August, and since the antlers of mature bucks will not be shed before mid-October, September, which is the best month for hunting Wapiti, would also be an excellent time for these species also.

TURKEY (ANATOLIA)

Local names: Fallow deer, *Alageyik*; Roe deer, *Kavaca*; Maral, *Kızılgeyik*.

There are three species of deer present in Turkey, but none of them are plentiful. Fallow deer *Dama dama dama*, although formerly abundant, are now restricted to the northern slopes of the Taurus Mountains. It has been suggested by some writers that the Fallow deer of Turkey are the Persian type *D.d.mesopotamica* but it is doubtful if the range of this latter deer ever extended as far north, latitude 36°N being about its limit in a northerly direction. Certainly none of the antlers that have come out of Turkey during this century bear any resemblance to the Persian Fallow. The doe is called *Ceylan* – pronounced *Jayan* – in Turkish.

Roe *Capreolus capreolus capreolus* also occur in some localities, and Turkey marks the natural limit of range westwards of the Maral *Cervus elaphus maral*, but nowhere are they plentiful.

At the present time (1980), therefore, all species of deer are protected, and the only large game animal permitted to be hunted by the Central Committee of Hunting is the wild boar. Foreign hunters can hunt only in parties organized by the Turkish travel agencies which have been authorized by the Ministry of Forestry.

U.S.S.R.

Note: Abbreviations of Principal Soviet Administrative Areas are as follows:

S.S.S.R. (Soyúz Sovetskikh Sotsialisticheskikh Respublik) Union of Soviet Socialist Republics.

R.S.F.S.R. (Rossiyskaya Sovétskaya Federativnaya Sotsialisticheskaya Respúblika) Russian Soviet Federated Socialist Republic.

S.S.R. (Sovétskaya Sotsialisticheskaya Respúblika) Soviet Socialist Republic.

All hunting in the U.S.S.R. is under the control of the Chief Administrator for Nature Protection, Reserves and Hunting, which is a department of the Ministry of Agriculture. There are over 6000 hunters' clubs in the Soviet Union, with a membership of several million. The Moscow Hunters' Society, for instance, with a membership of over 72,000 hunters and anglers, has about $7\frac{1}{2}$ million acres (just over 3 million hectares) at its disposal. The top authority is the Main Hunting and Wildlife Preserves Administration (Glavokhota) under the Council of Ministers of the R.S.F.S.R.

Hunting centres are staffed with wardens who are not only responsible for the stock of game, but also provide assistance, when required, by hunters. Before joining a hunters' society, candidates must be over eighteen years of age and pass an examination in weapon handling, safety rules and hunting legislation.

There are also a number of reserves set aside for the preservation of game, and these are being gradually extended. However, it should be appreciated that vast areas of the U.S.S.R. are actually undeclared reservations, because of their extreme inaccessibility.

In the vast hunting grounds of the Soviet Union are to be found a wealth of game animals, but facilities for hunting by visiting sportsmen are somewhat restricted and are being constantly changed. As an example, although there is a hunting reserve on the Krym peninsula (Crimea), facilities to hunt there by foreign visitors – although possible a few years ago – are at present no longer available.

In the Baltic Union Republics of Lithuanian S.S.R., Latvian S.S.R. and Estonian S.S.R., good hunting is available to members of various hunting societies. In Estonia the hunting season for Roe opens on 1 July, whilst Elk may be hunted during October and November. At present, however, hunting of Red deer in Estonia, where the present population is estimated to number about 500 head, is not permitted. Red deer, however, can be hunted in Latvia. The deer here are not indigenous stock, for the native stock became extinct many years ago. However, Red deer were re-introduced to Latvia during the middle of the last century and a large and stable population has been established, particularly in the Courlandia area. Some good trophies are produced, the antlers being long and well pearled, in strong contrast to some of the trophies produced by stags from the Ukraine, which are inclined to be short, thick and multipointed, with deep cups on top.

In Lithuania there are large populations of Elk, Red and Roe deer and hunting is available for all three species.

Hunting trips in the Soviet Union are organized by Intourist, and these include hunts for Red deer, European Roe deer, Siberian Roe, 'Isubra' Wapiti and Elk, and depending on the area to be hunted, other game animals such as tur, chamois, boar and bear may also be included in the 'all-in' seven to ten day package hunting trips, prices for which will vary according to the number of hunters in the party. There are also Reindeer and Sika deer in the Soviet Union, but none in the areas open for hunting by visiting sportsmen.

For instance, a week's hunt in the Krasney Reserve near the Black Sea after Red and Roe deer would cost (1979) a *single* hunter Rbs 460 (about £340) but if there were three in the party, the cost for each would be reduced to Rbs 395 (about £292).

A trip to the Baikal hunting reserve in the Irkutsk region after 'Isubra' Wapiti, Siberian Roe or Elk is rather more expensive, costing Rbs 500 (about £370) each for one or two hunters, but reduced to Rbs 453 (about £336) each for a party of three or more. All prices apply from Moscow and include two days' stay in Moscow, all food and accommodation during the hunting and provision of guides etc. but not air and other transport fares between Moscow and the hunting grounds. Trophy fees are also additional.

Each hunting party must be accompanied by a gamekeeper and this will be an additional charge, varying from about Rbs 191 to 214 (about £141 to £158) depending on the area and game to be hunted.

Accommodation varies from a hotel when hunting in the Krasny or Seliger State Forests, to 'a hunting cottage', tents or even on a boat when in the Baikal Forest area.

Suitable clothing for the area (fur jacket, fur trousers, fur cap and gloves as well as high boots) can all be hired on the spot. Rifles and ammunition are also available at a cost of Rbs 7 (about £5) for the former and Rbs 0.50 each (about 37 pence) for the latter.

Trophy prices are based on the score (number of points) each trophy obtains when assessed under the appropriate C.I.C. formula, and all trophies are measured and their value assessed in the presence of the hunter who will then be required to sign the card signifying his acceptance of the score.

Prior to the hunt, however, the following advance payments (1979) were required for each individual species to be hunted.

Species	Rbs	Rbs for trophy preparation	Total Rbs	Approx. sterling equivalent £
Red deer	1000 plus	20	1020	755
Isubra Wapiti	800 "	20	820	607
Elk (trophy head)	500 "	20	520	385
Elk (poor trophy)	130 "	20	150	111
Roe	300 "	8	308	228

Most of these prices refer to a trophy of Silver medal standard, so if, after measuring the head there should be a difference between the factual cost of the trophy and the advance payment, hunters will be given a receipt to guarantee payment upon their return home through the agency who organized the trip.

In the Gavrilovskoye State Forest for Red deer, and in the North Ossetian State Forest for Roe, advance payments are reduced to Rbs 480 (about £355) and Rbs 200 (about £148) respectively.

In a trip of such comparatively short duration it is probable that more

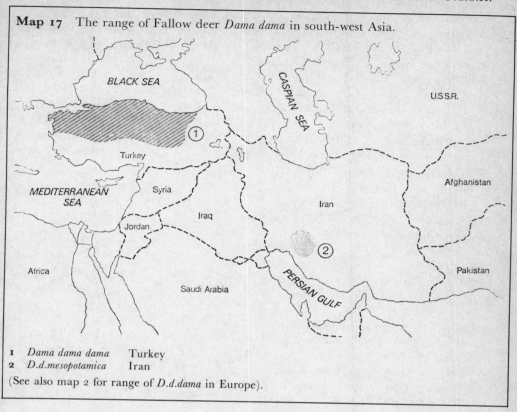

Map 17   The range of Fallow deer *Dama dama* in south-west Asia.

1   *Dama dama dama*   Turkey
2   *D.d.mesopotamica*   Iran
(See also map 2 for range of *D.d.dama* in Europe).

trophies will be taken below rather than above Silver medal standard, so the difference will generally require a refund rather than any further payment.

It will be noted, also, that a mandatory charge of Rbs 8 to 20 (about £6 to £14) is made for preliminary treatment (skinning and boiling) of the trophy.

In common practice with other European countries an animal that is wounded and not recovered will incur a fine, which varies from about £37 for a wounded Roe buck to about £150 for a Red deer stag or Wapiti. For a complete miss, the penalty will be about half these prices. Moreover, should a hunter refuse to 'shoot at an animal provided at his request' a fee is charged as though he had taken the shot and missed.

In some areas the minimum calibre permitted for Red deer is 7.62 mm but the most popular weapon in the Soviet Union for all species would appear to be a 9 mm 'Los' or 'Medved', and most rifles available for hiring are of this calibre. For Roe deer in the Ukranian Hunting Preserve of Gavrilovskoye, however, it is permissible to use 'a smooth-bore hunting gun'.

Red deer *Cervus elaphus* Sp.
Local name: *Blagoródnaya Olyén.*

The typical Red deer *C.e.hippelaphus* of Europe extends its range as far north as

137

the Baltic Republic states of Estoniya (Estonia), Latviya (Latvia) and Litva (Lithuania), and eastwards as far as about longitude 30°E in the Ukraine. There are also a few native Red deer on the Krym peninsula as well as some introduced Maral *C.e.maral*. This latter race replaces *C.e.hippelaphus* in the Bol'shoy Kavkaz mountains region (Caucasus).

A third member of the Red deer group – the Bactrian or Bukharian deer *C.e.bactrianus* – occurs in the forests of the lower Syr Darya of Kazakhskaya S.S.R. and in the Amu Darya basin of Turkmenskaya S.S.R., extending its range into northern Afghanistan. Nowhere is it plentiful and hunting is now prohibited throughout its range in U.S.S.R. The majority of deer are to be found in the Tigrovaya Reserve which extends to about 66,690 acres (27,000 hectares) in Tadzhikskaya S.S.R.

Red deer stalking is available in the following State forests.

Krasny Les Hunting Reserve, Krasnodar Territory R.S.F.S.R., 10 September to 30 November

Mityakino Hunting Reserve, Rostov Region, R.S.F.S.R., 17 September to 1 October

Gavrilovskoye Hunting Reserve, Kherson Region, Ukranian S.S.R., 1 October to 31 October.

Hunting is normally by stalking, particularly on the roar during the rut, but in the Mityakino forest 'high seats' are available.

All trophies are assessed in accordance with the C.I.C. formula and charged accordingly, starting at about £135 for a trophy of fewer than 130 C.I.C. points to a *minimum* of £288 Bronze, £555 Silver and £1318 Gold.

At the International Hunting Exhibition in Budapest (1971) ten of the twenty-four Gold medal trophies came from Ukrán Sz.Sz.K., the best, shot in 1969, having a score of 247.56 points. Priced under the 1979 charges, this stag would have cost the hunter about Rbs 8680 (about £6430). The best trophy yet obtained in Litva S.S.R. has a score of 237.04 C.I.C. points.

Roe deer *Capreolus capreolus*
Local name: *Kosúlya*.

Two races of Roe occur in the Soviet Union – the typical European Roe *C.c.capreolus* in the south and west, and the Siberian *C.c.pygargus* in the east.

In the southern part of its range the European Roe occurs in Gruziya S.S.R. (Georgia), Armeniya S.S.R. (Armenia) and Azerbaydzhan S.S.R. (Azerbaijan) as well as on the Krym (Crimea) peninsula. From here it spreads northwards through Ukraina S.S.R (Ukraine), White Russia into Estoniya, Latviya and Litvia along the Baltic coast, whilst in an easterly direction it occurs in all suitable localities as far as the Volga river and western slopes of the Ural mountains, beyond which it is replaced by the Siberian Roe. The best trophies come from the Republics bordering the Baltic coast.

In this area the stalking season for Roe is divided into two periods – the first, of a month, running from 15 May until 15 June, and the second, of four months, from 1 September until the end of the year. It will be noticed that stalking the bucks during the rut is not permitted.

Stalking the European Roe is available for visiting hunters in the Krasney Les Hunting Preserve which is situated some 42 miles (70 km) west of Krasnodar in the flood-plains of the River Kuban. This is a plain of dense mixed forest called 'Krasny' (red) because it is inhabited by Red deer and Roe deer as distinct from the Ghorny (black) forest with its wolves, boar and jackals.

Roe stalking is also available in the North-Ossetian Hunting preserve which is situated in the foothills of the Bol'shoy Kavkaz (Caucasus) mountains south-west of Ordzhonikidze. In both areas, however, stalking does not commence until about 10 September, by which date not only will the rut be over but only a few weeks remain before the older bucks will start to shed their antlers. In the Krasney Les Preserve the season only lasts about a month, but in the North-Ossetian Preserve, Roe stalking continues until the early part of December by which time all mature bucks will have their antlers in velvet.

Trophy prices are according to the score of the head when measured under the C.I.C. formula, starting at Rbs 16 (about £12) for a small European Roe head of under 70 C.I.C. points to at least Rbs 230 (£170) for a Gold medal trophy (130 C.I.C. points).

The best Roe trophy at the Budapest Exhibition (1971) shot in 1966 at Észt Sz.Sz.K had a score of 181.40 C.I.C. points. Priced under the 1979 trophy charges, this would have cost about Rbs 1200 (about £888) to shoot. The best trophy to date for the U.S.S.R. came from Estoniya S.S.R. with a score of 195.00 C.I.C. points. Another fine trophy from Litva S.S.R. comes a close second (194.00 points).

For antlers of Siberian Roe a slightly higher scale comes into operation, ranging from about £14 for a small head of under 70 C.I.C. points to about £450 for a trophy of 220 C.I.C. points, and increased thereafter at the rate of Rbs 20 (£14) per point.

Wapiti *Cervus canadensis*
Local name: *Izúbr*.

Of the three subspecies of Wapiti that occur in the U.S.S.R., the one most likely to be hunted by the visiting sportsman is the Asiatic Wapiti – *C.c.asiaticus* – generally referred to as the 'Isubra deer' which has a range extending from about Lake Baikal in the east to the Altai Mountains in the west. Intourist run a number of trips to the Baikal State Forest to hunt this deer, the season for which runs from about 20 September to 10 October. Siberian Roe and Elk are also in the same area, but it would only be possible to combine a hunt after Roe during the same trip, as the season for the latter does not open until the middle of October.

To the south and west of the range of the Asiatic Wapiti occurs the Tien Shan race *C.c.songaricus*, its principal location being, as its name suggests, the

Tien Shan mountains, where it occurs from about Syr Darya in Russian Turkestan to the Tarbagatai mountains in western Mongolia.

Of all the Asiatic Wapiti, the Manchurian race *C.c.xanthopygus* has the widest distribution, the habitat of this deer being the forested areas of eastern and northern Manchuria, ranging westwards and northwards into Mongolia and Chitinskaya Oblast province east of Lake Baikal in the U.S.S.R., which is the extent of its range in a westerly direction. In the east its distribution extends beyond the River Amur almost to the sea in the Gulf of Tartary.

Prices for shooting an Isubra deer range from Rbs 150 (about £111) to Rbs 1700 (about £1260) which is the *minimum* price for a trophy of Gold medal standard. All but one of the Gold medal winning trophies at Budapest (1971) came from Orosz F.SzK.

Elk *Alces alces* Sp.
Local name: *Los.*

The Elk has wide distribution throughout the U.S.S.R. Its range extends from Kamchatka and the Sea of Okhotsk in the east to Poland and the Baltic Sea in the west. An estimate taken in 1970 suggested that throughout the whole of its range the Elk population was just short of three-quarters of a million, with about two-thirds in the European part of the U.S.S.R. A century ago, however, due to over-hunting and, in some areas, contamination with various cattle diseases, the Elk had almost disappeared from much of its former habitat.

The recovery in the west started about 1919 when the Council of Peoples' Commissars banned not only Elk hunting but also Roe hunting in the European parts of the U.S.S.R., whilst in Siberia, although Elk hunting was permitted during the months of November and December, it was strictly forbidden to hunt during snow-crust conditions.

By 1930 the Elk population in European U.S.S.R. had significantly increased and it was starting to extend its range. The recovery in the east, however, was much slower and it wasn't until after the last war that any real increase was apparent in Siberia. Latterly, the Elk has now firmly established itself in Kamchatka, and some magnificent trophies, comparable to moose from British Columbia have recently been taken in this region.

The range of the typical European Elk *A.a.alces* extends from Karelia and the three Baltic Republics of Estonia (Estoniya S.S.R), Latvia (Latviya S.S.R.) and Lithuania (Litva S.S.R) in the west to the Urals in the east where it is replaced by the East Siberian Elk *A.a.cameloides.*

In Latvia the Elk is found both inland and along the coast and the position is much the same in Lithuania, the majority of deer occurring in the western part and in particular towards the delta of the Memel where they frequently wade out into the surf. In 1971 the Elk population in the three Baltic Republics was estimated as follows: Estonia 11,000; Latvia 17,000 and Lithuania 7000; whilst in adjacent Belorussiya (Byelorussia) or White Russia, the Elk were thought to number about 17,000.

The southern boundary of the European Elk is an irregular line extending westwards from the Urals to west of Pinsk in the Pripet Marshes and into Poland. It is numerous in much of its range, and occurs right up to the suburbs of Moscow. According to a recent estimate, there are probably around 10,000 Elk in the Moscow region. Further south the population is recovering in the Ukraine, and in 1970 were estimated to number about 13,000. It has also recently started to return to the Caucasus where it has been absent for many centuries. Throughout the U.S.S.R., it is suggested that the Elk population is now approaching the 800,000 mark.

The highest Elk population in the Asiatic part of the U.S.S.R. occurs in the boggy southern taiga of western Siberia and Amur basin, where the density varies from about 50 to 100 animals per 100 sq. km or even double the number in a few insular areas of the Ob forest steppe country. Access, however, for hunting in much of this area is extremely difficult. In the west, towards the Finnish frontier, good hunting for Elk can be had in Karelskaya A.S.S.R. (Karelia).

Intourist offer Elk hunting for the visiting sportsman in Mityakino Reserve, Rostov region R.S.F.S.R. and in the Seliger Reserve, Kalinin region R.S.F.S.R. from about mid-November to mid-December, and in the Baikal Reserve, Irkutsk region R.S.F.S.R. from mid-October to early November.

Trophies in the first two areas are described as 'poor' and in consequence demand a deposit of only Rbs 150 (about £111) as compared to Rbs 520 (about £385) in the Baikal Reserve, the former being the minimum price for an Elk with fewer than 200 C.I.C. points anywhere in the Soviet Union. Thereafter the price steadily increases from Rb 1 per point up to 240 (C.I.C. points) to Rbs 60 (about £44) per point after 370. The minimum price (1979), therefore, for a Bronze medal trophy (260 points) is Rbs 257 (about £190); for a Silver medal trophy (275 points) Rbs 470 (about £348) and for a Gold (300 C.I.C. points) Rbs 980 (about £726).

The best trophy shown at Budapest (1971) shot in 1934, had a score of 415.90 C.I.C. points – which, if charged at 1979 prices, would have cost about Rbs 5960 (approximately £4400). The best trophy from Yakutiya of the East Siberian elk *A.a.cameloides* on view at Plovdiv 1981 had a score of 551.70. It was shot in 1972.

5 Australasia

AUSTRALIA AND NEW GUINEA

It was not until the beginning of the last century that there were any deer in Australia, but since about 1803, as a result of numerous introductions, at least six different species of deer are now leading a wild existence in various parts of the country.

A similar situation exists, of course, in New Zealand, which, until about 1851 had no deer either, but there the similarity ends, for whereas many of the introduced deer to New Zealand increased to pest proportions in some areas, Australian deer have never spread to the same extent, and only about three species are sufficiently numerous to be of any real interest to the sport hunter.

The majority of the liberations were made by the various Acclimatization Societies, which were founded about the middle of the last century.

Eventually deer liberated by the Acclimatization Societies became established in the wild, and, together with those of private herds which had colonized Crown land, became public property subject to legislation which varied from State to State, as indeed, it still does today. However, it is only during the past twenty years or so that the interest of hunting and stalking deer in Australia, previously enjoyed by a comparatively small group of hunters, has become more widespread.

During the last century, 'the hunting of carted bucks and stags', writes Bentley (1967), 'was commonly practised and, on larger properties, as the privately owned herds increased, hunting deer on horseback or by stalking was a privilege enjoyed by the property owners and invited guests.' One such wealthy landowner was Thomas Chirnside who hunted Red deer from his property of Werribee Park.

Fallow deer were also kept in Werribee Park and it would appear that this species was perhaps more frequently the quarry for a carted deer hunt than the Red deer. In England, however, during the eighteenth and nineteenth centuries, when hunting the carted deer was a popular sport among the gentry, Red deer was the favourite quarry.

The practice of hunting the carted deer in Victoria ended before the close of the century. However, hunting with hounds continued, and in Victoria is still the State's most popular form of hunting the Sambar, the only difference

Map 18   Range of introduced deer of Australasia.

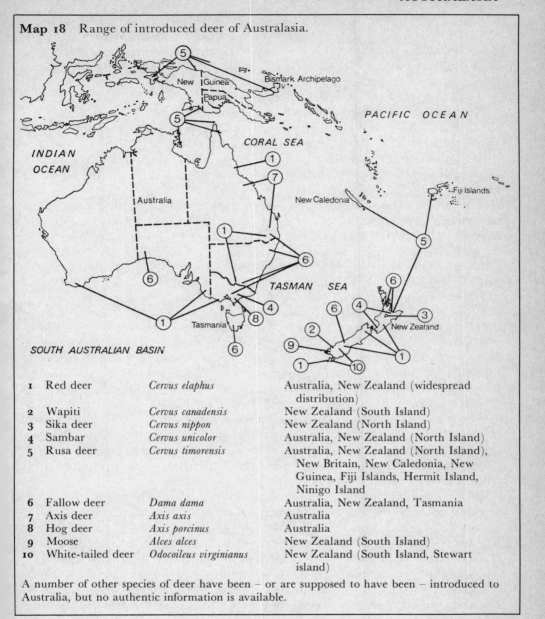

1	Red deer	*Cervus elaphus*
2	Wapiti	*Cervus canadensis*
3	Sika deer	*Cervus nippon*
4	Sambar	*Cervus unicolor*
5	Rusa deer	*Cervus timorensis*
6	Fallow deer	*Dama dama*
7	Axis deer	*Axis axis*
8	Hog deer	*Axis porcinus*
9	Moose	*Alces alces*
10	White-tailed deer	*Odocoileus virginianus*

Australia, New Zealand (widespread distribution)
New Zealand (South Island)
New Zealand (North Island)
Australia, New Zealand (North Island)
Australia, New Zealand (North Island), New Britain, New Caledonia, New Guinea, Fiji Islands, Hermit Island, Ninigo Island
Australia, New Zealand, Tasmania
Australia
Australia
New Zealand (South Island)
New Zealand (South Island, Stewart island)

A number of other species of deer have been – or are supposed to have been – introduced to Australia, but no authentic information is available.

today being that the quarry is wild rather than a carted beast and the hunters, armed with rifles, are on foot instead of being mounted on horses.

It is not known when hounds were first used to move the wild deer to riflemen posted at strategic places in the bush, but it was probably soon after the First World War, when the farmers of Gippsland started to complain about deer damage to crops and permits were issued for the deer to be shot in a number of areas. Previously, the deer had enjoyed almost complete protection – on paper anyway – and these permits only legalized something that was being carried out anyway.

Thus the deer became a public responsibility.

At first many deer were shot, but it was not long before the deer realized that to stand about in open fields during daylight was asking for trouble, and they became more elusive, taking refuge in deep gullies of thick scrub where silent approach on foot was virtually an impossibility. To shift the deer from these impenetrable thickets, the dog was the answer, so once more the hound returned to the deer hunting scene.

The increase and improvement in country roads in recent years has considerably helped the hunter to keep up with the hunt, for as often as not, if a vehicle is handy, it can be used to regain contact with hounds, and cut off the deer.

Hunting any deer with hounds undoubtedly disturbs the area more than just stalking with a rifle, and there is little doubt that hound hunting has been one of the major factors in the spread of Sambar into new country.

Probably the major criticism is that hounds generally hunt indiscriminately and run any deer irrespective of age or sex – the run and the meat often being of far more importance to the hunters than the trophy. Whatever criticism there may be, hound hunting up to date has been found to be the most effective method of coming to terms with the Sambar in the Australian bush, and over a period of time, the sexes of animals taken will probably even themselves out.

The very first deer to reach Australia were some Chital or Axis deer *Axis axis* from India which arrived in New South Wales about 1803. A year later one of the stags escaped from the enclosure and was subsequently shot one January evening by an unnamed gentleman who could thus claim to have been Australia's first 'deer hunter'.

During the next twenty-seven years or so at least thirteen different species – some represented by two or more subspecies – were introduced, and these included Axis deer *Axis axis*; Fallow deer *Dama dama*; Hog deer *Axis porcinus*; Red deer *Cervus elaphus*; Rusa deer *Cervus timorensis* and Sambar *Cervus unicolor*, all of which were eventually liberated into the Australian bush and remain today as wild populations. Among those which either failed to survive when liberated, or remained in confinement during their brief existence in Australia were Chinese Water-deer *Hydropotes inermis*; Mule deer *Odocoileus hemionus*; Musk deer *Moschus moschiferus*; Roe deer *Capreolus capreolus*; Sika deer *Cervus nippon*; and Wapiti *Cervus canadensis*. To this list should also be added the Swamp deer or Barasingha *Cervus duvauceli* for as a result of an introduction to the Coburg peninsula, Northern Territory in 1912, a few *may* still survive in the area – but up to date definite confirmation is lacking.

Despite the widespread introduction of deer, nowhere on the Australian mainland can deer stocks be said to be excessive. Indeed it seems doubtful if the total population of any single species outside Tasmania and New Guinea exceeds about 6000 to 7000 animals, the Sambar being the most plentiful.

There is no doubt that a greater interest in the deer is now being taken at Government level, particularly in Victoria where, in 1973, a Deer Advisory Council was formed which included two Government and five non-Government members, the latter representing the deer hunter, the farmer and the conservationist. In the same year a Shooter's Licence costing $A2 – or 50c for pensioners – a year was introduced, and this could be obtained at any police station. Anyone intending to hunt deer or game birds in Victoria also had to purchase a Game Stamp, the cost of which for *deer* only, valid for the calendar year for which it is issued, was $A10. Since 1982, however, these Game Stamps have been discontinued and by paying an additional fee of $A10 the Shooter's Licence can be endorsed to hunt game, which includes deer, as apart from vermin. Nowhere in Victoria, however, may deer be hunted in sanctuaries, nor is it legal to carry or discharge a firearm anywhere on a Sunday. Anyone wishing to hunt Hog deer must also obtain a metal self-locking deer-tag equivalent to the bag limit in force at the time, from the Fisheries and Wildlife office, for attaching above the hock of any deer taken, and any unused tags must be returned within fourteen days of the end of the open season. These tags are issued free.

A Shooter's Licence is also required in New South Wales, but not a deer stamp.

Other Victorian hunting regulations include the complete ban on night shooting, either by artificial light or by moonlight and no hunting is permitted between the hours of one hour after sunset and one hour before sunrise.

Although dogs may not be used for hunting Red deer anywhere in the State they may, however, be used for hunting Sambar in that part of Victoria bounded on the south by the Princes Highway and the west by the Hume Highway, provided it is wearing a collar to which is securely attached a metal tag on which is legibly printed the name and address of the owner. It is also recommended that a number registered with the Australian Deer Association should be tattooed inside the ear as an additional aid to trace lost dogs, and return them to their owners.

With regard to firearms, in Victoria a minimum calibre for both Red deer and Sambar is .270 in. (6.85 mm) firing a bullet of not less than 130 grains (8.42 g) in weight. For Hog deer, however, a slightly smaller calibre may be used (.243 in. or 6.17 mm) with a bullet no lighter than 100 grains (6.48 g). The minimum case length for a deer cartridge is 2 in. (51 mm). The shotgun is banned for deer, even with rifled slug.

For all the above mentioned deer it is legal to use either a long bow or crossbow provided the former has a pull weight of no less than 50 lb (22.7 kg) with a minimum draw of $27\frac{1}{2}$ in. (70 cm), and the latter a pull weight of no less than 80 lb (36.3 kg). For either weapon the projectile must be a broadhead arrow having a minimum of two sharpened cutting blades. A bow-hunter's licence, available from the Fisheries and Wildlife Division, costs $A2 per year from the date of issue. If, however, the archer owns a centre-fire rifle he is covered by a shooter's licence which specifies three categories – rim-fire .22, shotgun and centre-fire rifle – but does not include a bow. In order to hunt deer, however, the bow-hunter must attach a $A10 deer stamp to whichever licence he holds.

Sambar *Cervus unicolor*

The most important deer for sport hunting in Australia is the Sambar, the majority of which are to be found in Victoria. The original Sambar came to Victoria about 1861 with some animals from Sri Lanka, *C.u.unicolor* and peninsula India *C.u.equinus*, and these were introduced to a number of localities which included the Grampians and the timbered country around Mount Cole in western Victoria, and to Gippsland in the south-east. Others were liberated on Snake Island, lying east of Wilson's Promontory and to French Island, which is situated some 40 miles (64 km) south of Melbourne. In all these districts the deer acclimatized themselves well and at present are described as plentiful in Gippsland but are now rarely seen in the Grampians. Their status on the islands is less secure and indeed they are already extinct on Snake Island, which is, however, a stronghold for the smaller Hog deer.

For the most part, the Sambar's habitat in Victoria is mountainous and heavily timbered, and since much of it has been logged, there are vast areas of secondary growth providing not only good food but also dense cover for the deer. 'To stalk or still hunt this sort of country', writes Bentley (1967), 'requires a patience and application possessed by very few, and a tremendous amount of hunting time has to be worked up for any success. Very many men start their deer hunting in this way: many give up, others find their way into the hound teams where the work is strenuous yet more relaxed and the success ratio considerably higher. The really dedicated few persist with stalking. However, the number of Sambar stalkers has increased in the past few years'.

In States other than Victoria still hunting or stalking is the more normal method of hunting deer, particularly Hog deer, Fallow deer and Red deer. Indeed the use of hounds for hunting any deer other than Sambar in Victoria is now illegal and even for Sambar they cannot be used outside an area bounded on the west by the Hume Highway and on the south by the Princes Highway.

Sitting up and waiting for deer to visit a well-used feeding place can be productive if the area has not been previously hunted over with hounds. Until 1975, when the use of an artificial light for hunting deer in Victoria was made illegal, spot lighting was much practised and probably over 60 percent of the Sambar killed each season were taken in this manner. In 1978 further legislation in Victoria followed, making it illegal to shoot deer between one hour after sunset and one hour before sunrise, thus preventing the shooting of deer by moonlight.

From about Easter until October or November are the usual months for Sambar hunting, as the weather is cooler for both hound and hunter. A cool, wet day in summer may also tempt a hunter to take out his hounds, for at present there is no close season for hunting Sambar.

In 1977 it was estimated that the average number of deer taken per hunter was 1.19, the most successful being those who employed a combination of stalking and hunting with hounds (2 deer per hunter), closely followed by those who hunted with hounds only (1.72 deer each). Stalker success, however, was considerably lower, only about 0.62 deer per hunter being achieved.

A combination of hunting with hounds and stalking also gave the highest average number of deer taken per hunter per trip (0.275) and stalking only the lowest (0.068). There is no doubt that whatever method is used, to bag a Sambar in Victoria requires patience and perseverance.

The rut, as in New Zealand, can occur at almost any time of the year, but the majority of mating would appear to take place during the months of September and October. Antler shedding is likewise variable, but it would seem that the best chance of taking a stag in hard antler would be during the second half of the year, and in particular during the months of July to October.

Hog deer *Axis porcinus porcinus*

Hog deer, which were obtained from India and Sri Lanka about 1870 were introduced to a number of localities in the coastal region of south-western Victoria and are now well established in the national park area, on Wilson's Promontory, on Snake Island and one or two other islands in the district. In 1947, on Snake Island, it was estimated that the stock of deer on the island was approximately 3000 head, but since then, due to much illegal hunting, deer stocks have been considerably reduced.

In 1973, following an investigation by the Deer Advisory Council of Victoria into the apparent decline in the mainland population of Hog deer, the Fisheries and Wildlife Division agreed to implement a number of the Council's proposals which included that not only should every hunter restrict his kill, during a one-month open season (1 to 30 April) to one stag and one hind, but that there should be a complete ban on the use of hounds and spotlights for hunting. As a result, stalking is now the accepted method of hunting Hog deer in Victoria.

Hog deer stags generally cast their antlers about September or October, and the new growth should be clean of velvet and hard by the end of January in readiness for the rut which normally takes place during February and March.

Fallow deer *Dama dama dama*

The exact year of introduction of Fallow deer to the Australian mainland is not known, but since the original source appears to have been from

Tasmania, it cannot have been earlier than about 1836, which was the date the first Fallow reached that island. Today wild Fallow deer are present in four, and possibly five States.

In New South Wales Fallow deer are reported as being fairly plentiful on the New England range near Glen Innes as well as in the district of Albury and surrounding timbered country which runs along the boundary of Victoria. There are also a number in the national park.

In Victoria a small number are said to be frequenting an area in south Gippsland whilst in the west of the State a few are still to be found in the Grampians region, but nowhere can they be said to be plentiful, and the hunting of this deer is now prohibited in Victoria throughout the entire year.

In South Australia Fallow deer are fairly plentiful in the extreme south-eastern part of the State but in the hills around Adelaide they were probably shot out about 1953.

In recent years, however, the clearance of scrubland which has been their principal stronghold for cultivation has now placed the status of the Fallow deer in South Australia in jeopardy. Fortunately the Australian Deer Association is aware of their plight and in 1974 initiated a scheme with private landowners to rehabilitate some Fallow deer on their properties.

Over the years there have been several releases of Fallow deer in Queensland and at the present time there are small herds in Toowoomba district which is located some 60 miles (96 km) west of Brisbane and near Stanthorpe which lies some 80 miles (129 km) to the south.

In 1912 the Gilruth Administration liberated some Fallow deer on the Coburg Peninsula, Northern Territory, but little is known of their present status and it is doubtful if any remain, the dingo being a formidable predator.

Fallow deer were first introduced to Tasmania in 1829 and for a time were kept in parks, the primary intention being to release animals when required for hunting with hounds. Subsequently, as the stock of deer exceeded the carrying capacity of the parks, a number were liberated and it was not long before about 600–800 deer were running wild in Tasmania (*Second Annual Report*, Acclimatization Society of Victoria, 1863).

Today Fallow deer are well established in Tasmania, particularly in the Eastern Midlands around Campbell Town, Ross and Lake Leake and this is where most hunting is carried out. Throughout the whole of their range it was estimated a few years ago that the population of Fallow deer in Tasmania was in the region of 7000 to 8000 head (Wapstra 1975) (*Deer Management & Research in Tasmania*, Fisheries & Wildlife Paper, Victoria No. 8).

There is no doubt that Tasmania has taken a greater interest in the management and conservation of deer than any other State of Australia, and as long ago as 1928 the *Animals and Birds Protection Act* required that no one could hunt deer unless in possession of a proper licence, and then only one 'adult male deer' could be taken on any one day of an open season. Having shot his deer, the hunter then had, within forty-eight hours, to take the complete carcase, with head still attached, to a police officer for identification and registering.

For many years it was a case of bucks only and this naturally resulted in a marked imbalance in the sex ratio. In 1970, therefore, a research programme was instituted by the Animals and Birds Protection Board – subsequently taken over by the National Parks and Wildlife Service in 1971 to see what steps should be taken to adjust the sex ratio, and this resulted in hunters, during the 1974 and 1975 seasons, having their annual bag limit reduced from five bucks to one buck and two does per season. In 1976 this was again changed to three deer per hunter of *any* sex.

In 1977 a Hunter's Authority Card system was introduced, which specified the number and sex of deer which the hunter could take off any particular property. The season limit was fixed at two deer per licence, which had to be taken during the following open seasons: bucks, 12 to 27 March; does 12 March to 10 April. A tagging system was also in operation. In 1978 the three weeks open season for bucks and four weeks for does followed, to within a few days, a similar pattern, the season limit again being fixed to two adult deer, but only one could be shot on any one day.

As the deer in Tasmania are largely on private property, the hunter must obtain the owner's permission to hunt on his land – which is, in effect, the Hunter's Authority Card – before he can purchase his deer licence. It is up to the property owner to decide how many hunters he can allow on his land and for what period during the open season. A licence costs $A10.

Although the season may vary slightly from one year to another, the Fallow rut in Australia generally commences around April, with the fawns being born in late November or December. The bucks start to cast their antlers in early October.

Stalking is the usual method of hunting Fallow deer in those States where this deer may legally be shot. Waiting at some vantage point covering a regular feeding or passing point is also much favoured by the less active hunter.

Australian Fallow deer antlers are inclined to be light and cannot be compared to the best in Europe.

Red deer *Cervus elaphus*

Red deer are to be found in the following five States of Australia, but their presence in the last two is somewhat precarious, Victoria, New South Wales, Queensland, South Australia and Western Australia.

The first Red deer to reach Australia were six animals from Windsor Great Park, which were presented in 1860, by Prince Albert to Thomas Chirnside to stock his park at Werribee. Subsequently deer from Werribee Park were hunted by the Melbourne Hunt. The Red deer in Victoria today undoubtedly owe their origin to them, their principal haunts being in the Grampians and Ararat area.

The original Red deer came to Queensland in 1873 when Queen Victoria presented the Queensland Acclimatization Society with two stags and four hinds from her Windsor Park herd. A further presentation was made by Lord Lamington who was Governor of Queensland about this time, and all these deer were liberated at Cressbrook, subsequently to spread out into the mountainous country around the head of the Brisbane river where they are now said to be quite plentiful. In 1976, as it was considered that stocks were getting too high, the Queensland National Park and Wildlife Service proclaimed for the first time since their introduction over a century ago, a trial open season for Red deer from 29 March until 26 April inclusive, with the intention of removing 500 animals. Provided a hunter had bought a $A5 hunting permit, he could apply for one or more deer tags at a cost of $A20 each. As things turned out, only 265 deer tags were purchased by 211 licensed hunters who applied, so the eventual cull was only about half the number planned. An open season for Red deer, however, was not repeated in 1977, and the Queensland Government has proclaimed that Red deer are to be considered a commercial resource for deer farming. Movement of Red deer from Queensland to other States is prohibited. In 1979 a live stag was fetching about $A1500.

In South Australia a few Red deer may still survive in the scrub country around Naracoorte in the extreme south-east corner near the border with Victoria, but there can't be many.

Their status in Western Australia is equally precarious and it seems possible that the once well-established herd near Pinjarra, which lies near the coast some 50 miles (80 km) south of Perth may be approaching extinction.

In Australia stags cast their antlers about the middle of September, and by February the new growth should be complete. The rut takes place toward the end of March, extending into April.

The usual method for hunting Red deer is by stalking but since in Victoria the hunting of Red deer is only legal during the month of June, the rut will be over so the hunter will not have the aid of a stag's roar to guide him to his quarry.

Axis deer or Chital *Axis axis*

As already mentioned, the very first deer to have been introduced to Australia seem to have been Chital or Axis deer from India, which reached New South Wales about 1803. They obviously did well, and within ten years a herd of about 400 animals had been established on Dr John Harris's property near Bathhurst.

Since that date Axis deer have been introduced to a number of localities but in Queensland only does the species appear to have survived in a wild state with any certainty.

Probably the largest concentration of Axis deer in Queensland is that centred about the Maryvale Creek Valley, near Charters Towers. These deer, *A.a.ceylonensis*, are descended from a stag and two hinds released in 1866 by

William Hann, and despite the undoubted ravages of dingoes, not to mention years of drought, a fine herd was soon established. In 1953 the deer in this area were estimated to number about 600 animals.

In 1979 legal hunting for Axis deer on Niall Station in Queensland became available for the first time, but on a very limited basis, and only those individuals with a current membership of at least one year's duration in the Australian Deer Association could apply for a permit costing about $A300 (about £150) per stag from the Queensland branch of the A.D.A., the fee being paid subsequently to Mr M G Anning, the owner of the Station.

As elsewhere in the world where this species has been introduced, there is no set breeding pattern, and calves can be dropped any time. Fresh cast antlers have, however, often been picked up during July and August, so the best chance of obtaining a stag in hard antler would be during April or May.

Rusa deer *Cervus timorensis*

Rusa deer were first introduced to Victoria about 1868, and by the end of the century, as a result of further releases being made at Gembrook and elsewhere, were said to be established in various parts of the State. Unfortunately some of the releases were made in localities occupied by Sambar, so interbreeding undoubtedly occurred. Until 1948 an occasional Rusa deer was still being taken in West Gippsland, but today the species is probably extinct in Victoria.

As a result of introductions early in the century Rusa deer now occur on a number of islands which include Friday and Prince of Wales, off Cape York Peninsula of northern Queensland, but they are not plentiful.

Rusa deer, obtained from New Caledonia, were released in the national park of New South Wales towards the close of the last century, and today are tolerably numerous. In New South Wales the Rusa is the only species of deer which is protected throughout the year.

Between north and south of Australia, there is a difference of about three months in the time of the rut, which on Thursday Island takes place during September and October, as compared to late June and July in New South Wales, the shedding of antlers being some five months later.

Undoubtedly the most successful introduction of Rusa deer has been to Papua New Guinea, and in some areas the deer population runs into many thousands.

In West Irian, which was formerly Netherlands New Guinea, a number of liberations have been made during the past seventy years to various localities around the coast. They are particularly plentiful around Merauke in the south-east corner from where they have extended their range into western Papua. Between 1969 and 1973 a number of aerial surveys carried out at three to six monthly intervals, were made of the deer frequenting the Bula Plains/Fly River area in extreme south-west Papua and as a result it was estimated that 'as many as 20,000 deer may be present in the trans-Fly area of Papua and perhaps up to 100,000 in the Digul-Fly River Swamplands' with an overall density of about twenty deer per square kilometre (E. Lindgren 1975).* It would appear that the deer are not much hunted by the natives of the area. The original deer in this area were brought from Aru Island, which lies in the Arafura Sea, about 1920. Aru Island itself had received its initial stock of Rusa deer from the island of Ceram (Seram) about 1855, so the type would have been *C.t.moluccensis*. The Moluccan Rusa deer is also well established on the east coast of Vogel kop, particularly around Manokwari and on the Onin Peninsula. These deer also came from the Island of Ceram in 1913. Seven years later a further liberation of Moluccan Rusa took place near Hollandia, on the north coast, the deer having been obtained from Halmahera in the Moluccas.

In 1975 a hunting lodge – the Bensbach Wildlife Lodge – was established on the Bensbach River in south-west Papua – thus providing accommodation for up to sixteen hunters visiting the area. Deer are very plentiful and 'wherever we stood on the plains' writes Bruce Slater, 'there were always at least one hundred deer in view. . . . It was difficult to get a shot at the deer of your choice because of the number of deer milling around'.

Tariff at the lodge costs (1979) K80 (approximately £40) per person per day, and this includes the use of a guide for hunting, accommodation, meals, park entrance fee and hire of rifle (if required).

The shooting is licensed with a bag limit of five trophies per hunter, royalties being collected for the Wildlife Management Committee on a basis of K15 (approximately £7.50) for the first head ranging up to K60 (approximately £30) for a fifth head.

North of New Guinea, a few Rusa deer are present on the Hermit Islands in the Bismarck Sea, as well as on Ninigo Island, the former being descendants from some deer originally introduced about 1909. About 1910 some Rusa deer were liberated near Rabaul in New Britain and successfully survived severe hunting pressure from the Japanese during their wartime occupation of the island.

Despite the variety of deer in Australia, lack of numbers and the relatively inferior trophies of most species would hardly warrant a special trip, unless a visit could be combined with, say, a trip to New Zealand – in which case a Fallow buck from Tasmania or a Hog deer from Victoria would obviously be the kind of trophies to go for. Rusa stalking in New Guinea is undoubtedly an attractive proposition, for facilities there are probably as good as anywhere in the world, and certainly more accessible than in their native country of Indonesia.

NEW ZEALAND
Prior to 1851 there were no deer of any description on either the North or

* *An Introduction to the Biology of the Rusa Deer (Cervus timorensis) in the Western District, Papua, New Guinea.* Fisheries & Wildlife Paper, Victoria No. 8.

South Islands of New Zealand. In that year a pair of Red deer from Lord Petre's park at Thorndon in Essex were sent to Nelson, South Island, but unfortunately the hind succombed either during the journey or shortly after arrival, the stag being released in the Matai valley. Since that date, many liberations have been made in both islands. not only of Red deer but several other species as well, and the result has been that at present no fewer than eight different species of deer, which include Fallow, Sika, Rusa, Sambar, Wapiti and White-tailed deer, are completely acclimatized and leading a wild existence there. Moose from North America have also been introduced to the South Island, but have never really established themselves. Attempts, however, to acclimatize Mule deer and Huemul failed completely. For a time it appears that the Axis deer or Chital from India had managed to establish itself, but latest reports suggest that the species is now extinct.

Whilst some of the earlier introductions were made privately, the majority of liberations were effected by Acclimatization Societies. In the final stages of acclimatization, however, the Tourist Department of the Government was the responsible party.

In contrast to the New Zealand Government's former desire to populate the country with as many game animals as possible, within seventy years there were regrets that deer and other game animals such as Tahr and Chamois had ever been allowed to set foot in the country, for many of the *cervidae*, Red deer in particular, had increased to such an extent that they had become a pest.

In 1927 the State Forest Service inaugurated a campaign for the destruction of deer in their plantations and a bounty of 2 shillings (10 pence) subsequently reduced to 1 shilling 6 pence ($7\frac{1}{2}$ pence) – per tail was paid to private hunters. Until this time the management of the herds had been the responsibility of the Acclimatization Societies. Three years later all protection was removed and in 1931 the first Government control operations were commenced by the newly formed Deer Control Section of the Department of Internal Affairs. Between 1931 and 31 March 1975, the total number of deer killed on official operations was 1,124,297. In 1977–8 it is estimated that about 75,000 deer were killed by the commercial meat exporters.

Not all culling has been done by shooting, and in the early sixties a new method of control was tried. This was the use of 1080 poison, which for many years had been used extensively in New Zealand for rabbit control.

At this period the expanding export trade of venison to Europe had not yet got under way, so the recovery of meat was not a problem, and even if shot, the majority of carcases were left in the bush to rot.

Nothing, of course, could be less selective than poisoning, good or bad types of deer being equally affected. However, when the policy is complete extermination, then the question of selective culling does not have to be considered. The disappointing results, however, of this poison method of control did not warrant the high cost involved, and it has not been pursued in recent times.

More recently, culling with the aid of helicopters has produced some spectacular results, but as deer stocks get less, this method will also have to be abandoned on grounds of economy.

Describing this method, Mr Newton McConochie writes (*in litt*):

The larger exporting companies generally use two helicopters which go low into the bush country at a point where the tall timber verges on to the Alpine scrub, and scared by the noise of the machines, the deer are driven up towards the open clearings. Deer cannot travel fast for any great distance uphill, and they soon start to tire, with the machines operating like two sheepdogs just above tree level. Eventually the deer, tired out by their uphill climb, soon stand, and it is then the time for the shooters in the helicopters to start work. The majority of them are very skilled in their work, and as the pilot navigates the machine at ranges varying from a few yards to fifty [45 metres] from the deer, the deer are shot down one after another to near extinction.

After the deer have been shot the animals are gutted and then, with the skin on, the carcasses are flown back to base on hooks that are suspended under the helicopter and supplied for that purpose. Three small animals, or two large matured stags, can be taken out on each trip by this method. At first, when they first started to operate and the deer were more plentiful, a hundred or even more a day was a satisfactory kill, but this tally is slowly dwindling as time goes on and the deer get fewer. The helicopter has at least prevented many thousands of tons of venison being left to rot in the bush.

Introduced game animals belong to the Crown and provided the private hunter obtains a permit – which is free – he has complete freedom of access to all Crown land. Permits to hunt in the State forests are supplied by the New Zealand Forest Service, but since there is no limit to the number of permits issued, this frequently results in an unlimited number of hunters operating in a single block, which is obviously unsatisfactory from the hunter's point of view.

Permits to hunt on Unoccupied Crown Land, or in a national park have to be obtained from the Department of Lands and Survey, and since these are issued on a block system, a strict control is kept on the number of hunters permitted to hunt in any one area. Wapiti hunting in the Fiordland National Park is the best example of a block system, the twenty or so hunting blocks being drawn for each season by ballot. Anyone wishing to hunt in Fiordland, therefore, has to apply to the Secretary of the National Park Board in Invercargill.

On occupied land, hunting is permitted only at the discretion of the owner or occupier and it is believed that land tenure could well hold the key to the future of game in New Zealand. Unfortunately, even on private land the deer is not safe from the airborne poacher, and many a deer has been shot and picked up by hunters operating from a helicopter. At first it was for meat, but latterly, with the increasing interest in deer farming, the deer are being shot with tranquilizing darts, and then transported away live.

The Wapiti, therefore – provided you are successful in the ballot – would seem to be the most challenging trophy to go for in New Zealand today, but the stalker *must* be fit for the going is very rough.

Furthermore, in Fiordland the average annual rainfall can be anything from 100 to over 300 in. (254 to 762 cm) and when it does rain, it does so in real earnest! In a matter of hours the streams running off the steep mountains become raging torrents and with this quick influx of water the lakes rise rapidly. As a case in point, Lake Thomson near where we were camped one night, rose as much as 20 ft (6 metres) after two days of continuous rain, but it was surprising how quickly the level fell once the rain had ceased. With such high rainfall it is not surprising that many days can be wasted just sitting around in the tent waiting for the weather to clear – and to add to the discomfort, the sandflies do their best to make life pretty unbearable at times.

In the 1920s, when the first British sportsmen started to go deer stalking in New Zealand, not only were trophy animals more plentiful, but competent guides, particularly in Otago, were available at about £1 to 25 shillings (£1.25) a day, as well as pack horses to transport the party and gear into the mountains. Application to hunt had to be made to one of the Acclimatization Societies, who issued each sportsman with a licence entitling him to two trophy heads, and allocated a block of country in which the party could hunt without interference from other hunters.

But not so today, for there will be no guarantee that other hunters are not in the same area, and all equipment, tents, food, rifles etc. will probably have to be manually transported. True, the use of the light aircraft or helicopter has cut travelling time down from perhaps two or three days trekking to a matter of hours, and has enabled many previously inaccessible places to be reached. One cannot, however, just land a plane where fancy chooses and there are still many areas that are accessible only to the hunter sound in wind and limb.

There is no doubt that New Zealand has a large potential for developing big game as a tourist attraction, for the country is so lightly populated that it would be an easy matter to designate large areas of uninhabited country as hunting blocks where sportsmen would have to pay for what they shot. Indeed, a start in that direction has already been made, for with the passing of the *Wild Animal Control Act* in 1977, not only are deer now classed as 'wild' instead of 'noxious' animals but the Director General of Forests may set aside any area of State forest – or other tenure with the owner's permission – as a recreational hunting area where hunting as a means of recreation is to be used to control – though not exclusively – the numbers of wild animals.

Comfortable huts as bases for fly camps, and transport either by boat or aircraft must be available to reach the hunting areas, and whilst the Forest Service has certainly tried to encourage the sportsman by providing huts and improving access to some areas previously inaccessible, until this latest project nothing outside Fiordland has been done to reserve certain blocks for sport hunting *only*. Really competent guides should be available. Unless these facilities are available, New Zealand can never hope to attract the overseas sportsman anxious to acquire a good trophy.

As things are at present, no one needs a licence to hunt deer anywhere in New Zealand, the only requirement being a permit to enter any particular area. Unless one goes far into the bush, however, prospects of taking a good trophy are not very good, and will not be improved if the demand for live deer sales to the deer farmer – particularly for the velvet trade – continues to increase.

A summary of the successful deer introductions that have taken place since the middle of the last century are as follows.

Red deer *Cervus elaphus*

As already mentioned, the first Red deer to reach New Zealand arrived on the South Island in 1851. Twelve years later the first introduction of Red deer to the North Island took place – a stag and two hinds from Windsor Park – and these were subsequently liberated on the Taratahi plain near Wellington, from where they crossed over to the Maungaraki Range and formed what is known as the Wairarapa herd.

Other introductions quickly followed, and between 1851 and 1923 there were over 200 liberations of Red deer from Britain, which included wild Scottish blood from Invermark deer forest (Angus) and English park deer from Windsor (Berkshire), Knowsley (Lancashire), Richmond (Surrey), Stoke (Buckinghamshire), Bushy (Middlesex), Warnham (Sussex) and Woburn (Bedfordshire). Deer were also obtained from Australia, whose original stock had also come from England.

In common with other introductions to the southern hemisphere, the Red deer rut in New Zealand during the months of April and May, the antlers being cast about September. Calves are born in November and December.

By the turn of the century, and until about 1930 the Red deer stags in New Zealand were producing antlers of real trophy class and in particular, far superior to what the original wild strain had been capable of in Scotland. Eventually, however, overpopulation caused a general decline in quality, and although a few fine trophies can still be found it will be a waste of time going to the more accessible areas for few really mature stags will have been able to survive the recent cull of the commercial meat hunter or catch-up of live animals for the deer farmer.

However, as a result of the drastic culling operations that have taken place during recent years, and with fewer deer and less erosion, the feed should increase, and this should result in more favourable conditions for the deer and, hopefully, a return to the better class animal.

Despite the general lowering of quality, several trophy heads with antlers over 40 in. (102 cm) long have been taken in recent years. Most of the best trophies have come out of the South Island.

Wapiti *Cervus canadensis*

The Wapiti introduction in the South Island dates back to 1905, when about eighteen deer were released at the head of George Sound in the Fiordland

National Park, where they soon established themselves, and within fifteen years had crossed over into the Lake Te Anau district. It is recorded that the original strain was *C.c.nelsoni*.

At present, apart from an occasional straggler which has been seen east of the lake, the Wapiti is confined to an area of approximately 500,000 acres (202,000 hectares) of the Fiordland National Park, bounded in the east by Lake Te Anau, in the north by Sutherland Sound and in the south by Thompson Sound.

Unfortunately, Wapiti have to share Fiordland with Red deer and the two have interbred, to the detriment of both. Indeed, a large bull I shot on the shores of Lake Thompson I am certain was such an animal, for his $42\frac{3}{4}$ in. (108.5 cm) antlers were topped by typical Red deer cups. When shot, he was bugling, yet when seen in the area a few days previously I had passed him over as I considered his voice more of a roar than a bugle.

The rut commences from about mid-March onwards, and will continue throughout April – the majority of the calves being born around mid-November, by which time the older bulls will have cast their antlers.

Hunting in the Fiordland National Park is controlled by a permit system, and anyone wishing to arrange an expedition into the area must apply to the Secretary of the Fiordland National Park Board in Invercargill for full details and application form. Inquiries should be made well in advance for invariably applications far exceed the number of hunting blocks available, which are distributed by ballot.

Due to the prolonged periods of torrential rain which may be encountered in Fiordland, many regular hunters of the area have discarded the telescopic sight in favour of trouble-free aperture or open sights, and even when hunting on the high tops above the timber line, the terrain is generally sufficiently broken for a close-in stalk to be made, thus avoiding long shots.

Most Wapiti are shot during the rut, when the sound of a bugling bull will indicate its presence to the hunter, followed by a careful stalk. A few hunters, however, try to simulate a bugle in order to entice the bull to them.

Similar to Red deer trophies, Wapiti heads coming out of Fiordland have deteriorated in recent years, and it is seldom that one is taken today with a length measurement in excess of 50 in. (127 cm).

Adult bulls in New Zealand do not achieve the weights of similar aged beasts in North America, and will average around 600 to 700 lb (272 to 318 kg) in weight.

Sika deer *Cervus nippon*

Sika deer were first introduced to New Zealand in 1885, when three deer were liberated by the Otago Acclimatization Society at Otekaiki near Oamaru, and although a small herd was established, it appears that owing to crop damage, the deer were subsequently shot out.

In 1905 the eleventh Duke of Bedford presented to the Government of New Zealand three pairs of Manchurian Sika deer *C.c.mantchuricus* which had been bred at Woburn in England. These deer were liberated at Taharua, near Lake Taupo in North Island, and at the present time their approximate distribution extends from the Kaingaroa State Forest in the north to the northern Ruahine Range in the south, and from the Maungaharuru Range in the east to Lake Taupo and the Tongariro National Park in the west.

The Sika start to rut during the early part of April and this will continue until about mid-May. Antlers are shed about October.

The standard of trophy produced by some of the New Zealand Sika stags is as good as anywhere in the world, and several heads measuring over 30 in. (76 cm) have been shot, the longest being an 8-pointer from Puketitiri with a length of $33\frac{1}{4}$ in. (84.5 cm).

Probably the best area to hunt Sika deer is in the northern part of the Kaimanawa Forest Park, for not only has it the highest stable population, but the area is well supplied with tracks and paths, some of the former being suitable for all-weather vehicles. Three huts, maintained by the Forest Service, are also available for use by hunters and others visiting the park.

In 1979 the New Zealand Government Tourist Bureau were offering to Australian deer hunters guided hunting trips after Sika deer and Red deer on leased private and Maori land, guaranteed free from other hunters in the area, for \$A525 (about £218) (8 days) or \$A725 (about £302) (15 days). These charges include all hotel/motel accommodation (but not food) en route, transport *within* New Zealand, guides, use of cabins and provisions during the hunt.

Fallow deer *Dama dama*

Fallow deer occur in both North and South Islands. The first introduction to the North Island took place about 1870 when Sir George Grey introduced some to Kawau Island. About the same time other deer were introduced to Motutapu Island. Both these islands are situated in the Haukari Gulf on the east coast of Auckland. Other liberations were made about this time to some of the other islands, including Selwyn Island, but it was not until 1877 that Fallow first appeared on the North Island mainland. In this year eighteen deer were liberated on the Maungakawa and Matamata ranges, Waikato. By 1940 the Fallow in this area had reached several thousand in number and in 1945 1368 were shot. It now numbers only a few animals.

Other Fallow herds in the North Island are found at Wanganui, Tauranga, the south Kaipara peninsula near Auckland, and in one or two other areas.

In the South Island a number of Fallow liberations have been made, the first taking place in 1864 when three deer from Richmond Park, Surrey, were released in the Aniseed Valley near Nelson and where their descendants still remain. A few Fallow deer are to be found in the vicinity of Fairlie, about 35 miles (56 km) west of Timaru in South Canterbury. Their territory is principally on farm land. There are also moderate concentrations of Fallow deer around the north end of Lake Wakatipu.

One of the best herds in the South Island is to be found in the Blue Mountains near Tapanui in Otago and at the present time about 1000 deer are killed annually in this district. A small herd is also to be found on the Paparoa Range, which is situated in North Westland.

The bucks go to rut about March and this will continue until about mid-May. Antlers are shed during the latter part of October and early November, the older bucks casting first.

The Wanganui Fallow would seem to offer the best potential for stalking in the North Island, and even though they are subjected to considerable hunting pressure, they continue to spread their range, particularly in a westward direction. However, there is considerable diversity of land use in this area, for much of the habitat is private farm land, scenic reserve, Maori land or Crown land, so intending hunters may have to obtain permission from more than one party before entry.

In the South Island the best prospects for hunting are in the Blue Mountains of Otago – an area which is entirely State forest – and hunting therein is administered by the Forest Service. The whole of this State forest has been divided into thirty-five separate hunting areas, which vary in size from about 1000 to 2000 acres (404 to 808 hectares) and thus the hunting pressure in any one area is restricted.

In the Woodhill State Forest near Auckland, owing to forestry activity, hunting permits are issued only for non-working days between 1 May and 30 September, and owing to the great demand are for one day only and are issued by ballot, hunting parties being restricted to three in number.

Although the Blue Mountains have probably produced more trophy heads than any other area, in recent years some of the best trophies have come out of the Greenstone area, which lies on the north-west side of Lake Wakatipu in Central Otago.

White-tailed deer *Odocoileus virginianus*

The first White-tailed deer to reach New Zealand were two pairs which were released in the Takaka Valley, north-west of Nelson in 1901, and were followed four years later by a consignment of twenty-two deer which were purchased from New Hampshire, United States of America, and all but three survived the long sea journey. These deer, which presumably were *O.v.borealis* were released into three localities – nine (two bucks and seven does) at Port Pegasus, Stewart Island; nine in the Rees Valley on the north-west side of Lake Wakatipu, South Island, and the remaining animal, a buck, was liberated in the Takaka Valley to join up with those previously released there. It was not long before the Rees Valley and Stewart Island White-tailed deer became well established, but it seems that those in the Takaka Valley only survived a few years. There have been no liberations of White-tailed deer in the North Island.

During the early years the Whitetail on Stewart Island, which extends to about 425,000 acres (172,000 hectares) kept mainly to the area around

159

Mason Bay and south of Paterson Inlet, but have now spread to practically all the western portions of the island except the Ruggedy Mountains and Mount Anglem in the north, the latter rising to some 3214 ft (980 metres). The majority keep near the coastal belt, and in the evening or early morning a number of them can be seen feeding out on to the shore to eat seaweed.

By 1920 the White-tailed deer on Stewart Island, which until then had been afforded complete protection, were sufficiently numerous for harvesting, and so in that year the first hunting licences were granted. Hunting by licence holders, however, did not keep pace with the increase, and as a result the Government started, in 1930, a number of control shooting operations, both against Red deer and White-tailed deer and this continued, spasmodically, for the next twenty-three years, when a 'bounty' was introduced in an effort to encourage the private hunter to increase his kill. It seems to have failed to produce the desired effect, and so after five years, was abandoned in 1958.

Whitetail bucks go to the rut about May, which is about a month after the Red deer rut on Stewart Island. Antlers are shed during October and November, a few weeks before the fawns are born.

Hunting Whitetail on Stewart Island is tough going, as most of the island away from the beaches is covered by dense bush interspersed by dangerous waterways. The weather can also be very unpredictable with sudden storms raging in from the Antarctic and snow in the mountains during the winter. The sandflies can also make life pretty intolerable at times.

Although land tenure on Stewart Island includes State forest, Crown land, Maori and private land, the majority of permits to hunt there are issued by the Conservator of Forests, New Zealand Forest Service in Invercargill as well as by a resident forest ranger on the island. Permits are issued on an open basis, the old hunting block system having been discontinued. Stalking on private land is also available, and one agency in Victoria, Australia, was recently offering 'Stewart Island Safaris' for hunting Whitetail and Red deer on 10,000 acres (4000 hectares) of private land from 1 April to the end of June, at a price of about A$15 (about £7.50) per day.

There are a number of Forest Service huts dotted around the island which can be used as a base camp by hunting parties who prefer to have a roof of corrugated tin rather than canvas over their heads at night.

Shotguns and low-power .22 rim fire rifles are not permitted on the Island.

Rusa deer *Cervus timorensis*

In 1907 eight Rusa deer – probably *C.t.russa* – were obtained from Noumea in New Caledonia and in January of the following year were released at Galatea in the foothills of the Urewera Range, which lies south-east of Rotorua in North Island. Rusa deer are not indigenous to New Caledonia, the original animals having been introduced from Java about 1870. It is probable, therefore, that the Rusa deer in Galatea are *C.t.russa*. Their distribution is generally limited to the area of liberation, being bounded in the south by the Whirinaki river, in the north by Waiohau State Forest, and in the east and

Above Mule deer buck.
(*Leonard Lee Rue III.*)

Left Black-tailed buck – a close
relative of the Mule deer.
(*Leonard Lee Rue III.*)

Bow hunter aiming at Whitetail buck from a tree. (*Leonard Lee Rue III.*)

Hunting in British Columbia. *Above* bringing back a Caribou trophy to camp and *below* caping out a large Moose head shot by the author.

Trophy exhibitions frequently take place in Europe, and at some of the larger ones, several thousand trophies have to be assessed under the appropriate C.I.C. formula. This picture shows some of the Red deer trophies awaiting assessment at Nitra, Czechoslovakia, 1980.

The world record Red deer – *C.e. hippelaphus* – trophy from Romania – shot by N. Ceausesu in 1980 – with a C.I.C. score of 261.25 points.

The best recorded Red deer trophy from south-west England, killed by accident in 1950, with a score of 224.50 C.I.C. points.

The world record Roe deer – *C.c. capreous* – trophy from Hungary – shot by Lajos Cseterki in 1965 – with a C.I.C. score of 228.68 points.

A well-pearled Roe trophy from Perthshire, shot by P Wilson in 1976, with a provisional score of 203.6 C.I.C. points, is probably the best head taken in Scotland this century.

This massive antlered Roe buck, shot by Major Hon. P Baillie in Hampshire in 1974, has been provisionally assessed at 238.55 C.I.C. points – the highest on record.

Siberian Roe head – *C.c. pygargus* – with 'typical' forked back tine (C.I.C. score 246,40 points).

Peruke Roe head – a malformation
caused by injury to the testicle.

The world record Fallow buck trophy –
D.d. dama from Hungary – shot by Janos
Kadar in 1972 – with a C.I.C. score of
220.31 points.

Good Japanese Sika trophy (*C.n.
nippon*) from Rundhof/Schleswig in
north Germany.

'Typical' trophy of Reeves Muntjac
(*M. reevesi*).

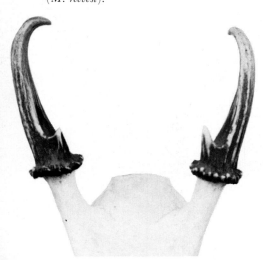

The world record Elk trophy – *A. a. alces* – from U.S.S.R. – shot in 1934 – with a C.I.C. score of 415.90 points.

A magnificent Elk trophy – *A. a. cameloides* – from Kamchatka, eastern Siberia – C.I.C. score 495.50 points.

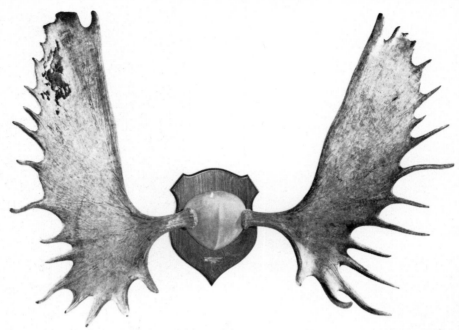

A fine Canadian Moose trophy – *A. a. americana* – shot at Cold Fish Lake, British Columbia, in 1974 by George and Phil Halvorson (Boone and Crockett score $219\frac{1}{8}$). (*Boone & Crockett Club.*)

The world record Alaskan–Yukon Moose trophy – *A. a. gigas* – shot at McGrath, Alaska, in 1978 by Kenneth Best (Boone and Crockett score 255). (*Boone & Crockett Club.*)

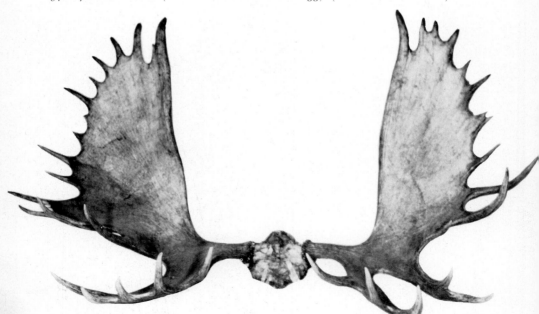

west by the Whakatane River and Kaingaroa State Forest respectively. Their habitat is mainly scrubland, consisting of manuka, toetoe and bracken, adjacent to farmlands, although a few are found in true forest. They are extremely shy and retiring, and like the Sambar seldom leave cover before nightfall.

The rut, which apparently only lasts about two or three weeks, generally commences about mid-July and may extend into early August.

Due to their habitat and nocturnal habits, stalking Rusa during daylight hours in the bush cannot be very rewarding, and most success has been achieved by watching, at dawn and dusk, places where the deer leave or re-enter the bush after a night of foraging on adjacent farmlands. Spotlighting at night on open farmland can also be very successful at times, but few farmers now permit this form of hunting.

Permits for hunting in either the State forest areas or Urewera National Park can be obtained from the New Zealand Forest Service in Rotorua. The Ureweru National Park is not divided into specific hunting blocks, so any hunting permit for the park – which extends for a maximum period of one month – automatically includes the area inhabited by Rusa deer.

Sambar *Cervus unicolor unicolor*

The first Sambar to reach New Zealand were a pair from Sri Lanka which were released in the Manawatu/Rangitikei district, north of Wellington in 1875, and descendants of these animals still remain in the area but they are not plentiful. Other Sambar were subsequently liberated to the Rotorua district, as well as near the Waikato River, south of Auckland, and whilst the former managed to establish themselves and still remain there today, the deer around Waikato were soon shot out by local hunters. All Sambar releases were made in the North Island.

As elsewhere in the world, the Sambar rut does not seem to follow any fixed pattern and may occur at any time between May and December, with most activity occurring during the period June to August. Although stags with antlers in velvet have been seen during any time of the year, the best chance of shooting one in hard antler would seem to be between April and September.

Throughout most of the day the Sambar lie up in thick cover which they are loathe to leave unless literally walked upon. There are, therefore, few opportunities for a conventional stalk in daylight, and in consequence, spot lighting at night has been found to be the most productive method of bagging a Sambar. Another successful way is to have small areas of cover driven to one or two concealed rifles, whilst on private land, some hunters, armed with shotguns using solid slug, walk though suitable scrubland hoping to flush a deer and get a close-range shot at it. Shotguns, however, are *not* permitted in State forests.

Compared to Sambar trophies that have been obtained in India and Sri Lanka, New Zealand heads are small, and anything with antlers over 32 in. (81 cm) in length is considered good, the record being a trophy shot pre-1924 from Shannon near Foxton in the Manawatu region with a length of $39\frac{3}{4}$ in. (101 cm). One or two non-typical heads of up to ten points have occasionally been shot in Kaingaroa State Forest, Rotorua.

Moose *Alces alces andersoni*

Moose, which were first introduced from North America in 1899, with a second introduction in 1910, are barely holding their own in the Dusky Sound area of south-west South Island, and so far as is known, only about three or four bulls and two cows have been legally taken, the first bull being shot in 1929 by EJ Herrick.

The heavy rainfall and competition for available forage from Red deer, which were liberated in the Dusky Sound area in 1909, are believed to be the main reasons why the Moose has failed to establish itself.

It must be appreciated, therefore, that big game hunting in New Zealand for the overseas visitor can be extremely difficult, for not only must he compete with local hunters, both commercial and trophy, but also with a country that owing to its extremely rugged nature, requires a high degree of physical fitness. It must be about the only country in the world where there are no 'close seasons' and no bag limits on deer shot, and as a result, any person may shoot as many deer, at any season and just about anywhere he wishes, provided he is not trespassing on private property. The challenge is certainly there, but unless time and good fortune are on the side of the hunter, the results may be disappointing.

NEW CALEDONIA

In 1870 twelve Rusa deer *Cervus timorensis russa* from Java were liberated in New Caledonia – one of the largest islands in the Pacific, and the introduction was not only a success but within thirteen years there were already complaints of serious damage to crops, etc.

Forty years ago it was estimated that the Rusa population on the whole island – which is about 250 miles (402 km) long and 31 miles (50 km) wide, numbered some 225,000 animals, and at that time about 46,000 hides were being exported annually. By 1951 the number had fallen slightly to about 200,000, since when there has been a drastic reduction, a recent estimate (1979) suggesting that the total population is now only about 30,000 head – but still more than sufficient for hunting. Moreover, the law now reserves the deer for sport, and the sale of venison or other deer products is not permitted.

Much of New Caledonia, which has a semi-tropical climate, is not only extremely rugged but also covered by dense bush, which makes spying for trophy heads difficult. However, the country around Ouaco is more open and there is ample opportunity to select a deer from a distance with binoculars and plan a stalk.

Deer hunting is available all the year round, but the best time to hunt the stags is during the rut, which starts about the middle of July and continues for about two months. At this time of year the weather is normally dry, with temperatures about 22° to 25° C during the day, but dropping as low as 8° C at night.

The stags generally start to cast their antlers during January, so stags in hard antler can still be found until the end of the year, but by October the capes will have lost a lot of hair and in consequence will not be suitable for a full head mount.

Since about 1976 a Canadian by the name of Jack Shepherd has been taking out visiting sportsmen from Australia and New Zealand on guided hunts on the Lafleur ranch, Ouaco. These hunts, each of which lasts about four days, take place during the months of July, August and September, and cost (1979) about $A600 (about £300). There is no shortage of deer around Ouaco, for it is not unusual for upwards of 500 deer to be seen during the day's hunt. Many of the stags carry fine trophies – far better, on average – than those in New South Wales, Australia – but with so many to choose from, selecting the best can be a problem to any hunter anxious to shoot his first Rusa.

An average trophy head from New Caledonia will measure about 30 to 32 in. (about 76–81 cm) in length, and under the Douglas scoring system score about 195 to 205 points. A really top class trophy, however, might make 37 in. (94 cm) and have a Douglas Score of around 230. The best one so far taken on the Lafleur ranch had a score of 241.6 Douglas points.

Recently, an area of about 2470 acres (1000 hectares) on the Lafleur ranch has been surrounded by a 6-foot (1.8 metres) deer proof fence and a number of exotic species introduced, with the intention of providing exotic game hunting for visiting sportsmen, as is currently being practised on the game ranches of Texas (*see page 262–6*). Already the Reserve, in addition to Rusa deer, contains Fallow deer, Red deer, Sika deer and Chital, and in the near future it is intended to add Blackbuck and Aoudad (Barbary sheep). At present numbers of each species are being allowed to build up, but by the mid-eighties it is hoped that the first trophy heads will be available for hunting.

At present it is not permitted to bring a firearm into New Caledonia, but rifles are available at the Lafleur ranch for visiting sportsmen to use.

Part III
THE AMERICAS

6 Hunting and Stalking the Deer of North America

North America, and in particular Alaska, British Columbia and Yukon, offer some of the finest hunting obtainable anywhere in the world, for in addition to several species of deer, fine hunting after wild sheep, Rocky Mountain goat and bear is also available. In this vast continent, particularly in the far north, there are millions of acres of uninhabited wild country, some of it only accessible by float plane or pack horse. Much of this wild terrain is divided into Big Game Management Zones, and in those areas where hunting is permitted, arrangements to do so can only be made through a licensed outfitter, thus ensuring that not more than one hunting party is out in any one area at the same time and the game is not over-cropped. Needless to say, there are vast areas in Canada still largely unexplored by the non-resident hunter, and it is only in comparatively recent years that outfitters have been sending parties into Yukon and the Northwest Territories.

Although it is correct to describe all species of the *Cervidae* as 'deer', when anyone speaks about hunting deer in North America it invariably refers to the pursuit of Whitetail, Mule or Black-tailed deer and not Moose, Caribou or Wapiti (Elk), which complete the indigenous species that frequent the North American continent. Moreover, you will seldom hear the word 'Wapiti' used in the States, for this large relative of the European Red deer is called an 'Elk' – a name which should strictly be reserved for the European Moose – *Alces alces alces*. However, in view of the increasing number of American sportsmen visiting Scandinavia for hunting, the Elk and Reindeer of Norway are now frequently referred to as Moose and European Caribou respectively.

Quite apart from the cost of outfitting a hunt in these remote areas, one must be prepared to spend at least three weeks on the trip – in fact, many outfitters stipulate that the minimum time for a hunt in areas like the Cassiar in British Columbia or in parts of Yukon Territory is twenty-one days, but if extra time can be spared, a full month is recommended. Quite obviously, the longer the hunt, the better chance there is of finding trophy animals in areas that have been too far distant for the 'short-duration' hunter. Irrespective of whether the trip is of one, two, three or four weeks duration, the cost of travel to reach the hunting ground remains the same, and although a longer stay will increase the overall cost of the hunt, if by doing so a really worthwhile trophy can be taken instead of just an ordinary one, or perhaps none at all, the money has been well spent.

Unfortunately not all hunting in North America can be enjoyed in such solitude, for hunting in the more accessible parts of the United States, particularly during the first few days of the deer hunting season, can be like opening day of the winter sales in one of our towns or cities, with every hunter queuing up to get a shot, which may result in not every hunter returning home alive! In fact, just as there are people who keep out of town during sales week so are there those who give the woods a miss during the early days of the deer hunting season.

Although many resident hunters, particularly when after Mule or Black-tailed deer, and to a lesser extent after Wapiti, organize their own hunt, for a non-resident hunter it is essential that he should be accompanied by a good guide, and probably a packer as well – a service which is supplied by a licensed outfitter. Indeed, in many western States and Canadian Provinces or Territories the use of a resident guide by a non-resident hunter is mandatory, and although the service may cost money, it improves the chance of success considerably. A few years ago a survey was made by Byron W. Dalrymple and revealed that among Wapiti hunters the success of guided non-residents, over a three-year period, averaged out at 97 percent as compared to 25 to 40 percent of the non-guided resident hunters. The obvious advantage of being accompanied by a *competent* resident guide is that he knows the country and where game is most likely to be found, thus avoiding precious holiday time being wasted by a hunter who would otherwise have to seek out such information for himself.

I say *competent*, for the increasing interest in hunting North American game by overseas visitors has inevitably produced a number of bogus outfitters and guides anxious to step in on the bandwaggon and so make a fast buck or two before the protests of disappointed clients eventually drive them out of business. True, in some States and most Provinces and Territories, outfitters have to be licensed by law, and although no stringent credentials are required, the chances are that most licensed ones will be reliable.

Some years ago, in order to combat these fly-by-night outfitters, Idaho set up a State agency called the Idaho Outfitters and Guide Licence Board, whereby all guides and outfitters within the State had to be licensed by law. As a result, a licence could be revoked at any time for fraudulent advertising, failure to perform a contract, or for 'immoral, unethical, or dishonourable conduct in the licensee's relations to a guest or patron'. It is now general practice for guides to be licensed and this has undoubtedly improved the standard of guiding. A licence, however, will not, overnight, turn a poor guide into a good one, for some can never make top grade.

Guides, however, are not mandatory in the United States of America, though some landowners may require non-residents to have a guide when hunting on their land. In Wyoming, a non-resident hunting a 'designated wilderness area' is, however, required to have either a resident acting as a guide, or a licensed professional guide.

In Alaska, non-residents are required to have a guide, or be accompanied by an Alaskan resident over 19 years of age 'within the second degree of kindred' when hunting brown/grizzly bear and Dall sheep, but not deer. No visiting sportsman to Alaska, however, should ever consider hunting there without a guide.

Having decided on what game to hunt, and in which State, Province or Territory the hunt is to be made, application should be made to the appropriate Game Department (*see Appendix B*) for a list of licensed guides and outfitters, on receipt of which enquiries should be directed to at least three so that a comparison can be made between prices and facilities etc. offered. Reference should also be obtained, where possible, from other sportsmen for whom the outfitter or guide has previously arranged a hunt. It is essential, also, to ascertain in writing *exactly* what the outfitter will provide, and also whether the charge includes hunting licences and permits. Normally a pack-trip outfitter should provide everything except the hunter's personal gear. It is essential that any arrangements to hunt must be made with the outfitter well in advance, for *good* guides are relatively few, and consequently get booked up. This particularly applies to areas of northern British Columbia, Yukon and the Northwest Territories, for hunting in some of these more remote areas has in the past been considered too difficult and expensive for the average hunter to reach, and it is only in recent years that outfitters have paid much attention to the last two mentioned Territories.

Dalrymple (1974) gives a word of warning about the so-called 'guaranteed hunts', for it is difficult to know whether the guarantee ends at the shot, which could be taken at any range from 50 to 500 yards (45 to 450 metres) if the guide so insists, or only when the trophy is obtained. True, most of these 'guaranteed trophy' hunts are after such game as Mountain lion, bear or boar, but what the hunter does not know, states Dalrymple 'is that after he and the guide have undergone a certain amount, but not too much, of riding or searching, usually with a pack of hounds, a captive animal is released from a hidden pen and a short chase begins and the target is brought to bay.' I cannot imagine, however, that any guide will have a trophy Moose or Caribou hidden away somewhere for release when his client is starting to show signs of fatigue!

In addition to the use of modern weapons, there is an increasing interest throughout North America for hunting with primitive weapons, which include the bow and arrow, handgun and the muzzle loader, and in those States and Provinces where this form of hunting is permitted, certain regulations have been drawn up.

The typical deer of North America are Moose, Caribou, Wapiti (Elk), Mule deer, Black-tailed deer and White-tailed deer, and all are legal game in both Canada and the United States of America. British Columbia, however, is the only Province in which all six may be found.

In addition to the indigenous species of deer, hunting of exotics is available in some of the extensive game ranches of Texas and New Mexico and elsewhere (*see Chapter 10*).

167

Anyone anxious of seeking a trophy head of any species should study Appendix A as well as the latest edition of *Records of North American Big Game* (1981), and find out the areas which have yielded the best trophies in recent years. It might then be possible to contact, via the appropriate Fish and Game Department (*see Appendix*) the outfitter responsible for the area, and ascertain what the prospect of a trophy hunt might be.

Wapiti *Cervus canadensis*

Wapiti – the Red deer of North America which the Americans call 'Elk' – is the second largest deer in the world, with good bulls standing over 5 ft (152 cm) at the shoulder and exceptional beasts weighing well over 1000 lb (545 kg) live weight. Unlike the Red deer, however, male and female Wapiti are referred to as bull and cow instead of stag and hind, but calf is correct for the young of both species.

During the seventeenth century the Wapiti was one of the most widely distributed deer in North America, with a range stretching from the Pacific Ocean in the west to almost the Atlantic in the east, and from about what is now Mexico and Georgia in the south to northern Alberta in Canada. At this period it was estimated that its population may have been about 10 million head. Three centuries later it was on the verge of extinction for during the latter part of the last century a great slaughter took place, first by the hide hunters and then at the close of the century by 'tusk hunters' who killed the bulls just for the sake of their canine teeth, for which there was a profitable market among members of the Elk's Lodge who had them mounted in gold caps and wore them suspended from their watch chains. The canine teeth of Red deer – referred to as *Grandeln* in Europe – are likewise much prized by the European hunter.

Eventually this wanton slaughter was checked, but not before the typical race *C.c.canadensis* which frequented the eastern parts of North America and Merriam's Wapiti *C.c.meriami* of Arizona and northern Mexico had become extinct, and the Wapiti elsewhere had disappeared from about 90 percent of its former range.

Now, as a result of introductions during the present century, many of the former haunts of the Wapiti have been repopulated, and by 1955 the Wapiti was present in over twenty States of the United States as well as in parts of Canada, principally in the national parks.

Over the whole of North America, including Canada, four subspecies are represented as follows: Roosevelt's or Olympic Wapiti *C.c.roosevelti* in the coastal regions of the west from Vancouver Island in the north to California in the south; the Rocky Mountain Wapiti *C.c.nelsoni*, which is the most plentiful in North America, its principal range being centred around the Rocky Mountain chain from south-western Alberta and south-east British Columbia in the north to New Mexico in the south; the Saskatchewan Wapiti *C.c.manitobensis* which has a restricted distribution in southern Saskatchewan and south-west Manitoba; and the small Tule or Dwarf Wapiti *C.c.nannodes* of

Map 19   The range of Wapiti *Cervus canadensis* in North America.

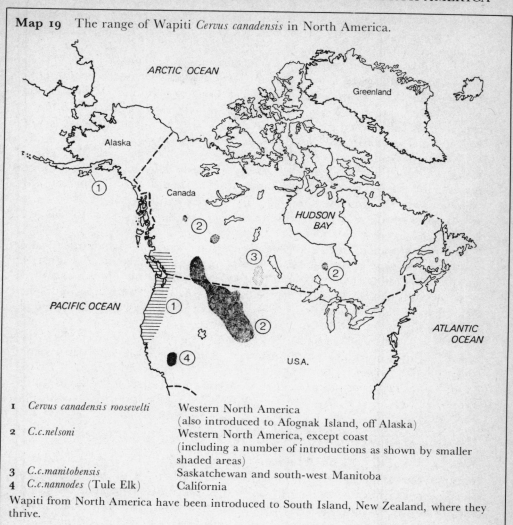

1	*Cervus canadensis roosevelti*	Western North America (also introduced to Afognak Island, off Alaska)
2	*C.c.nelsoni*	Western North America, except coast (including a number of introductions as shown by smaller shaded areas)
3	*C.c.manitobensis*	Saskatchewan and south-west Manitoba
4	*C.c.nannodes* (Tule Elk)	California

Wapiti from North America have been introduced to South Island, New Zealand, where they thrive.

California, which has a population of only about 650 and is totally protected.

Life cycle of the Wapiti

The rut starts in September and reaches its peak about the end of the month. Just prior to the rut – about the last week in August – the bulls start their distinctive bugling, and this will continue until the end of October, by which time most bulls will have finished with the rut. Intermittent bugling may, however, still be heard during early November.

The Wapiti, similar to the Red deer, is a polygamous animal and during the rut the older bulls round up as many cows as they are able to hold against local opposition. As a result, battles between males are of fairly frequent occurrence.

The calves, normally only one, are born mainly in June.

In some parts of its range, and in particular in the more mountainous districts, the Wapiti can be considered as a migratory animal for the snows of winter soon make it abandon its summer range for lower altitudes. In many areas the Wapiti, when journeying from summer to winter territory, follow well-defined migration routes. They are good swimmers.

Although Wapiti usually herd in winter, they do not 'yard' like White-tailed deer, for their extra size and strength enable them to press on through heavy snow. They have few predators, and although a few – principally weaker ones or calves – will be taken by wolves, mountain lions or coyotes, winter starvation – generally brought on by over-population – is the biggest killer.

By mid-March most of the older bulls will have cast their antlers, and growth of the new antler should be complete by about the end of August. A typical bull's antlers – or 'rack' as it is called in America – should have six tines or points, but heads with as many as nineteen tines have been recorded. The Americans today also refer to the brow and bay tines, which old timers used to call 'dog-killers' or 'war-tines', as 'lifters'.

A typical feature of Wapiti antlers is the placing of the top tines, called 'sur-royals', which normally point upwards in the same plane as the beam. Occasionally, however, these upper tines will terminate in a crown or cup, similar to a Red deer, and this is most apparent on trophies of Roosevelt's Wapiti as well as in areas where Red and Wapiti have interbred, such as in New Zealand.

Hunting Wapiti

Although Wapiti may often be seen near the roads which pass through the national parks, such as in Yellowstone or Banff where, with the exception of the Grand Teton National Park in Wyoming, hunting is prohibited, elsewhere they become extremely elusive once the hunting season has commenced, and take refuge in the remote mountainous country well away from the highways. Hunting, however, is permitted in the Grand Teton National Park but by the time the hunters are in the area the tourists have mostly departed. There seems little doubt that this practice has been to the benefit of both hunter and hunted, and could well be extended to other national parks.

The summer range of the Wapiti is generally around the 8000 to 10,000 ft (about 3000 metres) altitude, and provided the weather remains fairly open, they will remain at this level throughout the rut. In late September and early October, however, the weather can be very unpredictable in the mountains.

Just prior to the commencement of the hunting season, Wapiti may be seen on pastures bordering the timber line, and in the more accessible areas their presence in these localities will not have escaped the notice of hunters, many of whom will probably take up a position in the locality on the day prior to the season opening, in the hope of getting an early shot before hunting pressure in the area will force the deer to move out. In fact, a few years ago I was in Wapiti terrain near Longview, Oregon, on the day prior to the opening of the hunting season, and a number of hunters were already setting up camp. When I was told that by morning there would be several hundred in the district all hoping to get a shot, I was thankful I was not to be one of them! Snow and blizzard conditions will often force the Wapiti to leave the high country and move into timbered areas where they can often be hunted by sportsmen operating from base camps accessible by mechanical transport.

For a non-resident it is essential and, indeed, in most areas mandatory, that he should be accompanied by a good guide and packer – a service which is supplied by a licensed outfitter. A good guide for sheep, mule or White-tailed deer will not necessarily mean that he is any good on Wapiti, so it is always advantageous to find out what success has been achieved by previous clients during the past two or three seasons. Really good Wapiti guides are in the minority, so in order to ensure getting the best available, all arrangements for the hunt should be made well in advance – and preferably during the previous season. Good packhorses are also at a premium, but if you have been able to fix up with a good guide, you can be pretty sure that he will not allow the hunt to be ruined by useless horses.

For hunting in heavy timber on steep hillsides, however, horses can be a handicap, particularly when there is snow about, but in other circumstances the horse can play an important role, not only to carry the hunter over a large and often rugged terrain, but also to bring out the trophy and venison. Some hunters dismount only when a Wapiti has been located, and the shot is to be taken. Others dismount when fresh tracks have been found, and then proceed to hunt on foot. This is obviously preferable, for not only is the approach more silent, but as soon as the beast has been spotted, less time will be wasted in taking a carefully placed shot. And for success, well-placed it must be, for a Wapiti is a large animal and can take a lot of punishment. It is extremely important, therefore, if a long and perhaps abortive chase after a wounded beast is to be avoided, that the first shot must be the last, for in many cases dense cover may prevent a second one being speedily taken.

During the rutting season the sound of a bull bugling will often be the first indication that Wapiti are in the vicinity, and at this time of year, a travelling bull can always be expected. In mountainous country, therefore, time spent watching from a good spy point, any grassy clearing or sparsely wooded hillside is time well spent, for sooner or later a bull will appear, and if out of shot, give the opportunity for a stalk or 'still hunt', should it move into denser cover.

During the rut it is possible, as with many other species of deer, to attract bulls to the area of the hunter by imitating their call. Commercial whistles are available in sporting stores, but many hunters prefer to make their own.

A calling place should be selected that allows a large area to be watched, and where the sound will carry. It is, apparently, most effective early in the season and in areas that have not been heavily hunted. Opinions vary, however, as to the value of this method of hunting, and there are those who 'feel that its only good for calling up other hunters!' and it has occasionally resulted in a fatality at the hands of a trigger-happy hunter.

A hunt during the rut has to be carefully timed, for latitude can affect the dates. Weather, too, can play an important part.

In some areas, however, the Wapiti hunting season does not open until 1 November, by which time the rut will be over, so 'calling' would then be unproductive. In the United States, with few exceptions, the bag limit per hunter is one Wapiti, irrespective of sex. During the bull Wapiti season, only male animals 'with visible antlers' may be shot, but in either-sex seasons, any animal may be taken. On several occasions unlimited Wapiti licences for bulls only have been permitted in New Mexico where the annual cull is about 1000 to 1500 animals.

Some States such as Washington, in addition to areas which are open to all Wapiti hunters, have other zones which are reserved for permit holders only. Anyone wishing to obtain a permit must apply not later than 1 September at any Game Department office, and about three weeks later the draw will be made, at which all applicants may attend. In 1977 some 6550 permits were issued to Wapiti hunters, the largest number in any one hunting unit being 600. These numbers alone give some indication of the destiny of hunters that are about during the hunting season. Anyone drawing a permit for a controlled Wapiti season is not permitted to apply for another permit until after the next two succeeding seasons, and anyone found applying for a permit during this period will automatically be disqualified for an additional two years.

The best trophies are produced by the Rocky Mountain Wapiti, the majority being shot in Montana. Good heads have also come out of Alberta, Colorado, Idaho and Wyoming, but trophies from British Columbia are disappointing and none can find a place in the Record Book. The same is also true of heads from Vancouver Island.

So far as Roosevelt's Olympic Wapiti is concerned, the best trophies have come from Oregon State, and in particular Grant Co. Trophies of the Manitoba Wapiti are similar in size to Roosevelt's and most of the best trophies have been taken in the Duck Mountains of Manitoba.

Success in Wapiti hunting is probably lower than in any other hunt after deer in North America, and Byron W Dalrymple (1974) suggests that in any given year 'not more than one out of five, sometimes less, will bag an Elk'. Statistics kept by several game departments show, however, that hunters with guides are invariably more successful than those hunting on their own.

The Wapiti is certainly not a scarce animal in many parts of its distribution – in fact its total population in North America must be around the half million mark, of which about 90,000 to 100,000 of both sexes will probably be shot annually by hunters. Quite apart from those frequenting the national parks, a considerable area of Wapiti territory, although open to hunting, cannot be reached due to the fact that it may be adjacent to private lands through which access is not allowed. Of course, the pressure of hunting in the more accessible areas obviously reduces the chance of success, thus restricting the manner of the hunt, for it can happen that the same bull may be the target of two or more hunting parties – not a very inviting prospect for any hunter!

For success, therefore, it is essential to pack out as far away from civilization as time and money will allow.

For approximate hunting seasons of the Wapiti, see pages 213–4 for Canada and pages 238–40 for the United States of America. Seasonal dates, however, vary from year to year, and up-to-date information for any particular area can only be supplied by the Fish and Game Department of the State, Province or Territory concerned (*see Appendix B*).

Moose *Alces alces*

The Moose, a close relation of the Elk *A.a.alces* of northern Europe, is the largest living deer in the world, with exceptional specimens from Alaska weighing up to 1800 lb (816 kg).

The Moose has a much wider range in North America than the Wapiti though numerically, in any one area, Moose density is never as high as that reached by Wapiti in parts of their range. The total Moose population is probably around the half-million mark, of which about two-thirds will be in Canada.

In Canada the Moose – which is an old Algonquin name – occurs in all the mainland provinces except the northern half of the Labrador peninsula. It was introduced to Newfoundland in 1878 but is absent from the other larger islands situated around Canada's coastline except Cape Breton, off Nova Scotia, where several introductions have taken place and recent reports suggest they are on the increase.

During the present century the Moose has extended its range, particularly in a northerly and westerly direction, at the expense of the more central parts of its former range, and this has resulted in the Moose being numerous in parts of northern Alberta, British Columbia and Yukon, whilst in the area between Lake Winnipeg and the Great Slave Lake of Mackenzie it is much less numerous than formerly. In British Columbia the average annual harvest of Moose killed in recent years has been about 20,000 to 25,000 whilst in Alberta and Yukon it has been about 15,000 and 800 respectively.

In 1968 it was estimated that Ontario had a Moose population of about 125,000 animals, with a ratio of identified bulls to cows of about one to two. In 1970 the legal Moose kill amounted to about 12,300, a quarter of which were taken by non-residents.

In the United States by far the greatest density of Moose is found in Alaska, and it is from this area that the largest trophy bulls have come. Here the Moose has almost unlimited excellent range, extending from the Peninsula to the Brooks Range and the Arctic Slope.

173

Map 20 The range of Moose *Alces alces* in North America.

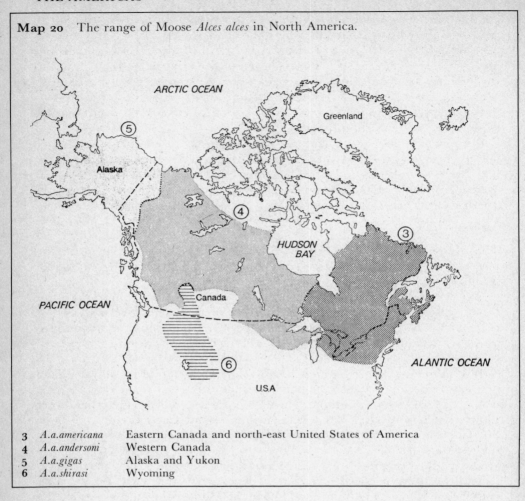

3	*A.a.americana*	Eastern Canada and north-east United States of America
4	*A.a.andersoni*	Western Canada
5	*A.a.gigas*	Alaska and Yukon
6	*A.a.shirasi*	Wyoming

Within the Rockies, Wyoming has the largest Moose population, and the average seasonal kill will be around the 1000 mark – which is about a tenth of the number being harvested each year in Alaska.

The Moose of North America are divided into four subspecies, distributed as follows.

1 The Eastern Moose *A.a.americana*

This Moose, which has a shoulder height of around 70 to 72 in. (about 180 cm) frequents those Provinces to the east of and including part of Ontario. These include Quebec, Labrador, Newfoundland, Nova Scotia and New Brunswick, whilst the State of Maine now has a small but expanding Moose population. This Moose also has a limited distribution in the State of New Hampshire and Vermont.

One of the best Eastern Moose trophies taken in recent years was a 27-pointer shot in Quebec Province in 1949, with a spread of 65 in. (165.1 cm) (B & C Score $211\frac{4}{8}$).

2 The Western Moose *A.a.andersoni*

This type has the widest distribution in North America, extending from British Columbia and Yukon in the west, to Manitoba and probably western Ontario in the east, after which it is replaced by *A.a.americana*. In the extreme south-eastern part of its range, the States of Michigan (including Isle Royale) and Minnesota are included.

The best trophy, shot in Alberta in 1960, was a 22-pointer with a spread of 60 inches (152.4 cm) (B&C 225).

3 The Wyoming or Shiras Moose *A.a.shirasi*

This Moose is restricted to the Rocky Mountains, from southern British Columbia and Alberta in Canada to Wyoming, Utah, Idaho and Montana in the United States of America, being most plentiful in the first mentioned State where approximately 1200 animals will be taken in a season. Trophies of the Shiras Moose are not so large as the other types, and any head with a spread of about 55 in. (140 cm) is good, whilst over 60 in. (152 cm) is quite exceptional.

4 The Alaskan Moose *A.a.gigas*

This is the largest, both in body and antler, of the four types of Moose to be found in North America, with large bulls standing as high as $6\frac{1}{2}$ ft (200 cm) at the shoulder, and antlers with a 74 in (188 cm) spread being not uncommon. It occurs in all suitable localities throughout Alaska, extending its range into south-west Yukon and north-west British Columbia. Comparing the present-day distribution of Moose in Alaska with a century ago, it would appear that whereas the Moose was formerly concentrated in the interior away from the coast, the position today is rather the reverse, and we find the species present in many coastal regions where, half a century ago, it was unknown, whilst many of its former haunts are now practically deserted. Indeed, at the beginning of the last century the Moose was almost unheard of in Alaska, and yet today it can be described as plentiful, with an annual harvest of about 10,000 animals.

Between 1949 and 1957 a number of calves were caught up from the Kenai Peninsula and general Anchorage area, and released in the Copper River Delta area near Cordova. Survival and reproduction was good, and a limited harvest of this newly established herd was initiated in the fall of 1960, when twenty-five bulls were shot. There was no hunting in 1961 but in the following year twenty-five bulls were again taken.

Life cycle of the Moose

The rut of the Moose in North America commences about the middle of September, and will last about a month. At this season, when a bull is following a cow, it will often utter a succession of low grunts. When in season, the cow will also make a few low, vibrant calls. At all other times of the year adult Moose are normally silent.

During the rut the bulls will frequently fight with each other for the favours of a cow, and the sound of crashing antlers can often be heard over a wide distance. Indeed, it was the sound of battle that enabled me to shoot a large bull with a 60-in. (152.4-cm) spread of antlers in British Columbia. We first heard the clashing of antlers late one afternoon, whilst setting up camp, but there was insufficient daylight left to allow a hunt that evening. The following morning the bulls were still at it – or it may have been a new opponent – and it continued on and off for the next hour, by which time we had made our approach and a shot from my .30–06 brought an abrupt end to the fight.

During the rutting season the matured bulls will paw out small depressions or wallows and after urinating in them several times, will have a good roll. Cows will also use the wallows, and after rolling in them, like the bulls, will emerge covered in mud.

By the end of the year the older bulls will have started to shed their antlers, but new growth will not commence until the spring. It may be February or early March, however, before the younger bulls will shed. Once started, the growth of the antler continues at a remarkable rate, and before the end of August the older bulls will be rubbing their antlers, now hard, against shrubs and trees to remove the velvet.

Moose are excellent swimmers and there are numerous records of them having swum distances of up to eight or nine miles (13 to 14 km) whilst crossing bays and lakes. Although Moose are browsers, they are very fond of aquatic vegetation and frequently have their heads completely submerged for thirty seconds or more whilst feeding on vegetation growing below the surface. Peterson (1955)* even records that they will 'occasionally dive for plants in water over 18 ft (549 cm) deep'.

In the depth of winter, when the snow gets really deep, several animals may congregate together if a good supply of food is available, and up to twenty animals have been reported in such gatherings, but this is unusual. The presence of several animals moving from one area to another in deep snow causes well-defined tracks to be cut through the snow and creates what is known as a 'Moose-yard'. 'Yarding', however, is a temporary situation, and as soon as the food runs out, the gatherings disperse. At other times of the year one seldom sees any number of Moose together, although just prior to the rut, several bulls may congregate in one area for a short time.

Moose hunting

For a hunter anxious to get a really big trophy, there is no question that his best chance of success would be a trip to Alaska or north-west British Columbia, but he must be accompanied by a guide familiar with the country.

Most Moose hunting in North America, and particularly in Canada and

* Peterson, Randolph L (1955), *North American Moose*

A fine Wyoming or Shiras Moose head – *A. a. shirasi* – from Madison County, Idaho, shot by Vicki Grover in 1976 (Boone and Crockett score $188\frac{4}{8}$). (*Boone & Crockett Club.*)

The third largest Wapiti antlers – *C. c. nelsoni* – shot in 1977 by Clarence Brown in Panther River district, Alberta (Boone and Crockett score $419\frac{5}{8}$). (*Boone & Crockett Club.*)

The world record Reindeer trophy – *R. tarandus* – from the U.S.S.R. with a C.I.C. score of 989.0 points.

A fine Barren-ground Caribou trophy – *R. t. groenlandicus* – from Becharof Lake area, Alaska, shot in 1978 by Kenneth Best (Boone and Crockett score 456 $\frac{1}{8}$). (*Boone & Crockett Club.*)

The world record Woodland Caribou trophy – *R. t. caribou* – shot by H. Casimir DeRham in Newfoundland prior to 1910 (Boone and Crockett score $419\frac{5}{8}$). (*Boone & Crockett Club.*)

The world record Mountain Caribou trophy – *R. t. caribou* – shot near Turnagain River, British Columbia, in 1976 by Garry Beaubien (Boone and Crockett score 452). (*Boone & Crockett Club.*)

The world record Mule deer trophy –
O. h. hemionus – ('typical' antlers) shot
in 1972 by Douglas Burris Jr in Dolores
County, Colorado (Boone and Crockett
score $225\frac{6}{8}$). (*Boone & Crockett Club.*)

Below left The third largest Mule deer
antlers (non-typical) – *O. h. californicus* –
shot in 1972 by Harold Ray Laird in
Mariposa County, California (Boone and
Crockett score $319\frac{4}{8}$). (*Boone & Crockett Club.*)

Below right A fine Columbia Blacktail
trophy – *O. h. columbianus* – shot in 1972
by G Scott Jennings in Jackson
County, Oregon (Boone and Crockett
score $160\frac{7}{8}$). (*Boone & Crockett Club.*)

A fine White-tailed deer trophy – *O. v. dacotensis* – from Missoula County, Montana, shot in 1974 by Thomas H Dellwo (Boone and Crockett score $199\frac{3}{8}$). (*Boone & Crockett Club.*)

The second largest White-tailed deer antlers ('non-typical') – *O. v. macrourus* – shot in Clay County, Iowa, in 1973 by Larry Reveling (Boone and Crockett score 282). (*Boone & Crockett Club.*)

A fine Coues' White-tailed deer antlers – *O. v. couesi* – from Pima County, Arizona, shot in 1975 by T Reed Scott (Boone and Crockett score $121\frac{1}{8}$). (*Boone & Crockett Club.*)

A good 'non-typical' Coues' White-tailed deer head – *O. v. couesi* – from Santa Cruz County, Arizona, shot in 1968 by Carlos G Touche (Boone and Crockett score 128). (*Boone & Crockett Club.*)

A fine Sambar deer trophy – *C. u. niger*
– from India – (C.I.C. score
517.90 points).

A good Rusa deer trophy – *C. t. russa* –
from North Island, New Zealand.
(C.I.C. score 293.20 points).

A good Axis deer trophy – *A. a. axis* –
from Madhya Pradesh, India, with
additional tines frequently grown at
base of brows (C.I.C. score 350.40 points).

A 'typical' Hog deer trophy – *A. p.
porcinus* – from India (C.I.C. score
173.20 points.)

A 'typical' Huemul – *H. bisulens* – from the Peruvian Andes. (C.I.C score 189.20 points.)

Pampas deer – *Ozotoceros bezoarticus bezoarticus* – antlers from Argentina (C.I.C. score 204.10 points.)

Marsh deer – *B. dichotomus* – antlers from Brazil. (C.I.C. score 417.00 points.)

Brown Brocket deer – *M. gouazoubira* – antlers from Argentina, shot by N Franco with a C.I.C. score of 32.40 points.

Swamp deer – *C. d. branderi* – shot early in the century by Col. A S Colley in Madhya Pradesh, India. (C.I.C. score 449.50 points.)

A 'typical' Hangul or Kashmir stag – *C. e. hanglu* – shot in Kashmir by Captain R Smales in 1919. (C.I.C. score 590.70 points.)

'Typical' Eld's deer *C. e. siamensis* antlers from Thailand (C.I.C. score 427.20 points.)

A fine pair of Père David's deer *E. davidianus* antlers from Woburn. (C.I.C. score 503.30 points.).

Alaska, is done from a horse, the hunter dismounting when a suitable beast has been selected. From then on it is a stalk in the conventional manner. The advantage of using a horse is that the hunter can cover considerably more territory in the day than could be accomplished on foot. Throughout the day frequent stops will be made to spy any large tracts of open hillside or valley in order to pick up any animal that may be browsing or on the move. Even when riding along in cover an animal may be encountered at fairly close range, and if in an area that has been subject to little or no hunting pressure, it will probably be little disturbed by the sight of a horse, and may remain in the vicinity sufficiently long for the hunter to dismount and take a shot if so desired.

In the eastern part of their range, where the terrain is less mountainous, calling during the rut is a favourite method of hunting Moose. So far as I am aware an artificial Moose call is one of the few animal lures which cannot be purchased from a sports outfitter, so the hunter has to improvise either by fashioning a type of megaphone made out of birch bark or similar material, or by calling through cupped hands. In common with many other species of deer, young males tend to lose their normal caution on hearing a call, and will recklessly rush up to the caller, whilst the older bulls will probably make a careful and quiet circle to test the wind before coming in too close. The best time for calling is probably late afternoon or evening.

As in Europe, when hunting deer from a *Hochsitz*, elevation is of considerable importance when calling Moose, for not only does sound carry further when made from an elevated position, but there is less chance of the hunter's scent reaching the deer. On occasions, therefore, the caller may climb a tree to make the first calls, whilst the hunter remains concealed on the ground.

In calling, one can either imitate the deep toned grunt of the male, or the quavering, drawn-out wail of the cow, which can at times, as with Red deer in Europe, be more effective than using the bull sound.

Another ruse to attract bulls is by rattling old antlers together, or thrashing the undergrowth with a stick in order to give the impression of a bull thrashing the bush with its antlers. It is often worthwhile to intersperse 'bull calling' with a bit of bush bashing.

I understand, however, that calling Moose is seldom, if ever, done in the Rockies or north-western part of its range. It is, however, sometimes practised in Yukon Territory.

In some areas Moose are killed by being driven out of thickets and clumps of timber through open terrain around which two or more hunters have been strategically posted, but this method is only possible when 'group hunting' is permitted, and is more for the meat than the trophy hunter.

Before the lakes and streams are frozen over, Moose can often be hunted very successfully from canoes but this can only be done in a country such as Ontario where a conglomeration of lakes connected by streams and channels allows the hunter to proceed over and spy a large tract of country. West of

Prince George in British Columbia, however, Moose hunting by boat or canoe can be enjoyed on Stuart Lake and other lakes in the area.

Calling, during the rut, from a canoe can often bring results, for away from the shore the sound of the call will be audible over a considerable distance, but as soon as the call is answered the canoe should be paddled as quickly and quietly as possible to a place of concealment along the shore. Hunting by canoe can be particularly useful in country that abounds in dense bush – otherwise a shot or even to get sight of Moose in such terrain would be almost an impossibility.

In addition to calling, another ploy sometimes used whilst hunting Moose from canoe is to keep splashing the water with the paddle so as to imitate the sound of an animal wading in shallow water whilst feeding.

In areas where there has been little hunting pressure it is not unusual to spot a Moose across a small lake, and even though it may have seen the canoe, will remain standing, and allow the canoe to approach within range for a shot. It would seem, therefore, that in much the same way as other game animals will often allow a close approach to be made by car or other transport, so does the Moose fail to associate danger coming from a canoe on a lake. At one time a successful way of hunting Moose was at night from canoes equipped with strong lights, but this practice is now illegal.

Hunter success depends very much on the area being hunted, for lack of access to many of the Moose's best haunts results in over-crowding of hunters in areas accessible by road, thus leaving vast areas well away from the highways completely unhunted. In Ontario, for instance, about 12,000 to 15,000 Moose will be killed each fall by the 50,000 to 60,000 licensed hunters which represents a hunter success of about one in four. For many years now about 70 to 80 percent of the entire Moose kill in Ontario has been taken during the first two weeks of the season which commences about the middle of September, when the weather is still pleasant for hunting and the bulls are on the move because of the rut. In less populated areas, with a good guide, success for a non-resident hunter should be almost 100 percent, but whether the bull has trophy antlers or not depends very much on patience, perseverance and luck. Until recently, hunters and guides looking for a really big head in Alaska used to cruise around in a light aeroplane, and having spotted one, land in the vicinity – a method of hunting that significantly reduced the proportion of large trophy bulls in the Moose population as a whole. Regulations have now put a stop to this practice for it is forbidden for hunters to shoot a Moose on the same day as being airborne.

Recently, some concern has been expressed in Ontario about the effect on Moose of hunters using power toboggans for access. These machines are used during the latter part of the season, mostly in December, when it is estimated that only about 10 to 20 percent of the total Moose harvest occurs, so it is concluded that any detrimental effect on the Moose population must be minimal. It is, of course, illegal to chase Moose or any deer with power toboggans.

In 1964 the Boone & Crockett Club decided to classify the Moose of North America, for record-keeping purposes only, into three categories based on geographical lines as follows.

1 Canadian Moose. This includes both the Western Canadian Moose *A.a.andersoni* and the eastern type *A.a.americana*. This category, therefore, covers all Moose from Newfoundland in the east to British Columbia in the west, but excludes any trophies taken in Alaska, Yukon or Northwest Territories which are classified as Alaska-Yukon Moose.

2 Alaska-Yukon Moose *A.a.gigas*. This group covers all trophies taken in Alaska, Yukon and Northwest Territories. It is realized that there are probably some pure examples of *A.a.gigas* in north-west British Columbia, but up to date no trophy has yet to come out of British Columbia even to qualify for inclusion in the Record Book.

3 Wyoming-Shiras Moose *A.a.shirasi*. Only animals taken south of the boundary between Canada and the United States are eligible for this category.

Of the above three categories, by far the largest trophy is produced by the Alaska-Yukon Moose, and the majority of best trophies have come from south-west Alaska and in particular from the Kenai and Alaska Peninsulae, but this is probably due to its accessibility from Anchorage. Recently, however, a number of new roads have been built on the peninsula by people prospecting for oil, so increased human activity in the area will doubtless affect the Moose population, and future trophy hunters would probably be well advised to go further afield. Compared to Alaska, comparatively little hunting for Moose has been done in Yukon but three of the best trophies yet recorded have all come from around Mayo, which lies right in the centre of the Territory.

So far as the Canadian Moose is concerned, the best chance of a good trophy of the western race *A.a.andersoni* would be either Alberta or British Columbia, and if it was a combined hunt after Moose and Caribou, then unquestionably the latter, and in particular in the Cassiar region where excellent specimens of both can be found.

Of the eastern type *A.a.americana*, all the best trophies have come out of Quebec Province.

The Wyoming-Shiras Moose *A.a.shirasi* has the smallest trophy of all the North American Moose, the maximum antler spread yet recorded being $62\frac{3}{8}$ in. (158 cm) on a trophy shot in Idaho in 1957.

A seven-day hunt after Moose in Manitoba, which includes camp accommodation, one guide per two hunters, use of boat, flights in and out of Thompson and hunting licence, costs $1050 (about £500), 50 percent of which must be paid as a deposit – refundable on ninety days advance notice of cancellation. Less luxurious trips are, of course, available and another outfitter in Manitoba is offering a minimum four-day package hunt for Moose for $100 per day – a price which includes all transportation, to and from, and within the hunting area either by boat or 'all-terrain' vehicles, food, tent-camps, cooking and guides etc., but not the licence fee ($150). A seven-day hunt, therefore, with this outfitter would cost about $850 (about £425).

For those who wish to share in the chores of camp life etc., one Manitoba outfitter, who claims a hunter success rate of about 80 percent, is offering a canoe hunting trip after Moose, during which the hunters, limited to two, 'will be expected to help the guide paddle and even set up camp'. Intending hunters should take note of the footnote to the brochure which states, 'Remember: you will have to carry all your gear over the *many* portages we will make – so keep it as light as possible'!

N & N Safaris run a ten-day hunt after Moose in Alaska for $2500 (about £1250) (1979), a third of which has to be deposited to confirm the trip. If the hunt is extended to fifteen days, Caribou can be included for an extra $1450 (about £725). These prices do not include transportation to and from the hunting lodges, nor the cost of the hunting licence and tags.

The hunting season for Moose not only varies throughout its range but also within each Province, Territory or State, depending on latitude and population. Some areas are open to residents only, some permit either sex to be taken, whilst in others all hunting of Moose is closed.

The earliest Moose hunting anywhere in Canada can be obtained in Yukon Territory, the season for males generally opening on 1 August and in recent years, terminating at the end of October – a season lasting about thirteen weeks. It is very doubtful, however, if any bull can be found with antlers entirely free of velvet before the latter part of August, so early hunting in that month is best suited for the meat hunter.

In British Columbia, which provides over a fifth of the total number of Moose killed annually in North America, the open season for bulls in some northern areas commences about mid-August – a full month earlier than in many hunting areas in the south. In areas where cows or antlerless deer are allowed to be shot, the open season for these generally commences in mid-September, but in the more southerly regions, not until late October or November.

For hunting seasons in Canada, *see pages 213–4*; for hunting seasons in the United States of America, *see pages 238–40*. Precise and up to date information, however, can only be supplied by the Fish and Game Department, and by the outfitter, once the area of the hunt has been decided upon.

Caribou *Rangifer tarandus*

Caribou – the equivalent of the Reindeer of Europe – were members of the late Pleistocene fauna of North America, and at the present time two types – the Barren-ground and the Woodland – are recognized on this continent, the former being divided into three subspecies.

A full grown Caribou bull will vary in height at the shoulder from about 42 in. (107 cm) to just over 50 in. (127 cm) according to subspecies, whilst the weight will also vary accordingly from about 200 lb (91 kg) of a Barren-ground bull to as much as 600 lb (272 kg) for an extremely large Woodland specimen, the males of which *average* about 400 lb (180 kg). Caribou, therefore, are much larger than the Reindeer of Europe. Generally speaking, it would appear that the Caribou of northern British Columbia – which some authorities refer to as the Mountain Caribou – attain the largest size both as regards body weight and antlers.

The Barren-ground Caribou – which consists of three subspecies and which Banfield (1961) calls Tundra Reindeer – are distributed throughout northern Canada from Baffin Island in the east to Unimak Island, Alaska, in the west. In the eastern part of its range, and as far west as Yukon Territory, the type is known as *R.t.groenlandicus*, but beyond the Mackenzie mountains in Alaska, this form is replaced by *R.t.granti*.

Included in the range of the former are the Canadian islands of Ellesmere

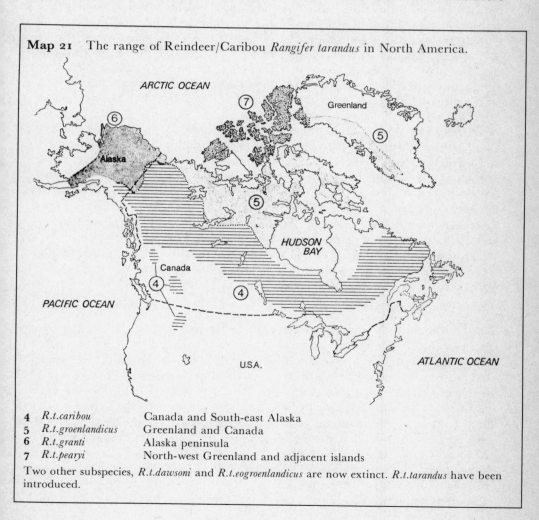

Map 21   The range of Reindeer/Caribou *Rangifer tarandus* in North America.

4	*R.t.caribou*	Canada and South-east Alaska
5	*R.t.groenlandicus*	Greenland and Canada
6	*R.t.granti*	Alaska peninsula
7	*R.t.pearyi*	North-west Greenland and adjacent islands

Two other subspecies, *R.t.dawsoni* and *R.t.eogroenlandicus* are now extinct. *R.t.tarandus* have been introduced.

and Baffin. This Caribou also occurs in Greenland, but in the extreme north-west of Greenland and adjacent islands, another form, *R.t.pearyi* is recognized.

At one time the range of the Woodland Caribou *R.t.caribou* extended from Newfoundland in the east to British Columbia and Queen Charlotte Islands in the west. Included in this range were all the southern provinces of Canada as well as some of the northern states of the United States of America, such as Maine, New Hampshire, Vermont, Michigan, Wisconsin, Minnesota, North Dakota, Montana, Idaho and Washington State.

The present distribution of the Woodland Caribou is much reduced, the southern limits of their range having been pushed northward, with the result that excluding Alaska, only about a hundred or so still remain in the United States of America, the majority of which are in northern Idaho. In Alaska the Woodland Caribou is now extinct on the Kenai Peninsula, but a few may still remain in the Copper River area in the south-western part of the State.

In Canada, Woodland Caribou are present in all Provinces except Nova Scotia and New Brunswick, in both of which it became extinct during the early part of the present century. Altogether, throughout the whole of its range in North America, Banfield (1961) suggested that the total population of Woodland Caribou may be about 43,000 animals, of which about 5000 to 6000 are on the island of Newfoundland.

In addition to Caribou, there are some domestic and feral Reindeer *C.t.tarandus* in parts of northern Canada and Alaska as a result of introductions which have been made during the past ninety years. The first Reindeer reached Alaska about 1890 and came from Siberia. By about 1930 the herds had increased to more than 600,000 animals but this was followed by a decline, and currently number about 35,000. The range of herding activities extends along the coast of Alaska from as far south as the Yukon-Kuskorwim Delta to the Seward Peninsula and islands in the Bering Sea.

Domestication of Caribou has not been seriously considered, and the closest thing would be the maintenance of a captive research herd at the University of British Columbia, but this project has now been disbanded.

The life cycle of Caribou

The Caribou rut commences during the latter part of September or early October and by the middle of the latter month will have reached its peak, continuing in some areas to early November. As with the Reindeer, the bulls are continuously on the move at this period, rounding up their herd of cows and meeting challengers. In consequence there is little time for feeding and their reserve of fat acquired during the summer months is soon used up. Thus, by the time November arrives, the bulls are hardly in the best condition to face a long and bitter winter, but somehow the majority manage to do so.

Caribou are usually silent, and during the rut the bulls have no special challenge call. When surprised, both sexes may give a loud snort, whilst some grunt-like noises may sometimes be heard coming from a large group.

There is a marked variation in the dates of shedding the antlers, according to sex, age and physiological conditions of the individual. The first to shed will be the older bulls, and this may start from mid-November onwards. By mid-December only the younger bulls will still retain their antlers, and by February all but the yearlings should have shed, although it may be late March or early April before the youngest will have lost their antlers. The antlers of the cows, however, will not be shed until about the time of calving in late May or June, the older animals generally being the first to lose them. For about three months during mid-winter replacement of antler on the older bulls is held in suspense and it will not be until March that any growth will be visible. By mid-September growth will be complete and any velvet still adhering to the antler, rubbed off.

A feature of a good trophy, besides length and span, is the wide, low shovel tine, and whilst this is normally present on one side only occasionally there will be a double shovel.

The Woodland or Mountain Caribou does not congregate into such immense herds nor undertake such long migrations as the Barren-ground Caribou. The former does, of course, move periodically from one grazing ground to another, but the area covered is nothing like so extensive as that of the Barren-ground Caribou, which may extend up to 800 miles (1280 kilometres) in distance between the summer and winter ranges.

The only real predator of the Caribou is the wolf. Wolf packs follow the migrating herds and take their toll of aged or weak animals. It has been estimated that a wolf requires food equivalent to, and may kill, eleven to fourteen Caribou a year.

Hunting the Caribou

Few hunters make a trip to the Barrens with the express purpose of hunting Caribou only – the majority are shot in conjunction with a hunt after other game animals such as Moose, bear, goat or wild sheep. Nevertheless, the Caribou has an outstanding trophy, the best of which will measure over 55 in. (140 cm) in length and perhaps have fifty points or more. Moreover, no two heads are alike, and it is their variability which is one of the chief attractions; it is also this variability which, on a one-bull only hunt, can make selection of the beast to take extremely difficult.

Once in good Caribou country, to bag a bull of sorts is not difficult – in fact, the Caribou is probably the easiest of all the game animals of North America to shoot.

Invariably, Caribou are first spotted whilst riding across the tundra or around the timber line, and provided a direct approach is not made, it is generally possible, by riding a slowly converging course, to get within range before dismounting to take the shot. On sighting a herd that holds a good bull, some people prefer to dismount and make a stalk – this, in my opinion, makes the eventual shooting of a good trophy more rewarding, for some physical effort will have been expended before success has been achieved. It would appear that Caribou in large herds are easier to approach than those in small groups, presumably the animals are under the impression that there is safety in numbers!

The Caribou possess a very keen sense of smell, so when stalking it is essential that the wind is favourable. Its sense of hearing is good, but not exceptional whilst its eyesight is poor compared to other game animals that frequent wide open spaces. Its 'curiosity' is well known, and has been the downfall of many a good trophy, for many hunters have discovered that by adopting some unusual behaviour, such as waving their arms or a flag, a group of animals can at times be enticed to approach rather than flee in terror. When alarmed, a Caribou will probably run only a short distance before stopping and taking a further look at the intruder.

On their migration routes, Caribou have favourite crossing places over rivers, narrow lakes or between high passes – it is therefore possible to play a waiting game overlooking one of these places in the hope that a good bull will come your way.

In Yukon Territory, however, except during the last fortnight of October, any form of hunting or activity designed to prevent or interfere with Caribou crossing the Dempster Highway within a 5-mile (8-km) corridor on either

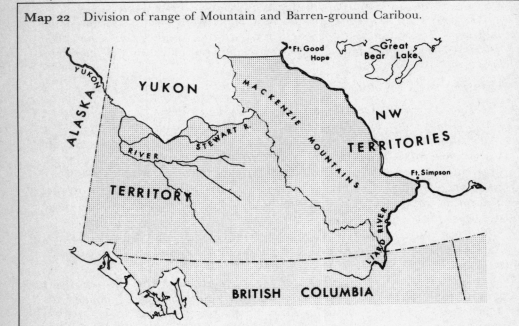

Map 22 Division of range of Mountain and Barren-ground Caribou.

The new Mountain Caribou area encompasses the southern two-thirds of the Yukon and the Mackenzie Mountains of the North-west Territories. Trophy Barren-ground Caribou taken there previously are now ranked in the Mountain Caribou category.

side, starting at Mile 41.6 (Highway Camp) and extending to the Yukon/Northwest Territories border, is prohibited.

All the largest Barren-ground trophies have come from Alaska and indeed, 360 out of 385 trophies listed in the Record Book have come from this State.

For a good Mountain-type Caribou trophy, northern British Columbia, particularly around Cold Fish Lake and the Spatsizi region during September is as good an area as any. Moreover, good trophies of Moose, Stone sheep and Rocky Mountain goat can also be got there. Most hunting in this part of British Columbia is done on horseback and a mixed game hunt is generally of three weeks' duration, with the party sleeping in tents. Access to Cold Fish Lake from Prince George is by plane.

A five-day hunt for Caribou in Alaska (1979) cost about $1750 (about £875). The price did *not* include transportation to and from the hunting lodge – nor the non-resident cost of hunting licence ($60) (about £30) and Caribou game tag ($200) (about £100).

Most Caribou hunting in Yukon Territory will also be done from horseback and, as in British Columbia, will generally be part of a mixed game hunt of minimum duration of about fifteen to twenty-one days, many outfitters even refusing to accommodate trips of less than three weeks. On the other hand, in both Alaska and Northwest Territories, after a fly-in by plane, much of the Caribou hunting will probably be done on foot, which at times can be physically demanding. However, there is some horseback hunting in both areas, particularly in the Wrangells and Talkeetnas of eastern Alaska. On the Alaska peninsula, and other areas in the south, track and all-terrain vehicles (A.T.V.) have been used and similar transport has also been tried in Northwest Territories as well as jet boat and dog sledge.

Newfoundland is a good area in which to hunt the Woodland Caribou, but non-resident alien licences are expensive, and only a limited number available, selection being made on a draw basis. For the so-called Quebec-Labrador Caribou, the George River area of Quebec has produced some of the best trophies taken in recent years.

In British Columbia it is possible to have a late season hunt after Caribou and Moose during the latter part of October, through November to early December, the hunters being accommodated in hutted camps at lower elevations to the autumn hunts.

One of the main difficulties in hunting Caribou for a good trophy is that with only one bull permitted on a licence, when a good trophy is seen, a decision has to be made on the spot whether or not to take it, for unlike other species of deer, one cannot pass over a head temporarily with the intention of coming back the following day or so should nothing better be seen. It will just not be there, for Caribou, being nomadic creatures, seldom stay in the same area for two days running, so if a good trophy is seen and time is getting short, take it if the guide says so. This is where the judgement of one's guide is invaluable, for if he is a good man, he will know how the head compares to the *best* bulls in the area.

THE AMERICAS

Some hunters search for a trophy with a double shovel, but such heads are rare, particularly in Barren-ground Caribou, where it has been estimated that only about one in every 5000 or more bulls will have such brows.

For recording trophies in *Records of North American Big Game*, categories of Caribou are recognized with boundaries based on geographical lines, rather than by taxonomic classification. This treatment has, unfortunately, caused some confusion, particularly as regards the subspecies *Rangifer tarandus caribou* which, in British Columbia and Alberta is referred to as the Mountain Caribou, whereas in Newfoundland it is called the Woodland Caribou, the former having a higher minimum score (390) to qualify for inclusion in the Record Book than the latter (295).

Until 1980 the Caribou of the whole of Yukon and Northwest Territories were considered to be Barren-ground, but for record keeping purposes trophies taken in the southern third of Yukon and in the Mackenzie mountains will now be classified as Mountain Caribou – the same type as occurs in neighbouring British Columbia and Alberta.

With regard to trophies from Alaska, northern Yukon, northern Northwest Territories, Saskatchewan, Manitoba and Ontario, these will all be treated as Barren-ground (either *R.t.granti* or *R.t.groenlandicus*) whereas the Caribou in the last three mentioned Provinces are probably referable to as the Woodland type, *R.t.caribou* as are also the Caribou from Quebec and Labrador. Until 1971 the latter were, however, included among the Barren-ground Caribou; now 'for the convenience of record keeping only' they are considered separately as 'Quebec-Labrador Caribou' with a lower minimum score for inclusion in the Record Book of 375, as compared to 400 for the Barren-ground.

Mule deer *Odocoileus hemionus*

Mule deer, which include the Blacktail and Sitka deer of the Pacific coastal areas, are found over a vast expanse of western North America and in a variety of habitats, from the high mountains of the Rockies to the plains and deserts of New Mexico. Their range is confined almost entirely to the western half of the United States – say from about longitude 100° westwards – and extending northwards from about central Mexico in the south to southern Alaska and the Great Slave Lake in Northwest Territories in Canada. Throughout their distribution, eleven subspecies, two of which are Blacktail, are recognized, the typical type *O.h.hemionus* – generally referred to as the Rocky Mountain Mule deer – having the greatest range in both Canada and the United States. Generally speaking, it is a deer of the mountains and big open spaces, and a great animal to hunt.

In Canada the range of the Rocky Mountain Mule deer extends westwards from about the south-western shores of Lake Winnipeg in Manitoba, through Saskatchewan and Alberta to British Columbia where, towards the coast, it is replaced by the Sitka (Blacktail) deer *O.h.sitkensis*. In the United States the Rocky Mountain Mule deer also has a wide distribution, ranging from the

Map 23 The range of Mule deer/Black-tailed deer *Odocoileus hemionus* in North America.

I	*Odocoileus hemionus hemionus*	West and central North America
2	*O.h.sitkensis*	Coastal area and islands off British Columbia
3	*O.h.columbianus*	British Columbia to northern California
4	*O.h.californicus*	Mid California
5	*O.h.inyoensis*	California
6	*O.h.fuliginatus*	California
7	*O.h.eremicus*	North-west Mexico and Arizona
8	*O.h.crooki*	North Mexico
9	*O.h.peninsulae*	Baja California
10	*O.h.sheldoni*	Tiburón Island
11	*O.h.cerrosensis*	Cerros Island, Baja California

Based on Hall & Kelson (*The Mammals of North America*).

western boundary of Minnesota in the east, to Oregon and eastern Washington in the west, where it is replaced by the Columbian Black-tailed deer *O.h.columbianus*. Included in its distribution are the States of Colorado, Idaho, Kansas, Montana, Nebraska, Nevada, North and South Dakota, northern New Mexico, Oklahoma, Utah and Wyoming. In the south the Rocky Mountain Mule deer is replaced by the Desert or Gray Mule deer *O.h.crooki*, whose distribution covers northern Texas, southern New Mexico and Arizona, whilst in the south-west by the Inyo Mule deer *O.h.inyoensis* and in eastern California by the California Mule deer *O.h.californicus*. Southern California is frequented by the Southern Mule deer *O.h.fuliginatus*, which is replaced in Baja California by the Peninsula Mule deer *O.h.peninsulae*.

East and west of Baja California are situated two islands, Tiburón Island in the Gulf of California, and Cerros Island in the Pacific Ocean, and each has its own type of Mule deer, the Tiburón Island Mule deer *O.h.sheldoni* on the former, and the Cedros (Cerros) Island Mule deer *O.h.cerrosensis* on the latter.

East of the Gulf of California in Sonora, Mexico, is found the Burro (Mule) deer *O.h.eremicus*, whose range extends northwards into southern Arizona, being replaced here by the Desert Mule deer *O.h.crooki*. Intergradation between the Burro deer and the Southern Mule deer *O.h.fuliginatus* probably occurs where the two types converge.

In central Mexico, the Desert Mule deer extends its range as far as Zacatecas, which approximately marks the southern extent of the Mule deer's range in Central America.

The largest race – the Rocky Mountain Mule deer – stands about 40 in. (101.6 cm) high at the shoulder, and weighs about 250 lb to 350 lb (114 to 159 kg) live weight, according to locality, with exceptional bucks scaling up to 400 lb (181 kg). The smallest race is the Peninsula Mule deer – but the two insular types from the islands of Tiburón and Cedros, are not much bigger.

Generally speaking the races of Mule deer *Odocoileus hemionus* conform to Bergman's Law in that individual races inhabiting the colder localities are larger than those living in warmer regions, a possible exception being the Sitka Black-tailed deer *O.h.sitkensis*.

No one knows what the total Mule deer population is in North America, but it must be well over three million in the United States.

Life cycle of the Mule deer

The rut of the Mule deer varies from one geographical area to another, the northern subspecies having an earlier rut than those in the south. For instance, the rut of the Rocky Mountain Mule deer will start around October, reaching its peak in November and in most localities will be finished by early December. Maximum activity lasts only about three weeks in any one area. In New Mexico, however, the rut of the Desert Mule deer will not get under way until December, and extend into the New Year.

In mountainous localities, the Mule deer is a migratory animal, for it likes to spend the short summer months high up on the mountains where it can graze the rich grasses and herbage. In some localities, therefore, Mule deer, during the summer, can often be found at altitudes of around seven or eight thousand feet (about 2300 metres) or even higher – generally on a slope facing south-east or south-west where the early morning or late evening sunshine can be enjoyed to the full. In the middle hours of the day, however, when the weather is warm, they retire to shade, or perhaps to a northern slope where they can find a cooler temperature. Southern facing slopes are also much favoured for the same reason during the winter, which is spent in the valleys where food is still available and the snow not too deep. During their migration from summer to winter quarters, distances of 50, or even up to 100 miles (80 to 160 km) have been covered.

Antlers of bucks in the northern races are normally shed between January and March, depending on locality, the older bucks shedding first. Antler replacement, however, does not commence immediately, and it will be about April before signs of the new growth are visible. Antlers of the Desert Mule deer, however, will not be shed until about mid-March and into April, and the interval between shedding and commencement of growth of the new antler is only a matter of days.

Hunting Mule deer

Mule deer hunting in the more remote areas of its distribution can provide excellent sport, and deer populations have increased so dramatically in some localities that some States now allow two or more permits.

The Mule deer is generally hunted in more open terrain than the White-tailed deer, and during the autumn at dawn and dusk, they can often be spotted feeding or moving across clearings on a mountain side, and subsequently stalked. Shots at Mule deer in the mountains are, therefore, often taken at longer ranges than at White-tailed deer, and few American hunters will hesitate to take a chance at 300 yards (270 metres) or even more, regardless of whether the deer is standing or running. Some guides feel they have fulfilled their obligation if their client can have a shot, irrespective of the range.

On the opening day of the season, when thousands of hunters are afoot in the hills, probably the best chance to kill a Mule deer is to take up a position on a hillside from which an extensive area can be watched, for with so much disturbance going on all around, the deer are constantly on the move, and sooner or later one will probably pass your lookout. Many hunters arrive in the hunting area a day or so prior to the season opening in order to familiarize themselves with the ground and see if any good bucks have taken up their territory in the vicinity. In some States, however, there is some restriction on pre-hunt scouting. In Georgia, for instance, pre-hunt scouting (for Whitetail) or camping in the area is permitted only on the day immediately prior to the first day of the big game hunting season. In Nevada it is unlawful to camp within 100 yards (90 metres) of a water hole in any manner likely to restrict the access of wild or domestic stock.

Watching trails to streams or ponds that are frequented by deer is not likely to be very productive during the first few days of the season, for the deer will be so much harassed that they will have little time for drinking – anyway in daylight. Later in the season, when the initial stampede to shoot a deer has died down, and the woods are comparatively quiet, these areas can be profitably watched, particularly when the weather is hot and dry, and the deer more thirsty in consequence.

Some hunters have been following the European custom of shooting deer from a *Hochsitz* or high seat, and in some areas platforms have been erected in trees overlooking a game trail or a likely feeding area (*see page 223*).

Heavy snow storms during the late fall force the deer to move to their winter range, and if their accustomed migration route is known, watching one of these trails can be very rewarding.

Driving deer, particularly in the more densely afforested areas, is often restored to and can be very productive, but in districts where hunting pressure is considerable, it is best – and safest – not to attempt to do so until later in the season, when fewer hunters will be about, for not only can one drive get mixed up with another party's drive, but no one knows how many individual hunters there may be in the area.

Another method is for two hunters to work as a pair, one walking along one side of a ravine or narrow canyon, whilst his companion takes the other side. Any deer disturbed by a hunter on one side will often cross over to the other and so give the other rifle the chance of a shot. Sometimes the hunters will be on horseback, and this enables considerably more ground to be covered. Needless to say, a hunter should always dismount before attempting a shot, although by the time this has been accomplished the deer may have disappeared from view.

In the south where the terrain is not too mountainous, the deer is often hunted by motor vehicle, by which method a considerable area can be covered. Hunting, or discharging a firearm from any vehicle, however, whether moving or stationary, is illegal anywhere in Canada, and in most States of the United States.

During the rut, Mule deer bucks are probably less aggressive than Whitetail, and serious fighting between males seldom occurs. In consequence, rattling antlers to attract bucks during the rut does not seem to produce the result that it does with the White-tailed deer (*see page 201*).

If, however, it was possible to hunt in an area free of other hunters, then 'still hunting' and stalking undoubtedly provide the best sport. Furthermore, if natural coloured or camouflaged clothing could be worn, as is normal practice whilst hunting in Europe, the chance of success would be greatly improved. 'But nowadays', comments Rollo Robinson, 'only an idiot would hunt deer during the regular rifle season while clad in camouflage'. Anyway, such dress would be illegal in most western States, which require that anyone hunting with a rifle must be clad in red, orange or yellow. In seasons reserved solely for archery, however, these requirements do not apply.

It must not be thought that there are no areas in North America where Mule deer cannot be hunted without having to share the ground – and perhaps the deer you are stalking as well – with hundreds of other hunters. There are plenty of such areas but they will not be near a motorway or readily accessible to the weekend hunter. As when hunting many other species in North America, one has to pay in time and money for privacy!

The open season for hunting Mule deer varies so much from Province to Province and from State to State, as well as between individual Game Management areas that it is only possible to generalize. The open season for buck, however, begins in some areas before the antlers may be properly clear of velvet, so anyone wishing to trophy hunt, except in the more northerly parts, should not plan a trip after Mule deer before the latter part of September.

A typical Mule deer trophy will consist of short upright brows and double forks on each side thereby making it a 10-pointer (5 a-side). Frequently, instead of simple forking, numerous points or tines erupt throughout the length of the beam and produce what is referred to as a 'non-typical' trophy.

If measured under the Boone and Crockett formula for normal trophies, these non-typical heads would be severely penalized for abnormalities, and so it was decided to create a separate formula for non-typical antlers, and since 1952 Mule deer antlers fall into two categories – 'typical' and 'non-typical' – and are measured accordingly.

In any division, there must be a few border line heads which could qualify for either the 'typical' or 'non-typical' class, but this is solved by measuring the trophy under both formulae and placing it in the list in which it scores the highest.

The minimum score to qualify for inclusion in the Record Book under 'non-typical' antlers, is 240 as compared to 195 for the 'typical' trophy.

This rather questionable ruling must result in some anomalies. For instance, a trophy taken in Colorado in 1972 with sixteen tines $(7+9)$ is included in the 'typical' antler class, whilst a 12-pointer $(6+6)$ also killed in Colorado in 1960 appears in the 'non-typical' list. The highest number of tines of any Mule deer trophy recorded in the latter list is fifty $(23+27)$.

From trophies in *Records of North American Big Game*, 1981, it would seem that the highest number of 'non-typical' trophies have come from Arizona (29), Colorado (68) and Idaho (34). Since, however, over twice as many Mule deer are killed anually in both Colorado and Idaho than are taken in Arizona, the chance of shooting a 'non-typical' deer in the last named State would appear to be slightly better, particularly in the Kaibab Forest area, for no fewer than twenty-one of the twenty-nine 'non-typical' recorded trophies have come from this area, quite apart from any others which may have been taken but are not of sufficient merit to reach the Record Book. Another interesting point about these twenty-one 'non-typical' antlers from Kaibab is that twenty of them have been taken between 1940 and 1969, and during the five years 1949 to 1953, two trophy bucks were taken each season, suggesting that there may be a hereditary strain in the area for producing this type of antler.

For hunting seasons of the Mule deer, see pages 213–4 for Canada, and pages 238–40 for the United States of America. Seasonal dates, however, vary from year to year, and up to date information for any particular area can only be supplied by the Fish and Game Department of the State, Province or Territory concerned (*see Appendix B*).

Black-tailed or Sitka deer *Odocoileus hemionus*

Black-tailed deer are closely related to Mule deer, for they belong to the species *O.hemionus*, which is a name given to two races which inhabit a quite considerable strip of country along the Pacific coast, extending from southern Alaska in the north to northern California in the south. Over the northern part of its range the type is known as the Sitka deer *O.h.sitkensis*, taking its name from Sitka island, and is plentiful on many of the islands off southern Alaska and western British Columbia, including the Queen Charlotte Islands.

The southern race, referred to as the Columbian Blacktail or Coast deer – *O.h.columbianus* – has a range extending from south-west British Columbia, including Vancouver Island, southwards along the coast through Washington, Oregon into north-west California.

The average live weight of an adult Columbian Blacktail buck is about 140 to 150 lb (64 to 68 kg) in the northern part of its range, but in north California, 125 lb (56 kg) would be a good average. Adult does in good condition will be about 60 lb (27 kg) less. No weights are available for Sitka deer, but they will be slightly less.

The Black-tailed deer – so called because of the black upper surface of the tail in contrast to the light coloured tail with only a black tip of the Mule deer – frequently interbreeds with both the Rocky Mountain Mule deer *O.h.hemionus* and California Mule deer *O.h.californicus*, where their ranges overlap. In consequence certain areas have been designated as 'intergrade areas' and any buck killed in these areas, for the purpose of trophy assessment will be classed as Mule deer. Details of the boundaries of these 'intergrade areas' in British Columbia, Washington, Oregon and California are given in *Records of North American Big Game*, 1981, and anyone wishing to hunt Blacktail anywhere near its eastern boundaries would be advised to familiarize himself with these areas, otherwise the Blacktail shot with 'record' antlers may turn out to be a 'Mule deer'!

Throughout most of its range the Black-tailed deer is plentiful, particularly the Columbian Blacktail, which is estimated to number close on a million deer in Washington and Oregon alone where the hunters' annual kill is around 60,000 animals. In California the deer is abundant in the country north and south of San Francisco Bay, where the low mountain ranges are covered with a dense growth of brush – the chaparral.

Since 1916, when eight Black-tailed deer from the Sitka area were released on Hichinbrook and Hawkins Islands in Prince William Sound, there have been a number of transplants of this deer to Alaska where it is now well established on both the mainland and adjacent islands of Prince William Sound. In recent years the annual harvest of Sitka Blacktail has been about

12,000 deer, but four bad winters resulted in hunting being banned in some areas. British Columbia probably has about half a million Blacktail along its western sea board.

In 1961 ten Black-tailed deer *O.h.columbianus* caught up as fawns in Oregon were introduced to the island of Kauai in Hawaii, and these were followed by other releases in 1962 and 1965. By 1970 the number of deer on Kauai had increased to 400 and in that year the first hunting permits were issued.

On the northern part of its range the Blacktail ruts from about September to November, but in Hawaii it commences in October and may continue until January.

Hunting the Black-tailed deer

Due to the habitat of the Black-tailed deer, which over much of its range consists of dense brush and rain forest with heavy undergrowth, the hunting of this deer along the Pacific coast is completely different from hunting Mule deer elsewhere, and in many instances can best be compared to hunting White-tailed deer only in denser undergrowth. 'The habits of these deer', writes Dalrymple (1974), 'are a consequence of the cover in which they live. On the southern end of the range this may be brush so awesomely dense a man cannot walk through it, but has to crawl. Farther north in some of the coastal rain forest, the under storey is like a wall.' Continuing, he says, 'Some hunters take great pride in their prowess at beating the Blacktail on its own terms. They sneak and crawl through openings and trails in thick cover, sometimes even surprising a deer in its bed. This is tough hunting, however, and it is

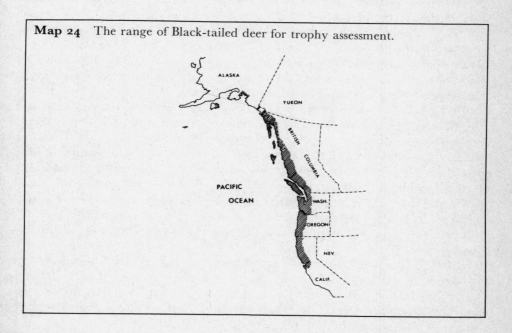

Map 24   The range of Black-tailed deer for trophy assessment.

important to bear in mind that portions of the range have a substantial number of rattlesnakes.'

Much of the Blacktail country consists of narrow bush-filled canyons, and it is possible for one or two hunters to work their way through the bush and move the deer out to other hunters posted along the rim of the canyon.

There are also some places in the Blacktail country, particularly in the north-west, where timber has been extracted, thus leaving comparatively open areas rich in low scrub attractive to the deer and a good place to make a stand.

In California the hunting season for this coastal deer has traditionally started during the early part of August, but will have terminated by the time the rut gets under way.

Columbian Black-tailed deer are particularly plentiful in Mendocino County yet hunter success averages only about one buck taken in every twelve to fourteen days' hunting. Only bucks with forked antlers or better are legal game, and it is estimated that only about 10 to 15 percent meet this requirement, the majority of which, during the hot days of August, lie up in dense cover. Furthermore, since about three-quarters of Mendocino County is privately owned, hunting on these lands is usually restricted to landowners and their friends, and as a result, areas where public hunting is permitted are much over-hunted.

The season for hunting Sitka deer on Vancouver Island and on the coastal part of British Columbia runs for about nine weeks from mid-September to early December. Normally two deer – one of which may be antlerless – are permitted on licence, but in part of Vancouver Island, three may be taken, two of which may be antlerless.

On the Queen Charlotte Islands there is an open season for about thirty-nine weeks during which ten deer of either sex may be shot.

In Alaska (mainland), where four deer may be shot, the open season for bucks commences on 1 August and for antlerless deer, about mid-September, the season for both terminating about mid-January.

On Kodiak Island (eastern part) the open season for bucks is the same as on the mainland but it is legal to start shooting antlerless deer on 1 September. At present the bag limit on Kodiak is two deer.

On the island of Kauai, Hawaii, the number of Blacktail available for hunting is strictly limited and hunting permits for bucks only are available through public drawing.

During the 1977–9 seasons, although a total of 1097 trips were made by hunters, only fifteen deer were accounted for – a hunter success of 1 percent.

Bucks average about 150 lb (68 kg) live weight, but weights of over 200 lb (90 kg) have been recorded.

Hunting Black-tailed deer on private land on Kauai is not permitted.

Dogs may only be used if a shotgun of under 20 bore gauge but not less than .410 gauge loaded with 00 buckshot or rifled slug is used, as well as any centre fire rifle of less than 1200 ft/lb muzzle energy. Dogs may also accompany the archer as well as any hunter armed only with a knife.

Knives are considered permissible weapons on both Molokai and Kauai – principally when hunting wild pig with dogs – for when an animal is held at bay, many hunters prefer to despatch it with a knife to avoid accidentally shooting one of the dogs.

Only one person is allowed to accompany a hunter at any time, and during such time he must carry on his person not only a valid hunting licence but also a non-hunter permit. Under no circumstances may he carry the hunter's firearm whilst loaded.

The antlers of Blacktail bucks are smaller than some Mule deer, and tend to have fewer tines – indeed, some antlers of the Sitka deer are difficult to distinguish from White-tailed deer. Just how rare 8-pointer $(4+4)$ Black-tailed bucks are in northern California is shown by figures from Mendocino County where, on the University of California 5000 acre (2000 hectare) research station which is open to controlled public hunting, not one buck out of 472 taken over a period of twelve years (1963–74) had four tines on each side, most of the antlers being just forks. Reference to the list of trophies in the eighth edition of *Records of North American Big Game* (1981) will show how small Blacktail antlers are in comparison to Mule deer; the maximum length of the former seldom exceeding 24 in. (61 cm) as compared to about 30 in. (76 cm) for Mule deer. Sitka Blacktail *O.h.sitkensis* trophies are even smaller than Columbian.

For hunting seasons of the Black-tailed deer in North America see pages 213–4 (Canada) and pages 238–40 (United States).

White-tailed deer *Odocoileus virginianus*

Once exterminated from much of its former range in eastern United States, the White-tailed deer by introduction and strictly controlled hunting legislation, has now been restored and is the most widespread of all the deer species in North America, for it is resident in every State in the United States of America except Alaska and Hawaii.

As an example of its dramatic recovery, take the State of Pennsylvania where, by the end of the last century the White-tailed deer had almost disappeared, and it was possible to walk for days through the mountains without seeing a single deer. Today, the deer numbering possibly 400,000 can be found in all sixty-seven counties of the State. How was this achieved?

After a complete ban on all forms of hunting in 1897, beginning in 1905, a number of refuges were established in various parts of the State and these were stocked with deer brought in from Michigan, Ohio, Kentucky, Maine, New Jersey, North Carolina, New Hampshire and game dealers in Pennsylvania. Between 1906 and 1924 nearly 1200 deer were released in the mountains, almost half of which had, in fact, been supplied by the Pennsylvanian dealers who had, no doubt, purchased their stock elsewhere.

A similar re-stocking programme was carried out in Virginia and as a result of the importation and transplantations of over 3500 deer which have been undertaken since 1931, virtually all the counties now have established herds in varying numbers, the total population in the State probably being just short of half a million deer.

In 1907 the *Buck Law* was passed, which prohibited the taking of antlerless deer, and this, no doubt, was a major factor in Pennsylvania's deer recovery.

Although the law was originally intended as a measure to make deer hunting safer and to increase the number of breeding females, within twenty years it became one of the greatest stumbling blocks in the way of sound deer management.

One of the first States to introduce a *Buck Law* was New Mexico some fifteen years before it became a State, for in 1897 a comprehensive law was passed for the protection of all game animals and fish. Under this Act the *Buck Law* was put into effect, and a deer season was set from September until the end of November in the northern counties, and from October to the end of December in the south. Two years later a bag limit of one buck was made law by the Territorial Legislature. The public, however, refused to accept these laws and the slaughter of deer and other game animals continued. Shortly before New Mexico became a State, a game licence system was eventually accepted, and season and bag limits established.

One of the objections by hunters to the *Buck Law* was the difficulty, it was claimed, to distinguish the sexes, which brought a Press comment that this was hardly surprising, since many hunters didn't seem able to tell the difference between a person and a deer, let alone the sex of the latter – or perhaps the former also!

The *Buck Law* remained in force until 1923 when for four years, antlerless deer were allowed to be shot. By this date the numbers of deer were already above the level of the true carrying capacity over much of their range, and it would have been prudent to have continued culling either sex thereafter. This, however, did not happen, and during the next twenty years, ten seasons were declared 'bucks only'.

Even more spectacular has been the recovery of deer in Mississippi where, in the late 1920s, it was estimated that fewer than 1500 deer remained in the State. In 1932, when the Mississippi Game and Fish Commission was inaugurated, the deer were scattered in small groups over some thirty-four counties of the State and hunting was prohibited in most areas.

The Commission immediately started to purchase deer and by 1940 it operated some forty refuge areas across the State where stocks of deer were built up prior to being released where good habitat existed.

Today as a result of these liberations, it is estimated that Mississippi's Whitetail population is close to a million deer, and deer hunting is now possible in at least part of all eighty-two counties of the State, with an annual harvest of over 96,000 deer – a considerable increase on the total of 2364 deer which were killed in 1955.

In the north, the range of the White-tailed deer extends into southern Canada to about latitude 48°, being present in the southern parts of British Columbia, Alberta, Saskatchewan, Manitoba, Ontario and Quebec. It also occurs in New Brunswick and Nova Scotia Island, but is absent from Newfoundland and Labrador, as well as Yukon and the Northwest Territories.

To the south, the range of the White-tailed deer extends through Mexico and Central America, and into the northern half of South America.

Throughout its entire range no fewer than thirty-eight subspecies are recognized, sixteen of which are resident in the United States of America and three in Canada.

Since the range of many of these subspecies overlaps, intergradation has occurred widely, and the situation has not been helped by the widespread transplanting of various subspecies into the geographic ranges belonging to others. However, similar to the Mule deer, it can be said that the larger forms of Whitetail are to be found in the north, and the smaller in the south. Thus the largest deer are to be found in those three races which occur in the northern part of the United States of America and southern Canada – namely *O.v.borealis*, *O.v.ochrourus* and *O.v.dacotensis*.

Accurate figures for the White-tailed deer population in North America are not available, but in the United States alone, their number probably exceeds 11,000,000 of which an estimated 3,100,000 are to be found in Texas. The estimated population of White-tailed deer in the seven Provinces of Canada where the species occurs is around half a million.

Vermont has a particular problem with its deer population, for as more and more deer range disappears under the spread of urbanization, little or no effort is made to control the wintering herds to the available winter range.

This is no new problem, the main cause of which has undoubtedly been the reluctance of hunters to shoot female deer. This was highlighted in a five-year trial period, starting in 1966, to kill not more than 8 percent of antlerless deer in each hunting zone, but the experiment failed miserably and the cull was well below the target. Yet, during the same period, more than 50 percent of the *available* bucks in the various zones were taken – and have continued to be taken – each year for decades. In at least one area of Vermont, the hunting pressure on bucks is so high that it is estimated that 'bucks rarely live past two years of age'.

After completion of the five-year trial, the shooting of antlerless deer was not continued. Antlerless deer, however, may now be taken during the special Bow and Arrow season.

A high doe population results in poor reproduction, and during a severe winter mortality is high. Thus, during the three successive winters of 1969–71, which were particularly hard, Vermont's deer population, estimated in 1968 at around 230,000, was cut down to almost half, many thousands being found dead in the deer yards during the spring dead-deer surveys.

Then followed a number of mild winters, until the winter of 1977–8 brought deer mortality that even exceeded the figures of 1969–71. The solution must be an overall reduction in numbers – particularly of female deer – which will mean a considerable number being harvested *every* year.

The life cycle of White-tailed deer

In North America the rut of the White-tailed deer commences during October and reaches its peak in November, the older bucks having finished by the end of the month, although rutting activity by some of the younger bucks will still be apparent in December or early January, particularly in the more southerly States such as Texas.

By the end of December the older bucks will have started to shed their antlers, followed by the younger bucks, and by the end of February or early March, antler shedding by all age groups should be complete. As with Mule deer, there is a time lag of a few months after shedding before the new growth will be visible, for it will not be until April that the velvet covered antler buds start to appear.

In the northern distribution of White-tailed deer adverse climatic conditions produce seasonal migrations from summer to winter range and vice versa in the spring. The distance travelled depends on the adequacy of shelter and the severity of the winter. Occasionally it may be 20 miles (32 km) or so but more generally under 5 miles (8 km).

Map 25 The range of White-tailed deer *Odocoileus virginianus* in North and Central America.

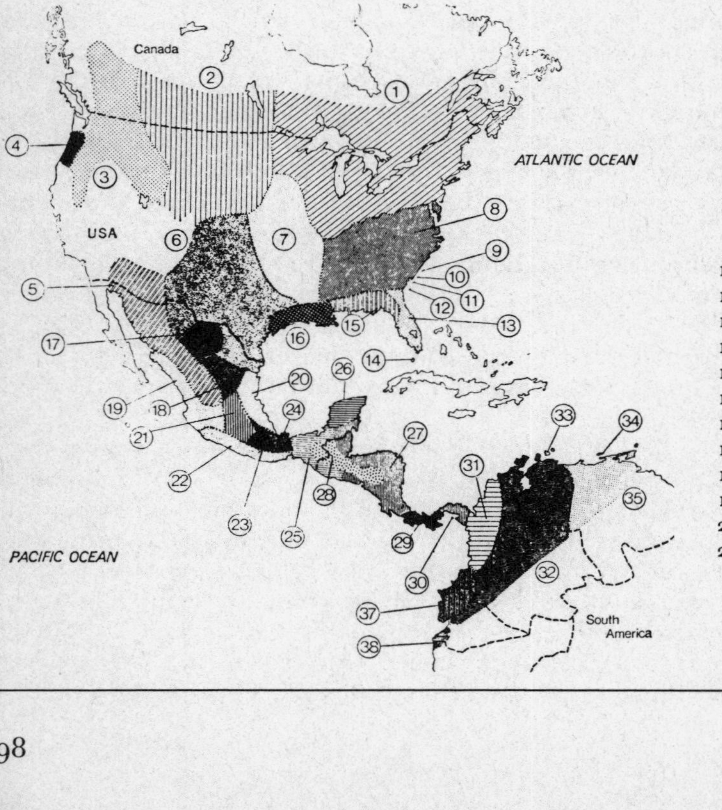

1   *Odocoileus virginianus borealis*
2   *O.v.dacotensis*
3   *O.v.ochrourus*
4   *O.v.leucurus*
5   *O.v.couesi*
6   *O.v.texanus*
7   *O.v.macrourus*
8   *O.v.virginianus*
9   *O.v.taurinsulae*
10   *O.v.venatorius*
11   *O.v.hiltonensis*
12   *O.v.nigribarbis*
13   *O.v.seminolus*
14   *O.v.clavium*
15   *O.v.osceola*
16   *O.v.mcilhennyi*
17   *O.v.carminis*
18   *O.v.miquihuanensis*
19   *O.v.sinaloae*
20   *O.v.veraecrucis*
21   *O.v.mexicanus*

In the more amenable southern range of this deer, seasonal migrations are almost non-existent, and if not too disturbed, the deer remain in a comparatively small area.

White-tailed deer are fond of water and are good swimmers, often taking to water to escape predators. Losses from natural predators, which include mountain lion, coyote, wolf and bobcat, are insignificant, although in former times, when mountain lion was more plentiful, they certainly took a heavy toll. Probably the most serious predator in some areas today is the domestic dog, which running wild, singly or in numbers, kill a number of deer, particularly does heavy in fawn, or young fawns – and in winter time, any deer that may get stuck in deep snow. Indeed during one January in New York State, dogs were estimated to have killed 1000 snow-bound deer.

Another significant 'predator' of the White-tailed deer in Texas is the motor car, and many hundreds are being killed on the roads each week. Indeed deer on the roads, particularly at night, are such a hazard that many cars are fitted with special bumpers to minimize the damage to the car when a deer is accidentally hit. During a trip to the Y.O. Ranch in Texas in 1978 I

outh-east Canada and north-east U.S.A.	22	*O.v.acapulcensis*	South-east Mexico
lberta to North Dakota	23	*O.v.oaxancensis*	South Mexico
orth-west U.S.A. and Canada	24	*O.v.toltecus*	South Mexico
regon and west coast	25	*O.v.thomasi*	South-east Mexico
rizona	26	*O.v.yucatanensis*	Honduras
exas and adjoining States	27	*O.v.truei*	Nicaragua and adjacent States
ansas and adjoining States	28	*O.v.nelsoni*	South Mexico and Guatemala
irginia and adjoining States	29	*O.v.chiriquensis*	Panama
ulls island	30	*O.v.rothschildi*	Coiba Island
unting Island	31	*O.v.tropicalis*	West Colombia
ilton Head Island	32	*O.v.guodotii*	Colombia and western Venezuela
ackbeard Island	33	*O.v.curassavicus*	Curaçao Island
lorida	34	*O.v.margaritae*	Margarita Island
lorida Keys	35	*O.v.gymnotis*	Venezuela and the Guianas
orth-west Florida	36	*O.v.cariacou*	French Guiana and northern Brazil
ouisiana	37	*O.v.ustus*	Ecuador (Andes)
orth Mexico	38	*O.v.peruvianus*	Peru and marginally
entral Mexico			
lid-west Mexico			
ast Mexico			
entral Mexico			

White-tailed deer have been introduced to New Zealand (South island) and to a number of other reas outside their normal habitat. See also map 29.

art based on map 491 E. Raymond Hall and K R Kelson (*The Mammals of North America*, Vol. II).

was told that an average of about three deer per day or night around Kerville became road casualties.

Hunting the White-tailed deer

'Bagging a Whitetail buck is surprisingly difficult in most parts of the country', comments Robert E. Donovan (1978). 'It is particularly difficult in the heavily hunted north-eastern and Central Atlantic states. In a recent year in Virginia, one deer hunter in eight was successful. In New York it was one in twelve; and in Vermont, one in ten. This means that in this part of the country something like nine out of ten deer hunters return from the field every year empty-handed.'

In Ontario about 13,000 to 15,000 deer are taken annually by approximately 85,000 licensed hunters – a hunter success ratio of about one in six. In Tennessee hunters both resident and non-resident, experience a 12 percent hunter success rate.

In 1949 it would appear that over the whole of the United States about one hunter in four could expect to kill a deer in the season, although much would depend on the region being hunted, success being greatest in the area adjacent to the mountains of the west and least in the more central areas.

Today large White-tailed deer populations are within easy driving distance of many of the large cities – Chicago, Detroit, Philadelphia and New York, etc. so many deer hunts are of only one day duration, and in an area where there is a bag limit of only one deer, success on the first day probably means the end of deer hunting for that year.

Methods of hunting Whitetail are varied, and whilst the majority of deer in the western states are mostly killed by stalking, still hunting, trail watching or in the course of a deer drive, in the east other methods are also used, and these include shooting from high seats or from a boat, or hunting with hounds. In some areas the shotgun is the only permissible weapon, in others its use against deer is prohibited.

In the more northern States, tracking deer in snow can be successful, but in the majority of cases it is not until you actually see the deer that you are aware of its sex, for tracks in snow can be very misleading. One way to avoid an abortive trek after a doe is to follow the fresh tracks of a buck that has just been spooked, but the disadvantage of this method is that an animal disturbed in this way may travel a considerable distance before settling down again.

In areas that abound in lakes and streams, if the deer have not been subject to much hunting pressure, they can often be found in the early morning or late evening feeding along the shoreline, and a good method of approach is to use a canoe or light boat, and drift or paddle along the waterways, spying for deer in much the same way as practised by Moose hunters. 'Float-hunting', as this method is sometimes called, is particularly useful for hunting areas where the undergrowth along the shoreline is so dense as to make travel on foot hardly a worthwhile proposition. In some areas, however, float-hunting is illegal. Early in the century, many deer were killed by headlighting from a boat – but the use of lights for hunting is now prohibited.

Of the two and a half million or so White-tailed deer shot in the United States in 1977, it was estimated that about 20 to 40 percent were killed during deer drives. Although selective shooting can seldom be practised during a deer drive, it is often the only practical way to hunt deer living in dense undergrowth.

In some of the south-eastern States and in the Canadian province of Ontario, it is legal to hunt deer with hounds – a method that is particularly useful in terrain that abounds in thickets and swamps.

One of the drawbacks of this form of hunting is that if the deer being chased by hounds is not shot, the hounds may continue to chase the deer long after it has passed through the line of hunters and the task then is to recover the pack before any further hunting can be done.

Hounding deer is a social way of hunting, usually done by clubs of perhaps twenty members or more on land that has been leased from private owners or forest companies.

The use of calls in hunting Whitetail is not much practised but does in particular can often be attracted by an imitation of the bleat of a fawn. Several commercial calls are on the market, and one firm provides a record with sample calls on it so that a beginner can have some idea of what is required. The game statutes of Texas, however, prohibit the use of artificial calls.

A better method to attract a buck, and one much practised in Texas, is to rattle a pair of antlers together in order to simulate a fight between two rival bucks. Obviously this method will normally produce results only during the rut, when it plays on the buck's natural instinct to defend its territory.

Not all bucks respond to rattling in the same manner, for some will come at the gallop, others at a trot, pausing every now and then to listen and test the wind, whilst some may sneak in silently and stealthily without giving any warning of their approach. As with calling, one shouldn't overdo it, for sound carries a long way.

Shooting deer from a high seat, either man-made or erected in a tree, is becoming increasingly popular, particularly in Texas, but in some areas elevated seats are not permitted. By way of contrast, some hunters, in cold weather, prefer to dig a foxhole in which to sit, exposing only the head and shoulders above ground level, and a few concerned about personal comfort even go to the extent of heating it with a catalytic heater. The chance of a deer winding a hunter concealed in a foxhole must obviously be far greater than one perched up in a tree, quite apart from the fact that in areas of heavy hunting pressure, the latter must be about the safest method for the hunter who prefers to wait for his deer rather than stalk or still hunt.

Sitting and waiting for a deer may be cold work, but one hunter suggests lighting a little fire for, he maintains, 'deer don't seem to mind wood smoke'. The main thing is to keep still, for even the slightest movement will probably be detected by an approaching deer.

In order to mask the human scent, commercial scents are now available in the States, but how effective they are I cannot say. Such scents, however, are widely accepted among the bow hunters, many of whom swear by them and liberally sprinkle their clothing before heading for the bush. Some scents are even credited with attracting deer, and stories have been told of bucks running with their noses to the ground following the footsteps of a hunter who had previously treated his boots to a musk scent.

Bob Ramsey, the author of *How to Rattle up a Buck* (1966), recommends placing a jar containing shredded paper, wool or cotton, to which a few drops of skunk musk have been applied, downwind of your position, and this, he claims, will prevent an approaching buck detecting human odour even at a distance of only 10 ft (3 metres).

Other ruses tried by hunters to dampen human scent include hanging clothes over a smoky camp fire; burying them overnight in a heap of pine needles, dabbing them with pitch-pine or putting them in a box of cut-up apples for a few days before going on a hunting trip. Personally I prefer to leave off the after shave lotion and make sure the wind is in my favour even if it entails a considerable detour.

Despite the fact that there are sixteen subspecies of Whitetail in North America, for record purposes the Boone and Crockett Club recognize only two – the typical White-tailed deer *Odocoileus virginianus virginianus* and certain related species, and Coues' White-tailed deer *O.v.couesi*. Each, however, is subdivided into two categories, 'typical' antlers and 'non-typical' antlers, the former since 1949 and the latter since 1968 when the Records Committee decided that the incidence of 'non-typical' antlers on Coues' deer – pronounced *cows* – occurred with sufficient frequency to justify a new classificaton. In 'typical' White-tailed deer antlers, in addition to the short upright brows, there should be three or four tines erupting upwards from each main beam with normally no bifurcation, as in Mule deer, thus producing a head of about ten or twelve tines. Similar to Mule deer, however, White-tailed deer antlers are often multipointed and sometimes run to thirty or more points, the record being a buck killed in Texas in 1892 with no fewer than forty-nine (26 + 23) tines.

As with Mule deer antlers, there does not seem to be any fixed number of tines to enable a decision to be made as to whether the head should be treated as 'typical' or 'non-typical', for included in the 'typical' antler section of the Record Book are a number of trophies bearing sixteen or more tines, the highest being twenty-three (12 + 11) belonging to a buck taken in Michigan in 1963. Conversely, in the 'non-typical' section, there are a number of trophies with fewer than fourteen tines, the lowest being a 9-pointer (5 + 4) killed in South Dakota in 1964. Normally, where doubt exists, the matter is solved by measuring the trophy under both formulae and placing it in the list in which it scores the highest which resulted in the above anomalies.

In the case of 'non-typical' antlers of Mule deer, I suggested (*see page 191*) that since heads of this type were repeatedly cropping up in the same locality, the incidence might be hereditary. In White-tailed deer, however, the occurrence of 'non-typical' antlers in any one locality seems to be less noticeable, except in Crook County, Wyoming, which has been the source of seven of the nine 'non-typical' trophies recorded for this State. There must, of course, be many thousand of 'non-typical' heads taken which never reach the Record Book.

Not every subspecies of White-tailed deer can be hunted. The Key deer *O.v.clavium* which occurs on about eighteen islands of southern Florida Keys was once near extinction, and although now, fortunately, out of danger, it receives full legal protection. The Columbian White-tailed deer *O.v.leucurus*, which is restricted to an area along the lower Columbia River in Washington, was also in a similar plight, but numbers now appear to be increasing and it could well be taken off the 'endangered' list.

7 Regulations and Licences in Canada

Undoubtedly Canada, and in particular British Columbia, offers some of the finest big game hunting obtainable anywhere in North America, for with six indigenous deer species, not to mention other game animals such as wild sheep, goats and bear, etc. there is no lack of choice.

Canada is a huge country, holding vast areas of uninhabited terrain, much of which, until comparatively recently, has been inaccessible to the hunter.

Furthermore, even in the more accessible areas, it is mandatory for most non-resident hunters to be accompanied by a licensed guide, and since most guides have an allotted area in which to hunt, this ensures minimum of hunting pressure.

In some Provinces and Territories the hunting of certain big game animals is restricted to 'residents' only, i.e. Moose in Nova Scotia and New Brunswick; Caribou and Wapiti in Manitoba; and Wapiti and Barren-ground Caribou in Saskatchewan, although non-resident licences to hunt the Woodland Caribou are available. However, the qualifications required to be recognized as a resident are not the same everywhere.

The minimum age required before a hunting licence will be granted varies from one Province or Territory to another. In Yukon, for instance, no person under the age of fourteen is eligible for any licence, and anyone between the ages of fourteen and sixteen is eligible to hunt provided he is accompanied by a licensed person over twenty-one years of age. In Alberta, any fourteen to sixteen year old may hunt if accompanied by a parent or legal guardian, or any person of eighteen years of age or older who has the written permission of the parent or legal guardian. Fourteen years is also the minimum age in British Columbia. In Ontario, however, no one under sixteen years of age may hunt, and if the applicant is under twenty years of age, he must complete a hunting training course given by a certified hunting instructor prior to applying for a licence examination, the charge for which is $3. For anyone twenty years of age or older, a hunter training course is optional but recommended. In Quebec, a hunter's certificate is required by anyone wishing to hunt with a firearm, but not by those using longbow or crossbow. These certificates are issued by the Department of Tourism, Fish and Game, which is responsible for the firearms handling safety courses. A non-resident, however, must be in possession of a document from his province, state or country of residence, establishing that he is competent to handle a firearm for hunting.

In Newfoundland, before a big game licence can be issued, an applicant must be eighteen years of age by 31 August, and have successfully completed the following hunting capability tests:

1 Marksmanship test
2 Hunter's safety test
3 Big game regulations test

Successful applicants receive a numbered certificate and a big game application form.

Identification

Licences may be issued for male deer, female deer or 'antlerless' deer but as in the United States of America, the description of what may legally be shot for 'male' or an 'antlerless' deer may vary from one Province or Territory to another.

In Nova Scotia, for instance, a male White-tailed deer is described as one with visible antlers exposed above the skin, at least one of which must be 3 in. (7.5 cm) in length from the burr (coronet) to tip. During a 'male season only' in Alberta, however, it is unlawful to be in possession of any deer antlers (White-tailed or Mule deer) of length less than 4 in. (10 cm). An 'antlerless' deer means a female or any male deer with antlers less than 4 in. in length.

In British Columbia an 'antlered animal is a member of the deer family over one year of age bearing visible bony antlers. . . . The small skin or hair-covered protuberances of fawns and calves do not constitute antlers'. In Vancouver, bucks must have two or more prongs on at least one antler.

In Alberta a *trophy* Mule deer is a buck 'bearing antlers, one of which excluding the first point on the main beam commonly known as the brow tine, is composed of a main beam from the head branching out into *not less* than three or more prongs or tines not less than one inch (2.5 cm) in length'. The definition of a trophy Elk (Wapiti) is 'a male deer bearing antlers, one of which is composed of a main beam from the head off of which projects not less than four prongs or tines not less than 3 inches (7.6 cm) in length'.

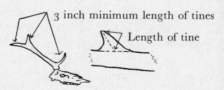

3 inch minimum length of tines

Length of tine

Minimum legal Wapiti (Elk) antlers in Kootenay (British Columbia)

In Saskatchewan an 'antlered' Elk means a Wapiti having one or both antlers measuring at least 6 in. (15 cm) in length, measured on the outside curve from the base to tip. In British Columbia (Kootenay) a bull Wapiti must have 'at least one branched antler which must consist of at least three tines (points) each of which is at least 3 inches (7.6 cm) in length.' (see sketch). In the same Province, in some areas, a bull Moose must have 'at least one branched or palmated antler, the longest of which is longer than the ear or a minimum of 10 in. (25 cm) before it can be shot.' The antlers, both bull Moose and Wapiti, must accompany the species licence when checking out. In Saskatchewan any male Moose of one or more years of age is considered a 'bull'.

In Yukon, although it is permissible to shoot either a male or a female Caribou during the hunting season, no animal of either sex may be shot that does not have forked antlers.

Tagging of carcases

In addition to any licence required to hunt deer of any species, all hunters, whether resident or non-resident, except Indians or Eskimos, are required to purchase the proper tag or seal for the desired species before the commencement of the hunt. In British Columbia it is mandatory to purchase the species licence before embarking on the hunt.

As soon as a kill is made the date notch on the appropriate tag, which corresponds to the date of the kill, must be cut out and the tag attached to the carcase, either through the tendon or around the base of the antler, where it must *remain* during transportation and until the carcase has been skinned out and cut up after inspection by a Fish and Wildlife officer or Game Guardian. The head should also remain attached to the carcase for as long as possible. No person may keep a deer carcase or any part of it, at his home or in any place of storage for more than twelve hours without it being registered. In British Columbia the lower jaw of all Caribou taken must be retained and submitted within ten days after the end of the hunt for inspection at one of the official checking stations in the Province. In Manitoba game taken by one person cannot be transported by another person unless it is accompanied by the licensee who took the game, or a special transportation permit has been obtained.

Tags are not normally transferable, but in Ontario, where group hunting is permitted, 'any member of the Group may take or kill the number of deer or Moose equal to the number of licences held by members of the Group.' In no case, however, 'shall the total number of big game taken exceed the total number of licences held by members of the party.'

Not everywhere is group hunting permitted. In Manitoba, for instance, residents may hunt Moose or deer in 'a party not exceeding two persons', each member being in possession of a valid hunting licence. Group hunting, however, is unlawful during the Elk (Wapiti), Moose or Caribou seasons.

Party licences are also available in Newfoundland for hunting Moose or Caribou and are issued under a system known as Party Licence Priority System. All applicants must have completed a hunter capability test and since applications for licences far exceed the actual number of licences available, it is recommended that hunters should apply for a party licence rather than an individual one, for the former are given priority over applications for individual licences. To illustrate this point, the results of the 1979 licence draw indicated that 98 percent (7915 out of 8136) of all applicants for a party licence received were successful, while only 6627 of the 13,311 applicants – or 50 percent – for individual licences were successful.

Hunters when applying, are invited to list as many area choices as possible in which they are prepared to hunt. Once a party licence has been issued names cannot be changed, but either person named on the licence is entitled to hunt alone.

When the person nominated on the party licence is accompanying the licensee, both may carry firearms and hunt. The word 'accompany', however, means hunting 'in the immediate area of and within sight of the licensee and the licensee and the other person named in the licence are both guilty of an offence if they are not in the immediate area and within sight of each other while both are hunting.'

Licences

The cost of licences varies not only from species to species but also from one Province or Territory to another and is, of course, subject to alteration from year to year, so any information given here can only serve as a rough guide. Up to date information *must*, therefore, be obtained from the appropriate Fish and Game Department at the time of the proposed hunt (*see Appendix B*).

Some Territories or Provinces such as Yukon require both a general hunting licence – which for a non-resident alien in 1978–9 cost $100 (about £43) as well as a non-resident trophy fee, which in the case of a Moose or Caribou, would cost a further $100 each.

Other Provinces, such as Alberta, British Columbia, Ontario and Quebec just issue a licence to hunt a certain species of big game, and this, for a non-resident may vary from about $50 for a Whitetail or Mule deer to $300 for a Moose in British Columbia. For a Caribou most Provinces or Territories charge $100 but in Newfoundland the cost is $500.

In Alberta, a Wildlife Certificate ($3) is a prerequisite for all hunting licences as well as a Fish and Wildlife Resource Development Stamp ($2), the proceeds of the former going to the Wildlife Damage Fund and the latter to 'Buck for Wildlife'.

The Buck for Wildlife Programme, initiated in 1973, is designed to maintain, improve and develop suitable habitat for various species of wildlife. A Wildlife Certificate is also required in Manitoba, but to be eligible for a certificate a person must have either graduated from the Manitoba Hunter and Firearm Safety Training course, or similar course from another Province or country, or have previously held a hunting licence. Anyone who has not reached his nineteenth birthday must be able to produce a Hunter and

Firearm Safety Training Certificate regardless of whether or not he has hunted before. Non-residents wishing to hunt in Saskatchewan must also produce a Firearm Safety Certificate before a hunting licence can be purchased.

Whilst hunting licences and game tags have to be obtained prior to the trip, trophy fees are generally payable only after the successful completion of the hunt.

Export permits, obtainable from most Ministry of Natural Resources offices in the area where the animals have been taken, are also required before any trophy can be taken out of a Province by a non-resident, and whilst these are generally issued free of charge, some Provinces such as Ontario make a charge of $15 for a Moose and $10 for a White-tailed deer.

Legal hunting weapons

Provided weapons are legal, it is not necessary to obtain a special permit to bring a firearm into Canada for hunting. This does not, however, remove the necessity of reporting firearms to Customs at the border. Fifty rounds of ammunition may normally be brought into the country by non-residents without having to pay any duty or taxes. The import by non-residents of pistols, revolvers and air pistols is prohibited unless required for an authorized revolver or pistol shoot, in which case a special permit may be released upon application to the Collector of Customs and Excise at the port of entry. Unlike the United States of America, handguns are not permitted for deer hunting in Canada. Fully automatic firearms are also prohibited.

Irrespective of whether the rifle is a legal one to bring into Canada, it need not necessarily be an acceptable one for hunting game, for certain firearms and ammunition are illegal in some Provinces and Territories.

In Alberta, for instance, any rifle of calibre less than .23 in. (5.8 cm) is illegal, as well as any cartridge case that measures less than 1.75 in. (4.4 cm) in length, or any non-expanding bullet. Nova Scotia and Saskatchewan also specify .23 in. as the minimum calibre, whilst British Columbia, Manitoba and New Brunswick all ban the use of any rim-fire rifle. In Yukon it is unlawful to use any rifle of less than .24 calibre whilst all solid pointed ammunition, including all hard point military type cartridges, are generally illegal.

In some Provinces, which include Nova Scotia, Saskatchewan and Yukon Territory, the shotgun, provided it is loaded with rifled slug or ball, may be used for deer, the last named specifying that the 'shotgun must not be smaller than 20 gauge'. Twenty gauge is also the minimum bore for shotguns in British Columbia, Newfoundland, Ontario and Quebec, but in Alberta any gun larger than the .410 is acceptable. Both British Columbia and Quebec prohibit the use of shotgun on Caribou and Moose, as well as for Wapiti in the former province.

Manitoba, Ontario, Quebec and Saskatchewan all permit the muzzle-loader to be used for deer hunting, although in Quebec it is not permitted for Moose. In Manitoba the minimum calibre for Moose and Wapiti is .50, but for White-tail .44 is acceptable.

Bow hunting for deer is permitted in the following Provinces and Territories:

Moose	Caribou	Wapiti (Elk)	White-tailed deer	Mule deer	Black-tailed deer
Alberta	Alberta	Alberta	Alberta	Alberta	British
British	Newfoundland	Manitoba	British	British	Columbia
Columbia	Northwest	Ontario	Columbia	Columbia	
Manitoba	Territories		Manitoba		
New Brunswick	*Yukon		New		
Newfoundland			Brunswick		
Northwest			Nova Scotia		
Territories			Ontario		
Ontario			Quebec		
Quebec			Saskatchewan		
Yukon					

*Residents only

With the exception of Newfoundland and Yukon, which specify a drawpull of not less than 45 lb (20.4 kg) elsewhere the requirement is a minimum of 40 lb (18 kg) drawpull.

For further details about bow hunting in North America, *see pages 225–8.*

Hunting with crossbow – a weapon described as a bow set transversely on a stock which has a trigger device used to hold the bow string for purposes of firing an arrow, stone or projectile – is permitted in British Columbia and Quebec.

In the former, a crossbow may be used during the special bow and arrow seasons unless excepted under regional schedules, to hunt all species of deer provided it meets the following requirements:

For Caribou, Moose and Wapiti it is illegal in British Columbia to use a bow having a pull of less than 150 lb (68 kg), but for the smaller species – Mule, Blacktail, Whitetail and the introduced Fallow deer, the minimum requirements are reduced to 120 lb (55 kg).

So far as the bolt (arrow) is concerned, provided it has a broadhead of at least $\frac{7}{8}$ in. (2.22 cm) at the widest point, and weighs not less than 250 grains (16.2 g) then it is legal for all species of deer.

In Quebec 80 lb (36 kg) pull is considered sufficient, whilst in Northwest Territories the draw weight must be at least 20 kg at 700 mm draw, the arrow having a broadhead point width of at least 25 mm at its widest point.

Visible clothing

In order to reduce accidents due to mistaken identity, hunting in some areas is only permitted provided visible clothing is worn by the hunters. In Alberta, for instance, a hunter 'must be visibly clothed in a long-sleeved coat or other long-sleeved outer garment and head dress of complete scarlet or blaze orange material' – an exception being any person hunting with bow and arrow in an area that has been reserved exclusively for the archers.

In Manitoba it is left to the hunter to decide whether he should wear 'a complete outer suit of white or hunter orange extending below the knees and a hunter-orange head covering. . . . A hunter-orange belt or vest may be worn if desired, in addition to the white suit.' Archers, likewise, are exempt only from this rule during the special archery seasons.

Archers hunting during the regular deer season in Saskatchewan, where they would be sharing the forest with riflemen, 'must wear a complete outer suit of white with a scarlet cap or a complete outer suit of bright-yellow or scarlet.' At other times they may wear a camouflaged suit, but never during the regular big game season. In New Brunswick, if a game warden sees any person or a licensed guide hunting without being properly attired in 'hunter orange' clothing, he may seize any such outer garment being worn and retain it for subsequent evidence.

In Nova Scotia, during the 1978–9 season the wearing of coloured clothing was not mandatory, but recommended, as it was probable that it would shortly become compulsory in the Province. In Quebec, hunters are also recommended to wear jackets of 'daylight fluorescent orange'.

Evidence of sex

Regulations of most Provinces state that it is unlawful to remove evidence of sex of any deer shot until the carcase is at home and cut up, or has been cleared by a Fish and Wildlife Officer or Game Guardian. To comply with this, the Big Game Regulations of Alberta suggest the following. Cut to one side of the scrotum or udder when opening animal for gutting. If the testicles and penis are removed, the entire scrotum should be left intact on one hind quarter. If the carcase has been skinned, then the scrotum or udder must remain attached to the meat. In British Columbia a portion of the udder or teats must be left attached to the carcase.

Any hunter in Yukon who kills a female Moose during an antlerless Moose season shall, when requested, forward the reproductive organs (ovaries and uterus), and also the lower jaw of such Moose, to a Conservation Officer or person authorized by the Director to receive them.

In order to ascertain the age groups of Wapiti being killed by hunters in Alberta, the incisors of all beasts shot are required by law to be mailed or taken personally to a Fish and Wildlife Office at the time of registration. It is also requested – but on a voluntary basis – to submit the incisor bar of all other game animals shot. Special envelopes are provided.

In Ontario the Ministry of Natural Resources is making a similar study but requires, at present, on a voluntary basis only, the complete lower jaw of all Moose or White-tailed deer shot, in return for which a 'deerhunter' or 'moose hunter' badge is given.

Moose and deer hides are also required by the Ministry of Natural Resources in Ontario for distribution to native people engaged in local crafts, and in exchange the hunter receives a blaze-orange hunting cap.

In the United States of America the law requires that all the meat from any deer killed must be taken out of the bush and none left to waste. In parts of Canada, however, it is different, for due to the inaccessibility of many of the hunting areas, it is not mandatory for hunters to bring out all the meat, so apart from that required for camp and identification purposes, the remainder is generally left for the bears and wolverines etc. to devour. Quebec regulations, however, require that 'every person who kills an animal while hunting shall take the necessary steps to prevent the edible flesh or the usable fur of such animal from spoiling.'

Dogs

In most localities the use of dogs for hunting is not permitted. In Ontario, however, their use has not been shown to have any harmful effects in good woodland range, but in farm country dogs are not permitted because deer may run into fences. Provided they are licensed, therefore, any number of dogs may be used for hunting deer or Moose, but during the close season they are not permitted to run at large in any area inhabited by deer or Moose.

In British Columbia dogs may be used when hunting Mule, Blacktail, Whitetail or Fallow deer, but they must be kept on leash. They are not, however, permitted to be taken on a hunt after Caribou, Moose or Wapiti.

General regulations

In Manitoba, New Brunswick, Newfoundland and Nova Scotia, it is illegal to hunt deer anywhere on a Sunday, but in Alberta and Ontario Sunday hunting is permitted only in certain Big Game zones. Some Provinces make no mention of Sunday hunting in their game regulations, so in such instances presumably it is legal.

Hunting or discharging a firearm from an aircraft, vehicle or power boat, whether moving or stationary, is illegal anywhere in Canada, or as the Manitoba game regulations state, 'A person may not use a vehicle driven by any means other than human power while hunting'. Snow-mobiles, however, may be used in certain areas to transport a kill out of an area to other means of transportation by the most direct route, but they may not be used to drive through deer or Moose yards (winter herding) or through a herd of Caribou. Most Provinces make it illegal to 'hunt, disturb or interfere with big game while such game is in a yard'. It is also illegal to fly in an aircraft or helicopter over a concentration of Caribou (Quebec regulations). In Northwest Territories, however, although in certain areas any aircraft may be used for locating game, a period of twelve hours must elapse before commencing any hunt. Helicopters, however, cannot be used for any purpose connected with hunting other than in an emergency.

Contravention of these regulations concerning the use of aircraft carries a minimum fine of $2000 (about £850) or fifteen month jail sentence.

It is illegal, everywhere, to hunt or kill any deer while swimming and this applies particularly to Moose and Caribou.

Hunting by artificial light is illegal, as indeed is any hunting between half an hour (or one hour) after sunset and half an hour (or one hour, as the case may be) before sunrise. Most regulations include a clause which states that it is unlawful to 'be intoxicated while hunting any wild life'! In Quebec, no person shall 'use any artificial means other than field glasses to detect, from a distance, the presence of an animal'.

As a general rule, it is unlawful to be in possession of a loaded firearm, or to discharge it without permission within about 200 to 300 yards (180 to 270 metres) of a farm building or dwelling house.

Outfitters and guides

Hunting and trophy fees may, however, be only a small part of the total cost involved for hunting big game in Canada, for with one or two exceptions, all non-resident alien hunters must book their hunts through a registered outfitter, and what their charges will be depends very much on the species and area to be hunted and also the duration of the hunt.

Names and addresses of registered outfitters can be obtained from the game branch of each Province or Territory, and it is helpful for the non-resident hunter to correspond with several of the outfitters listed, securing from them their open dates, prices and references. When contacting the outfitters, as much information as possible should be given, with respect to the number of hunters in the party, type of game required, time and duration of hunt. Most Provinces permit two non-resident hunters to share one resident guide. In British Columbia, a Canadian resident of the Province may take the place of a guide for a non-resident, provided a permit to do so has been obtained from the Fish and Wildlife Branch Office. In one or two areas of Alberta a resident of the Province may take the place of a licensed guide, and there are also some areas in Ontario where the use of a licensed guide is not mandatory. In Quebec non-residents are not allowed to hunt north of the 52nd parallel without the services of an outfitter. This includes the Caribou terrain.

In Manitoba, non-residents hunting Moose must not only be accompanied by a licensed guide, but also must hunt from a registered hunting lodge or outfitting camp. Non-resident Moose licences are only available from a registered lodge or outfitter, and must include the four-day package plan.

For residents, special Moose/Wapiti and Caribou hunts are issued on a draw basis only.

Most registered outfitters have their own registered hunting areas, and the majority are equipped with saddle and pack horses, as well as camping equipment, and will be responsible for providing guides and organizing the whole hunting trip.

For instance, in 1979 a twelve-day hunt in the Head Waters of the Muskwa River and Gathto Creek area south of Fort Nelson in British Columbia after

Moose, Wapiti, Caribou and Mule deer, as well as bear and wolf if required, would have cost about $3500 per hunter (about £1500). For this fee horses, camping equipment, saddles, food, cook and guide were supplied but it did not include either the species licence fee or non-resident hunting licence which, if all four species of deer were taken would have amounted to a further $425. The total costs, therefore, would have been around $4000 (about £1700).

For a seven-day hunt after Mule deer in British Columbia the cost would be about $1250 but a Whitetail hunt of similar duration would be slightly less – say $1000, whilst a combined seven-day hunt after both species would cost about $1500. To these prices must be added the cost of the non-resident licence ($75) and species licence fee ($50) for each deer – a total of around $1675. On all hunts, a deposit of one-third is required.

Dates of open hunting seasons and types of legal game available vary not only from one Province or Territory to another but also in different Game Management zones, and are subject to alteration on an annual basis. It must be realized, also, that where hunting with bow or other primitive weapon is permitted, a special open season for such weapons may be authorized outside the normal hunting season for modern rifle hunters. Seasons on a Special Draw licence for rifle hunters may also be arranged outside the normal hunting season.

Up-to-date information, therefore, on hunting seasons – as well as on legal weapons and licence fees etc. – can only be obtained from the Game branch concerned, a list of which appears in Appendix B.

As a rough guide, based on the 1979 hunting regulations, the open seasons for hunting deer in the Provinces and Territories of Canada are as follows:

Province or Territory	Caribou	Moose	Wapiti	Whitetail	Mule deer (Blacktail)
Alberta	Early Sept – end Nov	Early Sept – end Nov	Early Sept – end Nov	Early Sept – end Nov	Early Sept – end Nov
British Columbia[1]	Mid-Aug – mid-Nov	Mid-Aug – early Dec	Mid-Aug – end Nov	Begin Sept – early Dec	Begin Sept – end Feb. Early Sept – mid-Dec[2]
Manitoba	Begin Sept – early March	Begin Sept – late Nov	Early Sept – mid-Oct	Mid-Nov – begin Dec	—
New Brunswick	—	3 days end Sept	—	End Oct – end Nov	—
Northwest Territories	Mid-Aug[3] – end April End July – end Oct[4]	Begin Sept – end Oct	—	—	—

THE AMERICAS

Province or Territory	Caribou	Moose	Wapiti	Whitetail	Mule deer (Blacktail)
Nova Scotia	—	Few residents only	—	Begin to end Nov	—
Ontario	—	Mid-Sept – mid-Dec	Early Oct – mid-Dec	Early Oct – mid-Dec	—
Prince Edward Is.	—	—	—	—	—
Quebec	End Aug – end Sept	Begin Sept – end Oct	—	Early Sept[5] – end Nov End Oct[6] – mid-Nov	—
Saskat- chewan	Early Nov – begin March[7]	Begin Sept – begin Dec	Early Sept – late Nov	Early Nov – begin Dec	—
	Early Sept – begin Dec[8]	—	—	—	—
Yukon	Begin Aug – end Oct	Begin Aug – end Oct	—	—	—

[1] Some Fallow, Sept – mid-Dec
[2] Blacktail
[3] Barren-ground Caribou
[4] Woodland Caribou
[5] Anticosti Island
[6] Mainland
[7] Woodland Caribou
[8] Barren-ground Caribou

214

8 Regulations and Licences in the United States of America

Deer hunting in the United States of America is all on a licence basis, tags being issued by the appropriate Department of Fish and Game or Conservation etc. in each State to shoot a fixed number of each species – generally only one – during the hunting season.

For the resident, licences are comparatively cheap and cover all the commoner large game species of the State. For instance, a resident sportsman's licence in Montana costing $35 (1979) entitles the hunter to shoot one deer (either Mule or Whitetail but not both), one Wapiti (Elk) and one black bear, as well as some game birds and fishing. For these facilities, a non-resident has to pay $225 (about £112).

Most States permit only one deer – generally a male 'with visible antlers' to be shot during the regular hunting season, females and 'antlerless' deer being shot during special seasons arranged in areas where stocks are heavy.

One of the States that permits more than one deer per season on general licence is Louisiana which, although permitting six in a season, limits the kill per day to one. Over most of South Carolina the limit is five bucks per season, but there are some areas in this State where no limit is set.

In many States the number of Elk or deer tags available for non-residents is limited and once the applications reach the quota set, no more licences will be granted. For instance, in Idaho the quota of non-resident Elk and deer tags (Whitetail and Mule deer) in 1979 was set at 9500 and 8457 respectively. There is no limit, however, on general licences for residents.

In the following pages I have attempted to extract some of the most important points from the game laws of the fifty States each of which has its own game regulations and bag limits.

Licences and permits

In addition to permits issued for hunting during the normal gun or archery season, where deer stocks are high a number of special deer hunts are arranged, permits for which are generally distributed on a draw basis.

These hunts go by a variety of names. In Nevada, for instance, there are three types of hunts – Controlled, General and Special. The difference between a Controlled Hunt and a General Hunt is that in the former the number of hunters in any particular management area is limited, the permits, restricted in number, being issued by public drawing, whilst in a General Hunt there is no restriction on the number of hunters hunting in any particular area. A Special Season is similar to a Controlled Season, as only a limited number of permits are available for both residents and non-residents, distribution being on a draw basis.

A Controlled Hunt after Wapiti in the Wichita mountains of Oklahoma is certainly controlled on paper if not in practice.

Hunters will be grouped into parties and assigned an area and guide. Guides will not assist in actually locating or harvesting animals or in dressing or packing the carcase to an accessible area for vehicular pick up.

Hunters cannot take a companion into the hunt area. They will be accompanied by their assigned guides only. Hunters are permitted to have one companion available at the designated check station or Camp Doris to assist in the recovery of the carcase. The companions will be transported by refuge personnel to the hunt site after a kill is made.

Horses will not be permitted for hunting or packing purposes. Private vehicles will not be allowed on any of the hunt units. Vehicles will not be permitted to use any roads except improved roads as designated by the refuge manager.

The operation of such hunts is certainly 'controlled'!

A number of States operate what is known as Split Seasons – that is to say the general season might have a break in it of one or two weeks.

California have what they call Bonus Hunts and Exceptional Opportunity Hunts, the former being special 'permit hunts' arranged on private or military land for antlerless deer of either sex, whilst for the latter hunts a limited number of permits are available on specified days for trophy heads of three points or better.

Two special hunts are available in Alaska, one referred to as a Permit Drawing Hunt, for which permits costing $5 are issued on a drawing basis, and the other a Permit Registration Hunt, permits for which are issued throughout the season to an unlimited number of persons who must be in possession of a valid Alaskan hunting licence and apply in person at the Fish and Game Department Office. Applicants must agree to the conditions specified for each hunt, and understand that the season might be closed at short notice when a specified number of animals had been taken.

Successful applicants for a Permit Drawing Hunt may be required to demonstrate, to the satisfaction of the Fish and Game Department or Public Safety employee, their proficiency in firearms safety and marksmanship, unless they can show evidence of having completed an approved firearms safety course.

In Indiana a number of Special Controlled Hunts on military establishments are arranged on selected days during the open hunting season, permits for which are distributed by drawing. Depot employees from the military establishment may be assigned as hunting escorts and hunters must understand that for military reasons, any hunt is subject to cancellation or postponement.

Both Missouri and Florida have what is called a quota system, which is a method of rationing deer hunting opportunity. In Missouri there are two types of quota systems in operation; one to ration the antlerless deer harvest by issuing any-deer permits, and the other to limit the number of out-of-State hunters who can be directed to hunt in certain areas of the State.

The any-deer quota system has been found, under present hunting conditions, to be the best method of controlling the harvest of female deer, for it minimizes the variations in harvest that are caused by a change in hunting pressure or by the weather.

The non-resident quota system is required to limit the number of out-of-State hunters, particularly in the northern parts of Missouri. The non-resident quota system has resulted in these non-resident hunters being spread more proportionately throughout the State.

Utah reserve about 20,000 licences for non-residents, these being issued on a first-come-first-served basis. Montana also limit the number of licences available for non-residents.

In Florida, quota hunt permits are issued without charge on a first-come-first-served basis, the hunter selecting the area of his choice when submitting his application. The quota hunt permit system has limited the number of people hunting on each wildlife management area during the first nine days of the season, and with hunting pressure on the deer reduced, the quality of hunting has improved. Prior to the quota hunt system, 80 percent of legal deer were taken during the first two weeks of the season.

Special Deer Permits, limited in number, are also available in many States, selection generally being made by computer, thus giving all applicants the same chance of being selected.

Some people, however, seem to have more luck than others in draws, and to assist the unlucky ones, most States have what is called a preferential drawing whereby an applicant who has, perhaps, been unsuccessful over a number of years, can be given an advantage over applicants featuring for the first time in the draw.

Permits to hunt some of the less plentiful big game, such as Big Horn sheep or Moose, are also available only on a drawing basis. The number of permits available for any particular animal is strictly limited and most States limit the number of permits available to non-residents to only 10 percent in any district. Should the quota of Moose, say, in any particular area be under ten, then no permit in that district will be available for non-residents.

Depending on the number of applicants and game available, an applicant may well have to wait five or six years before drawing a permit. In Montana any person who has killed a Moose, Big Horn or 'Rocky Mountain' goat shall not be eligible to apply for a licence in any district for the next succeeding seven years.

Regulations

The hunting regulations issued annually by each State in addition to open season, tagging and firearms requirements, contain a list of practices which are unlawful whilst deer hunting. These include hunting near buildings and highways, hunting with firearms whilst under the influence of intoxicating liquor, disguising sex identification of the animal shot and shooting from vehicles, etc. Not all States require the same.

With regard to hunting or discharging a firearm *without permission* near an occupied building, distances vary from about 100 yards (91 metres) in New Hampshire and Delaware, to 440 yards (396 metres) in North Dakota.

In all States it is illegal to shoot deer from a public highway. Pennsylvania specify within 25 yards (23 metres) of the road, but New Mexico reduce this to only 6 ft (about 2 metres). In Wisconsin, except for a qualified, disabled person under permit, no other hunter may discharge any firearm or bow and arrow from or across any public road within 50 ft (15 metres) from the centre line, or fence line, whichever is the shorter.

Night shooting of deer everywhere is completely banned, the hunting hours normally running from day-break to sunset, or half an hour to an hour before sunrise and sunset. In Indiana hunting with guns is restricted to the hours between sunrise and sunset, but the archers have an extension of half an hour at each end of the day. The use of artificial light – often referred to as jacking – is therefore illegal.

In Kentucky no hunting is permitted on Mondays or Tuesdays, unless the Monday happens to be a federal holiday.

The question of Sunday hunting varies, not only from State to State, but also within an individual State. States which ban all Sunday hunting for deer include Delaware, Maine, Maryland, Massachusetts, New Jersey, North Carolina, Ohio, Pennsylvania, South Carolina, Virginia and West Virginia.

Georgia, New York and Rhode Island all open up a few areas for Sunday hunting, whilst in Connecticut Sunday hunting is permitted only on licensed private shooting reserves, and then only after permission has been obtained from the town.

Use of mechanical and other approach aids

Most State game laws ban the shooting of any wild animal from a vehicle which include all terrain vehicles (A.T.V.s) and snow-mobiles. In Mississippi it is prohibited to wound, drown, shoot, capture, take or otherwise kill any deer from a boat, and a similar law operates in both Kentucky and North Carolina, the latter also include 'any other floating device'.

The shooting of a deer whilst swimming is also generally banned, and in Kentucky it is illegal to shoot a deer whilst standing 'in water up to its neck'.

In addition to the ban on dogs for hunting, Kentucky also makes it illegal for 'any other domestic animal' to be used whilst hunting deer which presumably refers principally to the horse, though there are instances of hunters having used a cow to provide 'cover' for a stalk in an open field.

In Alaska aircraft may be used for Moose hunting in Unit 15 (A) – the area south of Anchorage on the Kenai peninsula – but only north of the Sterling Highway after midnight on the morning of 11 September. Otherwise, in Alaska 'a person who has been airborne may not thereafter take or assist in taking big game until after 3 a.m. following the day in which the flying occurred' except Sitka Black-tailed deer in the coastal region of the Alexander archipelago.

In Kansas it is illegal to use a two-way radio while hunting deer.

Tagging carcases

The tagging of deer carcases is universal throughout the States and immediately any deer is killed the tag must be attached to the carcase and remain there until the carcase is cut up. Even deer killed by a farmer, who is not required to obtain a permit to shoot deer on his own land, must be tagged in the normal way. The composition of the tag and point of attachment varies from State to State. In Wisconsin, for instance, the tag is of metal and must be attached to 'the gambrel [hock of hind leg] of the deer . . .' where it must remain until the carcase is consumed. In Vermont, however, the point recommended for the tag is inside the ear.

In Kentucky the tags – three of them – form part of the deer permit, and as soon as a deer is killed the appropriate tag will be attached to the hind leg as above, where it must remain until the carcase has been processed and packaged. Another tag must be attached to the raw hide as soon as the deer is skinned, whilst a third tag will be attached to any part of the deer – generally the head – which has been separated from the carcase to be despatched to the taxidermist for mounting. No head, however, may be detached from the carcase until the complete deer has been removed from the field. Tagged hides from lawfully taken deer may be bought and sold.

As far as the venison is concerned, in most States it is illegal to buy, sell or 'barter' any edible part of a deer, thus making the disposal of venison difficult and as a result there is very little commercial poaching for financial gain. A rather strange law exists in Vermont whereby it is illegal to dispose of any venison taken during the archery season (15–29 October). Had the deer, however, been shot about a fortnight later during the regular season (11–26 November) the venison may be sold or given away during the season and during a period of twenty days thereafter, *provided* it remains in the State.

Anyone wishing to donate venison in Utah becomes involved in a certain amount of paper work for the donor has to endorse the gift with a signed certificate stating what portion of the deer was being donated, the number of the deer licence upon which the deer was lawfully taken, the date of the kill and date of donation. This certificate has to be retained by the donor as *prima facie* evidence of lawful possession.

As soon as a deer has been killed, after the tag has been attached, it must be reported to the nearest checking-out station for registration, some of which, during the hunting season, remain open for the full twenty-four hours, whilst others close about 10 p.m.

Most States require each licence holder personally to accompany the carcase to its final destination. If, however, it is to be transported by anyone else, then the carcase must not only be tagged with the regular tag, but also with another tag, indicating the names of both the consignor and consignee, as well as the source of origin and final distribution. Normally, a deer carcase may only be transported during the official open hunting season and twenty days thereafter.

Identification

In Europe, sex decides the time of year when a deer may be shot, and the hunting seasons are arranged accordingly. In North America, however, except in an open season for both sexes, the deer are divided into two categories – buck (or bull) with visible antlers, and antlerless deer, and any deer, therefore, which does not fulfill the former definition, even though it may be a male, can legally be shot during the open season for antlerless deer. In other words an 'antlerless' deer does not necessarily mean a female, and in fact an antlerless deer in, say, the States of Florida and Ohio where the minimum antler length for a legal Whitetail buck is 5 in. (12.7 cm) could be any deer with antlers shorter than this figure. In the State of Washington, on the other hand, a legal buck with a visible antler 'is defined as one having a horn-like growth with velvet shed that is visible above the hair'.

In Nevada, a legal buck is 'any deer with at least one branched antler' thus designating all spike bucks as 'antlerless' deer. The following is a summary of what some States consider to be a legal buck 'with visible antlers' – one antler meeting the required length being sufficient:

5 in. (12.7 cm) antler length minimum	4 in. (10.2 cm) antler length minimum	3 in. (7.6 cm) antler length minimum	2 in. (5.0 cm) antler length minimum	Antler just visible above hair line
Florida	Arkansas	Indiana	New Mexico	Georgia
Ohio	Colorado	Massachusetts	Virginia	Louisiana
	Kentucky	New Jersey		North Carolina
	Montana	New York		South Carolina*
		Pennsylvania		South Dakota
		South Carolina*		Texas
		Tennessee		Washington
		Vermont		
		West Virginia		
		Wisconsin		

* In Game Zone areas 3-in. antlers is minimum – elsewhere an 'antler above the hair line only' would qualify.

The following States define an antlered deer as one having at least one branched or forked antler: Idaho, Iowa, Nevada and North Dakota.

It can be assumed, therefore, that in all the States mentioned above, any deer that does not fulfill the minimum antler specification is considered for hunting purposes to be an 'antlerless' deer.

So far as the Wapiti (Elk) is concerned, in New Mexico a legal bull is described as one having either a forked antler or a brow tine on at least one side, either of which must be at least 6 in. (15.2 cm) long. In Colorado an 'antlerless' Elk means either a Wapiti without any antlers or with one or both antlers, neither of which measures 6 in. (15.2 cm) in length. A legal bull is, therefore, one having one antler – or both – of at least 6 in. (15.2 cm) in length.

In Utah a 'bull' Elk is one with antlers over 5 in. (12.7 cm) in length, whilst the antlers of a Moose must be longer than the ears before it can be described as a 'bull'.

Juveniles

Whilst juveniles generally are not allowed to hunt unaccompanied by an adult until they are fourteen to sixteen years of age, some States do permit youngsters to go after deer with firearm or bow as early as ten years and even arrange special hunts for them. Tennessee is one of them, and for five days in early December hunts are arranged for youths of ten to sixteen years during which period each is allowed to shoot one deer of either sex. In order to participate in these hunts each juvenile, who must throughout the hunt be accompanied by a non-hunting adult, must have a hunting licence, a big game licence and a hunter safety certificate. Youth gun hunts are also arranged in the Land between Lakes area of Kentucky for two days in late November for youths in the same age category, each having to be in possession of a hunter safety certificate and be accompanied by an adult. Both must have a valid licence.

At the other end of the scale, free hunting, or reduced licence fees, are available in many States for senior citizens. In Hawaii, Kentucky and Rhode Island, once a resident has reached the age of sixty-five he can hunt without payment. In New Hampshire and New York, however, a licence does not become free until the ages of sixty-eight and seventy respectively have been reached.

In Vermont, a sixty-five year old resident may buy a permanent hunting licence for $1.75 but in Ohio a similar licence will cost a senior citizen $7.

Disabled

Some States make special provision for hunting by disabled persons, either by arranging special hunts for them or allowing them to purchase hunting licences at much reduced rates.

On Prudence Island, in the State of Rhode Island, a four-day hunt in early December is arranged for paraplegics and double amputees for which a normal hunting licence is required. None of the hunter's assistants are allowed to hunt or carry firearms at any time during this period, and if any deer is wounded and not recovered, it must be reported to the officer in charge.

In Vermont, provided a special permit has been obtained from the Commissioner, a paraplegic may hunt with either a firearm or a bow from a motor driven vehicle or craft. A similar facility is available in New Hampshire for paraplegics, disabled veterans or anyone who has suffered from the loss of, or 'use of both lower extremities'. On these hunts, however, it is not permitted to hunt from 'boats with motor attached or aircraft'. Furthermore, at no time whilst the vehicle is in motion, may the firearm be loaded. In Maryland, disabled persons may obtain a free special permit from the Wildlife Administration to hunt from an automobile, whilst a special three-day hunt is arranged in Massachusetts at the end of October for paraplegics.

In a number of States, occupants of farms and members of the family may hunt Whitetail or Mule deer without licence. In New Jersey an area of only 5 acres (2 hectares) is considered large enough to qualify as a farm but in Missouri it must be an area of more than 80 acres (32 hectares).

Party hunting

Some States have strict rules about the number of persons who may hunt together as a party. In South Dakota, for instance, it is unlawful to hunt in groups numbering more than twenty persons, whilst in Pennsylvania, twenty-five is the maximum number that may hunt together. Furthermore, in the latter State, if five or more persons hunt deer together, a roster must be maintained in duplicate, giving the full name and address of every member of the party, and full details of weight, sex, dates etc. of all deer shot.

In Rhode Island it is prohibited 'for more than five persons to hunt in unison', whilst six is the maximum number of persons permitted to hunt together in New Hampshire.

In Wisconsin 'deer hunting party permits' may be issued in certain zones to parties of at least four persons for taking *one* deer of either sex in addition to the individual bag limit of the party members. When party hunting, each member must wear a special armband on the sleeve of his outer garment.

No person, when party hunting for deer in Minnesota, may kill more deer than the total number of valid licences held by members of the party. Party hunting for antlerless deer is not permitted except among those persons who must *each* have an antlerless deer permit for the same area.

Both Kansas and Nebraska invite 'Buddy Applications' whereby not more than three applications in the former State and two in the latter may be submitted together in order to be considered as a group. The group will be considered as a unit in the drawing for permits. If the group number is drawn, then all will receive permits; if not, all will be rejected.

On the islands of Sapelo and Ossabaw in Georgia, a number of parent/child hunting permits of three day duration are arranged, distribution being by computer. Permits are limited to 100 on Sapelo and 75 on Ossabaw. Each pair shall consist of one child (12–16 years) and a responsible adult, but only one firearm is permitted per pair, either of which may do the shooting. Three-day parent/child hunting permits are also available in the Cedar Creek management area, but in this area only the child is authorized to discharge the firearm.

Deer drives

Many States prohibit or restrict the methods which may be used to drive or move deer to hunters. In Maine, for instance, it is unlawful for any hunter to drive or participate in a deer drive, whilst in New Hampshire no person is permitted to drive deer by the use of horns, whistles or other noise-making devices or by the use of snow travelling vehicles.

In Alabama, where dogs are permitted to move deer, should the total number of hunters exceed 300 in the Covington Wildlife Management area, then only one drive per day will be allowed.

On game management area lands in South Carolina, man-drives are permitted between 10 a.m. and 2 p.m. only.

High seats

Although long practised in Europe, it is only in comparatively recent years that shooting deer from high seats, or Tree Stands, has become popular in the United States, and although this method is still illegal in some areas, I believe it will not be long before high seat shooting will be an acceptable method of deer hunting in every State.

There is no doubt that many State Fish and Game departments are much concerned about the damage the high seats might do to the trees, and most instructions ban the use of nails in the construction of tree stands. 'No nails, spikes, screw-in devices, wire or tree climbers may be used to attach tree stands or to climb trees' states the Kentucky *Deer Hunting Guide* and this is typical of many. Most States that permit hunting from stands recommend or insist that they must be portable, and whilst some like Kentucky, permit the stand to be 'placed in trees no more than two weeks before the opening day of each hunting period, and must be removed within one week after that hunting period ends' others, like Wisconsin, Maryland and Louisiana, to mention but three, allow their use only provided they are completely removed each day at close of hunting hours.

Indiana permit the use of fasteners 'to attach a tree blind' to a living tree provided they do not penetrate more than $\frac{1}{2}$ in. (1.25 cm), whilst in South Carolina no wire may be wrapped around a tree to secure the stand in position.

Michigan and Kentucky require that the owner's name and address should be clearly marked on each platform, and in the latter's hunting regulations it states that any permanent stand that had been erected before 1979 could be used during that season but could not be repaired or maintained for future use.

Minnesota restrict the height of the platform from the ground to no more than 6 ft (1.8 metres) whilst in North Carolina, any deer hunting with rifles must be from stands at least 8 ft (2.4 metres) high.

Road casualties

In many States, particularly in Texas, a considerable number of deer become road casualties and with few exceptions, it is illegal to remove the victim, so this results in many thousands of carcases being left to waste. The Vermont game laws clearly state that 'it is unlawful to pick up deer carcases found on or along the highway'. A friend of mine who once motored from east to west Texas – a distance of over 700 miles (1200 km) – said he counted over 200 deer carcases en route in various stages of decomposition, lying by the roadside, and he himself had been responsible for one casualty. This sad state of affairs, of course, has been brought about by the fact that nowhere in the United States can deer be killed without an official tag, and those who have game tags have probably used them up on hunted deer. Furthermore, just as many deer and more are killed on the road during the close season, when a game tag, anyway, would no longer be operative.

It does seem, however, that some States are becoming aware of this waste of venison, and Indiana for one, has recently issued a Discretionary Order (no. W-17) which enables a deer killed by collision with a motor vehicle to be released to the owner or driver of the vehicle, or to anyone else at the discretion of the officer investigating the incident. A permit from the Department of Natural Resources will be issued to each donee and this will allow him to possess the carcase for his *own personal* consumption, for a period limited to sixty days. He is not, however, entitled to give any part of it away. If two or more highway deer are involved, a donee shall be eligible for only one deer.

A permit shall not be issued, however, to possess a young spotted fawn. Non-residents are not eligible as donees unless they intend to remain in Indiana for thirty days or more. In Delaware, the situation is similar and any deer killed by a motor vehicle may be retained by the motorist hitting the deer, upon official tagging by the State Police or Division Personnel. The Fish and Game Commission of Kansas issue 'accidental deer tags' so as to authorize legal possession of the venison.

Fines

Penalties for illegal killing of game or violation of the game laws vary considerably from State to State. In Utah, for instance, the wildlife is considered the property of the State, and the Wildlife Board has, therefore, authorized the Division of Wildlife Resources to reclaim the estimated value of any wild life illegally taken. In addition to heavy monetary fines and possible jail sentence, a 'monetary replacement' of wildlife taken illegally will be claimed by the Division through civil proceedings. In 1979, therefore, the replacement value of Moose, as established by the Board, was $1000, whilst for Wapiti and Mule deer, $750 and $500 respectively.

For unlawful killing of Wapiti in South Dakota and Pennsylvania, the fine is $300 and $400 respectively, as compared to $100 for a Whitetail in South Dakota. In Indiana, however, anyone who illegally takes a Whitetail 'shall reimburse the State the sum of $500'.

In New Jersey, anyone causing damage to crops is liable to a fine of up to $500 and loss of hunting privilege for two years.

The minimum fine for the violation of any of the game laws in Manitoba is $50 and this can be increased for more serious offences, up to a maximum of $1000 and up to six months' jail sentence. Similar sentences operate in Maine.

Colorado operate what is known as an '18 point Licence Revocation' scheme. Each conviction of a wildlife law has a specific point value. When a person has accumulated eighteen points or more within any five year period, the Wildlife Commission is authorized to suspend that person's licence privilege in Colorado.

The Colorado Division of Wildlife has recently transplanted several Moose into the Illinois River drainage area, and these animals are protected by law. If, therefore, any person is convicted of pursuing, wounding or killing one of these animals, he 'shall be punished by a fine of not less than one thousand dollars nor more than five thousand dollars, or by imprisonment in the State penitentiary for not less than one year nor more than three years, or by both such fine and imprisonment'.

Compared to almost a century ago these fines are not particularly severe, for as long ago as 1897 the fine for hunting without a licence in Wisconsin could be anything from $50 to $200, whilst for illegal transportation, $100 to $500. The penalty for false swearing was $500 to $1000.

With regard to accidents whilst hunting which result in injury or death to human beings, the New Hampshire Fish and Game Law states 'Any person, while on a hunting trip, or in pursuit of wild animals or wild birds, who carelessly shoots and wounds or kills any human being, shall be guilty of a misdemeanour, and in addition thereto his licence shall be revoked and he shall not be granted a licence to hunt for a period of ten years.' After which 'it may be restored at the discretion of the director and the Commission'!

Any person who carelessly discharges his firearm and thereby endangers life and property of another person shall lose his licence for a period not to exceed three years. If, however, any person abandons a wounded, or killed human being 'his licence to hunt shall be revoked for life'.

These penalties are in addition to any penalty imposed as conviction in court.

In an effort to combat game law breakers, some States offer rewards to encourage hunters to report any illegal actions they may happen to see whilst hunting. New Mexico is one, their scheme Operation Game Thief (O.G.T.) will pay up to $250 for information leading to the arrest of a law violator.

Bow hunting

Hunting deer and other game animals with bow and arrow is becoming increasingly popular in North America, and provided the weapon and arrows fulfil certain specifications and the hunter has the necessary licence, it is perfectly legal to do so in most Provinces and States, many of which have certain areas reserved solely for the archers. In others there may be a special bow-hunting season before the rifle shooters move in, and a few may permit both forms of hunting to run concurrently, but with special regulations about dress to be worn.

Wisconsin was the first State to allow bow hunting, when, in 1934, two counties were opened up for a short archery season. Forty applicants hunted, but only one buck was reported taken. Since their first season, Wisconsin has had an annual season, except in 1935, when all hunting was suspended. In 1945, during a forty-five day season, 146 deer were killed, and this was increased to over a thousand during a total of eighty-nine days of bow hunting, spread over two separate seasons during the course of one year in the early sixties. Approximately a quarter of these were taken by non-resident hunters.

Michigan was probably the next State to allow bow hunting and 186 archers turned out for the first season. During the early sixties a total of 36,420 archery licences were sold, of which 3777 were to non-residents, the total number of deer being killed by archers being 1230.

More recently, in Iowa about 16 percent of the deer hunters were archers.

In Wyoming, in addition to a regular hunting licence, an archer must also possess a valid bow-hunting licence for the species he wishes to hunt, one licence being necessary for 'big game' – which includes *all* species of deer – and the other for 'trophy game' (bear and mountain lion).

Nowadays, all States which have open deer seasons have special archery seasons of varying length, and in particular the States of New York, New Jersey and Pennsylvania can all offer good bow hunting for Whitetails.

The majority of States have the archery season before the general firearms season but some States, which include Maryland and Washington, allow the bow to be used during the firearm season. No hunter, however, may carry both firearms and bow whilst hunting.

A longbow suitable for one State may be illegal in another. For instance, the minimum requirement for pull or draw weight varies from 30 lb (13.6 kg) in Maryland, Louisiana and Wisconsin to 45 lb (20.25 kg) in Alaska, Kansas and Hawaii. Yukon also specifies 45 lb. For Wapiti (Elk) and Moose in Wyoming it must be 50 lb (22.6 kg).

The draw weight is the number of pounds pull required to draw an arrow of 28 in. (71 cm) in length to its head; 35 lb is generally considered suitable for a laminated full-recurved bow.

The specification for the legal arrow required for big game also varies from one State to another, some States requiring the full 28 in. whilst others, such as North and South Dakota and Tennessee, allow a minimum length of 24 in. (60.9 cm). Tennessee also require 'sharpened steel broad head blades of barbless (non-expanding upon retraction) design. The blade(s) shall not be less than $\frac{7}{8}$ in. (2.22 cm) nor more than 2 in. (5.08 cm) at widest point for single two-edge blades, or less than $3\frac{1}{2}$ in. (8.89 cm) in circumference for three or more blades. The minimum weight for all broadheads shall be 100 grains'. Whilst 100 grain minimum weight for the broadhead is also acceptable in Alabama and Tennessee, Wyoming require 400 grain for deer and 500 grain for Moose and Wapiti.

Rhode Island specify that the broadhead arrows must have at least two cutting edges, $\frac{7}{8}$ in. (2.22 cm) or greater in width constructed without rivets. Each arrow must also carry the name and address of the licensed hunter – a stipulation also required by New Hampshire and Texas.

Range requirements also vary considerably, for whilst 125 yards (114 metres) is acceptable for Virginia, New Jersey and South Dakota, the archery regulations for New Mexico and Wyoming require the arrow to be propelled a minimum distance of 160 yards (146 metres).

Apropos pull weight and range, the Fish and Game Department of Vermont decrees that a 40-lb bow is to be the minimum for deer. A good rule of thumb for maximum yardage for your bow is a pound-pull per yard – 50 lb pull 50 yard maximum target distance.

All State bow-hunting regulations are in agreement, however, that with neither the conventional nor compound bow may the arrow be held or triggered mechanically. It is also illegal to treat the arrow with any chemical or poison, or use an explosive head.

One of the advantages – a very dubious one I must admit – claimed by bow enthusiasts of the bow over the rifle, is that deer crippled with arrows are much less likely to die than those wounded with bullets, simply because the shock hasn't ruptured vital vessels which generally would bring eventual death.

Commenting on this subject, the Vermont *Fish and Game Law* booklet states the following.

Unlike a bullet, the broadhead arrow has no shocking power barring a hit on the spinal column. Because there is no shock, there is no muscle spasm to stop bleeding which starts instantly. There is also no plugging effect with a broadhead since there is no pushing action, only cutting. A deer hit by a broadhead in almost any fleshy area will usually bleed to death in short order. If sufficient bleed-out is not gained, the wound will heal quickly as a rule.

Very few arrow heads found in the thousands of deer examined at the checking stations or otherwise brought to the attention of the department, have either started to cover over with protecting gristle or have been completely encased.

Apropos wounded deer and bow hunting in general, the following remarks, released some years ago by the Wisconsin Conservation Department, were quoted by H R Wambold (1964).

There is little verification as to any considerable number of deer found dead later as the result of arrow wounds. Undoubtedly there are more crippled and wasted deer than are reported. Instances of these undesirable conditions are not as evident as the number of wasted deer resulting from other types of hunting.

Average killing distance figured to 25.7 yards [23 metres], whilst six out of ten deer shot were shot while running. Average distance of recovery of deer after being hit was 162.7 yards [146.4 metres].

Overall hunter success is probably under 5 percent, so the bow hunter's contribution to cropping deer in problem areas is negligible. Some years ago a poll, conducted by the Pennsylvania Game Commission, revealed that out of 2141 licensed archers, only 5 percent were successful in tagging their venison with a further 10 percent who recorded hits but failure to recover. The average distance for kills was 32 yards (28.8 metres) and the average time spent hunting, 36 hours. During the 1978 season, a total of 5053 deer (2122 bucks, 2931 does) were taken by archers. In Michigan the bow hunter's success ratio over the whole State was 3.5 percent, each hunter averaging approximately seven days' hunting during the season.

Bow hunting for exotics on the game ranches of Texas is becoming increasingly popular but at least one – the Priour Ranch, recognizing that this form of hunting inevitably results in an increase in wounding, has stipulated that a hunter may only hunt with bow provided he agrees to pay the full listed price for any animal that is wounded and not recovered.

There is no doubt that to achieve success, the bow hunter has to display considerably more patience, skill and fieldcraft to get within an effective range of about 30 yards (27 metres) to ensure a clean kill, than the hunter armed with a telescopic-sighted rifle, who can place a bullet with accuracy at over six times this distance.

Hunting, however, is not a test of marksmanship but of fieldcraft, and in my opinion, for any sport that involves the taking of life, the most efficient weapon should be used so as to reduce wounding and suffering to a minimum. The results of the Pennsylvanian Game Commission poll quoted above, revealed that *twice* as many animals got away wounded from the bow hunters as were accounted for – and I see no reason to believe that this is not a true picture of what happens elsewhere when the arrow replaces the bullet. Indeed, it could be considerably worse as more and more young and inexperienced hunters take up the sport.

The archers claim that the appeal of bow hunting is not so much the kill as the challenge to get up close to a wild animal. If that is so, then the same challenge would still be there for the man armed with a camera, but when the interest becomes venison or a trophy for his wall, then the rifle should be the weapon and not the bow.

Many countries prohibit the use of bow and arrow on deer, and I am thankful that I live in one of them!

Crossbow

At the moment the crossbow is not generally accepted as an approved hunting weapon, and it is not permitted for hunting in over a third of the States and Provinces of North America.

In Wyoming, where the crossbow is permitted, it must have at least 90 lb (41 kg) draw weight, be at least 14 in. (35.5 cm) draw length and have a positive safety mechanism. The butt must be at least 16 in. (40.6 cm) in length, and cocking must be by hand, without any leverage gaining device. The steel broadhead must have at least 1 in. (2.5 cm) cutting width. In Kentucky the minimum pull weight must be 100 lb (45 kg) but the minimum width of the barbless broadhead is reduced to $\frac{7}{8}$ in. (2.2 cm). The minimum pull weight for a crossbow in Arkansas, however, is only 75 lb (34 kg).

In Oklahoma, although the crossbow is normally illegal for hunting, its use may be allowed to an applicant who has 'a permanent disability of either hand to the extent that he cannot physically use a conventional longbow, as certified by a medical doctor'. Paraplegics, and those who have lost the use of one or both arms, provided they have a permit from the Game and Fish Commissioner, may also hunt with a crossbow during the deer bow season in North Dakota.

Muzzle-loader

In some Provinces and States, a special season is reserved for hunters who wish to use a muzzle-loading rifle, and to take advantage of these seasons, a special muzzle-loading licence is required. This licence is required for seasons established *exclusively* for muzzle-loaders, and may not be used for hunting during the general open season for modern firearms, even though the hunter may wish to use his primitive weapon. Conversely, no hunter is permitted to hunt any game during the season set aside for muzzle-loaders with a weapon that does not fulfil the following definitions of a muzzle-loader:

1 A muzzle-loader means any single or double barrel wheel lock, match-lock, flint-lock or percussion rifle with exposed ignition in which the black powder and ball or bullet must be loaded from the muzzle. If the rifle has a removal breech plug, such removal must require the use of tools. Minimum barrel length must be 20 in. (50.8 cm) but the minimum calibre required may vary according to the species to be hunted, the minimum for any deer being .38 (.40 preferred), such measurements being taken from land to land in the barrel. Ignition is to be wheel-lock, match-lock, flint-lock or percussion, using original style percussion caps that fit on the nipple and are exposed to the elements. Sights are to be iron sights. Telescopic sights or sights containing glass are prohibited.

2 Only one barrel of a double barrel muzzle-loader may be loaded at one time whilst hunting in a special primitive muzzle-loading season.

Variations to the above occur in some State regulations. In Delaware, for instance, the minimum length of barrel for a muzzle-loader must be 28 in. (71 cm) and it is unlawful to use a powder charge of less than 62 grains. In both New Jersey and Wyoming, however, the minimum powder charge is 50 grains.

Special seasons set aside for muzzle-loading rifles are of short duration. Thus in Washington State there is a three-week open season on Mule and White-tailed deer (bucks only) during the latter part of November and early December, whilst in another area both sexes may be shot during an eleven-day open season at the beginning of December.

For hunting Wapiti with muzzle-loaders, Washington State has a special open season lasting about nine days, during the middle part of December in which deer of either sex may be shot. In Manitoba the minimum calibre for Moose and Wapiti is .50, but for Whitetail and Mule deer a minimum calibre of .44 is sufficient. Colorado also specifies .50 as minimum calibre for Wapiti, but permits .40 for the smaller deer. In Yukon it is unlawful to hunt big game with a muzzle-loader or black powder rifle of less than .45 calibre. One hunting zone in Ontario has a ten-week open season (six weeks for non-residents), commencing early October reserved exclusively for hunting Moose with primitive weapons, which include both archery and muzzle-loaders, but the latter cannot be used for hunting White-tailed deer anywhere in the Province.

In Pennsylvania during the 1978 season, a total of 1570 deer (111 bucks, 1459 does) were taken by hunters using muzzle-loaders.

Muzzle-loading shotguns are also legal in a number of States, the usual stipulation being that buckshot or ball must be used.

In Texas, at a cost of (1979) about $50 per weekend, a hunting agency will arrange archery hunting on a few selected ranches during the month of October. Each hunter is assigned to an area consisting of approximately 100 acres (40 hectares) and during the three-year period up to 1979, with about 1600 archers participating, hunter success has been approximately 10 percent. Bag limits have been set at two bucks and one doe, one buck and two does or three does, depending on the area and availability. There is no extra charge for any deer taken.

Handguns

Handguns, described as any firearm having a barrel less than 12 in. (30.5 cm) in length, are permitted for use whilst deer hunting in a number of States. Colorado's definition of a lawful handgun is any short pistol or revolver intended to be held and fired from one hand and having no shoulder stock or attachment. The muzzle-loading handgun, however, is not permitted for use while deer hunting.

Handguns, referred to as 'sidearms' in Indiana and Mississippi, come in all shapes and calibres, and to find out what weapons – if any – are legal in any particular State, the hunting regulations will have to be studied.

Some States, which include Arkansas, Nevada and Tennessee, specify that the handgun must have a minimum barrel length of 4 in. (10.1 cm) but both Georgia and North Dakota require a slightly longer minimum length, namely 5.9 in. (14.9 cm) and 6 in. (15.2 cm) respectively. Kentucky go to the other extreme with a minimum barrel length of 3.9 in. (9.8 cm).

Both Kentucky and Tennessee give a full list of revolvers and pistols that are legal for deer hunting. These include .30 Herrett, .357 Herrett, .357 magnum; .41 magnum and .44 magnum. Kentucky also include the .41 auto mag; .44 auto mag; .45 auto mag; and the .357 auto mag; and any cartridge using a bullet of at least 110 grains weight and developing at least 500 ft lb of muzzle-energy. Maryland allow the use of any handgun providing it is 'capable of giving a muzzle-energy of 1200 or more foot pounds'. It permits, also, the use of the .44 magnum with a $6\frac{1}{2}$ in. (16.5 cm) barrel.

Shotguns

Although almost every State permits the use of shotguns for deer, the majority limit the bore to not larger than 10 gauge or smaller than 20 gauge. In both Arkansas and Hawaii, however, the .410 gun can be used provided the ammunition is rifled slug, although for Blacktail in Hawaii, buckshot may also be used. Slug, single ball (pumpkin ball) or buckshot is also mandatory ammunition in most States although pellet shot up to no.4 size is legal for Whitetail in Arkansas, whilst in Connecticut no shot larger or heavier than no.2 size is permissible.

In both Oregon and Washington, although the shotgun can be used for hunting the smaller deer, it is prohibited for Wapiti. No species of deer, however, may be killed with a shotgun of any description in Utah.

The use of automatic or hand-operated repeating shotguns capable of holding more than three cartridges, is prohibited in the majority of States and any gun capable of holding more than three cartridges must be plugged to limit them to a maximum capacity of three in the magazine and chamber combined. The plug must be of one piece, incapable of being removed through the loading end of the magazine. Georgia, however, permit a maximum of five cartridges for deer hunting whilst in Maryland the number of cartridges held in the chamber and magazine is unrestricted.

In West Virginia a combination rifle/shotgun (over and under) is permitted for deer hunting.

Rifles

In some States there is no restriction on rifle calibres, in others the .22 may be the largest permissible calibre, whilst some States may only allow deer to be hunted with shotgun, bow or muzzle-loader. Oregon, for instance, specify .24 as the minimum calibre for Wapiti provided it develops at least 1220 ft lb of energy at 100 yards. For Whitetail and Mule deer, however, a rifle of .23 calibre developing not less than 900 ft lb at 100 yards is acceptable. In both Connecticut and Idaho, no calibre larger than .22 is permitted, and although the latter allow rimfire ammunition to be used, most States that permit the use of this small rifle, specify 'centre fire' only.

Fully automatic, or semi-automatic rifles that take a clip holding more than eight cartridges are generally illegal, as is also the use of solid or military-type ammunition. Silencers, or sound moderators, are also illegal.

In order to ascertain what weapons are legal in any particular State the appropriate Fish and Game Department should be approached.

Dogs

The use of dogs for hunting varies from one State to another, but this is not a problem that is likely to confront a visiting sportsman. In most States it is illegal to hunt or pursue any wild animal with a dog in any area during the hunting season. One cannot, therefore, use a dog, as is common practice in Europe, to follow up a wounded deer, and when on a visit to Washington State I suggested that this must result in a number of deer being lost, the reply was 'not necessarily – for with so many hunters about, particularly during the early days of the season, a wounded beast has a good chance of being found by another hunter'. The snag here is, of course, that if the hunter finding a wounded animal has already used up his game tag, he will not be able to take home an untagged carcase, so it will probably be wasted unless he can find a friend who does not intend to use his licence.

During the latter part of the last century, when deer had almost disappeared from Pennsylvania, one of the first steps taken by the Game Commission in 1897, in an attempt to restore the Whitetail to a reasonable degree of abundance, was to ban the use of dogs for hunting deer, and also the shooting of deer at salt licks. It is still not permissible to be accompanied by a dog whilst hunting in this State.

The dog was also much used in former times for hunting deer in Wisconsin – in fact, a hound was considered standard equipment in those days and most hunters had one or more. 'Deer hunting without a hound was the same as dancing without a fiddle' observed one old Wisconsin hunter. The use of hound for hunting in this State is no longer permitted either.

In California, the law allows one dog per hunter, and these are often used to move deer out of dense cover, or trail a crippled deer. In 1965 Guy Connolly circulated a questionnaire to hunters in Mendocino County, and found that 12 percent were accompanied by a dog at all times, while 31 percent generally only took their dogs out when hunting in parties. The dog users claimed a higher hunting success than the hunters without dogs. The use of dogs during the archery season, however, is prohibited.

In many south-eastern States, dogs are the accepted method to bring deer up to the hunters posted at strategic points – in fact, they are invaluable to move the deer out of heavy brush country or coastal swamplands. In Arkansas there are special hunts in which Beagles are the only legal dogs for deer.

In eastern Virginia a traditional method for hunting deer is with the use of dogs. Their use, however, is not permitted during the bow and muzzle-loader seasons.

In South Carolina, although dogs are not generally permitted while deer hunting, in the Moultrie Game Management area, dogs are permitted to accompany the hunter on Wednesdays and Saturdays only during the period 16 October to 1 January.

In Georgia the Board of Natural Resources have designated certain areas where dogs may be used whilst hunting deer, but with certain restrictions as to weapons. For instance, if the party hunting deer with dogs consists of more than four hunters, then it is illegal to use a rifle or handgun and shotguns must be used.

The State of Louisiana does not permit anyone 'still hunting' to be accompanied by a dog, whilst in Florida the use of unleashed dogs during the bow season is prohibited.

Anyone wishing to use a dog to hunt deer in Oklahoma has to buy a $5 dog hunting licence tag. Dogs are also permitted during two of the three gun hunting seasons in Mississippi, the first of which commences shortly after mid-November. In the north of Mississippi most Whitetail fawns are born in July, but in the south a good month later, so when the season starts these southern fawns will only be about three months old, and many fall to hunting dogs.

Dogs, where allowed, are generally used for driving deer rather than finding one crippled and as a result, many a buck is wounded, only to escape and die. This loss, suggest R D Taber and R F Dasmann (*The Black-tailed Deer of the Chaparral*),

amounts to 40 percent of the take-home kill – two bucks left dead for every five packed out. A number of things contribute to this high loss. There is much shooting at long range; the hardness of the ground makes tracking difficult; the heaviness of the brush makes it easy for the deer to escape and hard for the hunter to follow.

Most important of all is the unwillingness of some hunters to look very hard for deer which have been hit. The weather is hot, the hunter is tired, and too often yields to the temptation to let that one go and look for another. Losses of this sort are inevitable in brushy country, but they could be scaled down considerably if the hunter made that extra effort.

Rollo S Robinson, in *Shots at Mule Deer*, gives further evidence of this wastage.

Concerned sportsmen were startled to learn in a Minnesota study that 68 White-tailed deer were wounded or left in the woods (both legal and illegal kills) for every 100 legal bucks harvested. Results of a questionnaire sent to New Mexico sportsmen disclosed that crippling losses ran about 21 percent, but it was believed by Wildlife Managers that the percentage ran approximately 30 percent because many hunters would not admit they had crippled deer. Similar losses on the Kaibab Forest were estimated to be 10 to 15 percent. Forest Service personnel working Utah's Fishlake district discovered that 2568 muleys, or 18 percent had gone down the drain through crippling. Colorado in a similar survey came up with a 15 percent loss. During a special removal of deer by game wardens in Utah's Twelve-mile Canyon, crippling losses were found to be 19 percent.

Similar losses are reported from California where, it would seem, there is strong anti-hunting and anti-firearms sentiment. 'Unfortunately', observes Guy Connolly (1979) 'the conduct of some hunters adds fuel to the antihunting position. Too many hunters are poor marksmen, and too many impossible shots are taken at long range or running deer. The result is a high rate of crippling loss – at least 20 percent of the recorded kill on the University of California Research Station, and perhaps 40 percent on some ranges.' He concludes by saying that 'unless hunters voluntarily act to improve their skill I forecast that sooner or later the State will require hunters to pass a marksmanship test'.*

A study in southern Utah revealed that on a buck only area the range loss expressed as a percentage of the removal, was double that of an adjacent area where bucks and does could be taken. Commenting on the significance of these figures, Jim Bond in *The Mule Deer*, writes

On the Oak Creek area about 30 deer are left dead on the range for every 100 legally bagged. Even though both sexes are hunted, an excessively high proportion of the range loss in this area consists of antlerless deer. For example, among the tagged bucks which have been killed and reported, range hunting losses amounted to only 8 percent of those legally taken, compared to 32 percent for does and 80 percent for fawns. Obviously where any deer is legal, such as the Oak Creek area, the recovery of wounded antlerless deer by hunters could be as high for antlered deer. Making it illegal to kill does and fawns does not correct the situation as numerous surveys have shown. On the contrary, even heavier wastage results not only during the hunting season but from starvation during the winter because of over-populations which develop through inadequate removals.

The State of Wisconsin has recognized the value of dogs for locating wounded game, and in 1978 the Department of Wildlife Management sponsored dog training sessions for hunters, and if successful the Department intends to establish a formal programme for dog training along the lines of their Hunter Safety Programme. Let's hope it is a success and that other States follow suit, for the proper use of a dog as a 'finder' rather than a 'flusher' will undoubtedly save much venison, and at the same time prevent the unnecessary cruelty of leaving a wounded deer in the bush.

With so many hunters out in the more accessible forests during the first few days of the hunting season, disputes over ownership of dead or wounded deer inevitably arise, and several cases have been taken to the American Courts for decision. One such case came before a Court in Wisconsin, which ruled that 'game belongs to the person who has it in circumstances that escape is improbable, if not impossible'. Thus, mortal wounding and immediate pursuit has been deemed possession.

The advice of one Michigan hunter is 'Take your buck straight away to the butcher, for if left hanging you could well find it had disappeared when you returned to collect'!

Hunting accidents

The Americans have, unfortunately, gained the reputation of being rather

---

* 'Deer Hunting in Mendocino County, California' *Deer* Vol. 4, Feb '79 No. 8

trigger-happy, and there are many areas in the States where people who value their lives will not venture into the bush during the hunting season. The trouble is the system – too many hunters having access to the same hunting area and none knowing where the other fellow is.

In many States only one deer is allowed on licence, and the majority of hunters – particularly the 'backyard hunters' who don't like to travel far from human habitation – are anxious to get their deer on the opening day of the season. Perhaps, prior to the opening date, a deer has been noticed frequenting a particular clump of trees or thicket – then at first light on the opening day, something is seen – or even heard – to move in the spot usually frequented by the deer, and a shot is taken – with the result that perhaps another hunter joins the 'dear departed'.

A number of hunters have been killed whilst attempting to stalk a calling Moose, for in some instances two hunters have been calling and answering each other, each believing the other to be a Moose. The man doing the stalking is usually the one to be killed and C E Hagie's advice is 'never attempt to stalk a moose you have been calling if you want to live' (*How to Hunt North American Big Game*).

I understand the majority of hunting accidents occur during impromptu deer drives – indeed my guide in British Columbia had lost his brother a year or two previously during a Mule deer drive.

Unfortunately, many hunters go into the bush for the first time without really knowing what a deer looks like and there are many stories of objects, animate and inanimate, that have been shot for deer.

One story that could have had a tragic ending concerns a hunter who shot what he thought was an Elk, but without going over to inspect his kill, went straight to a nearby farm and enquired of the farmer if he could possibly collect the deer for him on his tractor, to which the farmer agreed. When the carcase was reached, however, the farmer discovered to his horror that the hunter had shot a pony and although being ridden at the time by his young daughter she, fortunately, had not suffered any injury apart from fright.

Realizing how trigger-happy some hunters are around farms, one farmer put up a large notice at the entrance to his farmstead to the effect that 'if it moos it's not a moose but a cow'!

George Laycock in *The Deer Hunter's Bible* mentions a stuffed deer that an Illinois farmer, with a sense of humour, stood up in his field in order to see how many hunters would grind to a stop and take a shot. Several dozen did. Others have shot Jersey heifers and have even taken them into the deer-checking station, tagged and ready for weighing!

Some hunters never take binoculars with them into the bush, relying on their rifle 'scope' to look at game. As many hunters, when stalking or 'still hunting' in thick bush frequently carry their rifle with the safety catch off ready for instant action on a spooked deer, the danger of this practice cannot be over-stressed.

THE AMERICAS

Coloured clothing

In order to reduce the number of casualties among hunters, the wearing of coloured clothing by big game hunters was introduced, and is now mandatory in the majority of States during the gun season but not during the season reserved for bow and arrow only. 'It shall be unlawful' states the Regulations of the Montana Department of Fish and Game 'for any person to hunt big game animals or to accompany any hunter as an outfitter or guide, without wearing exterior garments above the waist totalling not less than four hundred (400) square inches (2580 sq.cm) of hunter orange material visible at all times while hunting.' Some States, which include Massachusetts, Oklahoma, Georgia, Tennessee and Rhode Island require 500 sq.in. (3225 sq.cm) whilst 200 sq.in. (1280 sq.cm) 'visible from all sides' is sufficient for New Jersey. In Hawaii it is even less, and provided any hunter or person accompanying a hunter displays a piece of orange-coloured material of at least 12 in. (77.4 sq.cm) square affixed front and back, and above the waist, he is within the law.

The hunting regulations of Rhode Island are particularly explicit in their requirements, for it states 'During the muzzle-loading and shotgun seasons for deer, all hunters must wear a minimum of 500 sq. in. of daylight fluorescent orange clothing on head, chest and back. Such clothing must have a dominant weave length between 595 and 605 nanometers, all excitation purity not less than 85 percent and a lumination factor not less than 40 percent.'

In Utah, the 400 sq. in. must be of Hunter Orange, as no other red and yellow colour will comply with the regulations.

In New Jersey, anyone seen not wearing fluorescent clothing can be fined $50 for each offence.

Even in States where the wearing of coloured clothing is not mandatory, the position is admirably summed up in the Pennsylvania Hunting Regulations, which state 'For your own enjoyment, peace of mind, and the fact that your life may depend on it, wear a bright color when hunting. Daylight fluorescent orange is recommended, and *be seen*.'

Ohio, Maryland and one or two other States make it mandatory for the hunting licence to be displayed between the shoulders on the back of the garment when hunting.

Hunter training

In the interests of safety, more and more States are introducing a hunter training scheme, and eventually no-one will be able to obtain a hunting licence without producing a Certificate of Competency in Firearm and Hunter Safety.

In Delaware, for instance, a Hunter Safety Programme was started in 1970 and it is now mandatory for any resident under the age of eighteen to complete successfully a six-hour course before applying for a hunting licence. Since 1970 over 14,000 Delaware hunters have taken the training programme. Maryland only commenced their hunter safety programme in 1978, but since that year anyone wishing to purchase a hunter's licence must produce either a certificate of competency in firearm and hunter safety, or a hunter's licence that had been purchased prior to 1 July 1978. This applies to everyone, irrespective of age.

In Rhode Island both gun hunters and archers are required to undergo hunter training. In Colorado, persons born after 1 June 1949 will have to complete successfully a hunter education course before applying for a firearm hunting licence and the certificate has to be carried on that person at all times when hunting. Appropriate training certificates from other States will be honoured in Colorado.

In South Carolina, the Department offers a twelve-hour Hunter Education programme which includes instruction in the principles of Hunter Safety and Conservation. Students gain, in addition to firearms and hunting safety, knowledge of basic wildlife management, principles of hunting ethics, hunter-landowner relations and hunting techniques.

In Utah, residents under the age of twenty-one must show proof of having completed an accepted hunter education course before a hunting licence can be purchased. The blue card issued after completion of the course must be produced when applying for a licence and the number recorded on it. Non-residents, however, need not present proof of completion of a hunter education course in order to obtain a hunter licence.

In Wyoming, although the State does not have a mandatory hunter safety requirement, the Department of the Interior does, however, require hunter safety certification to hunt in the Grand Teton National Park, or on the Federal Elk Refuge. This requirement, however, only affects the Wapiti hunters.

Deer hunting seasons

Hunting seasons and regulations are set by the individual State game commissions, or are passed by their State legislature, so no two States are alike. Furthermore, few States have determined permanent opening dates for their game species, and so new dates may be established each year following a game production survey. The dates are usually set in late summer, with very little notice, in some instances, to hunters before the season actually opens.

Some States arrange for the hunting season to commence near a particular weekend or holiday. In Vermont, for instance, the Bow and Arrow Season runs for '16 consecutive days beginning the second Saturday in October', whilst the Regular Gun Season runs 'for 16 consecutive days beginning 12 days before Thanksgiving'. This is not particularly helpful for a hunter from Europe or Australasia, who may not know the date of Thanksgiving (23 November). In New York State the regular deer season commences on the 'next to last Saturday in October and runs through to the first Sunday in

December'. The muzzle-loader season is fixed for 'the seven days immediately preceding the opening of the regular season'.

Whilst the approximate open hunting seasons for the various species of deer in individual States are as follows, it is essential for the hunter to obtain from the Game Department of the State in which he intends to hunt, the latest hunting regulations. For the addresses of the various State Game Departments, refer to Appendix B.

APPROXIMATE HUNTING SEASONS IN THE UNITED STATES OF AMERICA

State	Caribou	Moose	Wapiti	Whitetail	Mule deer (Blacktail)
Alabama	—	—	—	Mid-Nov – latter Jan	
Alaska	Early Aug – end March	Begin Sept – end March	Begin Aug – end Dec	—	Begin Aug – mid-Jan[1]
Arizona	—	—	Mid-Sept – mid-Dec	Late Oct – late Dec	Late Oct – end Nov
Arkansas	—	—	—	Split season: Nov & Dec	—
California	—	—	—	Early Aug – mid-Sept	Early Aug – mid-Sept Early Aug – mid-Sept[2]
Colorado	—	—	Late Oct – mid-Nov	Mid-Oct – mid-Nov	Mid-Oct – mid-Nov
Connecticut	—	—	—	About 15 days, Dec	—
Delaware	—	—	—	Split season: few days Nov & Jan	—
Florida	—	—	—	Early Nov – late Jan	—
Georgia[3]	—	—	—	Late Oct – early Jan	—
Hawaii[4]	—	—	—	—	Oct – Nov[5]
Idaho	Protected	Mid-Sept – mid-Nov	Mid-Sept – mid-Nov	Late Sept – late Nov	Late Sept – late Nov
Illinois	—	—	—	Split season: few days Nov & Dec	—
Indiana	—	—	—	Mid-Nov – begin Dec	—
Iowa	—	—	—	Few days Dec[6]	—
Kansas	—	—	—	Early Dec	Early Dec
Kentucky	—	—	—	Late Oct – early Nov	—

APPROXIMATE HUNTING SEASONS IN THE UNITED STATES OF AMERICA (*continued*)

State	Caribou	Moose	Wapiti	Whitetail	Mule deer (Blacktail)
Louisiana	—	—	—	Nov – mid-Jan	—
Maine	Protected	No general hunting[7]	—	End Oct – late Nov	—
Maryland[8]	—	—	—	End Nov – early Dec	—
Massachusetts	—	—	—	First week Dec	—
Michigan	—	Protected	Protected	Last fortnight Nov	—
Minnesota	—	No general hunting	—	Nov	—
Mississippi	—	—	—	Split seasons: Dec & Jan	—
Missouri	—	—	—	Late Nov	—
Montana	—	Mid-Sept – late Nov	Late Oct – late Nov	Late Oct – late Nov	Late Oct – late Nov
Nebraska	—	—	—	Mid-Nov	Mid-Nov
Nevada	—	—	Residents only	—	Mid-Oct – late Nov
New Hampshire	Protected	Protected	Protected	Early Nov	—
New Jersey	—	—	—	Few days Dec[9]	—
New Mexico	—	—	Early Oct – mid-Dec	Late Oct – mid-Jan	Late Oct – mid-Jan
New York	—	—	—	Late Oct – early Dec	—
North Carolina	—	—	—	Mid-Oct – end Dec	—
North Dakota	—	End Nov (one day)	—	Mid-Nov	Mid-Nov
Ohio	—	—	—	End Nov	—
Oklahoma	—	—	Mid-Dec[10]	End Nov	—
Oregon	—	—	Split season: end Oct; early Nov[11]	Protected	End Sept – early Oct
			Mid-Nov – end Nov[12]	—	End Sept – Nov[13]
Pennsylvania	—	—	—	End Nov	—
Rhode Is.	—	—	—	Early Dec[14]	—

APPROXIMATE HUNTING SEASONS IN THE UNITED STATES OF AMERICA (*continued*)

State	Caribou	Moose	Wapiti	Whitetail	Mule deer (Blacktail)
South Carolina	—	—	—	Mid-Aug – end Dec	—
South Dakota	—	—	Mid-Sept[15] – end Oct	Nov	Nov
Tennessee	—	—	—	Mid-Nov – early Dec	—
Texas	—	—	Permit only	Mid-Nov – end Dec	Mid-Nov – early Dec
Utah	—	Split season: Sept; early Nov	Split season: early Oct; Nov	—	Late Oct
Vermont	—	—	—	Nov	—
Virginia[16]	—	—	—	Late Nov – early Jan	—
Washington	—	Permit only	Split season: mid-Nov; late Nov to late Dec	Early Sept – early Dec	Early Sept – early Dec; Early Sept – early Dec[17]
West Virginia	—	—	—	Mid-Nov – early Dec	—
Wisconsin	—	—	—	Late Nov	
Wyoming	—	Begin Sept – end Nov	Begin Sept – end Nov	Begin Sept – end Nov	Begin Sept – end Nov

[1] Blacktail
[2] Blacktail
[3] Some Fallow, Oct–Feb
[4] Axis, March–April
[5] Blacktail
[6] Shotgun or muzzle-loader only
[7] Permit hunting may start in 1980
[8] Sika, end Nov
[9] No rifle permitted
[10] Permit only
[11] Rocky Mountain Wapiti
[12] Roosevelt Wapiti
[13] Blacktail
[14] No rifle
[15] Residents only
[16] Sika on permit only
[17] Blacktail

The above mentioned hunting seasons refer to firearms only.

Many states arrange special seasons for both archery and muzzle-loaders outside the firearm season.

Many States also have special permit seasons for reducing excess stock – particularly Wapiti.

9 Mexico, Central America, the West Indies and South America

MEXICO

Four species of deer – the two Brockets, Red and Brown, and the White-tailed and Mule deer which include many subspecies – are found in Mexico and although well distributed, due to over-hunting, especially by the peasants, none can be said to be plentiful in any of the more accessible areas.

A century ago the Wapiti also occurred in northern Mexico and adjacent parts of Arizona but this race, known as Merriam's Wapiti *Cervus canadensis merriami*, seems to have become extinct everywhere early in the present century. Since then there have been at least three abortive attempts to reintroduce the Wapiti into northern Mexico.

Until comparatively recently little attention was paid to sport hunting, and although, on paper, the game animals of Mexico should receive good legal protection, there are, unfortunately, not enough game wardens to ensure that the law is observed. Already, however, a start has been made on the Bighorn sheep in Sonora and Baja California, and this sheep is now being systematically hunted under Government supervision and constitutes a primary source of income for the Mexican Game Department. The Mexican Government, therefore, is fully aware of the economic value of sport hunting in the tourist industry, and doubtless encouraged by the success of sport hunting after the Bighorn sheep, will endeavour to improve the facilities for hunting deer, which is the most widespread game animal in the country.

In Mexico the Estado Mayor de la Secretariá de la Defensa has control over the purchase, possession and use of all types of firearms, including sporting guns. A gun permit must, therefore, be obtained from the Defence Department before a hunting licence, on which the number of the gun permit will be entered, may be purchased. By law, every licensed hunter must belong to a registered hunting club or association, and these clubs – numbering about 480 – are federated into a national organization – Federación Nacional de Caza, Tiro, y Pesca. Membership of a club will, therefore, endorse the credential of an applicant when applying for a gun permit from the Defence Department. It follows, therefore, that club membership becomes a prerequisite for obtaining the hunting permit. A non-resident, however, may purchase a hunting permit at the frontier by obtaining first a gun permit from an authorized representative of the Defence Department. He need not necessarily join a hunting club, although to do so would undoubtedly facilitate the issuing of permits, etc. Any non-resident wishing to hunt in Mexico will have to provide proof of citizenship, a certificate of good character from his home town police, sheriff or mayor, a photograph and complete physical description of himself and the type of weapon and ammunition which will be used, together with the area and duration of the hunt. Hunters may bring with them two rifles of smaller calibre than .30-06 together with fifty rounds of ammunition for each weapon. Handguns are prohibited. For a non-resident, a permit to shoot a White-tailed deer in Mexico cost (1979) $100 (£50) whilst for a Mule deer the cost was $500.

The open season for hunting both species is from about 10 December to 15 January.

For a hunter wishing to obtain specimens of all types of deer with the minimum amount of travel involved, Tamaulipas on the Gulf of Mexico is probably the only State where all three can be found, for although White-tailed deer occur throughout much of Mexico except Baja California, south-west Tamaulipas marks both the southern-most range of the Desert Mule deer and the northern limit of distribution of the Red Brocket.

Formerly game was hunted extensively for commercial purposes but since 1952, when the disposal of venison and deer hides was prohibited by Mexican law, hunting for food has now been the most important drain on deer populations.

White-tailed deer *Odocoileus virginianus*

The White-tailed deer, known locally as *Venado cola blanca*, is by far the most numerous and throughout Mexico twelve subspecies are recognized. There is little doubt, however, that intergradation with adjacent subspecies must occur throughout the entire range of the White-tailed deer, particularly in the more southern parts, but this should not cause concern to the average hunter whose prime concern is to bag a White-tailed deer.

Commenting on the White-tailed deer in Mexico, Leopold (1959) writes: 'White-tailed deer are hunted in Mexico by every conceivable device. Perhaps the most popular and effective method is driving the deer out of cover with dogs. But even when not hunting, every man who owns a gun carries it in the woods and shoots deer when he sees them, regardless of their sex or age or the season of the year. Spotlighting at night is widely practised either from an automobile or afoot, with a hand light.'

Other methods used include waiting, often perched in a tree, over water holes, customary feeding grounds or at salt licks. Some hunters in the Yucatán State use a wooden whistle to call their deer during the rutting season, whilst in southern Mexico it is standard practice to lure female deer within gunshot either by imitating the plaintive bleat of a fawn in distress, or by using a captured fawn as a live decoy. Other devices include snaring and pitfall traps.

Quite apart from hunter pressure, the White-tailed deer has many natural predators, and these include pumas, jaguars, coyotes, bears and wolves. Yet despite all this persecution, the deer has managed to survive throughout most of its range, and could increase rapidly if the game laws, excellent as they may appear on paper, could be properly enforced.

The rut varies considerably throughout Mexico. In the north it generally takes place around mid-winter (January) but in the south it will be about two months earlier. The season for antler shedding as well as for fawning, varies accordingly, the average gestation period being about 205 to 212 days.

Mule deer *Odocoileus hemionus*

The Mule deer – locally called *Venado bura* or *Cola prieta* – occurs in northern Mexico and Baja California, and throughout its range six subspecies, which include two insular types on the islands of Tiburón and Cedros, are recognized.

Of the mainland types both Burro *O.h.eremicus* and the Desert Mule deer *O.h.crooki* prefer desert ranges with scant variation, whilst the Mule deer on Baja California – *O.h.fuliginatus* and *O.h.peninsulae* in the south – show a preference for a habitat well vegetated with chaparral, oak or pine. The deer of Baja California are smaller than either Burro or Desert Mule deer, whilst the smallest of all are the deer – *O.h.cerrosensis* – on Cedros Island.

Generally speaking, Mule deer and White-tailed deer do not share the same habitat, and in northern Mexico, where desert conditions give way to forest on the lower slopes of the Sierra Madre in Sonora and Chihuahua the Mule deer is replaced by the White-tailed deer. The latter are completely absent from Baja California.

In Baja California, Leopold suggests that the rut probably takes place in November or December, a month earlier than in the desert areas of northern Mexico.

The Mule deer in Mexico is given the same treatment as the White-tailed deer, being hunted all the year round, and by similar methods (*see page 242*).

Brocket deer *Mazama*

Two species of Brocket occur in Mexico, the Red Brocket *Mazama americana temama* which inhabits the virgin rain forest of the south-east, and the Brown Brocket *Mazama gouazoubira pandora*. The approximate range of these two Brockets, which are locally referred to as *temazate, temazame, corzo* or *venadito rojo*, is as follows:

Red Brocket *M.a.temama* From about Chiapas, and Tabasco in the south, through Veracruz to southern Tamaulipas in the north.
Brown Brocket *M.g.pandora* Restricted to Yucatán peninsula.

Except for their difference in colour, both types are of similar size, adult bucks weighing about 37 to 45 lb (17 to 20 kg) live weight. Their flesh is said to be excellent, and in consequence they are hunted extensively, but owing to their predilection for impenetrable thickets – *monte* – native hunter success is considerably lower than on White-tailed deer. In Leopold's opinion 'dogs are virtually a necessity in hunting this elusive animal'.

Brocket are most abundant around small clearings in the rain forest, and tend to forsake tropical forest that has been impoverished by too much cutting or burning.

Brocket deer, owing to their small size, have many predators not only on the ground in the form of jaguar, puma and ocelot etc., but also in the air from the larger raptorial birds. Near villages, however, as in parts of North America, the dog is probably its worst enemy.

CENTRAL AMERICA AND THE WEST INDIES

Only two species of deer – the Red Brocket *Mazama americana* and the White-tailed *Odocoileus virginianus* – occur in Central America and both are widely distributed.

Of the former, two races occur, *M.a.cerasina* in Guatemala, El Salvador, Honduras, Nicaragua and Costa Rica, and *M.a.repertica* in Panama from where it extends its range into Colombia, South America.

Five subspecies of White-tailed deer are represented in Central America – the Chiriqui Whitetail *O.v.chiriquensis* in Panama, the Nicaragua Whitetail *O.v.truei* in Nicaragua, El Salvador and Costa Rica; the Chiapas Whitetail *O.v.nelsoni* in Guatemala, the Yucatán Whitetail *O.v.yucatanensis* in Honduras and Yucatán and the Coiba Island White-tail *O.v.rothschildi* on Coiba Island off the south-east coast of Panama.

From a hunting point of view none of the republics of Central America would seem to hold much prospect for the visiting sportsman, and both species have a wide distribution elsewhere in the Americas. In Costa Rica, Government and people are becoming increasingly conscious of conservation and are making a sincere effort to preserve the diminishing forests, flora and fauna. Recently a number of national parks have been established, which include some of the best remaining tracts of primeval forest.

The republics to the north of Costa Rica are, at present, in a very unsettled state. Nicaragua is just recovering from a bloody revolution and has been on the verge of war with Honduras. El Salvador is in turmoil, and there is considerable unrest in Guatemala. In such circumstances the arrival of a hunting party with firearms would probably be regarded unfavourably, if not with suspicion.

About 1850 White-tailed deer were introduced to Cuba, but have disappeared from many areas because of deforestation. It is believed the original deer came from Mexico, but since at least ten different subspecies are recognized for that country, it is impossible to suggest the race involved.

White-tailed deer have been introduced to a number of other Caribbean Islands which include the Dominican Republic (Hispaniola), Jamaica, the U.S. Virgin Islands, Barbuda (Leeward Islands), Dominica and Grenada (Windward Islands), but what their status is today is unknown.

There are also populations of free-ranging Fallow deer on the Leeward Islands of Barbuda and Guana, the deer on the former being descended from animals introduced by the Codrington family during the eighteenth century (Chapman, 1980).

Fallow deer have also been introduced to Cuba.

SOUTH AMERICA

Of the six indigenous species of deer to be found in South America, four – the Pampas deer, Huemul, Marsh deer and Pudu – are unique to this continent, and should, on that account alone, attract the overseas sportsman in search of a new species to hunt. Unfortunately, however, none are sufficiently numerous to withstand any hunting pressure whatever, and indeed, all four in Argentina are completely protected by law, if not in practice, in much of their range. The two species that are plentiful in suitable habitat in South America are the Brocket and White-tailed deer, but in view of the relatively insignificant trophy of the former and the availability of the Whitetail throughout North America, neither deer is likely to hold much attraction to the overseas hunter anxious to secure a species, rather than a subspecies.

In fact, were it not for the introduction of a number of exotic game animals – and in particular the European Red deer – it is unlikely that any European or North American hunters would ever visit South America to hunt deer alone. At present, about forty to sixty European and North American hunters regularly visit Argentina each March to hunt Red deer.

Even when game was more plentiful, remarkably few Europeans ever made hunting trips to South America, and in consequence, literature on the subject is limited.

The Red deer are all located in the mountainous country of western Argentina and adjoining Chile, and hunting is available on either national park reserves or on private ranches, during March and April. A small herd, estimated to number under 200 animals, also occurs in Peru, but antlers are said to be poor.

Other introduced deer include Fallow deer from Europe and Chital or Axis deer from India, and since populations of both species are on private land, opportunities for hunting either by a visiting sportsman can best be arranged by personal contact with an estate owner. With reasonable luck, five days should be sufficient to collect a representative trophy of each species, at a cost (1979) of about $400–600 (about £200–£300) per trophy. Klineburger Worldwide Travel agency, however, have been organizing a two to three day hunt in Buenos Aires province after both species at a cost (1979) of $1200 (about £600) for Axis deer in the Mar del Plata area, and $1100 (about £550) for Fallow deer at Bahia Blanca; the prices include the shooting of one trophy, full board and transportation during the trip. Additional trophies may be taken at a cost of $600 (about £300) and $550 (about £275) respectively. A $20 to $50 (about £10 to £25) exportation fee will be charged for each species.

Being 'introduced exotics', both Fallow and Chital are unprotected by law and can, therefore, be hunted quite legally throughout the twelve months. However, for the trophy hunter, April and May would be about the best time to hunt Fallow whilst for Chital, since their breeding habits follow no fixed pattern, probably any month between October and June would offer a good opportunity of finding a trophy stag in hard antler.

The only other species of deer that can be hunted legitimately in Argentina is the Brown Brocket which has a wide distribution in the northern part of the republic. The best hunting is on private ranches. Licences are not expensive, costing about U.S.$10–15 (about £5 to £7.50) with no trophy fee.

In Chile the only species of deer that can be hunted are the exotic Red deer and Fallow deer, both Pudu and Huemul being completely protected, and the latter being almost extinct.

There is no official open hunting season for the two exotic deer as they are concentrated on private estates and therefore come under the managership of the owners. These privately owned estates seldom exceed 10,000 acres (4000 hectares). In some areas isolated herds have wandered into adjoining *cordillera* or woods.

In Brazil the hunting of wild animals is protected by law (No.5. 197, dated 3 January 1967) Article 2 of which forbids all 'professional hunting'. 'Amateur' hunting, however, during specified months is permitted for the more plentiful game – which include both Brocket and Whitetail – in some States of the country, and these include Amazonas, Pará and Rio Grande do Sul.

Needless to say, however, in a country such as Brazil it is impossible to enforce any game law, and throughout the year the deer, in much of their range, are killed indiscriminately by the natives.

The Indian, writes Stanley E. Brock (1963), is a most indiscriminate hunter, and 'never knows when he has had enough to eat, and will never leave anything for another day. This is probably why he spends the best part of his life hungry'. He is nevertheless an excellent tracker of game.

The following is a brief description of the deer species of South America.

Brocket deer *Mazama*

The Brocket deer, whose range extends from Mexico in the north to Argentina in South America, has a wide distribution in the latter country, occurring in every republic except Chile and Uruguay. In South America four species – the Red *M.americana*, the Brown *M.gouazoubira*, the Little Red *M.rufina* and the Dwarf Brocket *M.chunyi* – and some twenty subspecies are found, with a further race *M.a.trinitatis* in the West Indies.

The exact range of the various species and subspecies of this deer has never been fully studied, and overlapping must occur in many areas.

The approximate distribution of the Brockets in South America is as follows:

Red Brocket *Mazama americana*
Local names: *Corzuelas, Veado*. In Argentina: *Venado colorado, Corzuela colorado*.
In Brazil: *Veado materio*. In Peru: *Venado colorado*.

This Brocket – sometimes referred to as the 'Bush deer' or 'Roe deer' (Brazil)
of which ten races occur in South America, has the widest distribution, being
found in all northern republics from Ecuador in the west, through Colombia,
Venezuela and the Guianas into Brazil. Its range also includes northern
Argentina, Paraguay and parts of Bolivia. In Peru this deer ocurs in the
Amazon region, and northern parts of the coastal region up to an altitude of
about 4900 ft (1500 metres). The southern limit of the Red Brocket in the
coastal area of Peru is about latitude 6.0 S.

The Red Brocket is still fairly abundant in many parts of its range, and in
some localities is subject to intensive commercial hunting for its hide. In Peru,
where 40,000 to 50,000 skins may be exported annually, it is particularly
vulnerable during the flood season when the population of large areas
congregate on small islands of dry ground to avoid being drowned.

In the tropical jungles of Brazil and the Guianas, however, the Brocket
enjoys seclusion and safety from hunters, and many millions must die without
ever having set eyes on man.

Basically, it can be said that in the Amazon area the Red Brocket lives in
humid forest to tropical rain forest whilst in the Andes it frequents the rainy
slopes, where humidity and annual rainfall is high.

In Argentina the Red Brocket is protected in all provinces, but hunting is
available in Paraguay, a good area being near the Paraguay river north of
San Pedro city. Raúl Lalo Mandojana, who has hunted the Red Brocket in
Paraguay tells me (*in litt*) that it is the most difficult bush stalking he has ever
done, the deer being almost entirely nocturnal in habit. It is an excellent
swimmer, and when pursued with dogs readily goes to a stream or river,
swimming with amazing velocity.

The Red Brocket is the largest of the Brockets; a good buck will weigh
about 77 to 88 lb (35 to 40 kg). A good trophy will measure about $4\frac{3}{4}$ to 6 in.
(12 to 15 cm) in length.

Little Red Brocket *Mazama rufina*
Local name in Argentina: *Pororo*.

Two widely separated subspecies of Little Red Brocket are found in South
America – the typical race *M.r.rufina* being found in Ecuador, south-east
Brazil and adjacent republics, and *M.r.bricenii* in north-west Venezuela.

In Argentina it is scarce and now protected by law. A good pair of antlers
will measure about 4 to $4\frac{1}{2}$ in. (10 to 11.5 cm) in length.

Brown Brocket *Mazama gouazoubira*
Local names: In Argentina: *Corzuela, parda, sachacabra, venado pardo*. In Brazil:
Venado catingeiro. In Paraguay: *Venado pardo*. In Peru: *Venado Cenizo, Venado
Plomo, Uchpa Lluichu, Nerenare* (Campa). In British Guiana: *Souai*.

247

THE AMERICAS

This deer, represented by eight subspecies in South America, occurs in western Brazil and adjacent parts of the Guianas, Venezuela, Colombia, Ecuador, Bolivia, Paraguay and northern Argentina. In Peru it is confined to the Amazon region. In British Guiana, where it is often referred to as the Lesser Bush deer or Grey Brocket, it is very numerous in favourable environments, which is the big forest rather than in savannah country. It is also found in semi-open brush type country as well as in desert Texas-like terrain.

The Brown Brocket is plentiful in northern Argentina from Cordoba province northwards, and compared to the Red Brocket, has much better adaptability to climate varations from humid to sub-desert ecosystems.

Very few stalkers hunt this little deer for sport, the majority of hunters being local people hunting for meat, which is said to be quite excellent.

The hunting season may vary slightly from year to year, but it mainly takes place during the winter months, May to August.

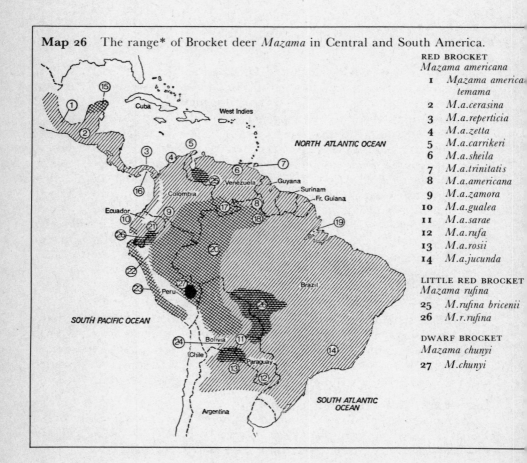

Map 26   The range* of Brocket deer *Mazama* in Central and South America.

RED BROCKET
Mazama americana

1   *Mazama america temama*
2   *M.a.cerasina*
3   *M.a.reperticia*
4   *M.a.zetta*
5   *M.a.carrikeri*
6   *M.a.sheila*
7   *M.a.trinitatis*
8   *M.a.americana*
9   *M.a.zamora*
10 *M.a.gualea*
11 *M.a.sarae*
12 *M.a.rufa*
13 *M.a.rosii*
14 *M.a.jucunda*

LITTLE RED BROCKET
Mazama rufina

25 *M.rufina bricenii*
26 *M.r.rufina*

DWARF BROCKET
Mazama chunyi

27 *M.chunyi*

Any trophy with an antler length of $4\frac{1}{8}$ in. (11 cm) is very good for the Brown Brocket, the longest yet recorded measuring just over 13 cm. One trophy with antler lengths of 12.2 cm (left) and 11.8 cm (right), had exceptionally large coronets, each measuring 10.2 cm in circumference.

Dwarf Brocket *Mazama chunyi*
Local names: *Tanka, Sani*, or *Chuni Taruca*; *Waiquo*.

This small Brocket has a limited distribution in the Andes of northern Bolivia and south Peru, where it occurs in some provinces of the Department of Puno and Cuzco. In the latter, the Dwarf Brocket is reported to be common from about 10,500 ft (3200 metres) – which is below the tree line – down to about 5900 ft (1800 metres) and occasionally may be encountered a little lower.

The Brocket is exclusively a forest dweller and hunting it in thick bush can be difficult and frustrating.

A method that will often be successful is to erect a high seat or platform in a

		BROWN BROCKET *Mazama gouazoubira*	
Mexico	15	*M.gouazoubira pandora*	Yucatán, Mexico
Guatemala to Costa Rica	16	*M.g.permira*	Isla San José
Panama to South America	17	*M.g.citus*	Venezuela
North Colombia	18	*M.g.nemorivaga*	South-east Venezuela and the Guianas
North Colombia			
North Venezuela	19	*M.g.mexianae*	Mexiana Island
Trinidad Island	20	*M.g.superciliaris*	Brazil
North-east of South America	21	*M.g.murelia*	South-west Colombia and Ecuador
South-east Colombia to north-east Peru			
West Ecuador	22	*M.g.tschudii*	Peru
Bolivia and north-west Argentina	23	*M.g.whitelyi*	Peru
Paraguay and Argentina	24	*M.g.gouazoubira*	Paraguay and North Argentina
North Argentina			
Brazil			

North Venezuela
Ecuador, South-east Brazil and adjacent republics

Andes of north Bolivia and South Peru

* The exact range of the various species and subspecies of the genus *Mazama* has never been fully studied and this map is only an indication of the general range of the four species: *Mazama mericana* (Red Brocket); *Mazama rufina* (Little Red Brocket); *Mazama gouazoubira* (Brown Brocket) and *Mazama chunyi* (Dward Brocket). Overlapping occurs in many areas.

tree overlooking a drinking place, and sit there during the night with a flashlight. On a dark night one has to rely solely on hearing to know when an animal is approaching, and when to switch on the light – the best moment being when it is actually drinking.

A buck with antlers is generally referred to as *macho* throughout South America; the Wapishana tribe, however, call it *massiro*.

There does not appear to be any fixed season for the shedding and development of the antlers, and this irregularity has caused some observers to suggest that these deer never shed their antlers. In Argentina, about 80 percent of the bucks shed their antlers in the spring, the new growth being hard and clean of velvet by late January.

Brocket deer are included among the animals that can be hunted during a ten to fourteen day 'jungle hunt' in Peru organized by Klineburger Worldwide Travel at a cost (1979) of $3500 (about £1750) per person.

Pampas deer *Ozotoceros bezoarticus*
Local names: *Venado, Ciervo de las pampas*; *Venadillo de Campo*; *Gama* (females) *Guazú-ti* (Guarani).
In Brazil: *Venado campeiro* (camping deer); *Veado branco*.

As the name suggests, this is a deer of the open plains and it avoids as far as possible woodlands and mountainous country. It is, in fact, sometimes referred to as the 'Field deer'. Three subspecies are recognized – the typical form *O.b.bezoarticus* which is reasonably well distributed in central and eastern Brazil practically up to the Amazon River; *O.b.leucogaster* which occurs in the northern part of Argentina, south-east Bolivia and Paraguay from where it spreads into the southern part of the Mato Grosso in western Brazil; and the rarest of the three, *O.b.celer*, which although once quite common in the northern and central pampas zones of Argentina, have now been reduced to under a hundred animals, the majority of which are in the two private estates of La Corona and General Lavalle in Buenos Aires province. There is also a small wild population in Uruguay, estimated to number about 200 animals.

The rut seems to be variable because fawns, particularly on the pampas south of Buenos Aires, have been reported for almost every month of the year, although the majority appear to be born between September and November, suggesting that most bucks go to the rut between January and March.

The Pampas deer carries a symmetrical head of six tines (points) very similar to that of a Roe buck, but less pearled and slightly larger – a good head measuring about 15 in (37.5 cm) in length. A few heads with ten to twelve points have been recorded, but such trophies are atypical. The majority of bucks start to shed their antlers during August and September.

In former times a favourite pastime of the 'gaucho' was to race the deer on horseback and catch them with their *bolas*, which consisted of three stones about as large as a big orange, attached to a common centre by strong cords about a yard or more long (about 1 to 1¾ metres). When within range these *bolas* are hurled at the deer and if the aim is true, become entangled in the

Map 27   The ranges of Pampas deer *Ozotoceros bezoarticus* and Pudu deer *Pudu* in South America.

Pampas deer *Ozotoceros bezoarticus*

1	*Ozotoceros bezoarticus bezoarticus*	Brazil
2	*O.b.leucogaster*	Central South America
3	*O.b.celer*	Argentina (Pampas)

Pudu deer *Pudu*

A	*Pudu pudu*	Chile and Argentina
B	*P.mephistophiles mephistophiles*	Ecuador and Peru
C	*P.m.wetmorei*	Colombia

antlers and around the neck, thus stopping the deer and so afford an opportunity for the 'gaucho' to lassoo the animal. When several hunters are chasing a single deer, he whose *bolas* first entangles the animal has claim to the skin even though another hunter may have finally lassooed it.

Probably the last occasion when the *boleadora* was used in an attempt to catch Pampas deer was about 1968 when Señor Manuel de Anchorina decided to catch up some deer frequenting a bleak marshland, called *cangrejales*, bordering the Bay of Sanboromon, to transfer to his estate at La Corona, Villaneuva in Argentina. The attempt to catch them with *boleadoras*, however, proved unsuccessful on the marshy ground, for the deer were able to run over the soft ground into which the horse and rider sank.

Eventually, in co-operation with the army, a helicopter was used to locate the animals, which were then chased into water and finally captured by a man jumping from the helicopter on to the deer.

Due to its strong smell, which resembles garlic, the Pampas deer has sometimes been referred to as the 'stinking deer'.

Pudu *Pudu*

Local names: *Ciervo enano*. In Argentina: *Pudu*. In Chile: *Venadito, Pudu*. In Peru: *Sacha Cabra* (Department of Huanuco), *Antagllo* (Tarma Province, Department of Junin).

The range of the Pudu – of which two species *P.pudu* and *P.mephistophiles* are recognized – follows a somewhat disjointed pattern, for some 2000 miles (3218 km) separates the two species, the range of the former being in parts of Argentina and Chile, whilst the latter, represented by two subspecies, *P.m.mephistophiles* occurring in Ecuador and Peru, and *P.m.wetmorei* in Columbia.

The Pudu is strictly protected (on paper, but not, unfortunately, in practice) in both Chile and Argentina, and a large number are illegally taken in *lazos* (snares) or with dogs. Pudu like terrain near lakes with plenty of under brush and high rainfall. They occur mostly between altitudes of 9900 ft (3000 metres) to about 6600 ft (2000 metres) below which the forest gives way to cultivation. According to local hunters it is also said to occur quite plentifully in the forested heights above San Ramón in the Department of Junin.

Pudu bucks, which weigh about 20 to 24 lb (about 9 to 11 kg) have small spike antlers of about 3 to 4 in. (7 to 10 cm) in length.

Huemul or **Guemal** *Hippocamelus*

Local name: *Shoan*

One of the most interesting deer of South America is the Huemul of which two species are recognized – *H.bisulcus* in the southern Andes, and *H.antisensis* in the north.

The range of the North Andean – or Peruvian – Huemul – sometimes referred to as *taruca, venado* – extends southwards along the high Andes chain from Ecuador in the north through Peru and western Bolivia into northern Chile and north-west Argentina as far south as Catamarca province.

Map 28   The ranges of Huemul or Guemal *Hippocamelus* and Marsh deer *Blastocerus dichotomus* in South America.

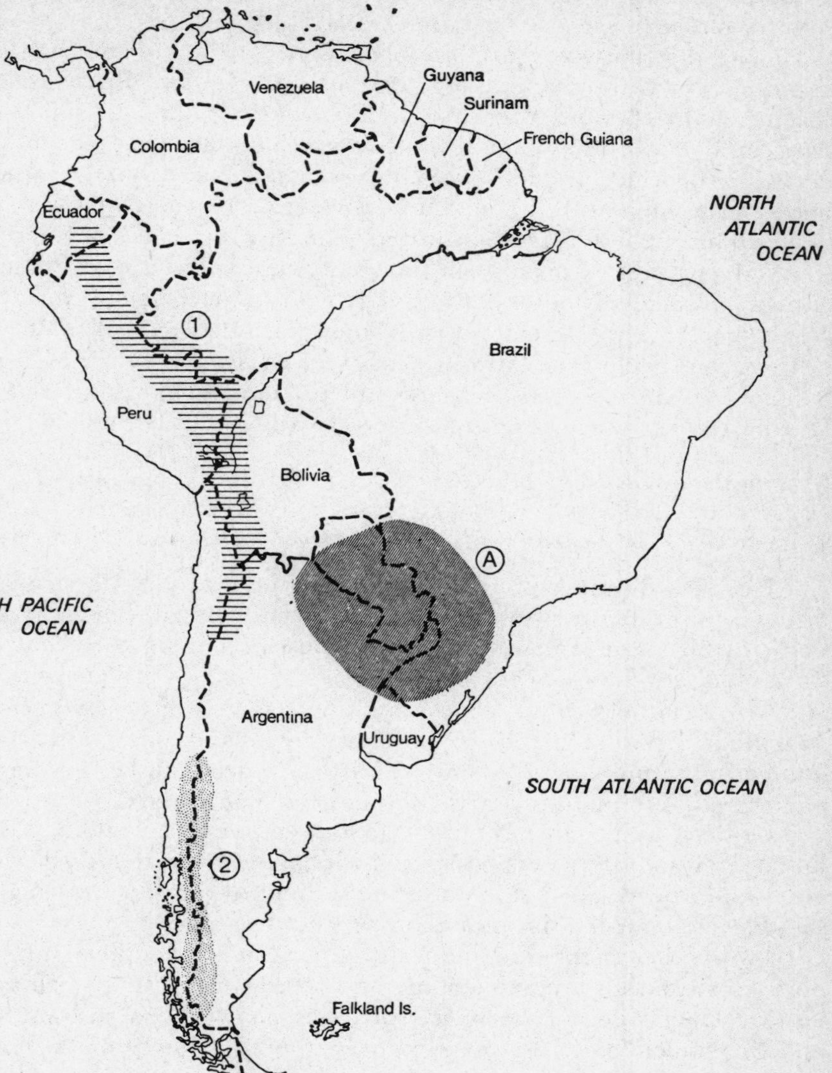

HUEMUL or GUEMAL DEER *Hippocamelus*

1   *Hippocamelus antisensis*   Northern Andes
2   *H. bisculus*   Southern Andes

MARSH DEER *Blastocerus dichotomus*

A   *Blastocerus dichotomus*   Central Brazil to north Argentina

In Peru, where the population is estimated to vary between 10,000 and 15,000 animals, the species is well distributed in the more central and southern parts of the Andean range, its principal habitat being mountainous country of over 14,000 ft (4200 metres) altitude.

During the rainy season (December to May) the Huemul move to the highest peaks, attracted by the green pastures. Hunters, therefore, have to reach great heights and travel, perhaps, two or three days' full ride before the deer can be successfully shot at this season. In consequence, the numbers of deer killed by white hunters is probably very small indeed, but the Indians who live at these high altitudes undoubtedly take a considerable toll.

The date of the rut varies according to locality, but in the northern part of the Andes it takes place between June and August. The approximate weight of a *taruca* male is about 154 lb (70 kg) with stomach removed.

A typical trophy has six tines, with antlers measuring about $13\frac{3}{4}$ in. (35 cm).

In 1979 Klineburger Worldwide Travel service were offering a ten-day 'High Andes Hunt' at a cost of $2500 (about £1250) per person, during which Huemul, White-tailed deer and Spectacle bear could be hunted.

Marsh deer *Blastocerus dichotomus*
Local names: In Argentina, Bolivia, Paraguay, Peru: *Guazuncho*; *Ciervo*; *Ciervo de los pantanos*. In Brazil: *Veado galheiro grande*; *Cervo*, *Guazú-púcu* (Guarani).

The largest of the indigenous deer of South America is the Marsh deer which is found in several areas of central and southern Brazil, Bolivia, Paraguay, Peru and northern Argentina where it is considered to be 'royal' game. In all these republics the species is protected on a number of private ranches, and although generally protected by law, there is very little enforcement. In Argentina, in particular, outside the Government and conservation areas, it is hunted indiscriminately. When wounded, this deer can be very aggressive, and there are numerous reports of hunters being charged.

This deer, as its name implies, is found on marshy ground and is seldom found far from water. Very occasionally it has been referred to as 'Delta deer' or 'Swamp deer'. An adult stag stands about 45 in (115 cm) high at the shoulder – about the size of a Scottish Red deer stag.

As with other members of the South American *cervidae*, there appears to be no fixed season for antler shedding and regrowth, for stags with antlers in various stages of growth can be seen at almost any month of the year. October and November, however, would appear to be the main months for rutting activity. A good pair of antlers – normally with eight points but occasionally up to twelve or more – and in many ways comparable to those of Mule deer – will measure about 24 in. (61 cm) in length.

Marsh deer are included among the game animals which may be hunted during a ten to fourteen day 'Jungle Hunt' organized by Klineburger Worldwide Travel in Peru at a cost of (1979) $3500 (about £1750) per person. On the fourteen-day hunt access to the hunting ground is by canoe –

otherwise a helicopter will be used for transportation in and out at an additional cost of approximately $500 (£250).

White-tailed deer *Odocoileus virginianus*
Local names: *Cariacus*, *Venado* (general); *Lluichu* (Peru), *Savannah deer* (Brazil and Guianas).

The White-tailed deer – generally referred to as *Venado* – has a wide distribution in the northern republics of South America north of about latitude 20° S, being entirely absent from Argentina, Paraguay, Uruguay and southern Brazil.

On the mainland six races have been recognized, whilst on two of the islands off the north coast of Venezuela two insular types occur, namely *O.v.margaritae* on Margarita Island and *O.v.curassavicus* on Curaçao Island. The latter may also occur on the Peninsula of La Goajira in northern Colombia.

On the mainland the distribution of the six races is approximately as follows: *O.v.cariacou* occurs in north Brazil and French Guiana, and its range probably extends into Surinam where it may intergrade with *O.v.gymnotis*. The typical locality of this race is stated to be the Savanna area of the lower Orinoco of eastern Venezuela. In western Venezuela *O.v.gymnotis* is replaced by *O.v.goudotii*, which extends its range to the Andes of Colombia. Two other races occur in Colombia: *O.v.tropicalis* which is confined to western parts, and *O.v.ustus* in the extreme south near the border with Ecuador. *O.v.peruvianus* also occurs in southern Ecuador, from where it penetrates its range along the coast to southern Peru. In Peru, from the north to the south of the country, it occurs on both the coastal plane and the western slopes of the Andes wherever there is adequate vegetation cover, right from sea level up to 13,100 ft (4000 metres) and even higher in the Andean region.

In some areas below about the 6600 ft (2000 metres) altitude the Whitetail co-exist with the Red Brocket.

The White-tailed deer is remorselessly hunted throughout the year wherever it occurs – bucks, does and fawns being killed indiscriminately. As a result, in some areas of extreme hunting pressure, it has become extremely retiring and almost entirely nocturnal. Nevertheless, it has shown remarkable tenacity and in very few areas has it been entirely eradicated.

In former days when deer were abundant in the Rupunini Valley (British Guiana), burning grass to hunt them was the Indian's biggest ritual. There were special times of the year for doing it; Christmas, height of the dry season, when the grass in the swamps was bone dry and long, was one of them. Brock (1963) said the following.

It was a wholesale slaughter and was largely responsible for the great diminishing in the deer's numbers. Popular places were mountain valleys where the wind, necked down, would howl through in the heat of the day. News of a hunt would be a sign for the whole tribe to gather, armed with their muzzle-loaders, and other ancient artillery. They would start at one end of the valley, up-wind, and lay a string of fires across it. Then the men would spread out, covering the whole front of the fire and some way ahead of it. The blaze, fanned by the strong breeze, would race through and put up every single animal lying in front of it. So intense would be the following barrage that only when so many deer began running away together could the odd one escape in the confusion.

This method is, apparently, still used today in some of the more remote areas but on a much reduced scale, with only about half a dozen hunters taking part.

Hunting deer with dogs is an activity much practised and in this field both the Brazilian and American Indian excel. The dogs are used to drive the deer from thick cover towards a line of guns, but on occasions will be allowed to run free after a deer, and in open savannah will generally succeed in pulling it down within a mile ($1\frac{1}{2}$ km).

In areas where, due to persecution, the deer has become largely nocturnal, the most effective method of hunting is to shoot at night with the aid of a flashlight.

Working on a large ranch, much of Brock's hunting was done from horseback, and he claimed to have 'had more action shotgunning from horseback than at any other form of hunting. . . . Riding through good deer country, carrying a rifle can provide excellent sport. The shots are usually snap off-hand ones at a bobbing Whitetail, and though you may miss more often than you hit, the action can be pretty hot.'

Hunting in cover, however, Brock considers that the shotgun, using cartridges loaded with AAA or SSG shot, is the best weapon.

Undoubtedly the most exciting sport is roping deer from horseback – a pursuit which has long been practised by the Brazilian *vaqueroes* – but not one that a visiting sportsman will be tempted to try.

This is a team game, and done properly, even the fleetest deer can be run down and roped. It is, of course, strictly a dry season pastime, and in British Guiana this means between October and the end of April. A good open plain of at least one mile (1.6 km) in length is necessary, and the better the *vaquero* is mounted the better the chance of success. Indeed, many deer have been lassoed by a single rider, completely unaided, but this calls for not only an exceptional mount, but also for the deer to have been roused close to the rider.

Describing the final capture of the deer, Brock states that should a *vaquero*, riding alongside the deer, miss with his loop, he 'may grasp it and throw it down by the tail, or even intentionally collide into it with his horse. . . . This technique of tailing comes from its use in cattle work, where cows that refuse to turn are often thrown down by their tails'.

There appears to be no particular rutting season, and in British Guiana and Brazil fawns can be seen at all times of the year, although the majority will probably be born during the dry season (between October and April).

Antlers bearing more than four tines aside are rare, whilst a good head will

Map 29 The range of White-tailed deer *Odocoileus virginianus* in South America.

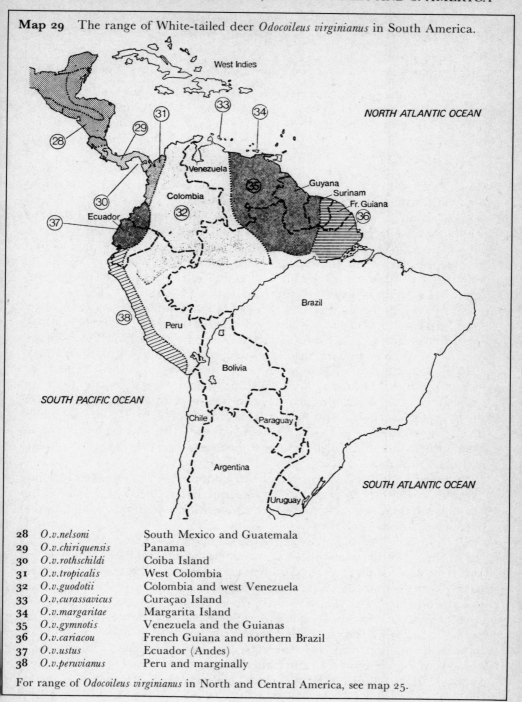

28	*O.v.nelsoni*	South Mexico and Guatemala
29	*O.v.chiriquensis*	Panama
30	*O.v.rothschildi*	Coiba Island
31	*O.v.tropicalis*	West Colombia
32	*O.v.guodotii*	Colombia and west Venezuela
33	*O.v.curassavicus*	Curaçao Island
34	*O.v.margaritae*	Margarita Island
35	*O.v.gymnotis*	Venezuela and the Guianas
36	*O.v.cariacou*	French Guiana and northern Brazil
37	*O.v.ustus*	Ecuador (Andes)
38	*O.v.peruvianus*	Peru and marginally

For range of *Odocoileus virginianus* in North and Central America, see map 25.

measure around 13 in. (32.5 cm) along the main beam, with a brow point measuring about 3 in. (7.5 cm) in length.

Red deer *Cervus elaphus*
Local names: *Ciervo colorado*; *Rojo*; *Noble*; *Europeo*.

The first Red deer to reach Argentina arrived about 1904 when Pedro Luro brought some deer from Europe to the province of La Pampa, the source of the animals being Murau in Austria and from Schönborn in the Carpathians. Shortly after the First World War Monsieur Hohmann imported about twenty-five deer from Germany and liberated them on an estate near San Martin de los Andes, Neuquén province in western Argentina. This estate, which extends to almost 200,000 acres (80,971 hectares) is a mountainous area lying at an altitude of about 3500 ft (1066 metres) above sea level. These deer acclimatized themselves well, and by the fifties it was estimated that the number of Red deer in the area was in the region of 3500 to 5000 head. During the winter of 1951, about 1000 deer (stags and hinds) were shot, as they had become too numerous, and were causing damage in the *estancia*. Normally, about fifty to sixty stags are killed annually on this estate during the rut, which takes place from about mid-March to mid-April.

By 1950 Red deer had spread to most of the Lanin National Park area south of Lago Quillen, as well as to a number of private estates, both in Argentina and across the Chilean border, where they have joined up with the deer between Lake Tromen in Argentina and 'Villa Rica' Volcan in Chile.

Red deer have also been introduced to other estates in Argentina, including two stags from Woburn, England, in 1972 to the Estancia Chacabuco at San Carlos de Bariloche in the province of Rió Negro. One of these stags – a 32-pointer – was decidedly cream coloured, but proved a bad breeder and was shot in 1978, in which year the other stag had twenty-five tines. Other stags in the district have come from Germany, Austria, Ukraine and the Carpathians.

Red deer have also been introduced to a number of estates in Chile. Some Wapiti have also been introduced to Parque Diana by Herr Adolf Vogel, but so far as is known, none were ever liberated outside the park, and all the deer have now been shot out.

In Chile the principal areas where the stag is hunted are in the south near the towns of Villarrica and Osorno. There is no organized hunting by outfitters, and hunters must make direct arrangements with the owners of the farm where the deer exist. Prices are reasonable and considerably lower than those currently operative in eastern Europe. Rural areas in Chile, however, compared to Argentina, are comparatively densely populated, and the average size of estates, in consequence, too small to provide satisfactory hunting areas. Many deer are taken by poachers and dogs running wild.

With the exception of approximately 395,000 acres (about 160,000 hectares) in the Lanin and Nahuel Huapi National Parks which are located in a mountainous range of country on the borders of Argentina with the Chile republic, all the remaining Red deer are on private ranches or *estancias*. Their range, extending over 5 million acres (about 2 million hectares) includes the provinces of Rio Negro, Neuquén, San Luis and La Pampa.

Every year, during November, the national parks authority make available for public auction blocks for hunting in their reserve in the Volcan Lanin area. These are let on a fixed ten-day period, the hunting season lasting from about 1 March to 1 May although in some blocks it may terminate somewhat earlier, depending on the game position. In some years, however, an entire block may be closed for hunting to allow the stock to recover. Hunting will be by pack horse.

Prices vary from one block to another, depending on the hunting prospects in any particular area, and also the period of the season, the hunting being best at the peak of the rut. A ten-day hunt in one of the best blocks, therefore, may cost about U.S.$2500 (about £1250) but in a less popular area it could be as little as U.S.$500 (£250), which would include guides, horses, food etc. During the last four years the hunter success ratio has been about 25 percent – all on ten-day guided hunts.

Probably the best chance of shooting a trophy animal would be in a private ranch or *estancia*, where the terrain is generally more open and less mountainous. In these circumstances the 'let' is based on the quality of the antler, and may cost anything from about U.S.$1000 (about £500) to U.S.$4000 (about £2000) for a particularly good trophy.

Most of the Red deer in La Pampa province, except in the Parque Luro, are on private ranches and a number of owners let their stalking. There is a large stock of Red deer in the 20,000 acres (about 8000 hectares) Parque Luro. The park is more or less surrounded by a deer-proof fence but up to date no sport-stalking has been permitted.

A six to eight day hunt after Red deer in the Bariloche area of western Argentina can be obtained from Klineburger Worldwide Travel at a cost (1979) of $4500 (about £2250) the price including the shooting of one trophy, full board and transportation during the trip. Additional trophies may be shot for $2250 (about £1125). If a stag is wounded and not recovered, 70 percent of the trophy fee will be charged, whilst the charge for a missed shot will be 5 percent.

On the *estancia* 'Los Helechos' in the province of Neuquén a much cheaper ten-day hunt is available for £500, which includes guide, horses, riding equipment, tent and 'basic' food – meat, bread and yerba 'mate' – and the opportunity to shoot a stag of twelve to sixteen-tines which should have a C.I.C. points score of around 190.00. Further stags may be shot at £250 each. From the camp, two hunters can operate simultaneously in independent areas, each extending to approximately 5000 acres (about 2000 hectares).

Despite the undoubted high quality of antler, a hunter has to be fortunate to shoot a trophy of more than 200 C.I.C. points. The two best Argentinian

Red deer trophies yet recorded were a 15-pointer from La Pampa province with 237.05 C.I.C. points (1970) and a 20-pointer from Nequén Province with 230.22 C.I.C. points (1967).

Axis deer or **Chital** *Axis axis*
Local names: *Ciervo axis*; *Chital*; *Morteado*.

Axis deer have been introduced to a few estates in Argentina and feral populations have been established in the provinces of Buenos Aires, Rio Negro and Nequén. A few have also been introduced to an estate in southern Brazil, and to Uruguay where they are established along the Uruguay River coast.

For a seven-day hunt after Chital, one outfitter from Buenos Aires is charging U.S.$1000 (about £500) for one hunter, or U.S.$1500 (about £750) for two, with an extra U.S.$130 (£65) per day should the trip be extended beyond the week. If the hunter is successful then a further U.S.$300–400 (£150–£200) is charged for the trophy, depending on its size. The best trophy yet recorded had an antler length of 90.5 cm (left) and 91.5 cm (right) (about $35\frac{1}{2}$ and 36 in. respectively).

Blackbuck antelope – another introduced exotic from India – may also be hunted during the same trip and the trophy fee for this species would be U.S.$300.

Sambar *Cervus unicolor*

About 1945 some Sambar were introduced to an area in the Sao Pablo State of Brazil, and in 1980 were said to number about 300 animals (R. Lalo Mandojana *in litt*). No further details are available.

Fallow deer *Dama dama*
Local names: *Ciervo dama*; *Gamo o paleto*.

Since about 1895 Fallow deer have been introduced to a number of estates in Argentina, and have acclimatized themselves well in the provinces of Rio Negro, Neuquén and Buenos Aires.

About 1930 some Fallow deer, which probably came from Germany, were introduced to northern Valdivia, Chile, and the species is well established there also. Some are fenced in, but others are free ranging.

The terrain occupied by Fallow deer in Buenos Aires province, all of which is privately owned, varies considerably, for whilst around Sierra de los Padres the country consists mostly of bush covered grassy plains and low hills of under 400 ft (120 metres) above sea level, in the Sierra de la Ventana and Cura-Malal areas it is more rocky, with mountains running up to about 3300 ft (1000 metres). Unfortunately, due to poaching and over-shooting, the deer in the Sierra de los Padres area are now near extinction.

Early in the century Fallow deer were introduced to an estate in Sierra de Volcán, but the species is now extinct there, the only deer in the area being Axis deer.

The bucks go to rut during April, so this month and the one following are the best times to hunt.

The best trophies come from Neuquén and Sierras Cura-Malal and Ventana, but the quality is generally poor, the best one so far measured obtaining 195.12 C.I.C. points.

In Peru Fallow deer were introduced in 1948 to the Huacraruco Ranch in the district of San Juan in Cajamarca Province, a few being subsequently released in the Chicamo river basin area. Due to poaching it is probable only a few remain.

A small number of Fallow deer also occur in two areas in the south-west of Uruguay (Chapman, 1980).

10 The Hunting of Exotics

At one time a sportsman anxious to shoot, perhaps, a Chital, Muntjac or Sika deer, had to travel many thousands of miles to India or east Asia to achieve his trophy. Those were the days when game was plentiful and available to be hunted by any person who had the time and wealth to do so. But not so today, for although air travel has reduced the travel time to reach these far off countries from months to a matter of days or even hours, many of the former hunting grounds – and this particularly applies to parts of India and Asia – are no longer open to the hunters of big game.

As a result, an increasing number of these fine game animals from the eastern hemisphere are being introduced to game ranches in Texas, New Mexico and elsewhere, and commercial hunting for exotics is now big business, attracting not only sportsmen from America but also from Europe and in particular from Germany and Spain.

Exotic game has been roaming the Texan ranches for close on half a century, and the manner in which exotic game hunting has developed is well illustrated by a survey of game ranches carried out by the Texas Parks and Wildlife Department in 1974 which showed that almost 60,000 exotic game animals, comprising thirty-nine different species, were present on the 316 private ranches. Today the number is nearer 80,000 head of game. Apart from stock fencing, few of the ranches, which vary in size from a few hundred acres to over 36,000 acres (14,400 hectares) are enclosed with high game-proof fences, and although the normal stock fence will contain Mouflon and Blackbuck – two of the most popular exotics within the ranches – the deer, for the most part, are free-ranging.

One of the largest enclosed private hunting areas in Texas is the Y.O. Ranch which has been in the possession of the Schreiner family for just on a hundred years. It takes its name from the mark which was, and still is, used for branding the cattle – the Texan Longhorn.

Surrounded by a 6 ft (1.8 metre) deer fence, the terrain is rocky and arid, with low hills and brushy draws, the typical vegetation being shinnoak, oak, cedar, cactus and tall grass. There is no natural water, and this has to be provided by windmills which are scattered throughout the ranch. During the summer months mid-day temperatures average around 90° F., but in mid-winter early morning and evening there can be 10 to 15 degrees of frost. Spring and autumn are undoubtedly the pleasantest times to visit the ranch.

In addition to the Texan Longhorns – which now number about 400 head – the ranch has always been an important producer of wool and mohair from sheep and goats. However, when in the early fifties a slump in the wool trade set in, a decision was made to launch out on commercial hunting, and the first exotic species were introduced. Today commercialized hunting for exotics would seem to be giving a better financial return than wool.

One of the most successful of the exotic introductions not only to Texan ranches but also to *estancias* in Argentina has been the Chital or Axis deer *Axis axis* of India, and a recent estimate suggested that the total population in Texas alone was in excess of 18,000, of which many thousand were 'free-ranging'. Indeed it has been suggested that perhaps the Axis deer population in Texas alone may now represent perhaps a tenth of the world's population of this species, and in some areas it is starting to compete with the native Whitetail.

Although the shedding and reproduction of antlers in Axis deer follows no set date pattern, it would seem that the majority of adult stags will be in hard antler from about April to November, thus providing a trophy to hunt during the summer months when the antlers of Whitetail bucks will still be in velvet.

Other species of exotic deer introduced to some of the Texan ranches are Red deer *Cervus elaphus* and Fallow deer *Dama dama* from Europe, and an assortment of subspecies of Sika deer from Asia, which include Dybowski *Cervus nippon hortulorum* from Manchuria, Formosan *C.n.taiouanus* from Taiwan and the typical deer of Japan, *C.n.nippon*. On the Y.O. Ranch there are a number of all black Sika deer, which would suggest that these may have originated from the Ryukyu Islands – the home of the endangered Karema Sika *C.n.keramae*, which is the most melanistic of the Sikine deer. It is a pity, therefore, that these black Sika cannot be segregated, instead of being allowed to mingle – and doubtless interbreed – with other Sika deer.

Mouflon, Barbary sheep (Aoudad), wild goat, Nilghai and Blackbuck antelope are included among the non-cervidae exotics that can be hunted on some of the ranches.

For many years the ambition of many American sheep hunters has been to achieve the 'grand slam' – i.e. trophy heads of the four types of wild sheep indigenous to North America (Bighorn, Dall, Stone and Desert sheep). When this has been achieved the hunter can join a club called the Grand Slam Club and up to date it is believed that 200 hunters have achieved the four kills. The 'grand slam' term has its origin in baseball and refers to a batter coming in to bat with all three bases 'loaded' – i.e. a runner on each – hitting a home run over the fence. It is a rare event seldom achieved by even the greatest hitters and results in the scoring of four runs.

Now the hunter of exotics has his own 'slams' to strive for – the Texan Slam which is to include one each of Mouflon, Corsican, White Corsican and Black Corsican sheep that make the Records of Exotics book, and the Exotic Super

Slam, which in addition to three types of sheep, (Corsican, Mouflon and Barbary or Aoudad), two wild goats (Catalina and Ibex), and Blackbuck antelope, will include Axis, Fallow, Sika and Red deer – a total of ten exotics, all of which must measure up to the standard required for entry in the Records book.

No State licence is required to hunt or shoot any of the exotic game animals, nor is there any State-controlled hunting season, so legitimately they can all be hunted throughout the twelve months of the year. However, it is pointless to shoot a trophy deer with antlers still in velvet, so the condition of antler growth really dictates the season. Apart from the Axis deer, therefore, whose antler growth is inclined to be variable, all the other deer should be in hard antler from about September to March. Hunting Whitetail and Wapiti, however, irrespective of whether within or outside a ranch fence, requires a State licence – which for a non-resident will cost $100.75 (about £50) (1979) – and the animal can only be shot during the State legal open season. In Texas there are, of course, no longer any free-ranging Wapiti.

On the majority of ranches, the firearm hunter will not be permitted to hunt without a guide, but during the special 'bow season' any archer wishing to hunt for Whitetail only, may be allotted a special hunting area extending, perhaps, to about 100 acres (40 hectares) and allowed to hunt on his own. He must, however, be accompanied by a guide when hunting any of the exotics.

The majority of ranches which organize 'hunts on a guaranteed basis' make no charge for the guide, as his services are included in the trophy fee. If, therefore, the guide fails to find an acceptable trophy, the hunter is under no obligation to shoot. 'It only costs to kill' is the claim of one ranch owner. On ranches that do make a charge, the cost of a guide works out at about $40 to $75 per day (about £20 to £37) depending on whether the guide is being shared between two hunters or not. At Llano, Wildlife Safaris make a charge of $150 to $200 per day (about £75 to £100) depending on the season, and this charge includes a guide, all transportation whilst hunting, food and accommodation, trophy fees being extra.

A few ranches, such as the Y.O. and Llano are able to provide comfortable accommodation for hunters, but in the majority of cases this has to be found in nearby motels. The duration of the hunt depends, of course, on the number of species to be hunted, but provided the weather remains open, a day to a day and half for each species should be sufficient.

Many ranches have a dirt landing strip available for the hunters flying in by private aircraft.

Trophy fees vary slightly from one ranch to another, but the following will serve as an approximate guide to the prices that were being used in 1979.

Axis deer	$500–$1000	(about £250–£500)
Fallow deer	$400–$750	(about £200–£375)
Sika deer, Formosan	$600	(about £300)
Sika deer, Dybowski	$1000	(about £500)

Sika deer (subspecies unspecified)	$400	(about £200)
Red deer	$1500–$2000	(about £750–£1000)
Wapiti (Elk)	$2500–$3000*	(about £1250–1500)

* One outfitter is offering a ranch hunt after Elk at $1500 for the hunt, and a further $1500 'for the shot' – which may be expensive if the bullet misses its target!

Good White-tailed deer hunting can also be obtained on most ranches, and in addition to the State hunting licence ($100.75 for non-residents) a species fee will also be charged, and this could vary from about $200 to $300 on ranches which operate a fixed price to as much as $1800 (about £900) or so on ranches where the price is calculated in accordance with the measurements of the trophy.

A price tag commensurate with the trophy has, of course, long been normal practice in Europe, but it is only recently that this system has been introduced to North America and at present applies mainly to White-tailed deer on a few ranches. I can, however, visualize it spreading to other species for it seems reasonable that a hunter who is successful in getting a really good trophy should have to pay more than one who is not in the least interested in antler measurements but is satisfied so long as he gets a buck. Already the Patio Ranch have increased the basic price for an Axis stag from $750 to $1000 for antlers measuring over 32 in. (80 cm).

Recently, therefore, a group of ranchers and outfitters developed a system, known as the Myers Point Pay for pricing Whitetail antlers, which takes into account not only antler points (tines) and measurements but also the body weight of the buck. Bucks are divided into two categories, the Trophy Class and the Mature Class, the factors sixty and forty respectively being used to calculate the price in each category as follows:

Any buck with antlers which meet *one* of the following requirements will be considered in the Trophy Class and charged accordingly, the number of points (tines) being multiplied by $60, and the weight by 60 cents.

1 Any head with 12 or more points (tines).
2 Any head with an antler base circumference of 5 in. (12.5 cm) or greater.
3 Any head with a spread of 20 in. (50 cm) or greater.
4 Any head with a drop point of 1 in. (2.5 cm) or greater.

An example of a Trophy Class buck would, therefore, be as follows:

Details		Factor	Price
Number of tines	10	× $60	$600
Spread	20½ in.	× $60	$1230
Weight of buck	150 lb	× 60¢	$90
			$1920 (about £960)

Note: The above head qualified only for Trophy Class because its spread exceeds 20 in.

Furthermore, if the head had had a drop point of 1 in. (2.5 cm) or greater, there would have been an additional charge of $500 (about £250).

Trophies in which none of the physical characteristics attain the minimum requirements for Trophy Class are considered Mature and the factor forty instead of sixty will be used as shown by the following example:

Details		Factor	Price
Number of tines	8	× $40	$320
Spread	18 in.	× $40	$720
Weight	120 lb	× 40¢	$48
			$1088 (about £544)

Using the Myers Point Pay system for the best Whitetail ('typical') trophy yet recorded for Texas (shot in 1963) the charge would have been about $2300 (about £1150). The best 'non-typical' White-tailed buck trophy for Texas had forty-nine tines (1892) and according to the Myers Point Pay system, would have been priced out at $3900 (about £1950). The number of tines on this head were, however, exceptional. The highest number of tines in recent years has been a 30-pointer, shot in Frio County in 1966, and priced in accordance with the above mentioned system, would have cost the hunter about $3000 (about £1500). In the above three examples the weight of the buck has been assumed to be 150 lb (68 kg).

The Myers Point Pay system is used for Whitetail shot on the thirteen ranches controlled by Texotic Wildlife Inc. who also charge 75 percent of the listed fee for any beast wounded and not recovered. This is an innovation to hunting in North America but is in general practice in Europe.

On the Guajolota Ranch, in addition to a day fee of $200 there is an equitable fee of $500 to $1500 (about £250 to £750) depending upon the size of the buck taken. This cost is determined by measuring the trophy under the Burkett System (*see page 275*), and multiplying the final score by $4. The final decision whether or not to take the trophy rests with the hunter for he alone knows what he is prepared to pay. During the first two years this trophy fee system has been in operation at Guajolota, the average total cost of a hunt after Whitetail has been around $1350 (about £675).

Compared to hunting game in other parts of the world, some of the charges for shooting exotics are not unreasonable, even though a 'ranch hunt' with a 'guaranteed trophy' at the end, undoubtedly lacks the excitement and challenge of hunting the wild animal in its native country. Moreover, a charge of $2000 for a trophy Whitetail buck on a Texan ranch may seem high, when the same animal can be shot elsewhere for the cost of only $100.75 (non-resident's licence). It must be appreciated, however, that on a private ranch where hunting is strictly controlled, the hunter, provided he can shoot straight, is virtually assured of a worthwhile trophy in a day or two, which, when hunting on public ground, would certainly not be the case. A figure of $2000 moreover, is comparable to the sort of price a visitor to eastern Europe would expect to pay for a Red deer stag of only Bronze medal standard, whilst for exceptional trophies the price could well be around £7000 to £8000 (*see page 108*). The proof is in the eating, and despite the charges, up to date there has been no shortage of clients anxious to shoot the Texan ranch Whitetail.

Some people suggest that to hunt any animal on a ranch, particularly surrounded by a 6-ft game-proof fence (1.8 metres) offers little sport. This is understandably true on a small fenced-in ranch or enclosure extending to perhaps a few hundred acres, but it must be appreciated that some ranches extend to 30,000 acres (12,000 hectares) or more – an area which is larger than many deer forests in Scotland – and within the boundary fences there can be an awful lot of extremely rough terrain in which the animal can take refuge. In my opinion, therefore, it is just as much an achievement to shoot a worthwhile trophy in one of these larger ranches as to kill, say, a medal class buck or stag from a high seat in Hungary or Yugoslavia. Undoubtedly the ban on all motorized transport for hunting within the ranch would make the venture even more sporting, but not only would considerably fewer animals be taken, but it would be virtually impossible to hunt the whole of the larger ranges properly without resorting to 'fly camps'. No one has yet suggested that it would be more sporting if, say, in Scotland, one did not take the landrover as far up the glen as possible before starting the day's stalk. There is no doubt, however, that shots at game are frequently taken from a vehicle, for Texan law at present is a bit ambiguous as to the extent a vehicle may be used within the confines of a ranch to pursue game. Generally speaking, therefore, most hunters feel that they are within their rights if they see game from a vehicle, to dismount and take their shot. On the Llano Ranch, which extends to about 12,000 acres (4800 hectares) hunting is, of necessity, mostly on foot and shooting from a vehicle is not usually permitted.

It is not only on the game ranches of Texas and New Mexico that these exotics flourish. Mention has already been made of the large number of Axis deer that now lead a feral life outside the ranches of Texas. This deer – known locally by the native names of *Kia* and *Dia* – has also been introduced to Hawaii and at the present time occurs in huntable population on the islands of Molokai and Lanai, and to a lesser extent on Oahu and Maui.

A non-resident licence to hunt in Hawaii costs $15 (1979) which is double the cost of a resident's licence. Licences to hunt deer are determined by public drawing and when issued, refer to a specific date. On each island the bag limit is one deer, and although this must be a male animal on Molokai, either sex may be taken on Lanai. Needless to say, hunter success, during recent years, has been considerably greater on Lanai as the following figures for 1977–8 deer season show:

Island	No. harvested	No. of hunter trips	Hunter success
Lanai	159 (either sex)	895	18%
Molokai	44 (male only)	1077	4%

These figures relate to Government-owned or controlled lands and do not include the deer which are shot on private lands on both Lanai and Kauai. Hunting is normally restricted to weekends during March and April so as not to conflict with the game bird season which takes place during December and January. All deer killed must be tagged immediately and the head or scrotum must be left attached to the carcase so as to enable the identification of sex. Breeding follows no fixed pattern, but the majority of stags will be rutting during April to August.

Permissive weapons include rifles of 1200 ft/lb muzzle energy or more, shotguns of 20 gauge or larger, loaded with oo buckshot or rifled slug; and bow and arrows of recognized hunting specification (*see page 226*). Whilst the use of dogs is forbidden on Lanai, they may accompany the hunter on Molokai provided he is hunting with any weapon other than the rifle mentioned above.

Axis deer have been introduced to the central coastal peninsula of California to an estate near Point Reyes National Sea Shore, Marin County, and in 1976 were estimated to number about 460 animals and increasing. Outside North America, Axis deer have also been successfully established in Argentina, on the island of Brioni in Yugoslavia and in Queensland, Australia.

Exotic deer are also present in other areas of North America. Early in the century Sika deer were imported to Maryland, and according to an eye witness account, four or five animals were released on James Island in 1916. They quickly established themselves, first spreading to nearby Taylors Island and then eventually, to the counties of Dorchester and Wicomico. In 1976 estimates put the number of Sika deer in Maryland at around 5000 and increasing.

In order to reduce the depredation caused by these deer, hunters in Dorchester County only, are permitted to shoot on licence one Whitetail and two Sika, which may be increased to three if no Whitetail has been taken. This bag limit applies to both the bow and arrow and the firearm season. Sika deer can be hunted in Maryland on the same hunting licence for White-tailed deer, the same open season applying for both species. About 300 to 500 Sika are being harvested each year.

Sika deer have also been introduced to the coastal islands of Virginia in the Chincoteague Island National Wildlife Refuge, and adjacent islands, where the overall population is estimated to number about 700.

Since 1964 public hunting has been permitted in the refuge, and although in the first two years 237 and 292 deer respectively were shot, the cull has since been drastically reduced, and in 1977 only twenty-two were taken, of which the bow-hunters claimed twelve. Limits for the bow hunters is one Sika per day, and three per licence year. At least one of the three must be a hind which will be tagged with a Virginia 'nuisance' tag.

One deer per day and three per licence year is also the limit for the gun hunters. The first deer must be an adult female or a buck with unbranched antlers. The second and third may be either an adult female, unbranched

268

buck or a trophy buck with five points or more. No hunter, however, may take more than one trophy stag or two adult females in a season.

There are also a few Sika deer in south-east Wisconsin but they are not numerous. A Sika deer can, however, be shot as a 'deer' during the regular hunting season.

In Europe Sika deer have been introduced into a number of countries and in many localities have established themselves well. These include England, Scotland, Ireland, Austria, Czechoslovakia, West Germany and Denmark. Sika deer have also been satisfactorily introduced to Morocco and to the forests of Madagascar.

Fallow deer, to the number of about 800, are to be found in an area known as Land Between the Lakes, in south-west Kentucky, and during the 1974 and 1975 seasons, 172 and 115 deer respectively were taken by hunters. Hunting of Fallow was then banned for two years but it was proposed to allow a few to be taken in 1979.

Fallow deer are also present in a small park at Prudenville, Michigan and on the islands of Little St Simons and Jekyll in Georgia. Although the former island is private land, State legislation requires the deer – estimated to number around 400 to 500 animals – to be shot between 20 October and 21 February, both sexes being taken.

In central Alabama, mostly in Wilcox County, as well as some in Dallas County, there is an estimated population of about 1000 Fallow deer, and for the purpose of hunting these are considered 'deer' to be taken during the regular season for Whitetail (*see page 238*). In New Mexico a wild population of Fallow deer is established in the Sacramento Mountains, having originated from animals which had escaped from a deer park.

Other areas in the United States where Fallow deer have been introduced outside the game ranches of Texas include the Boone and Wheeler counties of Nebraska, Eastern Shore in Cecil County, Maryland, on the McAester Army Ammunition Depot in Oklahoma and in two localities of California, one in the north coastal area of Mendocino County and the other on Point Keyes National Sea Shore. Except in the last mentioned area where the estimated population is around 500, herds in the remaining localities are small and probably number fewer than one hundred in any one area.

During the interwar years Fallow deer were introduced to counties Conejos, Larimer and Rio Blanco in Colorado, and to the islands of Martha's Vineyard and Nantucket, Massachusetts, but it is doubtful if any still survive (Chapman, 1980).

In Canada Fallow deer have been introduced to James, Sidney and Saltspring – three islands which lie adjacent to Vancouver in British Columbia – and these may be hunted during the normal open season for the Black-tailed deer in the area. Recent population estimates suggest that there may be up to 500 deer on James Island, with about half this number on Sidney.

In South Africa some Fallow deer – locally referred to as *Damhert* – were introduced to the Vereeniging estate in the Transvaal, and have remained there ever since. Fallow are also present in both Cape Province and Orange Free State, where they have been introduced to some estates to replace conventional farming for game ranching.

In Madagascar, about 1932, some Fallow deer from Czechoslovakia were released near Mamdjakatompo, and although surviving for about forty years, appear now to be extinct on this island (Chapman 1980).

In Australasia, Fallow deer have been introduced to Australia, Tasmania and New Zealand and hunting is available in all localities.

About 1880 some Fallow deer were introduced to Wakaya, in the Fiji group of islands, and are now believed to number about 400 animals (Chapman, 1980).

Fallow deer have also been introduced to South America and are now established in Argentina and Peru. This species has also been introduced to the Leeward Islands and Cuba.

Thirty years ago there were herds of Red deer at Land Between the Lakes area of south-west Kentucky, as well as on Bernheim Forest – a large privately endowed recreational area some 30 miles (48 km) south-west of Louisville and although a few still lingered on into the sixties, they are now extinct.

A few Sambar *Cervus unicolor* have been introduced to the Saint Vincent National Wildlife Refuge (Gulf Coast Island) in Florida, and to the Hearst Ranch in San Luis Obispo county of California, but in both areas numbers are small and what little hunting is done in the latter, is controlled by the landowner.

White-tailed deer have been liberated in Finland and Czechoslovakia whilst both Muntjac *Muntiacus* and Chinese Water-deer *Hydropotes inermis* are well established in many counties of England. Various species of exotic deer are kept in some of the game parks of Austria, and from time to time trophy animals are shot on licence.

Undoubtedly the most unique exotic deer is the Père David deer *Elaphurus davidianus* – sometimes referred to as Miliu – which became extinct in its native land of China at the beginning of the present century. Fortunately, before this occurred the 11th Duke of Bedford had been able to collect a few animals for his park at Woburn, from which the present day world population of about 800 deer – of which just over 300 are at Woburn, and the remainder scattered around the zoos of the world, owe their origin. As yet, none of the ranches of North America hold this species but as numbers build up in the zoos it is reasonable to assume that in the not too distant future the only outlet for surplus stock will be to the exotic game ranch.

There is little doubt that the exotic game ranch, when properly managed, does serve a most useful purpose in conservation, for it is obviously in the interests of the ranch owner that any particular species should flourish. As an example of the important role these game ranches have always played in increasing the world population of a species much diminished in its native country is the case of the Indian Blackbuck which, at one time, in India and

Pakistan, were estimated to number some four million animals but today it is doubtful if more than about 4000 to 5000 still remain. Fortunately, however, when one takes into account those feral animals which are now present on the ranches and *estancias* of North and South America, this figure can be more than doubled – a situation which could not possibly have arisen had there not been a demand for exotic hunting.

The Blackbuck, of course, is not considered an 'endangered animal' and its increasing population outside India is due solely to the fact that it can be hunted. If it had been on the Endangered Species list of the I.U.C.N. (International Union for the Conservation of Nature and Natural Resources), since the United States was a signatory to the Convention on Trade in Threatened Species of Animals and Plants, any animal on that list could no longer be commercialized. This, in my opinion, is probably a mistake, for although these immense ranches could undoubtedly provide a suitable habitat free from natural predators for quite a number of endangered animals, no ranch owner can be expected to go to the enormous expense of introducing and maintaining an animal, no matter how rare, from which there will not be any financial return. Take the position of the rare Indian Swamp deer or Barasingha *Cervus duvauceli* as an example. Small herds of this deer are present on one or two ranches in Texas, and an occasional trophy stag was available to the hunter. This is no longer possible so ranch owners have no inducement to maintain any stocks at all, so the species will eventually – if it has not already done so – disappear from the Texan ranch.

The introduction of exotics for hunting is nothing new. Over a century ago a wide range of deer from all over the world was introduced to both New Zealand and Australia. And what has been the result? Despite heavy hunting pressure, some of the species – particularly the Red deer – soon increased to pest proportions, and those of the same genus have interbred – namely the Red deer and Wapiti. The Rusa deer introduced to New Guinea, and Red deer to Argentina have also increased to near pest proportions.

The main lesson to be learnt from these and other such introductions is that most mammals – whether endangered or not – can breed successfully when introduced to a new and suitable habitat, and even if commercialism has prompted the introductions – i.e. exotic hunting – provided the venture is properly managed with only the oldest animals being culled, game ranching of exotics must, and will, play an important role in the conservation of any species.

The obvious advantage, therefore, of the game ranch over the liberation of any animal into a new habitat is that the game-proof fence, even though introducing some artificiality to the hunt, will at least control the movement of the deer, and prevent it becoming a pest to forestry and agriculture. My main criticism of the game ranch is that up to now there has not been any effort to select animals that will not interbreed.

Part IV
TROPHIES

11 The Measurement of Antlers and Trophy Awards

Throughout the world at least six different systems for the measurement of deer antlers exist, and none can be said to be ideal.

European deer trophies (Red, Roe, Fallow and Elk) are generally measured under the C.I.C. (Conseil International de la Chasse) formula, but occasionally the old Nadler formula, which gives a slightly lower final score value, is still used for Red deer antlers and was included in the evaluation of most of the Red deer trophies at the 1971 World Exhibition in Budapest. Until recently Spain had its own set of formulae, but in 1977 it was decided to adopt the C.I.C. formula. The old formula, however, is still being used by the Game Department when deciding trophy charges (*see page 78*).

In England, prior to the 1939 war, no formula as such was ever used for assessing the trophy value of British deer antlers, the three basic measurements of length, inside span and beam plus the number of tine ends and, perhaps, tip to tip measurements being thought sufficient. Now, however, sportsmen in Britain, particularly the Roe stalker, are beginning to use the C.I.C. formula, with the result that British trophies can now be compared with trophies shot in Europe. Moreover, the high standard of British Roe antlers has in recent years attracted an increasing number of continental sportsmen which has undoubtedly accelerated the acceptance of the C.I.C. method for assessing the trophies.

In North America deer trophies are measured in accordance with the Boone and Crockett Club formula but for Central and South American game trophies, apart from the Whitetail, until the publication of the C.I.C. book, *The Game-Trophies of the World* (1981), no recognized formula was available. Measurements in the Boone and Crockett formulae are at present taken in inches whilst C.I.C. measurements are metric. In International Exhibitions, therefore, such as the one in Budapest in 1971 where deer trophies from both hemispheres were on view, this further complicated the judging, particularly when it came to judging the Asiatic deer. Since 1952, however, the Boone and Crockett formula for Caribou has been used for the Reindeer of Europe, measurements being taken in metric instead of inches.

A still further set of formulae is used for New Zealand deer. There are, of course, no indigenous deer in that country and the exotic deer include Red,

Fallow, Sambar, Rusa, Sika, Whitetail, Moose and Wapiti. It would have been logical, perhaps, for existing C.I.C. formulae to have been used for the European deer, and the Boone and Crockett formulae for the American deer but this was not done. Instead, an entirely new formula for each species, but remarkably similar in some aspects to the Boone and Crockett system was formulated by Norman Douglas, and since 1958 has been accepted by the New Zealand Deerstalkers' Association as the official measuring system of the Association. It is also used in Australia.

Briefly, the Boone and Crockett Club system can be described as comparing the physical characteristics of one antler or horn against the other, and subtracting any differences. In typical deer heads, apart from Moose and Caribou, every individual tine is measured for length and the beam circumference taken at four places. It will be realized, therefore, that if, say, the bay or tray tine is missing on one side, it will also figure as a deduction and not score any points. Likewise, a single-antlered deer cannot score any points whatsoever.

The Douglas system does exactly the same, although the interpretation is somewhat different.

In the introduction to his system, Norman Douglas writes: 'The basic requirement of this scoring system is the recording of a *pair* – not a single antler, horn or tusk. . . .'

Continuing, he states: 'A single side is not even the part of a pair. It can only become a *pair* when a second side, or counterpart, appears. However small this counterpart may be, this is the beginning of a *pair*. At this point, thus, the score for a *pair* must begin.'

In other words, therefore, what Norman Douglas is saying is that any trophy, be it antlers of *Cervidae* or the horns of *Bovidae* that consist of one side only cannot score any points – and that, in effect, is the basis of the Boone and Crockett system.

Comparing the two, whereas in the Boone and Crockett system the measurements of both antlers are taken into account, and the difference subtracted, in the Douglas system only the antler or tine with the *lesser* measurement is considered, and this is *doubled* in the score. As an example, a Wapiti trophy with a left antler of, say, 50 in. in length as compared to 48 in. on the right side, will score 96 for this feature – which in effect, is exactly what it would have scored under the Boone and Crocket formula, i.e. a total of 98 for the two antler lengths, from which two will be deducted for a difference in lengths.

As in the Boone and Crockett method, all individual measurements – which are taken to the nearest eighth of an inch – are measured in the Douglas system, double the length of the lesser appearing in the score sheet. Furthermore, the measurement of *all* the top tines are included in the score and since this will include the terminal point of the main beam which has already been included in the overall length of the beam, one part of the antler is therefore being measured *twice*. The reason for doing this, writes Douglas, is that 'the true *length* of an antler reaches from the coronet base to the tip of the farthest tine point. . . . It will be found, however, that this does not always go to counter-parted tines on top . . . that is why, in the Douglas Score, all the top tines are measured separately, and, where possible are counter-parted after measuring *length*.' The true length goes to the tip of the royal tine on the left antler and to the tip of the back tine of the right antler.

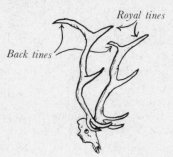

Royal tines

Back tines

The true length goes to the tip of the royal tine on the left antler and to the tip of the back tine on the right antler

For the majority of trophies in both the Boone and Crockett and Douglas Score systems, the number of points or tines are included only as supplementary data and do not count in the score. The number of tines on Moose antlers, however, figure in the score card of both systems. Supplementary data is included to indicate the conformation of the trophy, evaluation of which is generally a matter of personal opinion.

The hunting of exotics in Texas, which among the deer include Axis, Sika, Fallow and Red deer, is now becoming big business, and at least three different sets of formulae are currently being used to measure these trophies. In 1976 Thompson B Temple, who runs a sporting agency for this form of hunting, produced a number of formulae for measuring these exotic trophies, some of which include practices which are quite contrary to normal trophy measurement.

For instance, the beam circumference for the antlers of all species of deer except Fallow, are to be taken at the 'greatest circumference between points' – not the least. Presumably, therefore, this must be as close as possible to one or other of the two tines so as to take advantage of the area where the tine starts to branch. The beam circumference of Red deer antlers between the brow and bay tines (first and second) anyway, is a bad measurement to include in any score, for with this species the bay is frequently a branch tine of the brow, thus giving an abnormally large circumference where the two separate.

A still further system of trophy measurement has been evolved in recent years by a Texan by the name of Dr Joe Burkett. His system, known as the Burkett Trophy Game Records of the World (B.T.G.R.W.) is not only extremely complicated, requiring a special set of instruments, but the descriptive text contains a number of technical words and phrases, many of which I had never heard of before. For instance, he classifies Red deer, Roe deer and Sika deer, as well as several other species, in a group called 'Nontusked Posterolateral Monochotomous Non-Palmate Game', whilst the Fallow deer is designated as a 'Compound Palmate Antlered Game' which distinguishes it from the 'Compound-complex Palmate Antlered Game' of the Caribou and Reindeer, and the 'Simple Palmate Antlered Game', which includes Moose and Elk. Muntjac come into the 'Tusked Posterolateral Monochotomous Non-palmate Antlered Game', whilst those two non-antlered species, the Chinese Water-deer and the Musk deer are considered as 'Measured Two-tusked Game'. In his formula for what he calls 'Non-adorned Game' – and these include anything from a zebra, lion or bear down to a squirrel or weasel – he suggests that not only should the skull be measured for length and width, but also the femur saved so that its length and circumference could be recorded.

The basis of his system is volumetric displacement, and in the initial stages antlers and horns were submerged in water in much the same manner as the volume is currently taken in the C.I.C. formula for Roe deer antlers. From the figures obtained by submersion, Dr Burkett claims to have developed a system whereby comparable results can be taken by physical measurement with tape and callipers etc.

In measuring deer antlers, although the lengths of all individual tines are considered, no deductions are made when length or circumference differ from one side to the other, as in the Boone and Crockett system – nor are span or coronet circumference considered.

In Fallow deer, all tines, including those on the palm are measured, and this means that on exceptional trophies, when one includes the other measurements that have to be taken for circumference, palm widths, etc., well over sixty different measurements will have to be taken before a final score is reached – a very time consuming effort.

His method of measuring antler length not only differs from other methods, but his interpretation of antler length for such species as Red, Wapiti or Fallow is unique, for according to the instruction the length of any antler – or indeed tine – should be measured from 'its tip along its surface of greatest convexity as closely as possible parallel to the long axis, to the lowest point along the base and at right angles to the axis'. This means that in those instances where the coronet is at an angle, as on old Roe buck trophies, a main beam may not have an actual point of origin at the coronet, and in consequence, the length measurement will terminate at a point 'in space' which will be at right angles to the lowest edge of the coronet. Furthermore, since the line of measurement has to follow the surface of 'greatest convexity', this means that in any antler that has, along its length, one or more changes in direction – such as the antlers of Axis deer – the tape measure has to be continually switched from one side to the other in order to take advantage of the convex surface. These areas are called 'swing points'.

Since 1977 Dr Burkett has been running a number of seminars in order to train what he calls 'tropaeologists', who are then capable of measuring sportsmen's trophies at $25 per head, $5 of which the tropaeologist can retain, the remainder going to the B.T.G.R.W. Dr Burkett certainly has confidence in the future of his system for he gave up a quite lucrative veterinary job in order to travel around the country measuring trophies as a whole-time occupation. In May 1979 B.T.G.R.W. organized the Texas State Trophy Competition and Exhibition and their system was used for measuring the trophies.

The Safari Club International of America have yet another and far simpler system of measurement which is divided into eleven different categories covering most game animals of the world. A minimum score is set for each species, and any trophy that exceeds the minimum figure can, at $5 a time, be included in their Record Book – which is, of course, considerably cheaper than having a trophy measured by a Burkett tropaeologist. The Record Book, however, is open to members of the Safari Club International only.

The Burkett system is the first one in America which measures in metric, measurements in the Boone and Crockett for deer antlers being taken to the nearest eighth of an inch.

Big game hunting is an international sport and ideally there should be just one international system for measuring all the game trophies of the world, but at present each country is so attached to its own system that I cannot see this being achieved in the foreseeable future. In North America, apart from the measurement of exotics, I doubt if the Burkett system will ever find much following outside Texas, and of all the systems currently in use, I consider the Boone and Crockett to be the fairest to both hunter and trophy, for it only involves physical measurements. This system was used, therefore, in the preparation of the new C.I.C. formulae for both Asiatic and South American Cervidae (see *The Game Trophies of the World*).

So far as the formulae for European game under the C.I.C. system are concerned, inclusion of weight and award for so-called 'beauty points' must introduce a variable which would not occur if the result relied solely on physical data. For instance, in addition to physical measurements, European trophies measured under the C.I.C. system can have some credit points added to the total for beauty which include such features as colour, pearling, size of coronet, tine ends etc., and these can, in addition to the points allotted or subtracted for span, increase the score of a particular head by as much as 18 for Red deer, 19 for Roe and 13 for Fallow deer. Certain debit points can also be made to the score of these three species.

Beauty is, of course, only in the eye of the observer, and no two people's opinions are identical. The award of beauty points for deer antlers is certainly easier than, say, awarding beauty points for the skin of a European lynx which can be awarded beauty points for such features as length of fur, tips on ears, face and ear whiskers. The beauty and penalization section must, therefore, introduce some inaccuracy even though in international judging it is the opinion of a panel of judges (three to four) and not just an individual.

Measurements, if properly taken with a flexible steel rule, must be considered the most accurate method of assessment, and as both Boone and

Crockett and Douglas formulae rely solely on measurements for their evaluation, these methods are the most accurate.

Unfortunately, due to difference of opinion as to how individual measurements should be taken, results between one system and another are not comparable. As an example, take the measurement of the tray tine, which, in the Boone and Crockett method is measured along the outside of the tine from the nearest edge of the main beam to its tip. In the C.I.C. formula this measurement is taken along the *under*side of the tine 'from the place where it starts to emerge from the main beam to the extremity of the tine', whilst in Spain, where the I.C.O.N.A. system is used (*see page 78*) the length of the tray is taken along the *upper* side of the tine. The Douglas Score system, however, considers that 'the origin of the tine is at the beam centre, not at its outside edge'. This 'point of origin' is obtained with the aid of callipers (see sketch).

As a result, four different measurements can be obtained for the length of the same tine, and this could result in a difference of 7 cm or more as the following sketches show.

Variations in tine measurement

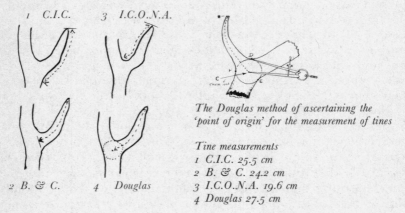

The Douglas method of ascertaining the 'point of origin' for the measurement of tines

Tine measurements
1 C.I.C. 25.5 cm
2 B. & C. 24.2 cm
3 I.C.O.N.A. 19.6 cm
4 Douglas 27.5 cm

It will be seen that the Douglas method produces the longest measurement, whilst the I.C.O.N.A. system the shortest.

A difficulty with the C.I.C. method is to gauge exactly 'the place where it (the tine) starts to emerge from the main beam', for in a number of cases the beam can start to thicken out well down on the main beam close to the bay, thus giving the tine a 'false' length. This thickening out of the beam can also make it a little difficult to judge exactly where to start the tine measurement when measured along the side (Boone and Crockett method). Measuring the tine length along the top (I.C.O.N.A. method) is certainly easier – and probably more accurate – whilst the Douglas system does at least provide an *accurate* starting point even though it does include about half the beam's diameter in the length of the tine (*see sketch*).

The most accurate way to measure a tine

X represents length when measured in accordance with B. & C. practice
X + Y represents length when measured in accordance with Douglas
score practice
Z represents length when measured in accordance with C.I.C. formula

Distance 'Y' represents part of beam not measured by the Boone and Crockett method. Since part of the beam thickness, therefore, is being taken into account when measuring a tine length, this could mean that a short tine projecting from a thick beam might have a slightly superior 'length' on paper than a longer one that erupts from a beam of small circumference. Furthermore, if part of the beam's thickness is to be taken into account when measuring a tine's length, then presumably if the tine is absent or broken off at the base, then this part of the beam's diameter should remain in the score.

For example, if the length of the left tray, when measured down the side (Boone and Crockett) is 20 cm compared to 23 cm when measured to centre of beam (Douglas), then if the tray tine had been broken off or was absent from the right antler, it would seem logic to give it a length of 3 cm – the amount by which it would have been credited had it been present.

In my opinion, therefore, the thickness of the beam should never be considered as part of a tine measurement, for the beam will *always* be present, even though tines may be absent.

I approve, however, of the Douglas method of using callipers to fix the point from where to start a tine measurement, but would suggest that the correct place to start measuring a tine would be the edge of the circle, and not its centre, as shown in the sketch. This point would, in fact, correspond very closely to that used by Boone and Crockett.

The use of callipers for tine measurement

Red deer, Wapiti and Sika deer all belong to the same genus and apart from size, produce antlers of similar format. It seems strange, therefore, that the Douglas score system should measure the brow tine of Sika antlers along the side in similar fashion to the other tines, but measure the brows of Red deer and Wapiti along the underside, from coronet to tip, as is normal practice in C.I.C. formulae.

TROPHIES

Measuring brow tines

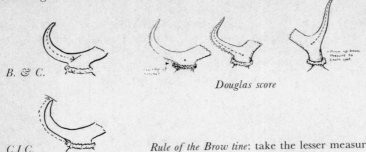

B. & C.

Douglas score

C.I.C.

Rule of the Brow tine: take the lesser measurement

So far as the measurement of the brow tines on Sambar and Rusa deer are concerned, it is left to the discretion of the measurer, for the Douglas score instruction states that they 'will probably require to be measured to a chalk spot rather than to the coronet'.

There is also a difference of opinion as to how the length measurement of both the antler and palm of Fallow deer trophies should be measured. In the C.I.C. method both measurements are taken to the highest indentation of the palm, whilst both the Douglas and I.C.O.N.A. methods measure the antler length to the tip of the longest point on top, but the length of the palm to the bottom of the highest indentation or 'top crutch' as in C.I.C. In the Douglas score the width of the palmation is also taken in two places – with and without points – but only the latter measurement is considered in the C.I.C. formula.

An exception to the Douglas method of measuring tines is in the measurement of the guard tine on Fallow deer, which is measured from the front edge of the palm to its extremity.

Measuring tines on Fallow antlers

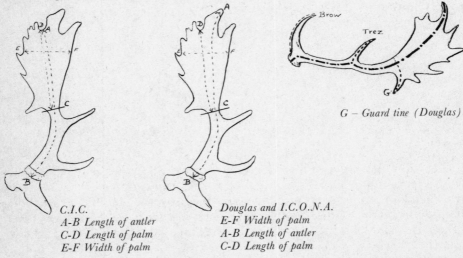

G – Guard tine (Douglas)

C.I.C.
A-B Length of antler
C-D Length of palm
E-F Width of palm

Douglas and I.C.O.N.A.
E-F Width of palm
A-B Length of antler
C-D Length of palm

All systems take into account the inside span measurement of all deer trophies except Elk and Moose, where only maximum *spread* is considered. The Douglas system, however, for all deer except Moose, includes both span and spread in its score. In the Boone and Crockett system the latter – except for Moose – appears only as supplementary data and is not included in the points score.

'Spread and Span together', writes Douglas, 'produce a spread factor, which, when taken into consideration with the length of the antlers provide a picture of the conformation of a head. As the ideal spread-to-length-proportion is obviously that which is the typical for the species, then some method must be used to penalize those which deviate from the mean. To this end a spread 'dead-line' has been set for each species. . . .'

Species	Spread dead line
1 Wapiti, Red, Sika, Sambar and White-tailed deer	Length of longer antler
2 Fallow deer	Length of longer antler plus 4 in. (10 cm)
3 Rusa and Axis deer	Length of longer antler minus 4 in. (10 cm)
4 Moose	No dead line

This means that provided the *spread* (not span) of trophies from deer in (1) do not exceed the length of the longer antler, no penalty will be incurred. Whilst the spread of Fallow deer antlers may exceed the length of the longer antler by 4 in. before any penalty will be incurred, the 'spread dead line' for both Rusa and Axis deer is 4 in. less than the length of the longer antler.

Whenever a spread exceeds the dead line set for that particular species, the difference between the spread and the length of the longer antler – plus or minus 4 in. for those species in (2) or (3) above – will be multiplied by 3 and the resulting figure deducted from the actual spread before entry into the score column.

The following two examples will illustrate the method.

Red deer
Spread	45	Length of longer antler 43
Spread dead line	43	
Difference	$2 \times 3 = 6$	

Deducting 6 from 45 (spread) gives a figure of 39 to be entered in score column.

Rusa deer
Spread	28	Length of longer antler 29
Spread dead line	(29–4) 25	
Difference	$3 \times 3 = 9$	

Deducting 9 from 28 (spread) gives a figure of 19 to be entered in score column.

In Boone and Crockett deer formulae (except Moose) any excess by which span exceeds length of longer antler is a deduction penalty, whilst in some C.I.C. deer formulae credit points: 0–4 for Roe; 0–3 for Red deer – and debit points – 0–6 for Fallow deer – are awarded if the inside span measurement achieves – or fails to achieve – a certain percentage of the *average* antler length. As an example, if the inside span of a Red deer trophy is 75 percent of the average length of the antlers, then 2 points will be awarded. If, however, the inside span of a Fallow buck trophy is only 75 percent of the average length, then a 3-point *penalty* is incurred (*see pages 292 for Red; 300 for Fallow; 302 for Roe*).

For all species of North American deer except Moose, should the inside span measurement exceed the length of the longer antler, this involves a double debit of the difference, for in the span credit column, *only* a figure equivalent to the length of the longer antler may be entered, whilst the excess – already deducted – has to be entered in the difference column. This is best explained by an example.

A Wapiti head with antlers measuring, say, 43 and 42 in. in length has an inside spread of 45 in., i.e. 2 in. more than the longer antler length: 43, therefore, is the maximum figure that can be entered in the span credit column (*page 294*), but as the excess of 2 has also been entered in the difference column – the score has, in fact, been debited by 4 points. To make a double debit is, in my opinion, being unnecessarily harsh.

So far as tip-to-tip measurement is concerned, unless it happens to be the equivalent of the inside span measurement for a Roe deer trophy, this measurement is not included in the score of any system. It is, however, included as supplementary data only in Boone and Crockett formulae, for all deer species except Moose.

The C.I.C. method is the only system which takes weight into consideration, and in the case of Roe deer antlers, volume as well.

The weight factor, unfortunately, can also lead to inaccuracies for not only are the antlers themselves weighed but also part of the skull, which is of no interest to the hunter anyway.

Skulls differ in size enormously, and it is possible to have *identical* antlers produced by either a broad skulled deer, or one with a comparatively small skull, and assuming that the same section of skull is present, the antlers produced by the broader skulled deer will have a superior points value for weight – not because it has superior antlers – which, after all, is what concerns the hunter, but because it has a bigger skull!

Skulls for assessment should be cut to what is referred to as the 'long nose cut', but if the cut has not been properly made certain arbitrary deductions can be made.

The normal cut for Red, Roe and Fallow deer, when being assessed under the C.I.C. formula, is from the back of the skull, through the centre of the eye cavity to the front of the nasal bone. If the trophy is weighed with full upper jaw intact, then up to 0.5 to 0.7 kg (about 1 to $1\frac{3}{4}$ lb) can be deducted for Red deer skulls; up to 0.25 kg (about $\frac{1}{2}$ lb) for Fallow deer and 65 to 90 g (about $2\frac{1}{4}$ to 3 oz) for Roe deer.

C.I.C. weight deductions for weighing deer skulls and antlers

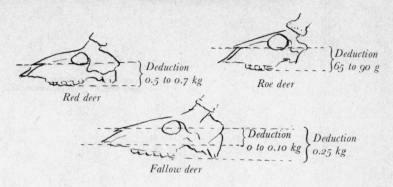

These deductions are, of course, very arbitrary, and so far as Roe deer, 90 g is quite insufficient for some of the big skulled animals which could probably warrant a deduction of as much as 140 to 150 g. As a result many more Roe trophies today are being submitted for evaluation with full upper skull, for if it happens to be a big skulled animal the stalker knows full well that it will attain a higher score with a maximum 90 g deduction, than if it had been properly cut, for the cut-off portion might have weighed as much as 120 to 130 g. In effect, therefore, the trophy was getting a 'bonus' weight of 30 to 40 g!

Another point which would favour the discontinuation of weight in Red and Fallow deer trophies is that fully mounted heads could then be included and properly measured in international exhibitions – and if the volume factor was also dropped for Roe trophy assessment, mounted Roe trophies could also be included. At present it is quite impossible to assess the C.I.C. score of any mounted deer trophy.

Considerable importance, however, in Europe is attached to the weight of the trophy and in Hungary and Poland the basic trophy fee is calculated on weight with, in the former country, a percentage supplement for those trophies reaching medal class.

Generally, the larger trophies owe much of their high score to weight, but it so happens that the existing world record Fallow buck trophy, although having a higher C.I.C. score of 220.31 against the previous best of 217.25, due to an inferior skull and antler weight of almost 1 kg (4.19 kg compared to 5.15 kg of the latter) would have had a trophy charge of but a third of the cost of the previous record (*see page 102*). This would confirm the folly of placing too much importance on weight rather than measurement.

The volume factor, however, is necessary for antlers with heavy pearling such as Roe deer trophies and although it does eliminate the judging of mounted trophies in international exhibitions, I think its retention is desirable, for it does take into account such features as heavy pearling, large coronets, etc. which cannot be accurately measured by tape. In the 1960s, in order to eliminate the work involved in taking the volume, it was suggested

Taking the volume of Roe buck antlers

that the same results might be achieved if the weight of the antlers was multiplied by 0.25 or 0.23 instead of 0.1, but detailed investigation showed that results were variable and unreliable, and the proposition was never approved by the C.I.C. Trophy Commission. Both weight *and* volume must, therefore, be taken before the C.I.C. score of any trophy can be officially recognized. Norway, however, has continued to use the weight only in the measurement of Roe trophies.

Even the definition of a point or tine – or the number of tines on a trophy – will vary from one country to another. In the C.I.C. formulae for all deer except Muntjac, the minimum length for a tine to qualify as such is $\frac{3}{4}$ in. (about 2 cm) whilst the definition of a tine under the Boone and Crockett formulae for all deer except Caribou is that the projection must be at least 2 cm ($\frac{3}{4}$ in.) long *and* its length must exceed the width of the base. For Muntjac and Caribou, half the above minimum lengths are sufficient to qualify as a tine.

Both Boone and Crockett, and Douglas systems, measure all crown tines and whilst in the former the beam tip is counted as a point but *not* measured, in the Douglas score it is included (*see page 274*).

Normally, the format of a deer's antlers follows a set pattern with tines being located at regular intervals, and any tines which emerge elsewhere are considered abnormal. Take the Moose, for instance. With this deer, normal tines are those which grow from the *edge* of the palm whilst those which arise from the face of the palm are considered abnormal.

In other deer normal tines arise from the top of the main beam, and any tines arising from the bottom or sides are probably abnormal.

There are, however, *no* abnormal tines on Caribou or Reindeer antlers.

For typical-type Whitetail and Mule deer, the total lengths of all abnormal tines figure as a debit in the score card, but in non-typical specimens as a credit.

Trophies which cannot be decided upon whether to treat as typical or non-typical, are measured by both formulae (Boone and Crockett) and the one giving the highest score is selected.

This option is, in my opinion, a mistake and can result only in anomalies (*see pages 191 and 202*). It would surely be preferable to have a specific minimum number of tines before a trophy could qualify as non-typical.

In the case of broken-off tines, all three systems stipulate that valuation is only permissible up to the place of breakage, and no allowance can be made for what *may* have been there. Damaged parts, however, do not count as irregular, and will not therefore be subject to any deduction in the C.I.C. formulae that include a beauty and penalty section.

However, with the exception of Red deer and Elk (C.I.C.), Caribou and Moose (B. & C.) and spellers on Fallow deer antlers (Douglas), the number of tines do not figure in the score charts of the three systems.

In Europe it is sometimes the practice to double the number of tines on the side carrying the most tines – thus a 10-pointer with six tines on one side and four on the other may be referred to as an 'uneven 12-pointer'.

It appears also, that American hunters are even more undecided on how to count the number of tines on a buck's head, those in the west counting only those, excluding the eye-guard, on one side of a trophy, which is sometimes referred to as the 'western count' – whilst in eastern States of the United States of America, hunters generally count all the tines on both sides of a buck's rack (antlers) including the eye-guards – and this is referred to as the 'eastern count'. Some hunters call anything from which you can hang a ring a point or tine, but if the antlers are held at the right angles it is, of course, possible to hang a ring from even the smallest lump or pearling!

In Japan hunters never consider the main beam as a point, but only the tines, so an 8-point Sika stag is always referred to as a 6-pointer.

The Boone and Crockett Club has long served as the international repository and clearing house for statistical data on North American big game. In 1973 an agreement was reached between the Boone and Crockett and the National Rifle Association of America to co-sponsor the record keeping for native North American big game trophies. This joint venture was called the North American Big Game Awards Programme (N.A.B.G.A.P.), their last awards programme – the seventeenth (1977–9) was the third to be jointly sponsored. For a trophy to be included in the Record Book it must have been entered in either a club competition (prior to 1973) or in one of the North American Big Game Awards Programmes which have been held at three-yearly intervals. Measurement is part of the entry procedure. The data secured from trophies officially entered in each Awards Programme entry is periodically summarized in editions of *Records of North American Big Game*, the latest edition being published in 1981. Once again, however, the Boone and Crockett Club has become totally responsible for the official record keeping for North American native big game, for with effect from 1 January 1981 the Boone and Crockett Club terminated the co-sponsorship agreement with the National Rifle Association of America and assumed full responsibility for the records-keeping programmes. The latest edition of the Record Book – the eight – has therefore been a product of the Boone and Crockett Club.

In North America trophies taken in 'fair chase', within five years of the closing date for the awards entry period, are eligible for awards of the Boone and Crockett Club Medal and/or the North American Big Game Awards Programme (N.A.B.G.A.P.) Certificates. Trophies taken earlier than five years prior to the closing date for the awards entry period, trophies of unknown origin and trophies not owned by the hunter, are eligible for Certificates of Merit only. Final scores and awards are made at the awards banquet which follows the close of a three-year period of trophy entry.

Should there be a trophy of exceptional merit, the judges panel *may* recommend the award of the Sagamore Hill Medal. It may also be awarded by the Executive Committee of the Boone and Crockett Club for distinguished devotion to the objectives of the Club, but only one may be given in any Final Awards Programme. This medal, created in 1948, is given by the Roosevelt family in memory of Theodore Roosevelt (founder and first president of the Boone and Crockett Club), Theodore Roosevelt Jr and Kermit Roosevelt, and is solely an award of the Boone and Crockett Club.

All entrants must submit a signed declaration of 'fair chase' that none of the following methods were used in acquiring the trophy:

1 Spotting or herding game from the air; followed by landing in its vicinity for pursuit.
2 Herding or pursuing game with motor powered vehicles.
3 Use of electronic communications for attracting, locating or observing game, or guiding the hunter to such.
4 Hunting game confined by artificial barriers, including escape-proof fencing; or hunting game transplanted solely for the purpose of commercial shooting.

In order to keep the number of recorded trophies under some sort of control, it soon became necessary to set a minimum score before a trophy could be recorded in the Record Book. Records are made to be broken, and it is not surprising that, from time to time during the past thirty years, the minimum score required for entry in the Record Book has had to be raised for each species. In 1951, however, the 'minimum' for five species of deer was lowered.

THE MEASUREMENT OF ANTLERS AND TROPHY AWARDS

A summary of the minimum entry scores necessary for a trophy to be included in the *Records of North American Big Game* (1981) are as follows:

	Minimum score
Wapiti (American Elk)	375
Mule deer (typical antlers)	195
Mule deer (non-typical antlers)	240
Black-tailed deer – Columbia	130
White-tailed deer (typical antlers)	170
White-tailed deer (non-typical antlers)	195
Coues' White-tailed deer (typical antlers)	110
Coues' White-tailed deer (non-typical antlers)	120
Moose, Canadian	195
Moose, Alaska-Yukon	224
Moose, Wyoming or Shiras	155
Caribou, Mountain	390
Caribou, Barren-ground	400
Caribou, Quebec-Labrador	375
Caribou, Woodland	295

Trophies for inclusion in the Records Book for which there is an entry fee of $20 must have been measured by an official measurer of the Boone and Crockett Club.

In order to encourage bow hunters to be more selective in their hunting and provide a system for record keeping and trophy award, the Pope and Young Club was formed in 1957, the well-established system of the Boone and Crockett Club being used for assessing trophies. Realizing that the bow hunter cannot be as selective as the rifleman, and in order to provide maximum competition, a lower point requirement has been set for each animal. The competition is open to anyone, and all trophies taken with bow and arrow under the rules of 'fair chase' during legal hunting seasons, are eligible. Their first Records book – *Bowhunting Big Game Records of North America* – listing about 2500 trophies, was published in 1975.

Quite apart from the triannual Awards Programme, the National Rifle Association started, in 1957, to issue to N.R.A. members, who had shot buck deer with antlers of four tines or more on a side, a gold lapel button. In the following year Whitetail, Mule deer and Pronghorn were included in the programme, since when it has been extended to cover all the deer species of North America, as well as most of the other game species. Members who duplicate their success in later years can receive a numbered tab – up to ten – to attach to their lapel pin, which depicts the species.

Members who hunt with bow or muzzle-loader can receive special recognition for their trophy by means of a tab which is attached to the lapel pin, bow hunting trophies being recognized by an arrow tab, whilst a powder horn tab identifies those taken by a muzzle-loader. Lapel pins cost (1980) $2 with identifying tab a further $1.

TROPHIES

The minimum requirements for a pin award for the various trophies taken by modern firearms are as follows: for Caribou, the minimum number of tines (counting both beams) shall be 24, whilst for Moose and Wapiti, ten (both beams). For other deer species, there must be at least four tines on one antler (western count).

The qualification for trophies taken by bow-hunting or muzzle-loader is that it 'must be a mature adult of the species'.

In 1959 the N.R.A. began issuing Silver Bullet Awards to members to recognize trophies that would make the Record Book. The first awards were for Whitetail and Mule deer only, but over the years the programme has been expanded so that there are now twenty-eight categories of acceptable trophies. The Silver Bullet Awards are on an annual basis, and apply to trophies taken during the *immediate* preceding season.

In addition to the Silver Bullet Award, a 'Leather Stocking Statuette Award', patterned after the fictional pioneer hunter, was established in 1970 to recognize the most outstanding single trophy entered each year in the N.R.A. Silver Bullet Awards Programme.

More recently, the N.R.A., in order to recognize trophies taken by N.R.A. members with bow and arrow, announced the award in 1978 (for 1979 season trophies) of Silver Broadhead Awards for twenty-six categories of North American big game the awards being, as for the Silver Bullet, on an annual basis for trophies taken during the immediate preceding season.

For a Silver Bullet plaque award, a trophy must score the minimum points required for inclusion in the *Records of North American Big Game* whilst for the Silver Broadhead plaque the lower scores required by the Pope and Young Club. Certificate awards are available for trophies that just fail to reach these requirements.

Hunters with rifle, gun or bow, wishing to have their trophy considered for acceptance of an award, must initially measure their trophy on an official score chart, obtainable, until recently, from the N.R.A. at a cost of 20 cents and if it makes the minimum acceptable score, apply for the trophy to be officially measured.

Some States have their own trophy buck programmes. In 1975 the Indiana Division of Fish and Wildlife established the Hoosier Record Buck Programme not only for the purpose of establishing a permanent record of the quality of White-tailed deer taken within the State, but also to recognize deer hunters who had been successful in taking a record class buck. Antlers are measured in accordance with the Boone and Crockett system.

Maine has a club for deer antlers called 'The Biggest Bucks in Maine Club', and in order to qualify for membership, a hunter must have shot a buck weighing at least 200 lb (91 kg) dressed.

New York State also has a Big Buck Club, an annual award being presented to the hunter whose trophy, taken during the year, has the highest Boone and Crockett score. Missouri's 'Show Me Big Buck's Club' now has a membership of over 600 hunters, whilst both Texas and Utah keep record books for deer under the titles of the *Big Rack* and *Biggest Bucks* record books respectively.

Every year since 1956 – with the exception of 1975 – the Weatherby Big Game Trophy is presented to a sportsman who, in the opinion of the Weatherby Selection Committee, has made a notable achievement in the world of big game hunting, not only by the number of species shot in different parts of the world, but also one who has made a valuable contribution to game conservation and hunting education.

First of all, to be even considered a nominee for the award, the hunter must have a substantial collection of most of the major game animals of the world. The amount of time and effort spent in building up the collection is also taken into account, and there is no doubt that to win the award, the hunter must have a considerable amount of time and money at his disposal. For instance, the last recipient of the award made no fewer than 128 hunts in forty-six different countries or States to collect his 209 species, eighty-eight of which were in the record class.

Up to date the majority of recipients of the award have been American (17), with two from Mexico and one each from Iran, Denmark, France and Spain.

More recently (1980) the Safari Club International has started a 'World's Greatest Hunter Award', the requirements of which are not very different from those of the Weatherby Award.

European sportsmen are very medal conscious and at all national and international game trophy exhibitions Gold, Silver and Bronze medals are awarded for trophies that reach the necessary standard.

The following are the scores necessary for medal awards at trophy exhibitions in Europe (1981):

	Gold	Silver	Bronze
Red deer (Eastern)	210 and over	190–209.99	170–189.99
Red deer (Western)	195 and over	180–194.99	165–179.99
Red deer (Scotland)	180 and over	168–179.99	160–167.99
Roe deer	130 and over	115–129.99	105–114.99
Fallow deer	180 and over	175–179.99	165–174.99
Elk	300 and over	275–299.99	260–274.99
Reindeer	800 and over	750–799.99	700–749.99
Exotics			
Sika deer (Japanese)*	255 and over	240–254.99	225–239.99
Sika deer (non-Japanese)*	400 and over	350–399.99	300–349.99
White-tailed deer (European)*	370 and over	350–369.99	330–349.99
Axis deer	300 and over	280–299.99	260–279.99

*Scores for medals at the International Hunting Exhibition at Plovdiv 1981.

For North American game trophies there are no such medal categories and the ambition of the North American trophy hunter is to shoot a head which is large enough for inclusion in the Record Book.

On the following pages are included examples of the formulae of the Boone and Crockett, C.I.C. and Douglas Score for measuring the trophies of deer species that can be hunted today, and where appropriate, the same trophy has been assessed by two systems for comparison. Final scores, however, are not comparable, for as already explained, no two systems measure identical areas of the antler.

All systems specify that a steel measuring tape should be used, and measurements recorded as follows:

C.I.C.
All measurements in metric, those taken in centimetres to the nearest 0.1 cm whilst those in millimetres to the nearest 0.1 mm. Weights, included in the score for certain European trophies are taken in kilograms to the nearest 10 g (Red, Fallow deer) whilst those taken in grams (Roe) to the nearest gram. In formulae that include a section for beauty or malformation, only whole or half points (1.0 or 0.5) will be given.

Boone and Crockett*
All measurements are taken in inches to the nearest eighth of an inch (.317cm) and recorded in the table as eighths, i.e. $40\frac{1}{8}$, $50\frac{4}{8}$ – not $50\frac{1}{2}$.
Weights, when taken, are for supplementary interest only and do not figure in the score of the trophy. Official measurements cannot be taken for at least sixty days after the animal has been killed.

Douglas score
All measurements are taken in inches to the nearest eighth of an inch, and will appear in the table as $\frac{1}{8}$, $\frac{1}{4}$, $\frac{1}{2}$ and $\frac{3}{4}$ and not $\frac{2}{8}$, $\frac{4}{8}$ or $\frac{6}{8}$ as in Boone and Crockett.

The purpose of this chapter is not to instruct the reader how to measure deer antlers by whatever system he chooses, but to explain and compare their difference. For more detailed instruction, reference should be made to *Records of North American Big Game* (1981) for North American trophies; to the *Douglas Score Handbook* (1959) for the deer of Australasia and to the C.I.C. book *The Game Trophies of the World* (1981) for the deer of Europe, Africa, Asia and South America.

*Note
Canada is converting to the metric system and by 1981 will have substantially completed the process. Eventually the metric system must inevitably be adopted throughout North America, but until this occurs, trophies taken in Canada and measured in metric will have to have the measurements converted to inches before being assessed by Boone and Crockett formulae.

A COMPARISON OF SOME FORMULAE FOR MEASURING DEER TROPHIES OF THE WORLD

Species	C.I.C. page	B.&C. page	Douglas score page
Red deer, European	292	—	293
Wapiti, American	—	294	295
Wapiti, Asiatic (*as B.&C. American but in metric)	—*	—	—
Asiatic Red deer types (Maral, Hangul etc.)	296	—	—
Roe deer, European	302	—	—
Roe deer, Siberian/Chinese	303	—	—
Sika deer	298	—	299
Fallow deer, European	300	—	301
Caribou	—	297	—
Reindeer (*as B. & C. for Caribou, but in metric)	—*	—	—
Elk	306	—	—
Moose, American	—	304	305
Axis / Hog deer / Rusa / Sambar	308	—	309
Mule deer & Blacktail (typical)	—	310	—
Mule deer (non-typical)	—	311	—
Whitetail and Coues, typical (*as B. & C. in metric)	—*	312	313
Whitetail and Coues, non-typical	—	314	—
Muntjac	307	—	—
Brocket	315	—	—
Chinese Water-deer / Musk deer	315	—	—

Note: In addition to the above, separate C.I.C. formulae exist for nine other species of deer which are either threatened or endangered, and since this book is concerned only with those deer which can be regularly hunted, they have been omitted on that account. They include: Eld's deer, Huemul, Marsh deer, Pampas deer, Père David's deer, Persian Fallow deer, Pudu, Swamp deer and Tufted deer.

The appropriate formulae for all these deer can be found in the C.I.C. book The Game Trophies of the World (1981).

C.I.C. formula (metric) for Red deer

		Left	Right	Average	Factor	Points
1.1	Length of main beam	104.1	109.2	106.65	×0.5	53.32
1.2	Length of brow tine	35.6	36.8	36.2	×0.25	9.05
1.3	Length of tray tine	39.4	42.6	41.0	×0.25	10.25
1.4	Circumference of coronet	26.6	25.4	26.0	×1.0	26.00
1.5	Circumference of beam (lower)	15.2	14.9		×1.0	30.10
1.6	Circumference of beam (upper)	14.0	14.0		×1.0	28.00
1.7	Weight of antlers (kg)		8.8−0.7=8.1		×2.0	16.20
1.8	Inside span 78.7 cm 77% of average length (see below)					2.00
1.9	Number of points (tine ends)		7+7 (1 tine end = 1 point)			14.00
2.1	Beauty points (0–18)					
2.1.1	Colour (0-2): light 0; medium 1; dark 2					1.5
2.1.2	Pearling (0–2): smooth 0; medium 1; good 2					2.0
2.1.3	Tine ends (0–2): blunt 0; brown tips 1; white tips 2					2.0
2.1.4	Bay tines (0–2): short (2–10 cm) 0.5; medium (10.1–15 cm) 1.0; long (over 15 cm) 2					2.0
2.1.5	Crown tines (0–10): 5–7 tines 1–5 points; 8–9 tines 4–7 points; 10 tines and over 6–10 points					6.0
						202.42
2.2	Penalty points (0–3): general defects and lack of symmetry					—
			Total score			202.42

Notes on measurement of Red deer antlers

1.7 Weight: According to amount of skull present, 0.5–0.7 kg may be deducted from the gross weight.

1.8 Span: Less than 60% of the average length of beam — 0 point
from 60–69.9% of average length of beam — 1 point
from 70–79.9% of average length of beam — 2 points
80% and over the average length of beam — 3 points

2.1.5 Crown tines

	Short (2–10 cm)	Medium (10.1–15.0 cm)	Long (over 15.0 cm)
5–7 tines in crown	1–2 points	3–4 points	4–5 points
8–9 tines in crown	4–5 points	5–6 points	6–7 points
10 tines and over in crown	6–7 points	7–8 points	9–10 points

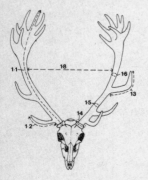

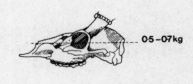

0·5 – 0·7 kg

Douglas score for Red deer

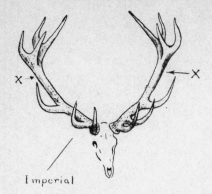

Imperial

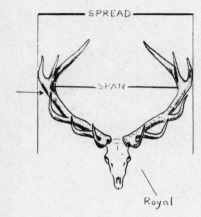

SPREAD

SPAN

Royal

	Shorter measurement doubled		
	Left	*Right*	*Score*
Length	41	43	82
Spread	$45 - (2 \times 3 = 6)$		39
Span			31
Beam	6	$5\frac{7}{8}$	$11\frac{3}{4}$
Coronet	$10\frac{1}{2}$	10	20
Brow	14	$14\frac{1}{2}$	28
Bay	$14\frac{1}{8}$	$14\frac{3}{8}$	$28\frac{1}{4}$
Tray	15	16	30
Tops			
Royal tine	·12	$11\frac{1}{2}$	23
Inner off royal	5	$4\frac{3}{4}$	$9\frac{1}{2}$
Back tine	17	16	32
Outer off back	8	$7\frac{3}{4}$	$15\frac{1}{2}$
	Total score		350

Spread: The dead line is the length of the longer
antler (43). Therefore, multiply difference (2) by 3
and deduct from spread, i.e. $45 - 6 = 39$ *(see page 281)*.

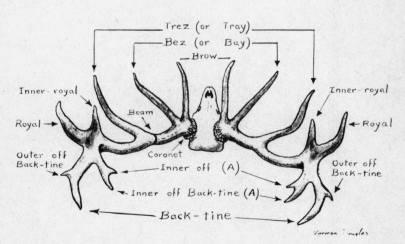

Trez (or Tray)

Bez (or Bay)

Brow

Inner-royal

Inner-royal

Royal

Beam

Royal

Outer off
Back-tine

Coronet

Inner off (A)

Outer off
Back-tine

Inner off Back-tine (A)

Back-tine

Norman Douglas

Tines below X are collectively known as the RIGHTS.

Tines above X are collectively known as the TOPS, or SURROYALS.

Boone and Crockett Club formula for Wapiti

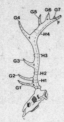 

	Supplementary data		Col. 1	Col. 2	Col. 3	Col. 4
	Left	Right	Span credit	Left antler	Right antler	Difference
A Number of points on each antler	6	6				
B Tip-to-tip spread		$45\frac{7}{8}$				
C Greatest spread		$50\frac{1}{8}$				
D Inside span [44] Span credit may equal but not exceed length of longer antler.			44			
If inside span of main beam exceeds longer antler length, enter difference						
E Total of lengths of all abnormal points						
F Length of main beam				$54\frac{6}{8}$	$56\frac{2}{8}$	$1\frac{4}{8}$
G-1 Length of first point				$18\frac{5}{8}$	$18\frac{7}{8}$	$\frac{2}{8}$
G-2 Length of second point				$16\frac{6}{8}$	$16\frac{2}{8}$	$\frac{4}{8}$
G-3 Length of third point				$20\frac{2}{8}$	22	$1\frac{6}{8}$
G-4 Length of fourth (royal) point				$18\frac{1}{8}$	$18\frac{4}{8}$	$\frac{3}{8}$
G-5 Length of fifth point				$12\frac{4}{8}$	$14\frac{4}{8}$	2
G-6 Length of sixth point, if present						
G-7 Length of seventh point, if present						
H-1 Circumference at smallest place between first and second points				$8\frac{6}{8}$	$8\frac{5}{8}$	$\frac{1}{8}$
H-2 Circumference at smallest place between second and third points				$7\frac{6}{8}$	$7\frac{6}{8}$	
H-3 Circumference at smallest place between third and fourth points				$7\frac{7}{8}$	$7\frac{7}{8}$	
H-4 Circumference at smallest place between fourth and fifth points				$6\frac{5}{8}$	$6\frac{4}{8}$	$\frac{1}{8}$
Totals			44	172	$177\frac{1}{8}$	$6\frac{5}{8}$

Add columns $1 + 2 + 3 =$ $393\frac{1}{8}$
Subtract column 4 $6\frac{5}{8}$

Final score $386\frac{4}{8}$

Note: This formula is used for the Asiatic Wapiti, the measurements being taken in metric.

Douglas score for Wapiti

		Left	Right	Shorter measurement doubled Left	Right	Score
Number of points (tines)		6	6			
Spread			$50\frac{1}{8}$			$50\frac{1}{8}$
Span						44
	Length of main beam			$54\frac{3}{4}$	$56\frac{1}{4}$	$109\frac{1}{2}$
C	Length of first tine, brow			$18\frac{5}{8}$	$18\frac{7}{8}$	$37\frac{1}{4}$
D	Length of second tine, bay			$17\frac{1}{4}$	$16\frac{1}{2}$	33
E	Length of third tine, tray			$20\frac{3}{4}$	$22\frac{1}{2}$	$41\frac{1}{2}$
F	Length of fourth tine, royal			$18\frac{5}{8}$	19	$37\frac{3}{4}$
G	Length of fifth tine (upper-back)			$12\frac{7}{8}$	$14\frac{7}{8}$	$25\frac{3}{4}$
H	Length of sixth tine (outer back)			—	—	—
I	Length of seventh tine (inner-off back)			—	—	—
J	Length of eighth tine (rear outer-off back)			—	—	—
A-B	Length of back tine			$26\frac{1}{4}$	28	$52\frac{1}{4}$
K	Circumference of beam			$7\frac{3}{4}$	$7\frac{3}{4}$	$15\frac{1}{2}$
L	Circumference of coronet			13	$12\frac{3}{4}$	$25\frac{1}{2}$
				Total score		$471\frac{7}{8}$

Comparing the scores of the same trophy measured under the two systems it will be noted that the Douglas score, which includes the measurements of spread ($50\frac{1}{8}$), coronets ($25\frac{1}{2}$) and back tine ($52\frac{1}{2}$), which has already been included in the measurement of the beam, has a final score of $471\frac{7}{8}$, compared to $386\frac{1}{2}$ of the Boone and Crockett. The latter system, however, omits the above three dimensions – which total some $128\frac{1}{8}$ points – but includes three additional beam circumferences, totalling 46. If one deducts these additional measurements from the two scores, the final comparison is $471\frac{7}{8} - 128\frac{1}{8} = 343\frac{3}{4}$ (Douglas) to $386\frac{3}{8} - 46 = 340\frac{4}{8}$ (Boone and Crockett), the small difference being due to the different method of measuring the tines.

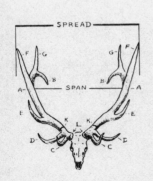

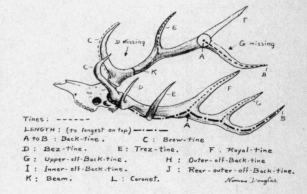

Tines : - - - - - -
LENGTH : (to longest on top) —·—·—
A to B : Back-tine .   C : Brow-tine
D : Bez-tine .   E : Trez-tine.   F . Royal-tine
G : Upper-off-Back-tine .   H : Outer-off-Back-tine
I : Inner-off-Back-tine.   J : Rear-outer-off-Back-tine.
K : Beam.   L : Coronet.
Norman Douglas.

TROPHIES

C.I.C. formula (metric) for all Asiatic Red deer types (Maral, Bactrian, Hangul, Shou, Thorold's, Yarkand)

Species: Hangul

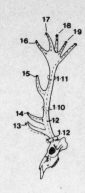

Supplementary data	Left	Right
A Number of tines	5	5
B Tip to tip		42.8
C Spread		106.7
D Weight antlers (kg): (optional) S/N/L.		

Cross out not applicable (*see below*)

Score data	Col. 1 Span credit	Col. 2 Left	Col. 3 Right	Col. 4 Difference
1.1 Inside span	76.2			—
1.2 Length, main beam		91.1	92.7	1.6
1.3 Length, brow tine		25.4	29.8	4.4
1.4 Length, bay tine		40.0	45.7	5.7
1.5 Length, tray tine		28.0	31.2	3.2
1.6 Length, fourth tine		21.2	27.0	5.8
1.7 Length, fifth tine		—	—	—
1.8 Length, sixth tine		—	—	—
1.9 Length, seventh tine		—	—	—
1.10 Circumference lower beam		14.3	14.3	—
1.11 Circumference upper beam		13.0	12.6	0.4
1.12 Circumference coronet		21.6	21.6	—
Total	76.2	254.6	274.9	21.1

Add columns 1 + 2 + 3 = 605.7
Subtract column 4   21.1

Final score   584.60

Note:
1.1 Inside span: If this measurement exceeds length of longer antler, difference will be entered in column 4.

Asiatic Wapiti To be measured in identical fashion as to American Wapiti, but measurements will be taken in metric.

*Skull cut – above eye-socket (small) – S
          through eye-socket (normal) – N
          Complete upper skull (large) – L

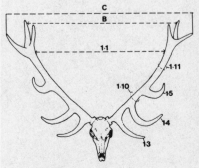

296

Boone and Crockett Club formula for Caribou/Reindeer

Type of Caribou: Quebec-Labrador

	Supplementary data	Col. 1 Span credit	Col. 2 Left antler	Col. 3 Right antler	Col. 4 Difference
A Tip-to-tip spread	$4 1\frac{3}{8}$				
B Greatest spread	$50\frac{7}{8}$				
C Inside span $49\frac{4}{8}$ — Span credit may equal but not exceed length of longer antler		$49\frac{4}{8}$			
If inside span of main beams exceeds longer antler length, enter difference					
D Number of points on each antler excluding brows			7	10	3
Number of points on each brow			4	2	
E Length of main beam			$55\frac{6}{8}$	$53\frac{5}{8}$	$2\frac{1}{8}$
F-1 Length of brow palm or first point			18	$18\frac{4}{8}$	
F-2 Length of bez or second point			$23\frac{1}{8}$	$22\frac{1}{8}$	1
F-3 Length of rear tine, if present				2	2
F-4 Length of second longest top point			$9\frac{7}{8}$	$12\frac{2}{8}$	$2\frac{3}{8}$
F-5 Length of longest top point			$10\frac{2}{8}$	$13\frac{4}{8}$	$3\frac{2}{8}$
G-1 Width of brow palm			$16\frac{4}{8}$	4	
G-2 Width of top palm			$5\frac{5}{8}$	$6\frac{3}{8}$	$\frac{6}{8}$
H-1 Circumference at smallest place between brow and bez points			$5\frac{5}{8}$	$5\frac{5}{8}$	$\frac{1}{8}$
H-2 Circumference at smallest place between bez and rear point, if present			$4\frac{4}{8}$	$5\frac{2}{8}$	$\frac{6}{8}$
H-3 Circumference at smallest place before first top point			$4\frac{4}{8}$	$4\frac{5}{8}$	$\frac{1}{8}$
H-4 Circumference at smallest place between two longest top palm points			$9\frac{1}{8}$	$13\frac{7}{8}$	$4\frac{6}{8}$
Totals		$49\frac{4}{8}$	$173\frac{7}{8}$	$173\frac{7}{8}$	$20\frac{2}{8}$

column 1	$49\frac{4}{8}$
Add column 2	$173\frac{7}{8}$
column 3	$173\frac{7}{8}$
Total	$397\frac{2}{8}$
Subtract column 4	$20\frac{2}{8}$
Final score	377

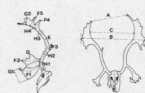
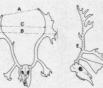

Reindeer

The same formula is used for the Reindeer of Europe and Siberia; the only difference being that the measurements are taken in metric.

In Norway it is the practice to multiply the number of tines on each antler, including those on the brow tine, by 2.5.

C.I.C. formula (metric) for Sika deer

Species: Manchurian Sika

			Col. 1 Span credit	Col. 2 Left	Col. 3 Right	Col. 4 Difference
Supplementary data	*Left*	*Right*				
A	No. of tines	5	4				
B	Tip to tip	73.2					
C	Greatest spread	80					

Score data

		Col. 1 Span credit	Col. 2 Left	Col. 3 Right	Col. 4 Difference
1.1	Inside span: If span exceeds length of longer antler, enter difference in column 4	60			—
1.2	Total of lengths of all abnormal tines between brow and third tine				—
1.3	Length of main beam		70.0	68.8	1.2
1.4	Length of first tine (brow)		25.5	24.5	1.0
1.5	Length, second (middle) tine		19.4	17.5	1.9
1.6	Length, third inner tine		12.5	13.0	0.5
1.7	Length, first extra crown tine		5.5	—	5.5
1.8	Length, second extra crown tine		—	—	—
1.9	Length, third extra crown tine		—	—	—
1.10	Circumference of beam (lower)		12.1	12.8	0.7
1.11	Circumference of beam (upper)		11.8	11.1	0.7
	Totals	60	156.8	147.7	11.5

Add columns 1 + 2 + 3   364.5
Deduct column 4   11.5

Final score   353.00

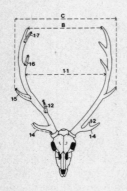
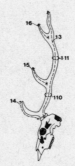
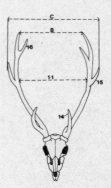

Douglas score for Sika deer

Species: Manchurian Sika

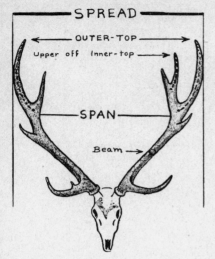

$5 + 4 = 9$

	Shorter measurement doubled		
	Left	*Right*	*Score*
Length	$27\frac{1}{2}$	$27\frac{1}{8}$	$54\frac{1}{4}$
Spread	$31\frac{1}{2} - (4 \times 3 = 12) =$		$19\frac{1}{2}$
Span			$23\frac{5}{8}$
Beam	$4\frac{3}{4}$	5	$9\frac{1}{2}$
Coronet	$7\frac{1}{2}$	$7\frac{1}{2}$	15
Brow	$9\frac{7}{8}$	$9\frac{1}{2}$	19
Tray	$7\frac{5}{8}$	$6\frac{7}{8}$	$13\frac{3}{4}$
Tops			
Inner top	$4\frac{7}{8}$	$5\frac{1}{8}$	$9\frac{3}{4}$
Outer top	11	$10\frac{7}{8}$	$21\frac{3}{4}$
Off-shoot tines	$2\frac{1}{8}$	—	—
Final score			$186\frac{1}{8}$

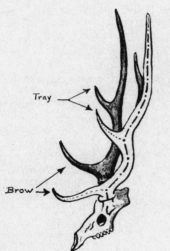

Converted to metric, this score is the equivalent of 472.75 compared to 353.00 of the C.I.C. Scores, however, are not comparable due to different features being taken into consideration.

Note: Spread. The dead line is the length of the longer antler $(27\frac{1}{2})$. Therefore, multiply difference (4) by 3 and deduct from spread, i.e. $31\frac{1}{2} - 12 = 19\frac{1}{2}$ (*see page 281*).

Tine lengths: – – – – – – – – – – – –

LENGTH (to longest tine on top) shown thus: — · — · — ·

Norman Douglas

C.I.C. formula (metric) for Fallow deer

		Left	Right	Average	Factor	Points
1.1	Length of main beam	79.4	74.3	76.85	×0.5	38.42
1.2	Length of brow tine	16.8	20.3	18.5	×0.25	4.63
1.3	Length of palm	33.0	38.1	35.55	×1.00	35.55
1.4	Width of palm	11.1	12.4	11.75	×1.5	17.62
1.5	Circumference, coronet	18.1	17.8	17.95	×1.0	17.95
1.6	Circumference, beam (lower)	9.5	9.8		×1.0	19.30
1.7	Circumference, beam (upper)	8.5	8.5		×1.0	17.00
1.8	Weight of antler	3.65 kg − 0.25 = 3.40			×2.0	6.80
2.1	Beauty points (0–13)					
2.1.1	Colour (0–2): pale 0; medium grey 1; dark 2					1.50
2.1.2	Spellers (0–6): Spellers must measure 2 cm to be considered (*see below*)					4.00
2.1.3	Mass, formation, regularity (0–5): mass 3; shape 2					2.50

Inside span 70.2

165.27

2.2	Penalty points (0–24)	
2.2.1	Insufficient span (0–6) (*see below*)	
2.2.2	Defective palm (0–10): bifurcated, jagged etc.	2.00
2.2.3	Edge of palm (0–2): smooth, worn, porous etc.	0.50
2.2.4	Irregularities (0–6): major differences in length etc.	0.00

Total penalty points 2.50   2.50

Final score   162.77

Notes on measurement of Fallow deer antlers

Length: Length of beam and palm, to be taken to highest point of *indentation* of palm.

Width of palm: Take circumference of palm at widest place and divide by 2.

Weight: According to amount of skull present, up to 0.25 kg may be deducted (*see sketch*).

Insufficient span: Span less than 85% of average length of beam   1 point penalty
Span less than 80% of average length of beam   2 points penalty
Span less than 75% of average length of beam   3 points penalty
Span less than 70% of average length of beam   4 points penalty
Span less than 65% of average length of beam   5 points penalty
Span less than 60% of average length of beam   6 points penalty

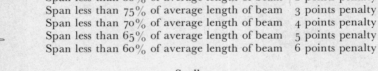

2.1.2 Spellers	one antler	both antlers
short, thin, few	0	0
along one-third of palm edge	1	2
along two-thirds of palm edge	2	4
along whole length of palm edge	3	6

0.1kg
0.25kg

Douglas score for Fallow deer antlers

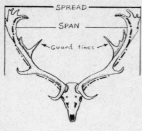

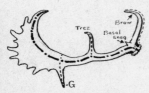

	Shorter measurement doubled		
	Left	*Right*	*Score*
Length	$31\frac{1}{4}$	$29\frac{1}{4}$	$58\frac{1}{2}$
Spread $32\frac{1}{2}$			$32\frac{1}{2}$
Span			$27\frac{1}{4}$
Beam	$3\frac{3}{4}$	$3\frac{7}{8}$	$7\frac{1}{2}$
Coronet	$7\frac{1}{8}$	7	14
Points			
Brow tines	$6\frac{5}{8}$	8	$13\frac{1}{4}$
Tray tines	$6\frac{1}{2}$	$6\frac{1}{4}$	$12\frac{1}{2}$
Guard tines	$8\frac{3}{8}$	$8\frac{1}{4}$	$16\frac{1}{2}$
Number of other palm points (Spellers)	6	5	10
Palms			
Length without points	13	15	26
Width without points	$4\frac{3}{8}$	$4\frac{7}{8}$	$8\frac{3}{4}$
Width with points	$5\frac{3}{4}$	$6\frac{3}{8}$	$11\frac{1}{2}$
Total score			$238\frac{1}{4}$

Length of beam: Measured to tip of longest point on top.
Spread: The dead line is the length of the longer antler plus 4 in.
(*see page 281*).
Palm points (Spellers): Any point or jag may be considered a
point 'if a finger ring or a strap can be hung upon it'.
Note: Any Fallow trophy with a score of 230 or more can be
considered a good one for New Zealand.

LENGTH shown thus: —·—·—.   Tines: ———————.
Length of palm without points: ——————. Guard tines:———— G.
width of palmation excluding points (below deepest crutch): <---->.
width of palmation including points: ——————|. *Norman Douglas.*

C.I.C. formula (metric) for Roe deer (European)

		Measure-ment	Average	Factor	Points
1.1	Length of main beam – left	27.8 ⎫	27.2	× 0.5	13.60
	Length, main beam – right	26.6 ⎭			
1.2	Weight of antlers (g) 605–70 = 535			× 0.1	53.50
1.3	Volume of antlers (in ccm)	255		× 0.3	76.50
1.4	Inside span (0–4 points)	9 cm			1.00
2.1	Beauty points (0–19)				
2.1.1	Colour (0–4): pale 0; yellow 1; brown 2; dark brown 3; very dark 4				3.50
2.1.2	Pearling (0–4): smooth 0; weak 1; average 2; good 3; very good 4				4.00
2.1.3	Coronets (0–4): weak 0; average 1; good 2; large 3; very large 4				4.00
2.1.4	Tine ends (0–2): blunt 0; medium 1; white tipped 2				1.50
2.1.5	Regularity (0–3) & quality (0–2) (total 0–5)				4.00
			Total		161.60
2.2	Penalties (0–5)				
	Unspecified abnormalities (0–3); tine defects (0–2)				—
			Final score		161.60

1.2 Weight: According to amount of skull present, 65–90 g can be deducted (*see sketch*).
1.3 Volume: Determined by immersing the antlers *only* in water (*see page 284*).
1.4 Span: Points (0–4) awarded as follows:

Very narrow – less than 30% of average length of beam	0 point
Narrow – from 30 to 34.9% of average length of beam	1 point
Average – from 35 to 39.9% of average length of beam	2 points
Good – from 40 to 44.9% of average length of beam	3 points
Very good – from 45 to 75% of average length of beam	4 points
Abnormal – too wide – more than 75% of average length of beam	0 point

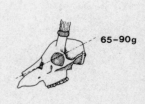

C.I.C. formula (metric) for Siberian and Chinese Roe deer

Species: Siberian Roe

Supplementary data

		Left	Right
A	Number of tines	4	4
B	Tip to tip spread	32.2	
C	Weight of antlers on skull*	575 g S	

Score data

1.1 Volume (in ccm) 325. Multiply by 0.3 and enter in Column 1.
1.2 Inside span. If span exceeds 75% of longer antler, enter difference in Column 5
1.3 Length of main beam
1.4 Length of brow tine
1.5 Length of upper back tine
1.6 Total of lengths of *all* additional tines

	Col. 1	Col. 2	Col. 3	Col. 4	Col. 5
	Volume	Span credit	Left	Right	Difference
1.1	97.5				
1.2		32.3			4.8
1.3			36.7	35.6	1.1
1.4			11.5	11.0	0.5
1.5			11.9	11.1	0.8
1.6			3.0	3.5	0.5
Total	97.5	32.3	63.1	61.2	7.7

Add columns 1 + 2 + 3 + 4   254.1
Subtract column 5   7.7

Final score   246.40

* Denotes whether weighed with full skull (L); normal cut (N) or short frontal bone cut (S).

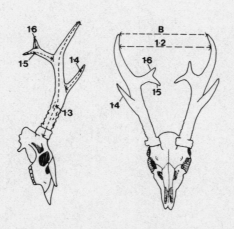

TROPHIES

Boone and Crockett Club formula for Moose
Type of Moose: Alaskan

	Col. 1 *Greatest* *spread*	*Col. 2* *Left*	*Col. 3* *Right*	*Col. 4* *Difference*
A Greatest spread	$70\frac{4}{8}$			
B Number of abnormal tines on both antlers				
C Number of normal points		19	17	2
D Width of palm		16	17	1
E Length of palm, including brow palm		$45\frac{1}{8}$	$44\frac{4}{8}$	$\frac{5}{8}$
F Circumference of beam at smallest place		$7\frac{7}{8}$	$7\frac{6}{8}$	$\frac{1}{8}$
Totals	$70\frac{4}{8}$	88	$86\frac{2}{8}$	$3\frac{6}{8}$

Add columns $1 + 2 + 3 =$ $244\frac{6}{8}$
Subtract column 4 $3\frac{6}{8}$

       Final score   241

Note:
D & E Width and length of palm: To be measured in contact with surface along the under side of the palm.
C Points: A projection must be at least 1 in. long, and the length must exceed the breadth of the points' base.
The reason that tine lengths are not measured but only recorded 'is that well developed palms with short points (tines) are more desirable trophies. Long points (tines) develop as a result of lack of palm material. Including point length measurements would thus discriminate against the more desirable characters of palm development' (Boone & Crockett).

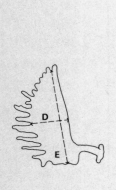
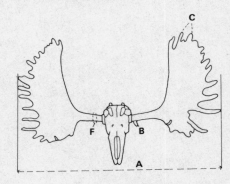

Douglas score for Moose

	Score equals smaller figure doubled		
	Left	*Right*	*Score*
A Length	$41\frac{1}{2}$	$43\frac{1}{2}$	83
B Spread			$70\frac{1}{2}$
C Beam	$7\frac{7}{8}$	$7\frac{3}{4}$	$15\frac{1}{2}$
D Coronet	$13\frac{1}{2}$	$12\frac{1}{2}$	25
Brow palmation			
E Length with points	$30\frac{1}{2}$	$29\frac{1}{8}$	$58\frac{1}{4}$
F Length, without points	$17\frac{1}{4}$	$18\frac{1}{4}$	$34\frac{1}{2}$
G Width at smallest place	$11\frac{1}{2}$	$9\frac{3}{4}$	$19\frac{1}{2}$
H Number of points	5	5	10
Main palmation			
I Length without points	34	33	66
J Width without points	16	17	32
K Width with points	$24\frac{3}{4}$	26	$49\frac{1}{2}$
L Number of points	14	12	24
Total score			$487\frac{3}{4}$

Note:
All measurements taken on the under side. This same trophy,
measured under Boone and Crockett formula, would have had a
score of 241.

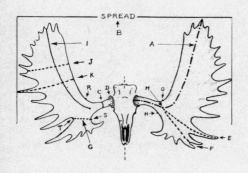

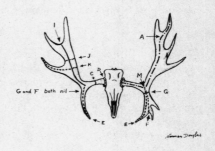

C.I.C. formula (metric) for Elk

Palmated antlers		Measurements		Total	Average	Factor	Points
		Left	Right				
1.1	Circumference of beam (4 cm *above* coronet)	17.0	17.3	34.3		× 1.0	34.3
1.2	Overall spread			94		× 0.5	47.0
1.3	Length of palm/beam	90.2	86.0	176.2	88.1	× 1.0	88.1
1.4.1	Width of palm	22.5	20.5	43.0		× 2.0	86.0
1.5	Average length of all tines (*see note below*)						11.0
1.6	Number of tines (16). One point for each tine above 10						6.0
						Total	272.4

2   *Penalty points* (0–8)
     Considerable difference in tine length (0–5)   1.0
     Asymmetry of one palm or beam compared to other (0–3)

						Final score	271.40

Non-palmated antlers		Left	Right	Total	Average	Factor	Points
1.1	Circumference of beam (4 cm *above* coronet)	21.5	22.5	44.0		× 1.0	44.0
1.2	Overall spread			124.6		× 0.5	62.3
1.3	Length of palm/beam	117.0	106.0	223.0	111.5	× 1.0	111.5
1.4.2	Circumference of tines (midway)	31.3	33.2	64.5		× 0.65	41.93
1.5	Average length of *all* tines (*see note below*)						36.6
1.6	Number of tines. One point awarded for each tine up to a *maximum* of 5 tines per beam						8.0
						Total	304.33

2   *Penalty Points* (0–8)
     Considerable difference in tine length (0–5)   —
     Asymmetry of one palm or beam compared to other (0–3)   —

						Final score	304.33

Notes on formula

1.4.1   Palmated antlers: Length and width to be measured along outer edge.

1.4.2   Non-palmated antlers: Circumference of *not more than* 5 of the longest tines, to be measured at mid-distance of length.

1.5   Palmated antlers: If average length of all tines amounts to 5 cm or more, one point is added for each centimetre up to a maximum of 15 points.

    Non-palmated antlers: For each centimetre of the average length of all tines, one point awarded.

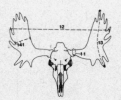 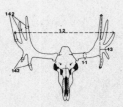

C.I.C. formula (metric) for Muntjac

	Left	Right	Col. 1 Span credit	Col. 2 Left	Col. 3 Right	Col. 4 Difference
Supplementary data						
A Number of tines	2	2				
B Tip to tip	10.0					
C Greatest spread	12.2					
Score data						
1.1 Inside span between main beams			8.0			
1.2 Length of main beam				9.5	9.1	0.4
1.3 Length of brow tine				1.7	1.1	0.6
1.4 Circumference of coronet				7.8	7.5	0.3
1.5 Circumference of beam at *mid*-distance				3.6	3.4	0.2
Total			8.0	22.6	21.1	1.5

Add columns 1 + 2 + 3 =   51.7
Deduct column 4   1.5
_____
56.20

Note: There is no Douglas score for this species. The above example is of Reeves Muntjac. Antlers of Indian Muntjac are considerably larger, and an outstanding specimen from Java has a score of 127.10 C.I.C. points.

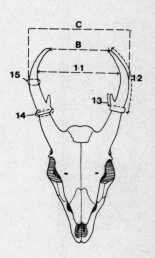

C.I.C. formula (metric) for Axis deer, Bawean deer, Calamian deer, Hog deer, Rusa and Sambar

Species: Rusa deer

Supplementary data

		Left	Right
A	number of tine ends	3	3
B	Tip to tip		50.2
C	Greatest speed		56.5

		Col. 1 Span credit	Col.2 Left antler	Col.3 Right antler	Col.4 Difference
Score data					
1.1	Inside span	40.6			
	If measurement exceeds length of longest antler, enter difference in Col. 4				
1.2	Length of beam		86.4	89.5	3.1
1.3	Length of first tine (brow		27.9	25.4	2.5
1.4	Length of second tine		26.2	20.7	5.5
1.5	Length of tines erupting from upper edge of brow if present		—	—	—
1.6	Circumference of beam		11.4	11.4	—
	Totals	40.6	151.9	147.0	11.1

Add columns 1 + 2 + 3 =   339.50
Subtract column 4   11.10
_____

Final score   328.40

A   Tines: Apart from small tines of minimum length 2.0 cm that may erupt on the upper edge of the brow, all other tines additional to 1.3 and 1.4 are considered in supplementary data only.

1.6   Beam circumference: To be measured at thinnest place between brow (1.3) and second tine (1.4). If latter absent, then mid-way between brow and tip of antler.

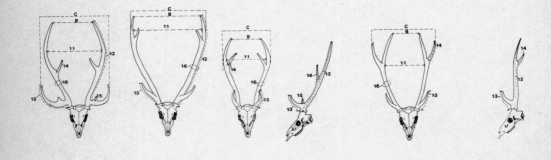

Note: C.I.C. scores for good trophies of Axis, Hog and Sambar are: Axis 450.00; Hog deer 175.00 and Indian Sambar 500.00.

Douglas score for Axis deer, Hog deer, Rusa deer and Sambar

Species: Rusa deer

No. of points: $3 + 3 = 6$

| | *Shorter measurement doubled* | | |
	Left	Right	Score
Length of beam	34	$35\frac{1}{4}$	68
Spread $22\frac{1}{4}$			$22\frac{1}{4}$
Span			16
Beam	$4\frac{1}{2}$	$4\frac{1}{2}$	9
Coronet	$8\frac{1}{2}$	$8\frac{3}{8}$	$16\frac{3}{4}$
Brow	$10\frac{3}{4}$	$9\frac{1}{2}$	19
Tops Inner	19	$19\frac{1}{2}$	38
Outer	$10\frac{1}{2}$	$8\frac{1}{4}$	$16\frac{1}{2}$
Total			$205\frac{1}{2}$

Beam is the smallest circumference of the main beam below the tops.
Span is the widest inside measurement between the main beams and below the tops.
Spread dead line (see page 281):
Sambar   Length of the longer antler.
Rusa   Length of the longer antler minus 4 in.
Axis deer   Length of the longer antler minus 4 in.
Hog deer

Converted to metric, the above score becomes 521.97, compared to 328.40 of the same trophy measured under the C.I.C. formula. The Douglas score includes the measurement of the spread, coronets and upper portion of the main beam which is measured twice. If these additional measurements are deducted, the comparison is 328.40 (C.I.C.) to 326.39.

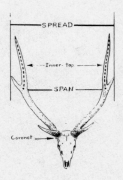

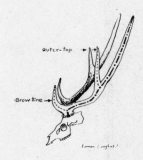

TROPHIES

Boone and Crockett club formula for Mule and Blacktail deer

Type of deer: Mule deer

		Supplementary data Left	Supplementary data Right	Col. 1 Span credit	Col. 2 Left antler	Col. 3 Right antler	Col. 4 Difference
A	Number of points on each antler	6	5				
B	Tip to tip spread		$24\frac{3}{8}$				
C	Greatest spread		$30\frac{4}{8}$				
D	Inside span $26\frac{5}{8}$ — Span credit may equal but not exceed length of longer antler			$26\frac{5}{8}$			
	If inside spread of main beams exceeds longer antler length enter difference						
E	Total of lengths of all abnormal points						$2\frac{7}{8}$
F	Length of main beam				28	$26\frac{7}{8}$	$1\frac{1}{8}$
G-1	Length of first point, if present				$2\frac{1}{8}$	2	$\frac{1}{8}$
G-2	Length of second point				$20\frac{1}{8}$	$20\frac{2}{8}$	$\frac{1}{8}$
G-3	Length of third point, if present				$9\frac{6}{8}$	$10\frac{7}{8}$	$1\frac{1}{8}$
G-4	Length of fourth point if present				$13\frac{7}{8}$	$13\frac{4}{8}$	$\frac{3}{8}$
H-1	Circumference at smallest place between burr (coronet) and first point				$5\frac{3}{8}$	$5\frac{3}{8}$	
H-2	Circumference at smallest place between first and second points				$4\frac{6}{8}$	$4\frac{6}{8}$	
H-3	Circumference at smallest place between main beam and third point				$4\frac{3}{8}$	$4\frac{2}{8}$	$\frac{1}{8}$
H-4	Circumference at smallest place between second and fourth points				5	$5\frac{4}{8}$	$\frac{4}{8}$
	Totals			$26\frac{5}{8}$	$93\frac{3}{8}$	$93\frac{3}{8}$	$6\frac{3}{8}$

Add columns $1+2+3=$ $213\frac{3}{8}$

Subtract column 4 $6\frac{3}{8}$

Final score   207

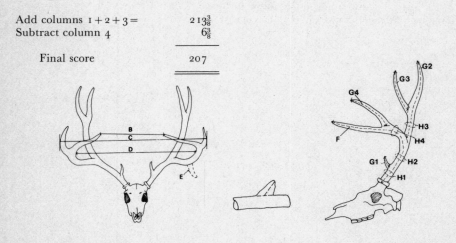

Boone and Crockett Club formula for 'non-typical' Mule deer

ABNORMAL POINTS

Left	Right
8	$3\frac{4}{8}$
$6\frac{5}{8}$	$3\frac{6}{8}$
$7\frac{7}{8}$	$1\frac{2}{8}$
$5\frac{1}{8}$	$3\frac{6}{8}$
$1\frac{1}{8}$	$6\frac{2}{8}$
2	$9\frac{2}{8}$
4	$9\frac{5}{8}$
$5\frac{6}{8}$	$2\frac{6}{8}$
$2\frac{2}{8}$	$7\frac{7}{8}$
$3\frac{1}{8}$	$2\frac{3}{8}$
	$4\frac{2}{8}$
	2
	$1\frac{2}{8}$
$45\frac{7}{8}$	$57\frac{7}{8}$

To Col. E $103\frac{6}{8}$

Supplementary data

	Left	Right
A Number of points on each antler	15	18
B Tip to tip spread	$19\frac{2}{8}$	
C Greatest spread	$40\frac{2}{8}$	

D Inside span of Main Beams $\boxed{22\frac{1}{8}}$ Span credit may equal but not exceed length of longer antler

If inside span of main beams exceeds longer antler length, enter difference

	Col. 1 Span credit	Col. 2 left antler	Col. 3 right antler	Col. 4 Difference
D Inside span of Main Beams	$22\frac{1}{8}$			
	Col. E			—
E Total lengths of all abnormal points	$103\frac{6}{8}$			
F Length of main beam		$21\frac{3}{8}$	$22\frac{5}{8}$	$1\frac{2}{8}$
G-1 Length of first point, if present		3	3	
G-2 Length of second point		$15\frac{2}{8}$	$14\frac{7}{8}$	$\frac{3}{8}$
G-3 Length of third point, if present		$11\frac{7}{8}$	$10\frac{5}{8}$	$1\frac{2}{8}$
G-4 Length of fourth point, if present		$9\frac{2}{8}$	10	$\frac{6}{8}$
H-1 Circumference at smallest place between burr (coronet) and first point		$5\frac{1}{8}$	$4\frac{6}{8}$	$\frac{3}{8}$
H-2 Circumference at smallest place between first and second points		$4\frac{7}{8}$	$5\frac{1}{8}$	$\frac{2}{8}$
H-3 Circumference at smallest place between main beam and third point		$4\frac{6}{8}$	$5\frac{3}{8}$	$\frac{5}{8}$
H-4 Circumference at smallest place between second and fourth points		$4\frac{6}{8}$	5	$\frac{2}{8}$
Totals	$103\frac{6}{8}$	$22\frac{1}{8}$	$80\frac{2}{8}$	$81\frac{3}{8}$	$5\frac{1}{8}$

Add columns 1, 2, 3 and E ($287\frac{4}{8}$), subtract column 4 ($5\frac{1}{8}$), thus giving Final Score $282\frac{3}{8}$.

Boone and Crockett formula for Whitetail and Coues' deer

Type of deer: Whitetail

		Supplementary Data		Col. 1 Span credit	Col. 2 Left antler	Col. 3 Right antler	Col. 4 Difference
		Left	Right				
A	Number of points on each antler	5	5				
B	Tip to tip spread	$9\frac{9}{8}$					
C	Greatest spread	$21\frac{4}{8}$					
D	Inside span $\boxed{18\frac{4}{8}}$ Span credit may equal but not exceed length of longer antler			$18\frac{4}{8}$			
	If inside span exceeds longer antler length, enter difference						—
E	Total of lengths of all abnormal points						
F	Length of main beam				$28\frac{4}{8}$	$28\frac{1}{8}$	$\frac{3}{8}$
G-1	Length of first point, if present				$4\frac{5}{8}$	$5\frac{1}{8}$	$\frac{4}{8}$
G-2	Length of second point				$11\frac{2}{8}$	$12\frac{5}{8}$	$1\frac{3}{8}$
G-3	Length of third point				$10\frac{4}{8}$	$10\frac{2}{8}$	$\frac{2}{8}$
G-4	Length of fourth point, if present				$6\frac{7}{8}$	$7\frac{1}{8}$	$\frac{2}{8}$
G-5	Length of fifth point, if present						
G-6	Length of sixth point, if present						
G-7	Length of seventh point, if present						
H-1	Circumference at smallest place between burr (coronet) and first point*				$4\frac{6}{8}$	$4\frac{6}{8}$	—
H-2	Circumference at smallest place between first and second points*				$4\frac{6}{8}$	$4\frac{6}{8}$	—
H-3	Circumference at smallest place between second and third points				$5\frac{4}{8}$	$5\frac{3}{8}$	$\frac{1}{8}$
H-4	Circumference at smallest place between third and fourth points, or half way between third point and beam tip if fourth point is missing				$4\frac{7}{8}$	5	$\frac{1}{8}$
	Totals			$18\frac{4}{8}$	$81\frac{5}{8}$	$83\frac{1}{8}$	3

Add columns 1 + 2 + 3 $183\frac{2}{8}$

Subtract column 4   3

Final score $180\frac{2}{8}$

Note: If brow point is missing, take H-1 and H-2 at smallest place between burr (coronet) and second point.

Douglas score for White-tailed deer

| | Shorter measurement doubled | | |
	Left	Right	Score
Length	$28\frac{1}{2}$	$28\frac{1}{8}$	$56\frac{1}{4}$
Spread $21\frac{1}{2}$			$21\frac{1}{2}$
Span, inside			$18\frac{3}{4}$
Beam	$4\frac{3}{4}$	$4\frac{3}{4}$	$9\frac{1}{2}$
Coronet	$7\frac{1}{2}$	$7\frac{5}{8}$	15
Length of (basal snag)	$4\frac{7}{8}$	$5\frac{3}{8}$	$9\frac{3}{4}$
Length (back tine)	$11\frac{5}{8}$	13	$23\frac{1}{4}$
Length First upper off	$10\frac{3}{4}$	$10\frac{1}{2}$	21
Length Second upper off	$7\frac{1}{8}$	$7\frac{3}{8}$	$14\frac{1}{4}$
Total score			$189\frac{1}{4}$

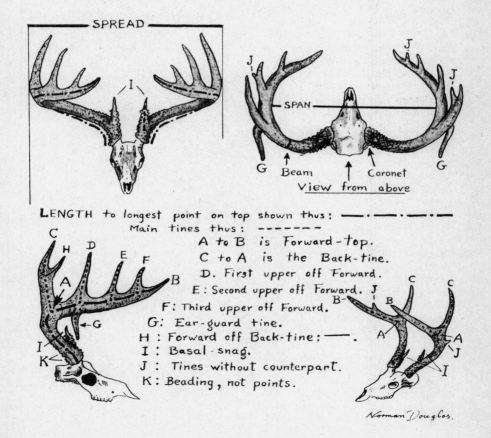

SPREAD

I

J
J
J
SPAN
G   G
Beam   Coronet
View from above

LENGTH to longest point on top shown thus: — · — · — · —
Main tines thus: - - - - - - -
A to B is Forward-top.
C to A is the Back-tine.
D. First upper off Forward.
E: Second upper off Forward.
F: Third upper off Forward.
G: Ear-guard tine.
H: Forward off Back-tine: —— .
I: Basal-snag.
J: Tines without counterpart.
K: Beading, not points.

C H D E F B A G I K

B J C C B A A J I

Norman Douglas.

313

TROPHIES

Boone and Crockett formula for 'non-typical' Whitetail and Coues deer

ABNORMAL POINTS

Left	Right
$1\frac{1}{8}$	$8\frac{2}{8}$
$3\frac{4}{8}$	$1\frac{2}{8}$
$9\frac{2}{8}$	$2\frac{2}{8}$
$5\frac{1}{8}$	$6\frac{3}{8}$
$2\frac{7}{8}$	$5\frac{3}{8}$
$2\frac{4}{8}$	$6\frac{7}{8}$
$3\frac{5}{8}$	$3\frac{7}{8}$
$5\frac{3}{8}$	$4\frac{1}{8}$
$1\frac{6}{8}$	
$35\frac{1}{8}$	$38\frac{3}{8}$

To Col. E $73\frac{4}{8}$

Supplementary data

		Left	Right
A	Number of points on each antler	14	13
B	Tip to tip		$15\frac{1}{8}$
C	Greatest spread		$29\frac{4}{8}$

		Col. 1 Spread credit	Col. 2 Left antler	Col. 3 Right antler	Col. 4 Difference
D	Inside span $21\frac{5}{8}$ Span credit may equal but not exceed length of longer antler	$21\frac{5}{8}$			
	If inside span of main beams exceeds longer antler length, enter difference				—
E	Total of lengths of all abnormal points	Col. E $73\frac{4}{8}$			
F	Length of main beam		$25\frac{1}{8}$	$25\frac{6}{8}$	$\frac{5}{8}$
G-1	Length of first point, if present		$3\frac{4}{8}$	$2\frac{6}{8}$	$\frac{6}{8}$
G-2	Length of second point		$10\frac{6}{8}$	$12\frac{5}{8}$	$1\frac{7}{8}$
G-3	Length of third point		$11\frac{5}{8}$	$12\frac{3}{8}$	$\frac{6}{8}$
G-4	Length of fourth point, if present		$12\frac{4}{8}$	$12\frac{3}{8}$	$\frac{1}{8}$
G-5	Length of fifth point, if present				
G-6	Length of sixth point, if present				
G-7	Length of seventh point, if present				
H-1	Circumference at smallest place between burr (coronet) and first point		$5\frac{3}{8}$	$5\frac{3}{8}$	
H-2	Circumference at smallest place between first and second points		$5\frac{6}{8}$	$5\frac{4}{8}$	$\frac{2}{8}$
H-3	Circumference at small place between second and third points		$6\frac{3}{8}$	$5\frac{7}{8}$	$\frac{4}{8}$
H-4	Circumference at smallest place between third and fourth points		$8\frac{3}{8}$	$5\frac{6}{8}$	$2\frac{5}{8}$
	Totals	$73\frac{4}{8}$	$21\frac{5}{8}$	$89\frac{3}{8}$	$88\frac{3}{8}$	$7\frac{4}{8}$

Add columns 1, 2, 3 and E ($272\frac{7}{8}$), subtract column 4 ($7\frac{4}{8}$), thus giving Final Score of $265\frac{3}{8}$.

C.I.C. formula (metric) for Brocket deer

Supplementary Data
A Tip to tip   4.9

Score data

	Col. 1	Col. 2	Col. 3
	Left	Right	Difference
1.1 Length, main beam	11.3	10.9	0.4
1.2 Circumference, lower beam (above coronet)	4.4	4.4	—
1.3 Circumference, upper beam (at mid-distance)	3.3	3.2	0.1
Total	19.0	18.5	0.5

Add columns 1 + 2   37.5
Subtract column 4   0.5

Final score   37.00

C.I.C. formula (metric) for Chinese Water-deer and Musk deer

Species: Chinese Water-deer

Score data

	Col. 1	Col. 2	Col. 3
	Left	Right	Difference
1.1 Length of canine tooth	56	57	1
1.2 Circumference of canine at point of eruption	30	29	1
Total	86	86	2

Add columns 1 + 2 =   172
Subtract column 3   2

Final score   170

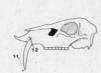

All measurements to be taken in millimetres.
Length of tooth: Measurement to be taken along front curve of tooth from point of eruption from jaw to tip.
Circumference: to be measured around tooth *as close as possible* to point of eruption from jaw.
Note: There is no Douglas score for this species.

Appendix A
Record Deer Trophies

The ultimate ambition of a trophy hunter is to shoot a world record head. So far as North American deer are concerned, these are assessed under the Boone and Crockett system and listed in *Records of North American Big Game* (1981). They can be considered the official world record for the species concerned.

All other deer are measured in accordance with the C.I.C. system, so the relative scores are not comparable. To be accepted as a world record, all European and Asiatic trophies must have been measured by a panel of judges at an International Exhibition of Trophies.

The following are the scores of the best trophies that have been *officially* measured by one or other of these two systems.

NORTH AMERICA

Species	B & C score	Locality killed	Owner or by whom killed	Date	Authority
Wapiti (American Elk)	$442\frac{3}{8}$	Dark Canyon, Colorado	John Plute	1899	NABG 1981[1]
Mule deer (typical antlers)	$225\frac{6}{8}$	Dolores Co., Colorado	D Burris Jr	1972	NABG 1981
Mule deer (non-typical antlers)	$355\frac{2}{8}$	Chip Lake, Alberta	E Broder	1926	NABG 1981
Columbia Blacktail	$172\frac{2}{8}$[2]	Marion Co., Oregon	B G Shurtleff	1969	NABG 1981
White-tail (typical antlers)	$206\frac{1}{8}$	Burnett Co., Wisconsin	J Jordan	1914	NABG 1981
White-tail (non-typical antlers)	286	Brady, Texas	J Benson	1892	NABG 1981
Coues' Whitetail (typical antlers)	143	Pima Co., Arizona	E Stockwell	1953	NABG 1981
Coues' Whitetail (non-typical antlers)	$151\frac{4}{8}$	Cochise Co., Arizona	C C Mabry	1929	NABG 1981
Moose, Canada	$238\frac{5}{8}$	Bear Lake, Quebec	S H Witherbee	1914	NABG 1981
Moose, Alaska-Yukon	255	McGrath, Alaska	K Best	1978	NABG 1981
Moose, Wyoming or Shiras	$205\frac{4}{8}$	Green River Lake, Wyoming	J M Oakley	1952	NABG 1981
Caribou, Mountain	452	Turnagain River, British Columbia	G Beaubien	1976	NABG 1981
Caribou, Woodland	$419\frac{5}{8}$	Newfoundland	National collection	pre-1910	NABG 1981
Caribou, Barren ground	$463\frac{6}{8}$	Ugashik, Lake Alaska	R Loesche	1967	NABG 1981
Caribou, Quebec-Labrador	$474\frac{6}{8}$	Nain, Labrador	Z Elbow	1931	NABG 1981

[1] For complete measurements see *Records of North American Big Game* (1981).
[2] Provisional.

EUROPE AND ASIA

Species	C.I.C. score	Locality killed	Owner or by whom killed	Date	Authority
Red deer	261.25*	Soveja-Vrancea, Romania	N Ceausescu	1980	Pl 1981
Roe deer	228.68*	Martonvásár, Hungary	Lajos Cseterki	1965	Bp 1971
Elk, European	415.90*	Orosz FSzK	L G Kaplanov	1934	Bp 1971
Elk, Siberian	551.70*	Yakutiya	Vnyoz-Girov	1972	Pl 1981
Reindeer	989.00*	?	P F Batickij	?	Bp 1971
Fallow deer	220.31*	Gyulaj, Hungary	Janos Kadar	1972	Bu 1978
Sika deer, Japanese	307.30	Nord Westfallen, F.R.G.	F Hake	1976	Pl 1981
Sika deer, Dybowski	457.80	Brovarski Rayon	A I Kipovkin	1979	Pl 1981
Wapiti, Asiatic	963.00	Kirgiz SSR	N G Leschenko	1966	Pl 1981

* Scores marked with asterisk are official world record trophies. For complete measurements of above trophies reference should be made to the appropriate Exhibition Catalogue of Trophies as follows:

Pl – World Exhibition, Plovdiv, Bulgaria, 1981
Bp – World Exhibition, Budapest, Hungary, 1971
Bu – International Exhibition, Bucharest, Romania, 1978

Appendix B
Addresses of Useful
Contacts for Deer Hunting

ASIA
Klineburger Worldwide Travel, 1519–12th Avenue, Seattle, Washington 98122, U.S.A.

Outfitters Inc., 8 South Michigan Avenue, Chicago, Illinois 60603, U.S.A.

AUSTRALIA
Australian Deer Association, P.O. Box 15, Doncaster, 3108 Melbourne, Victoria.
Bob Penfold, 72 Blanch Street, Shortland, 2307 New South Wales (Guide/Outfitter).

AUSTRIA
National Tourist Office, Hohenstaufengasse 3, A-1010 Wien 1.

BELGIUM
Only limited hunting available for visiting sportsmen.

BULGARIA
Union Bulgare des Chasseurs et des Pêcheurs, Conseil Central, 12 rue Gavril Ghénov, Sofia.

CANADA
Alberta Alberta Recreation, Parks & Wildlife, Fish & Wildlife Division, 10363–108 Street, Edmonton, Alberta T5J IL8.

British Columbia Fish & Wildlife Branch, 400–1019 Wharf Street, Victoria V8W 2Y1.

Manitoba Dept of Tourism and Cultural Affairs, 200 Vaughan Street, Winnipeg, Manitoba R3C IT5.

New Brunswick Dept of Natural Resources, Fish & Wildlife Branch, P.O. Box 12345, Fredericton, New Brunswick E3B 5C3.

Newfoundland Dept of Tourism, Wildlife Division, Building 810, Pleasantville, P.O. Box 4750, Newfoundland ALC 5T7.

Northwest Territories Superintendent of Game, Wildlife Service, Dept of Natural & Cultural Affairs, Government of the Northwest Territories, Yellowknife.

Nova Scotia Minister of Lands & Forests, P.O. Box 698, Halifax, Nova Scotia B3J 2T9.

Ontario Ministry of Natural Resources, Whitney Block, Queens Park, Toronto, Ontario M7A 1W3.

Quebec Ministère du Tourisme de la Chasse, et de la Pêche, Direction générale de la faune, 150 boulevard, Saint-Cyrille est, Quebec G1R 4Y3.

Saskatchewan Tourism & Renewable Resources, 1825 Lorne Street, St Regina, Saskatchewan S4P 3N1.

Yukon Government of the Yukon Territory, P.O. Box 2703, Whitehorse, Yukon Territory Y1A 2C6.

Miscellaneous Canadian Safari, P.O. Box 2678, Smithers, British Columbia.

CZECHOSLOVAKIA
Čedok, Jagdabteilung, 111 35 Praha 1, Na příkopě 18.

DENMARK
Diana Jagt-og Fiskerejser APS (Sport Agency) Skårupøre Strandvej 52, DK-5881 Skårup.
Vildtforvaltningen (Licence) Strandvejen 4, DK 8410, Rønde.

FINLAND
Finnish Game & Fisheries Research Institute, Game Division, Unioninkatu 45 B, 00170, Helsinki 17.

FRANCE
Société de Vénerie, 51 rue Dumont d'Urville, 75116 Paris.
Office National des Forêts (O.N.F.) 2 Avenue de Saint Mandé, 75570 Paris.

GERMANY, EAST
No organized hunting available.

GERMANY, WEST
Münchner Jagd-und Angelreisen, Schmidt & Hanrieder O.H.G., Lamonstr. 1, Postfach 86 07 11, 800 München 86.

GREAT BRITAIN
Major Neil Ramsay & Co., Farleyer, Aberfeldy, Perthshire PH15 2JE.
Sport in Scotland Ltd, 22 Market Brae, Inverness IV2 3AB.

HUNGARY
Mavad, Shooting Bureau, 1014 Budapest, Uri u.39.

ITALY
No organized hunting available.

NETHERLANDS
Koninklijke Nederlandse, Jagersvereniging, Amersfoort, Utrechtseureg 131.

NEW CALEDONIA
J A Shepherd, c/o Lafleur BP 37, Noumea.

APPENDIX B

NEW ZEALAND
Forestry Service, Director in General of Forests, New Zealand Forest Service, Private Bag, Wellington.

NORWAY
Direktoratet for viltogferskvannsfisk, Elgeseter gt.10, 7000 Trondheim.

POLAND
Centrala Turystyczna 'Orbis', Biuro Zagranicznej Turystyki Przyjazdowej, Sekija Polowán, Stawki 2, 00–193 Warszawa.

ROMANIA
Association Générale des Chasseurs et pêcheurs Sportifs, Calea Mosilor 128 70044 Bucarest.

SOUTH AMERICA
Servicio Nacional de Parques Nacionales, Sante Fe 690, Buenos Aires, Argentina.

SPAIN
Caza y Naturaleza, S/A (Cazatur), Apartado de Correos (P.O. Box) 50, 577 Madrid.

SWEDEN
Sverek, Sverige Rekreation A.B. Domäverket, S-171 93 Solna.

Värmland Tourist Association, Box 323, S-651 05 Karlstad.

SWITZERLAND
Limited hunting available for visiting sportsmen.

U.S.S.R.
Intourist, 16 Avenue Marx, Moscow.

UNITED STATES OF AMERICA
Alabama Department of Conservation, Game & Fish Division, Wildlife Section, Montgomery, Alabama 36130.

Alaska Department of Fish & Game, Subport Building, Juneau, Alaska 99801.

Arizona Arizona Game and Fish Dept, 2222 West Greenway Road, Phoenix, Arizona 85023.

Arkansas Arkansas Game & Fish Commission, Little Rock, Arkansas.

California Resources Agency, Dept of Fish & Game, Resources Building, 1416 Ninth Street, Sacramento, California 95814.

Colorado Division of Wildlife, Dept of Natural Resources, 6060 Broadway, Denver, Colorado 80216.

Connecticut Dept of Environmental Protection, State Office Buildings, Hartford, Connecticut 06115.

Delaware Dept of Natural Resources & Environmental Control, Division of Fish & Wildlife, P.O. Box 1401, Edward Tatnall Building, Dover, Delaware 19901.

Florida Game and Freshwater Fish Commission, Tallahassee, Florida 32301.

Georgia Dept of Natural Resources, Information Office, 270 Washington Street, S. W. Atlanta, Georgia 30334.

Hawaii Division of Fish & Game, Dept of Land and Natural Resources, 1151 Punchbowl Street, Honolulo, Hawaii 96813.

Idaho Dept of Fish & Game, 600 South Walnut Street, Box 25, Boise, Idaho 83707.

Illinois Dept of Conservation, 605 Wm. G. Stratton Building, Springfield, Illinois 62706.

Indiana Dept of Natural Resources, 607 State Office Building, Indianapolis, Indiana 46204.

Iowa Iowa Conservation Commission, Wallace State Office Building, Des Moines, Iowa 50319.

Kansas Fish & Game, Pratt Headquarters, Box 54A, Rural Route 2, Pratt, Kansas 67124

Kentucky Fish & Wildlife Resources, 592 East Main Street, Frankfort 40601.

Louisiana Department of Wildlife & Fisheries, 126 Wildlife & Fisheries Building, 400 Royal Street, New Orleans, Louisiana 70130.

Maine Dept of Inland Fisheries & Wildlife, 284 State Street, Augusta, Maine 04333.

Maryland Wildlife Admin. Dept of Natural Resources, Tawes State Office Building, -B2 Annapolis, Maryland 21401.

Massachusetts Division of Fisheries & Wildlife, Leverett Saltonstall Building, 100 Cambridge Street, Boston 02202.

Michigan Dept of Natural Resources, Box 30028, Lansing, Michigan 48909.

Minnesota Dept of Natural Resources, Division of Fish & Wildlife, Centennial Office Building, St Paul, Minnesota 55155.

Mississippi Game & Fish Commission, P.O. Box 451, Jackson, Mississippi 39205.

Missouri Dept of Conservation, 2901 North Ten Mile Drive, P.O. Box 180, Jefferson City, Missouri 65101.

Montana Dept of Fish & Game, Helena, Montana 59601.

Nebraska Game & Parks Commission, P.O. Box 508, Bassett, Nebraska 68714.

Nevada Dept of Wildlife, P.O. Box 10678, Reno, Nevada 89520.

New Hampshire Fish & Game Dept, 34 Bridge Street, Concord 03301.

New Jersey Dept of Environmental Protection, P.O. Box 1809, Trenton, New Jersey 08625.

New Mexico Dept of Game & Fish, State Capitol, Villagra Building, Santa Fe, New Mexico 87503.

New York Dept of Environmental Conservation, Albany, New York 12233.

North Carolina Wildlife Resources Commission, Raleigh, North Carolina 27611.

North Dakota Game & Fish Dept, 2121 Lovett Avenue, Bismarck, North Dakota 58505.

Ohio Dept of Natural Resources, Division of Wildlife, Fountain Square, Columbus, Ohio 43224.

Oklahoma Dept of Wildlife Conservation, 1801 North Lincoln, Box 53465, Oklahoma City 73105.

Oregon Dept of Fish & Wildlife, 506 S.W. Mill Street, P.O. Box 3503, Portland, Oregon 97208.

Pennsylvania Game Commission, P.O. Box 1567, Harrisburg, Pennsylvania 17120.

Rhode Island Dept of Environmental Management, Division of Fish & Wildlife, Washington County Government Centre, Tower Hill Road, Wakefield, Rhode Island 02879.

South Carolina Wildlife & Marine Resources Department, P.O. Box 167, Columbia, South Carolina 29202.

South Dakota Dept of Game, Fish & Parks, Pierre, Sigurd Anderson Building, South Dakota 57501.

Tennessee Wildlife Resources Agency, Ellington Agricultural Center, P.O. Box 40747, Nashville, Tennessee 37204.

Texas Parks & Wildlife Dept, 4200 Smith School Road, Austin, Texas 78744.

Utah Division of Wildlife Resources, 1596 West North Temple, Salt Lake City, Utah 84116.

Vermont Dept of Fish & Game, Montpelier, Vermont 05602.

Virginia Commission of Game & Inland Fisheries, P.O. Box 11104, Richmond 23230.

Washington Game Dept, 600 North Capitol Way, Olympia, Washington 98504.

West Virginia Dept of Natural Resources, Charleston, West Virginia 25305.

Wisconsin Wisconsin Natural Resources, P.O. Box 7191, Madison, Wisconsin 53707.

Wyoming Game & Fish Dept, 5400 Bishop Boulevard, Cheyenne, Wyoming 82002.

Miscellaneous
M & N Safaris, 3040 West Lomita Boulevard, Torrance, California 90505.

YUGOSLAVIA
'Lovska Zveza Slovenije', 61000 Ljubljana, Zupančičeva 9.

Bibliography

The following is a selection of books that give information about the deer and their trophies in those parts of the world where hunting is still available. Reference to the bibliographies in those books marked with an asterisk will provide titles for further study.

ALASKA BIG GAME TROPHY CLUB (1971), *Records of Alaska Big Game*, Anchorage, Petroleum Publications.

ASSOCIATION SPORTIVE DES CHASSEURS DE GRAND GIBIER ET COMITÉ DES FÉDÉRATIONS DÉPARTMENTALES DE GRAND GIBIER DE FRANCE (1975), *Meilleurs Trophées de Grand Gibier Français*.

*BANFIELD, A W F (1961), *A Revision of the Reindeer and Caribou*, Genus *Rangifer*, Ottowa, Nat. Museum of Canada, Bull. No. 177.

*BENTLEY, ARTHUR (1978), *An Introduction to the Deer of Australia*, Melbourne, The Koetung Trust.

BOISLAMBERT, Andrée Jacque Hettier de (1978), *Les Grands Trophées d'Europe*, France, Gerfaut Club.

BOND, Jim (c. 1960), *The Mule Deer*, Portland Oregon, Conger Printing Co.

BOONE AND CROCKETT CLUB (1981), 8th Edition, edited by W H Nesbitt and P L Wright, *Records of North American Big Game*, Alexandria, Virginia, The Boone and Crockett Club.

*BRAKEFIELD, Tom (1976), *Hunting Big Game Trophies*, New York, Outdoor Life, E P Dutton & Co.

BRANDER, A A Dunbar (1923), *Wild Animals in Central India*, London, Edward Arnold & Co.

BRANDER, Michael, ed. (1972), *The International Encyclopedia of Shooting*, London, Pelham Books.

BROCK, Stanley E (1963), *Hunting in the Wilderness*, London, Robert Hale.

BURRARD, Major G (1925), *Big Game Hunting in the Himalayas and Tibet*, London, Herbert Jenkins.

CARHART, A H (1946), *Hunting North American Deer*, New York, The Macmillan Co.

CHALMERS, Patrick R (1935), *Deerstalking*, Sportsman's Library London, Philip Allan.

*CHAPMAN, Norma G and D I (1980), 'The Distribution of Fallow Deer: a Worldwide Review'. *Mammal Review*, Vol. 10, Nos, 2 & 3 June/Sept. 1980. London, Mammal Society (Blackwell Scientific Publications).

BIBLIOGRAPHY

CONATSER, Dean (1977), *Bowhunting the Whitetail Deer*, New York, Winchester Press.

CONSEIL INTERNATIONAL DE LA CHASSE (1981), *The Game Trophies of the World*, compiled and edited by W. Trense, A J H de Boislambert and G Kenneth Whitehead (in one volume – English, French and German) Hamburg & Berlin, Paul Parey.

DALRYMPLE, Byron W (1973), *The Complete Book of Deer Hunting*, New York, Winchester Press.

DALRYMPLE, Byron W (1974), *North American Big Game Hunting*, New York, Winchester Press.

de CAÑETE, José Fernández (1969), *A Hunter's Guide to Spain* (1), Spain, Ministry of Information & Tourism Publications, The National Mint.

DE FALCO, Joe (1969), *The Complete Deer Hunt*, Long Island, Madison Publishing Co.

DONOVAN, Robert E (1978), *Hunting Whitetail Deer*, New York, Winchester Press.

DOUGLAS, Norman (1959), *The Douglas Score*, Auckland, New Zealand, New Zealand Deerstalkers Association.

EDMINSTER, Frank E (1954), *Hunting Whitetails*, New York, William Morrow & Co.

EDWARDS, Lionel & WALLACE, H Frank (1927), *Hunting and Stalking the Deer*, London, Longmans, Green & Co.

ELMAN, Robert (1976), *All About Deer Hunting in America*, New York, Winchester Press.

EXHIBITION CATALOGUES
 (1937) Munich – *Waidwerk der Welt*, Berlin, Paul Parey.
 (1954) Dusseldorf – *Jagd und Hege in Aller Welt*, Dusseldorf, Heinzwolf Kölzig.
 (1971) Budapest – *Waidwerk de Gegenwart* (1972) – Budapest, Kossuth.
 (1977) Marseilles – *Chassexpo Mediterrannée*.
 (1981) Plovdiv – *World Exhibition of Hunting*, volume 1.

FITZ, Grancel (1957), *North American Head Hunting*, New York, Oxford University Press.

FITZ, Grancel (1977), *How to Measure and Score Big Game Trophies*, New York, David McKay Co.

FORBES, J (1924), *New Zealand Deer Heads*, London, Country Life.

FORRESTER, Rex & ILLINGWORTH, Neil (1968), *Hunting in New Zealand*, Wellington, A H & A W Reed.

FREEMAN, E A (N D), *How to Hunt Deer*, Pennsylvania, The Stackpole Co.

GATES, Elgin T (1971), *Trophy Hunter in Asia*, New York, Winchester Press.

HAGIE, C E (1946), *How to Hunt North American Big Game*, New York, The Macmillan Co.

HALTENORTH, Th and TRENSE, W (1956), *Das Groszwild der Erde und seine Trophäen*, München, Bayerischer Landwirtschaftsverlag.

*HARRIS, L H (1973), *A Hunting Guide to Introduced Wild Animals of New Zealand*, Wellington, A R Shearer.

HAYES, Tom (1960), *Hunting the Whitetail Deer*, New York, A S Barnes & Co.
HEUSER, Ken (1972), *The Whitetail Deer Guide*, New York, Holt, Rinehart & Winston.

JAMSHEED, Rashid (1976), *Big Game of Iran (Persia)*, printed privately.
JOLL, Gary (1968), *Big Game Hunting in New Zealand*, Christchurch, Whitcombe & Tombs.

KIRCHHOFF, Anne (1976), *Wörterbuch der Jagd*; *Dictionnaire de la Chasse*; *Dictionary of Hunting*, München BLV.
KOLLER, L J (1952), *Shots at Whitetails*, Boston, Little, Brown & Co.

LANDIS, Sam W (1967), *A Hunter's Guide to Mexico*, Mexico, Minutiae Mexicana.
LÁSZLÓ, Bakkay, LÁSZLÓ, Szidnai & JÓZSEF, Szabolcs (1971), *10 Év Aranyérmes Trófeái Gold medaillen-Trophaën des Letzten Jahrzehntes (1960–1969)*, Budapest, Mezögazdasági Kiadó.
LAYCOCK, George (1963), *The Deer Hunter's Bible*, New York, Doubleday & Co.
*LEOPOLD, A STARKER (1959), *Wild Life of Mexico*, Berkeley & Los Angeles, University of California Press.

MANDOJANA, Lalo (1975), *Caza Major en la Argentina*, Buenos Aires, Gráficos D.K.L.
MISCELLANEOUS CONTRIBUTORS (1973), *The Book of Hunting*, New York and London, Paddington Press.

O'CONNOR, Jack (1967), *The Art of Hunting Big Game in North America*, New York, Alfred A Knopf.
*ORMOND, Clyde (1962), *Complete Book of Hunting*, New York, Outdoor Life, Harper & Brothers.
ORTUÑO, Francisco & JORGE de la PENA (1977), *Reservas Y Cotos Nacionales de Caza*. 2. Region Cantabrica, Madrid, Incafo.

PETZAL, David E, ed. (1976), *The Experts Book of Big Game Hunting in North America*, New York, Cord Communications Corp., Simon & Schuster.
POPE & YOUNG CLUB (1975), *Bowhunting Big Game Records of North America*, Colorado, Johnson Publishing Co.

RAMSEY, Bob (1966), *How to Rattle up a Buck*, Waco, Texas, Johnny Stewart.
ROBINSON, Rollo S (1970), *Shots at Mule Deer*, New York, Winchester Press.
ROSENBERG, Frantz (1928), *Big Game Shooting in British Columbia and Norway*, London, Martin Hopkinson & Co.
*RUE, Leonard Lee (1979), *The Deer of North America*, 2nd printing, New York, Outdoor Life, Crown Publishers.

SAFARI CLUB INTERNATIONAL (1980), edited by McElroy, C J, Arizona, Safari Club International.
SARTORIUS, Otto & LOTZE, Karl (1963), *Stärkste Rothirschgeweihe der Welt*, Hannover, M & H Schaper.
SARTORIUS, Otto (1970), *Stärkste Damschaufler der Welt*, Hannover, M & H Schaper.

BIBLIOGRAPHY

SISLEY, Nick, ed. (1975), *Deer Hunting Across North America*, New York, Freshet Press.

SLATER, Bruce (1975), 'Hunting in Papua, New Guinea', *New Zealand Wildlife*, Vol. 7 issues 50 and 51.

*SMITH, Richard P (1978), *Deer Hunting*, Harrisburg, Pennsylvania, Stackpole Books.

SZEDERJEI, Ákos & SARTORIUS, Otto (1960), *Die Goldmedaillen-Hirsche Ungarns*, Budapest, Terra.

TABER, Richard D & DASMANN, Raymond F (1958), *The Black-tailed Deer of the Chaparral*, Game Bull. No. 8 State of California Dept of Fish & Game Management Branch.

*TAYLOR, Walter P, ed. (1956), *The Deer of North America*, Pennsylvania, The Stackpole Co. and The Wildlife Management Institute, Washington DC

TEMPLE, Thomas B (1978), *Records of Exotics*, Vol. 2, Kerrville, Texas, Herring Printing Co.

THATE, J O (1955), *Het Reewild*, Zutphen, Netherlands, N V W J Thieme & Cie.

TINSLEY, Russell (1965), *Hunting the Whitetail Deer*, New York, Harper & Row.

*UECKERMANN, Dr Erhard (1956), *Das Damwild*, Hamburg & Berlin, Paul Parey.

UNITED STATES ARMY IN EUROPE (31 May 1971), *Guide to Hunting in Germany*, USAR EUR Pamphlet No. 28–148, USAFE Pamphlet No. 215–2.

VARICAK, Veljko (1972), *Lovske Trofeje na Slovenskem*, Ljubljana, Zlatorogova Knjizaica.

VARICAK, Veljko (1979), *Ocenjevanje Lovskih Trofej Evropska Divjad*, Ljubljana.

WALLACE, H Frank (1913), *British Deer Heads*, London, Country Life.

WALLACE, H Frank (1913), *The Big Game of Central & Western China*, London, John Murray.

WAMBOLD, H R 'Dutch' (1964), *Bowhunting for Deer*, Pennsylvania, The Stackpole Co.

WARD, Rowland (1935), DOLLMAN, J G & BURLACE, J B, eds. *Records of Big Game, African & Asiatic sections*, London, Rowland Ward.

WEISS, John (1979), *The Whitetail Deer Hunter's Handbook*, New York, Winchester Press.

*WHITEHEAD, G. Kenneth (1960), *The Deerstalking Grounds of Great Britain and Ireland*, London, Hollis & Carter.

*WHITEHEAD, G Kenneth (1964), *Deer Stalking in Scotland*, London, Percival Marshall & Co.

*WHITEHEAD, G Kenneth (1972), *Deer of the World*, London, Constable & Co.

*WHITEHEAD, G Kenneth (1980), *Hunting and Stalking Deer in Britain Through the Ages*, London, B T Batsford.

*WODZICKI, K A (1950), *Introduced Mammals of New Zealand*, Wellington, Dept of Scientific & Industrial Research, Bull. No. 98.

WOOTERS, John (1977), *Hunting Trophy Deer*, New York, Winchester Press.

YOUNG, G O (1947), *Alaskan-Yukon Trophies Won and Lost*, Huntingdon, W V Standard Publications.

General Index

Index of Countries and Place Names